ALBERTA

Marcus McGee

PEGASUS BOOKS

Pegasus Books
8165 Valley Green Drive
Sacramento, CA 95823
www.pegasusbooks.net

First Edition: October 2017

Published in North America by Pegasus Books. For information, please contact Pegasus Books c/o Marcus McGee, 8165 Valley Green Drive, Sacramento, CA 95823.

This book is a work of fiction. Any resemblance to actual persons, living or dead, events, or locales is entirely coincidental.

Library of Congress Cataloguing-In-Publication Data
Marcus McGee
Alberta/Marcus McGee 1st ed
p. cm.
Library of Congress Control Number: 2017950905

ISBN – 978-1-941859-67-4

1. NATURE / Animal Rights. 2. PSYCHOLOGY / Animal & Comparative Psychology. 3. SOCIAL SCIENCE / Anthropology / Cultural & Social. 4. SOCIAL SCIENCE / Discrimination & Race Relations. 5. POLITICAL SCIENCE / Civil Rights. 6. NATURE / Animals / Primates. 7. LAW / Discrimination.

10 9 8 7 6 5 4 3 2 1

Comments about *Alberta* and requests for additional copies, book club rates and author speaking appearances may be addressed to Marcus McGee or Pegasus Books c/o Marcus McGee, 8165 Valley Green Drive, Sacramento, CA, 95823, or you can send your comments and requests via e-mail to mmcgee@pegasusbooks.net.

Also available as an eBook from Internet retailers and from Pegasus Books

Printed in the United States of America

For Natsumi, my daughter,

I appreciate and admire the strength of your convictions, your dedication to helping others, your abiding interest in your history and your eternal optimism. The duty of the youth: Change the world before it changes you!

All we owe each other... is Truth.

What's important for my daughter to know is that... if you are fortunate to have opportunity, it is your duty to make sure other people have those opportunities as well.

> — Kamala Harris
> U.S. Senator
> State of California

Writ of Habeas Corpus

In common law, **habeas corpus** (Latin: [We command that] you have the body) is the name of a legal action or **writ** by means of which detainees can seek relief from unlawful imprisonment. Historically, the **writ of habeas corpus** has been an instrument for safeguarding individual freedom against arbitrary state action.

—Brennan Center for Justice at New York University School of Law

The Problem with Being a Thing

It is difficult, to handle simply as property, a creature possessing human passions and human feelings... while on the other hand, the absolute necessity of dealing with property as a thing, greatly embarrasses a man in any attempt to treat it is a person.

—Fredrick Law Olmsted, traveling in the American South before the Civil War

Preface to Chapter One
Rattling the Cage
Toward Legal Rights for Animals
By Steven M. Wise
The Nonhuman Rights Project

The goal has always been the same, with the approaches to it as different as mine and Dr. Martin Luther King's non-violent marching—that dramatizes the brutality and the evil of the white man against defenseless blacks. And in the racial climate of this country today, it is anybody's guess which of the "extremes" in approach to the black man's problems might personally meet a fatal catastrophe first — "non-violent" Dr. King, or so-called "violent" me."

You don't have a revolution in which you love your enemy, and you don't have a revolution in which you are begging the system of exploitation to integrate you into it. Revolutions overturn systems. Revolutions destroy systems.

— Malcom X

The ultimate weakness of violence is that it is a descending spiral, begetting the very thing it seeks to destroy. Instead of diminishing evil, it multiplies it. Through violence you may murder the liar, but you cannot murder the lie, nor establish the truth. Through violence you murder the hater, but you do not murder hate. In fact, violence merely increases hate.

Returning violence for violence multiplies violence, adding deeper darkness to a night already devoid of stars. Darkness cannot drive out darkness; only light can do that. Hate cannot drive out hate. Only love can do that.

— Dr. Martin Luther King, Jr.

ALBERTA

Marcus McGee

Alberta

Chapter 1

"Stop! You do not have a legal right to progress beyond this point!"

The stern officer's face was indiscernible behind the gas mask as he stood before an intimidating phalanx of police officers clad in military riot gear. He spoke through a bullhorn.

"This is your final warning!"

When the front line stopped, the ranks marching behind began to swell and extend out at both sides. The setting sun glowed at the horizon as dusk settled on the apartment neighborhoods and the eclectic mixture of buildings in the progressive city. The chanting crowd continued to gather behind determined leaders.

No Justice, No Peace! No Justice, No Peace! No Justice, No Peace!

In the distance, an officer knelt, handcuffing a blonde with dreadlocks as two other officers threatened her black boyfriend. The air smelled of CS gas and smoke from an old Chevy Caprice, burning on Telegraph Avenue. Red and blue lights flashed from squad cars parked along 14th Street across from Ogawa Plaza in Oakland.

The protest began as a meeting in the public space at the center of the city, which many attendees had renamed Oscar Grant Plaza. That afternoon, the midday news reported the fatal shooting of an unarmed black teenager just outside the 19th Street Oakland Bart Station. Sandoval "Sand-Man" Sanders, a nationally-recruited high school football quarterback, had been shot nine times when officers mistook him for a felon who had recently robbed a small community grocery store.

Angry Bay Area residents began to gather shortly after five o'clock, determined to make certain the city and the media did not ignore the event. The police chief had chosen to withhold the names of the officers involved until the investigation got underway, but local community leaders were incensed that the city was more concerned with damage control than justice for a wrongful death at the hands of the police... again.

"Turn around now! This is your final warning!"

Civil rights attorney Natsumi Mitchell stepped forward, presenting her card and legal documents as she approached the officer.

No Justice, No Peace! No Justice, No Peace!

"This is a peaceful protest, and we have a permit, signed by a judge, to proceed to Jack London Square."

"Why? So you people can burn and loot it? I'm sorry, but my captain has direct orders from the mayor to make sure this misunderstanding does not get out of hand. You're just gonna have to tell your judge to take the matter up with the mayor."

"We have the right to move forward. We have the right to march and protest. First Amendment of the U.S. Constitution. I'm sure you know how it works."

The officer sighed, disgusted.

"You might have the right, but do you see what's behind me? Do you think any of us care about your rights tonight? Do yourself a favor and go home before you're responsible for someone else getting hurt today. You're their leader. They'll listen to you. Take your troublemaking asses on home!"

Natsumi remained defiant.

"We ain't gonna let nobody turn us around. We are moving forward. So if you're going to arrest us for exercising our legal rights, you can start with me!"

The crowd cheered, following her as she stepped forward, but the police behind the officer had already reacted. Pandemonium ensued within seconds as the aggressive police force surged against the crowd, firing off tear gas canisters, pushing people to the ground and making arrests. Then without warning, a group of agitators at the left flank, separate from the protesters, converged on the scene, some intent on protecting people, while others attacked the officers, flailing with fists and trying to remove officers' gas masks.

It wasn't long before reinforcements arrived to help the officers under assault, which drew still more protesters into the fray. Television cameras rolled as police and news helicopters nearly collided overhead. Face-down on the asphalt, Natsumi heard cursing, screaming and gunshots fired.

It was never supposed to go like this! They'll never learn!

When the officer stood her up, she saw her friend and fellow attorney, Padmi Ravi, being restrained by a brutal, heavy-handed officer. Padmi was Natsumi's best friend through college and law school, and Padmi was seven months pregnant. *It was supposed to be a peaceful protest!*

Earlier in the afternoon, after the report of the Sandoval Sanders murder, Natsumi and Padmi sent out an email blast, encouraging friends and activists to meet at Oscar Grant Plaza to make a statement to the city, the nation and the world. They contacted a judge and managed to get a permit to march from the plaza to Jack London Square. If Natsumi had known the protests would turn violent, she would have insisted that Padmi stay home, but such admonition would have been unnecessary. Padmi would have never have knowingly exposed her unborn baby to such risk!

Natsumi recoiled at the sight of an officer striking Padmi on the back of her shoulders with a baton. At that point, it was obvious that Padmi wanted nothing more than to get out of harm's way—for herself, but more desperately for her baby. Yet once she fell, the officer continued striking her, on her back and shoulders and once on the head.

Desperate to get away, Padmi struggled to her feet and tried to run, but the officer shot her with a taser gun dart and dialed up the voltage. She fell, convulsing on the sidewalk as he maintained pressure on the trigger.

"Stop! You idiot! She's *pregnant!*" Natsumi screamed as she struggled against her restraints, only to be forced back to the ground. "You're killing her baby! She's pregnant! She's seven months pregnant, goddammit!"

By the time the officer who had pinned Natsumi to the ground made sense of her words, it was too late.

"Gates! Turn it off! She's *pregnant!* Kill the juice, goddammit!"

Padmi still convulsed on the ground even after the current no longer flowed through her body, with her spasms growing increasingly intense as she panted between deep moans of intense pain.

"I'm dying! Call 9-1-1! Help my baby!"

When the nervous, panicked officer turned her over, the crotch area of her pants was drenched with clear liquid and she foamed at the mouth.

"Oh my God! I'm sorry! Ma'am, are you okay? We'll get help!"

By that time, the officer who was restraining Natsumi softened his tone and posture.

"We didn't know she was pregnant. How far along is she?"

"Far enough! By the way, we're both civil rights lawyers. If you look to your left, this whole incident is being recorded by at least four people on cell phones! When will you guys ever learn? We're persons with rights. You can't do this to people! Our lives matter!"

As the police officer glanced over at the crowd toward the persons with phones poised, recording, a sick feeling flooded the pit of his gut. He knew the outcome would be bad, that he was helpless to halt the inevitable. Within hours, the recordings would go viral. There would be an investigation. He would be identified and condemned, labeled as violent and a racist.

And worse, Oakland's police chief and the city mayor, on the verge of succumbing to pressure from protesters and activists across the country, seemed poised to offer up a sacrificial victim, provided the circumstances were sufficiently egregious. It wouldn't matter to anyone that his favorite nephew was half-black.

"Is anyone a doctor?" one of the activists who crowded in screamed. "The ambulance won't make it in time! The baby is coming now!"

The officer turned back toward Natsumi.

"You have to understand, Miss. We were just doing our jobs. We didn't mean for any of this to happen."

"Of course you didn't!" Natsumi snapped. "You cops never do, but somehow we just keep on dying!"

****

On most days, Kendrick Vesey was a biological anthropologist, adjunct professor and lecturer at the University of California, Berkeley. He was the author of four renowned books relating to Animal Language Research, the Great Ape Language, Yerkish and case studies involving Washoe, Nim Chimski and Koko.

In recent weeks, he had appeared on *60 Minutes, 20/20, Nature, NPR Science* and as a guest on nightly news programs across networks and cable television stations. Yet the upcoming Wednesday would signal his crowning achievement, as he had flight reservations for Stockholm, Sweden, where the Committee and the King would present him with the Nobel Prize in Physiology or Medicine.

Kendrick repeated his words in American Sign Language as he spoke, a playful Jamaican accent flavoring his inflection.

"There is no reason to fear traveling to the ceremony in an airplane across the water. Yes, sometimes jets do crash in the water, but Kendrick and Alberta will not crash. It's no different than flying over land. Kendrick and Alberta will be safe. I promise."

Alberta frowned, unconvinced by his answer, and responded in sign language, which he translated aloud.

"Mi not happy to go to Stockholm inside an airplane over the water. Terrorist is on plane. Isis blow up plane! Boat is better. Better we sail on boat to Stockholm."

This time, Kendrick frowned.

"A boat would take too long. Besides, I've already booked our flight. We have to be there on Monday. Don't worry. We got this! Breathe easy now."

"What Tupac say? Mi no trust nobody. Maybe if Kendrick get Mai Tai for Alberta, then mi fly."

After a moment of hesitation and contemplation, he sighed, amused at her toothy smile.

"It's a deal. Legally, you're under age, but who's gonna know? Maybe we'll even let you have the window seat."

Kendrick's fiancée, Jennifer Alvarez, was passing through the room as he finished the remark, leaving in her wake the fragrance of her sweet *parfum*. Jennifer was 5'3" with an attractive face, mocha skin and a thick, shapely body. She was an impeccable dresser and her voice possessed a musical quality, flavored in Spanish.

"I think this whole thing is ridiculous. She doesn't need to go to Stockholm. There are plenty of tapes and other documentation available. Besides, it's embarrassing. This is supposed to be a big moment for you— for us, and you're putting that silly monkey front and center in all this."

Alberta's reaction was instant and angry. She pounded the table, half-snarling at the woman, as she screamed something unintelligible.

"That's right. *Monkey*! I said it," Jennifer taunted as she snatched her designer purse off the black leather sofa in the luxurious Oakland Hills home.

"Come on, baby," Kendrick sighed. "You know the difference. She's an ape, not a monkey. You know she doesn't like being called that."

Alberta continued in the garbled tirade, and then she fixed her fingers in a sign that even Jennifer could understand.

"You see? She's flippin me off. I told you. She's always startin that shit with me. Monkeys belong in the zoo!"

"Where are you going?" Kendrick asked. "I thought we were going to dinner?"

"Last minute shopping for the trip," she announced over the sound of Alberta's protests while slipping into a sleek jacket. "One hour, max."

She kissed him, lingering, while eyeing Alberta.

"When we get married, we're moving to Millennium Tower in downtown San Francisco. You need to tell her the bad news. They have a no pet policy."

Alberta was still angry fifteen minutes after Jennifer left.

"Why do I let Jennifer come here?" Kendrick translated aloud. "Why do I not chase Jennifer away?"

"Well," he answered, signing, "because Jennifer is my mate—you know that… because Kendrick love Jennifer."

"Jennifer no love Kendrick," Alberta signed. "Jennifer no love Alberta. Jennifer love Jennifer everything. Too much perfume always. Jennifer is stupid monkey!"

"Look," Kendrick answered, becoming annoyed. "It not good for Alberta fight against Jennifer. After Stockholm, Jennifer will be my wife."

"Why Kendrick need wife? Why him want wife?"

"A wife is a mate. For human, wife is mate. You know that. Jennifer will be mate for Kendrick until him old and die. For humans, 'marriage' is law. It's human law."

Frustrated, Alberta wagged her head.

"Mi no like human law. Human law no like mi, no like ape. Human law no like chimp" she signed, and then she frowned in confusion. "Human mate till die? This true or lie? Till die?"

"Yes. One human is a mate for one human… for life. That's what marriage is."

"Alberta not have mate. Mi not free."

"No," Kendrick protested. "Alberta will be free. Human law says Alberta will be free. We're so close now. Alberta is not like other apes. Alberta will never go to zoo or lab. Alberta will be free, like humans. This month, I promise. Alberta will be the first legal nonhuman person, by human law! If anyone's going to change the legal status of nonhuman persons, it will be you, Alberta."

****

Fifteen years earlier, American billionaire philanthropist Davis Franklin read a scientific, scholarly manuscript for publication about a young female chimpanzee that some scientists were calling a freak of nature. She was born different. Her brain was different. CT scans and neuroimaging revealed a brain that was denser than normal chimpanzee brains, and it was fifteen percent larger.

Scientists used the Encephalization Quotient, the measure of relative brain size, defined as the ratio between actual brain mass and predicted brain mass for an animal of a given size, to get a rough estimate of the intelligence, or cognition, of an animal. While the EQ for average chimpanzees ranged from 2.2 to 2.5, Alberta's EQ, at 7.26, was higher than that of the tucuxi, a freshwater Amazon River dolphin (smarter than a bottlenose), at 4.56, but slightly lower than that of humans, who ranged from 7.4 to 7.8.

Alberta's brain was denser, due in part to the greater number of glial cells that fed her brain neurons. This meant the nerve cells in her brain needed more fueling cells because they consumed more nourishment, resulting from higher brain activity.

Secondly, portions of Alberta's brain, such as the cerebral cortex, were thinner, yet more saturated with neurons, than corresponding areas inside mainstream brains. Imaging indicated that she had an enlarged prefrontal cortex, and deep furrows divided her wider brain in the right parietal lobe and the left parietal lobe, and the Sylvain fissure seemed truncated.

In short, she was a chimpanzee born with a brain like Albert Einstein's, which neurologists had labeled an "Einstein brain," and thus her name was changed from *Kipekee*, which meant "unique" in Swahili, to simply "Alberta."

"It's like someone cut open her head and literally dropped Einstein's brain in it," Dr. David Jacobs, the researcher who discovered her, proclaimed, "an exact match, except for the slightly smaller size!"

She was originally owned by the Southwest Foundation for Biomedical Primate Research Center in San Antonio, but Davis Franklin managed to buy her before the research paper and findings about her were published. By the time the scientific community realized how remarkable she was, Franklin and a fleet of his lawyers were well on their way to granting her relative emancipation, placing her in the moral category of a "person," rather than private property, meaning she would never be caged or studied.

Instead, Franklin sought out a sensitive, activist biological anthropologist who specialized in great ape language and/or Yerkish. After nearly nine months of vetting candidates, his team settled on a handsome, dark-skinned primate language researcher and adjunct Berkeley professor Kendrick Vesey, who welcomed the challenge of working with such an extraordinary primate subject.

When he was working, Kendrick and Alberta stayed in rooms at the opposite ends of the home that Franklin provided in the Oakland Hills, allowing the scientist access to primate facilities at Hlusko Laboratory in Berkeley. Kendrick returned to his upscale Midvale Drive Daly City apartment on his days off and for private time with Jennifer.

Over time, the scientist and his subject developed their own unique complex language that served for efficient communication in the home, though translated verbatim, it sounded unrefined and simple. The language was a fusion of Jamaican patois, literal ASL translation and Yerkish.

At birth, researchers selected Alberta as part of an animal language acquisition study, and a pair of primatologists raised her in an environment similar to that of a human child, complete with furniture, a refrigerator, dresser drawers and a bed, with sheets and blankets. She had access to clothing, combs, toys, books and a toothbrush. She had responsibilities in the home and travelled with a human family on car trips. Davis Franklin insisted on continuing the study in the Oakland Hills home.

Alberta was ten years old when Kendrick came to live in the home, so they had been together for seven years. During that time, she mastered American Sign Language so that she was completely conversant, marking a breakthrough in chimpanzee and human communication. Beyond signing and fully understanding human speech, comprehension testing confirmed that she could read and understand literature at or above proficiency for 12th grade student standards. She was also able to grasp and apply advanced math concepts.

Kendrick realized early on that Alberta was thirsty for learning, a quality that sometimes made his colleagues nervous. A few suggested that she was a monstrosity, created in a lab by the government, who would eventually return to claim their experiment. Others predicted that she would one day show her repressed animal side, resulting in a horrific bloodbath where some poor human would die. Undeterred by warnings and discouraging comments, Kendrick was a patient and compassionate teacher and friend, and Alberta prospered under his tutelage.

****

"Alberta make Kendrick proud in Stockholm," she signed.

"I'm already proud of you, Alberta. I just want the whole world to know how very special you are!"

As he reached over, rubbing one of her shoulders, she closed her eyes and tilted her head, relishing the feel of his fingers.

"One human mate one human? Till die?" she signed, repeating his words. "This human marriage law?"

"That's pretty much how it works," he nodded. "Why do you ask?"

"Mi ask to know," she answered, which was a response she repeated often. "Human marriage law is lie."

He laughed, scratching her scalp.

"Why does Alberta say that?"

"Mi watch movies and mi read news online. One human mate one human... till divorce—not die!"

Chapter 2

"How is she, doctor?"

"Who are you?"

"Natsumi Mitchell, her best friend. I was there when it happened."

"Then you should have advised her against doing something so dangerous."

Natsumi took a deep breath, regretting the day's events.

"Please, just tell me she's going to be okay."

"Well, she'll be fine. She'll pull through, but the baby didn't make it."

"No!" Natsumi cried. "What? What happened?"

"Apparently, she received at least 50,000 volts from the police taser. Normally, it shouldn't have presented a problem. In fact, there have been numerous cases of pregnant women being tasered at the same voltage with no harm to the baby. But in medicine, every case and every set of circumstances is different. You just never know."

"Is she conscious?"

"Yes. She's with her husband now. He's very upset. From everything we know, the trauma to the baby could have been the result of her falling to the ground, or she could have been struck in the abdomen by the officer. We just don't know. I understand there were people filming the incident?"

"At least five people, five cameras."

"So maybe we will find out what happened somewhere in the future. Unfortunately, that won't bring her baby back. Right now, she's not in good shape, mentally or emotionally—just not in a good place. She needs rest. You might want to consider visiting her tomorrow."

Numb as she headed along the corridor, Natsumi had summoned the elevator from the lobby by the time she realized that someone was shadowing her. She hardly recognized him in civilian clothing, but his face, with the Roman nose and dimpled chin, was unmistakable.

"You come to finish the job? You pigs killed her baby! What? Did you come to the hospital to make sure she doesn't talk?"

"Please!" Draco sighed. "It's not like that. That thing—what happened today—was wrong. I was there like you were there. I don't know what to say to you, or to her. I'm... I'm sorry."

"Her baby is dead! Her unborn son—who will never be! Sorry doesn't help."

The Oakland police officer glanced down the hall each way, hoping no one was paying attention to her angry outburst.

"Please! Can I buy you a cup of coffee? I'd like to talk to you. I am not the horrible person you think I am. Give me just ten minutes. I know who you are and what you do, Ms. Mitchell. I've followed you on the Internet for the past year. Please. You'll be glad you took the time to talk to me."

"I don't share my personal information on the Internet. You know nothing about me. No thanks on the coffee. Right now, I just want to stick around to be here for my friend when she needs me."

He glanced over at the elevator door as it opened.

"You were leaving. I heard the doctor tell you to come back tomorrow. Come on, I just want to talk to you for a few minutes."

He reached over, holding the elevator door to keep it in place.

"Another twenty-four hours and it'll be too late."

"What will be too late?" she demanded.

"All your friends with their video phones—depending on how it all gets portrayed—I won't have a job in twenty-four hours. That's why I need your help."

"If you lose your job, you'll be getting what you deserve! My friend lost her baby because of you!"

Confused, she looked into his pleading eyes.

"Why would I want to help you?"

"Because I'm trying to help you."

He lowered his voice to a whisper, leaning closer.

"Look, I know things. My old man taught me to be straight as an arrow, to call a spade a spade."

"A spade?" she asked, incredulous. "What? Is that where you learned to be a racist?"

"He taught me to be outspoken, to call a thing for what it is. What happened out there today was wrong, for at least fifteen reasons… and now a baby is dead."

"You were one of those reasons!" she scoffed.

"And so were you! It was a dangerous situation. You should have never had her out there."

She backed, raising her hands and shaking her head, shocked at his nerve.

"So why am I standing here talking to you? I hope you do get fired!"

"I'm sorry," he pleaded. "I told you I was blunt, and that's why you owe it to yourself and your cause to take a few minutes to talk to me."

She examined his face as she had studied the many faces of persons she interviewed in her career as an attorney. The most honest persons always sounded like they were lying, usually because they were trying too hard to be truthful, and it showed.

The professional liars, however, always seemed to be the *most* honest, the most truthful. They were the best storytellers, and the rest fell somewhere in between. This officer was blunt, and though the idea of going to coffee with him seemed absurd, she was curious about what he had to share.

"Okay, ten minutes, in the hospital cafeteria, but if after three minutes you haven't done anything but try to save your job, you'll be looking at the back of me!"

They chose a quiet corner of the cafeteria and sat opposed to each other, gourmet coffee steaming from fancy paper cups.

"My name's Johnnie Draco. I've been a cop in Oakland since I was twenty-three, so half my life. My dad was a cop, and when I made sergeant, he told me that was as far as I wanted to go. At captain, he said, things got too political. You just have to go along."

He bowed his head as he sipped his coffee.

"My dad was right. As a sergeant who's not trying to make lieutenant or captain, I'm far enough away to not go along when I know somethin's wrong. I need you to help me so I can stay on the force and make a difference. Believe me, I'm one of the few cops who understands what it's like to be on the slight-side of justice scales."

Natsumi turned as she saw several protesters from the event approach the register, hoping no one would recognize the man across from her.

"Okay, so what exactly are you asking me to do?"

"I need you to stand up for me. Tell everyone that what happened to your friend, Padmi Ravi, wasn't my fault. The video's already gone viral, so there's going to be hell to pay. They're gonna demand their pound of flesh. If you stand up for me, then the proper blame will fall on Trevor Gates, the cop who hit a pregnant woman and tasered her. I won't defend what he did."

"But you were on me."

"Don't exaggerate. I took you to the ground... with minimal force. But by the time I did that, I saw something."

"What was that?" she asked.

"Maybe you saw it too. There was a group of young men who looked like gangbangers, on the fringe, on the left—sagging pants, grills, colors, playin loud rap music. They weren't with you and they weren't protesting, but in that crucial moment, they came on all of a sudden. I've seen em before, throwin bricks and burnin cars, but they show up whenever and wherever you guys protest."

"Yeah, I've seen them," Natsumi nodded. "Locals, troublemakers."

"I don't think it's so innocent. They might be locals, but I believe there's someone out there who doesn't like your protests—someone big with government, legal and big business connections—he probably has politicians and cops like Trevor Gates on his payroll. That someone is paying thugs to sabotage your protests, to steal the national headlines and supply an alternate narrative. Someone's paying traitors to discredit your cause and movement."

"Now that I believe," Natsumi sighed. "I've seen it... in Ferguson, in Sanford, in Staten Island, in Baltimore, in North Charleston, in LA and here.

So, in exchange for me going out there and standing up for you, you're going to tell us who's behind all this? You would be willing to betray your own?"

"Like the traitors who betray your movement, people like Trevor Gates discredit our badge. I'm not a traitor. My first loyalty is to my police brethren. I'll always bleed blue, but I'm frustrated. All it takes lately is one day, one incident and one ignorant, bigoted asshole to get a whole department labeled as corrupt and racist, facing a federal investigation. That hurts cops as a whole and subtracts from all the good we do. I don't want to work with bigots, white or black."

"So what can you accomplish? Do you have any proof that someone is paying agitators to discredit our movement? Who's behind it?"

"I'm close, but I'm in a place where I need your help."

****

Kendrick had last minute issues with his passport, but the California governor, who had become quite fascinated with Alberta, assured him that if he came to Sacramento, the matter could be resolved within a few hours. Kendrick was born in a small village outside Negril, Jamaica, to a native mother and an American father, but his elderly mother had lost his birth certificate and the photocopy passport he had was suspect.

Leaving Alberta in the charge of Roland, his assistant, he and Jennifer set out at eleven a.m. with the hope of reaching the State Capitol by one o'clock. While the shopping in San Francisco was *nonpareil*, Jennifer appreciated the humbler, more helpful personal stylists and personal shoppers at the Nordstrom in Sacramento, and her favorite restaurant by far was Zocalo, on Capitol Avenue.

The governor seemed disappointed that Kendrick did not bring Alberta along, and though annoyed, he settled for small talk with Jennifer. It was Friday, so the governor's chief-of-staff managed to expedite the passport so that it would be ready on Wednesday—when Kendrick, Jennifer and Alberta were set to fly to Stockholm for the Nobel ceremony. The governor was also able to work out an arrangement so Alberta would not have to travel as "a pet," relegated to a kennel in the cargo area of the jumbo jet. The airline agreed to allow her to occupy a seat aboard the jet, much to Jennifer's displeasure.

"So when we get to the hotel, she's going to sleep in the room with us?"

"Don't be silly," he answered. "The Committee's already said she'd have her own room. She'll be next door, so we'll have our privacy. We can have a romantic night."

"With *her* listening through the walls! Now that's just creepy. I don't know how you're going to expect me to be turned on with that filthy, stinking sub-gorilla's ear against the common wall. I'd be too grossed out!"

Zocalo Restaurant in downtown Sacramento was one of the city's premiere dining spots. Named for a famous square in Mexico City, its exotic décor reflected the upscale opulence of that distant metropolis. High ceilings, tall plants, hammered copper accents and a pool with floating flowers made for a festive yet intimate atmosphere. They sat at a table on the enclosed sidewalk.

He reached across, taking her hand.

"I love you, Jennifer, and we're going to be married. You have to know you're the number one priority in my life, and…"

"But…" she interjected.

"I said, 'and.' But what?"

"But Alberta is your number *two* priority, and sometimes you tell 'unremarkable' number one to just sit her ass down while you're catering to your *oh so special* number two! And it's getting old."

"That's not true."

"She was with you before me, and she'll be with you after me, I suppose."

"Why you wanna act like that?" he groaned. "We're supposed to be out having a nice dinner. I thought you'd be happy going out to your favorite place."

"Just get me another Cadillac margarita, okay?"

They ate in silence for ten minutes.

"Tell me something," she began. "Why were you so against the plan to have her bred with another chimp? They were going to pay your boss over a million dollars for that."

"They wanted the baby for experiments, which wasn't going to happen," he answered. "It wasn't just me. Davis Franklin was against it, and Alberta wasn't having it."

"Baby? Don't you mean 'the puppy?' Isn't that what they call little monkeys? And who cares what Alberta wants? She's a pet!"

"She's emancipated. She'll have legal rights as a nonhuman person. She's allowed to make her own decisions."

"And why didn't she want to be bred? Was she saving herself for you?"

He moved her margarita to his side of the table.

"I think you've had enough to drink."

She glanced toward the bartender, smiling.

"Maybe I hit a nerve? A little too close to home, you think?"

"No, a little too much tequila."

She stood.

"You can't stop me from drinking, papi. I'll just go to the bar."

While Kendrick remained at the table, finishing dinner, Jennifer went inside the restaurant and joined a group of young men at the bar, where she slammed three of four *Patrón Silver* shots.

She wore a black pencil skirt with Christian Louboutin stilettos and a low-cut, maroon, button-up blouse. She had a shapely butt, with subtly muscular, well-toned legs and large breasts, so it wasn't long before one of the young men began touching her—first her hands, and then her hair, shoulders and back, but when his hands landed in her lap, Kendrick rose, went inside and approached.

"Ooh, that's nice perfume," the man said leaning in, inhaling, lingering. "Makes me wanna take a bite!"

"I'm sure the lady appreciates the drinks and all the attention, but fellas, the girl is mine. And now you've primed her up for me. I'll thank you later."

He removed the shot glass from in front of her.

"Hey! I was drinking that! Put it back!"

As she stood, struggling to reach for the glass, she fell over onto the man who had been flirting.

"Who are you? Ooh! I'm not feeling so good."

And before she could regain her balance, her face contorted and her eyes seemed to bulge. The explosion of warm tequila and lime ooze, laced with bits of chewed-up tortilla chips and salsa bits, surprised the man, whose face was immediately drenched in the frothy, bubbling liquid. Jennifer was mortified.

"I am so sorry!"

Without warning, she hurled on the cringing young man again, this time in his lap. Fearing a third assault, he scrambled to get out her line-of-fire as one of his friends was nearly doubled over, laughing, while the other took pictures of the spectacle with his smart phone.

"Is that *blood*?" Kendrick asked as he wrapped his arm around her waist to escort her away from the bar.

She examined the goop, embarrassed.

"No, that's the salsa. I am so sorry."

Kendrick paid the bill, ordered the car from the valet, and within minutes, they were headed back to the Bay via I-80 West. It wasn't the first time he had rushed her away from a bar. Three weeks earlier, she passed out in the bathroom of a Carmel restaurant. A week before that, she went off on him at his brother's retirement party dinner. The problem was getting worse.

"You okay? You all right?" he asked.

"I'm fine! Why did you do that?"

"Why did I do what?"

"Why did you take my drink? That's what started it all. It was all your fault!"

"My fault? I'll just leave that one alone."

She awoke an hour later.

"I'm sorry, Kendrick. I'm sorry, baby."

"I know. It's okay, sweetie."

He glanced over, exhaling.

"Jennifer, what's going on with you? You never used to be like this."

He reflected on the earlier oddity.

"That was blood I saw when you threw up. Something's not right. I think you need to go see a doctor tomorrow, definitely before we leave for Stockholm."

"I'm fine, papi. It's just I've been a little insecure lately. I know it makes no sense for me to be so jealous, but I don't trust her. She's evil and you're blinded to it. Everyone's blinded to it! She's this living miracle, and you can't see past that to understand what she really is. Stupid monkey!"

"That sums it all up."

"But do you ever think about how it all makes me feel?" she sobbed. "You dote on her! She's the only thing you ever want to talk about. She's all anyone ever asks you about. It's all about her! No one ever says, 'How's your fiancée? How's Jenny?' It's always Alberta! What woman in the world would want to be second-rate to a damned chimpanzee?"

"There's nothing second-rate about you, baby, and when we get married—"

"When we get married," she interrupted, "I'm going to have a little more say in this relationship! Things are going to change, and there may come a point when I'll say it's either her… or me!"

She glared over at him.

"But that's a no-brainer for you, isn't it, Kendrick? That's why you're not saying anything."

"It's a false choice," he answered. "There would never be a basis for such a decision."

"You say!"

"Yes, I say… it's a false choice."

She sighed, rolling her eyes.

"And you know I have abandonment issues. Say whatever you want to say, Kendrick. It's all going to come to a head very soon, and you're going to have to choose. You can get another job. Just get her out of my life! I'll give you exactly one month. Either she'll be gone… or *I'll* be gone."

Chapter 3

"And five, four…"

The cameraman counted down the last three numbers on his fingers without a sound. Conditioned to the emphatic gesture from the director, the languid host barely smiled as he glanced toward the teleprompter. Once the camera light came on, however, the transformation from casual to animate was instantaneous.

"We've got a great show for you today, people! Our guest this morning is Natsumi Mitchell, women's activist, civil rights attorney, social issues advocate—she answers to all three. And just two nights ago, Ms. Mitchell, along with attorney Padmi Ravi, were the victims of a brutal assault by Oakland Police officers—so brutal in fact that Ms. Ravi, over four months pregnant at the time, lost her unborn son. Hello Natsumi. I guess the first question anyone would ask: how is Padmi? She must be devastated."

"Ms. Ravi is obviously going through a difficult time right now, so it wouldn't be appropriate for me to make any comment about her this morning. I agreed to come on today to condemn and call out the actions of Police Officer Trevor Gates, who's a murderer in my opinion."

"A murderer, Ms. Mitchell? Now that's quite an accusation!" host Tony Gomez hedged. "Of course, that would involve willful intent."

"You've watched the video, Tony. We've all watched it. There was specific intent. Knowing that she was pregnant, Officer Gates tasered her with 50,000 volts of electricity, and then he slammed his baton into her pregnant stomach. After she was down, he dropped his full weight on his knee into her back while uttering a racial slur."

"As I understand," Gomez interrupted, sitting forward, "there a bit of confusion about the alleged racial slur. Do you have any direct knowledge of what he said to her? Did you actually hear it?"

"I heard it. He called her a nigger."

"The N-word? That's what you heard? But how can that be? Isn't she Indian? Ethnically East Indian? I understand her family moved from Fiji when she was young."

"It doesn't matter. It suggests that racial animus actuated his state of mind. More than just a murder, it should be charged as a hate crime. Gates is on record saying, and I quote, saying, 'Blacks are animals. The belong in jail, in cages. Every last one of them!'"

"Well," the host continued, "the police chief has condemned his actions. City officials, including the Mayor, have condemned him, and even the Governor has weighed in to that effect. Are you suggesting the district attorney should charge Trevor Gates with a murder as a hate crime?"

"This city has a very capable district attorney. I'm certain she will see this senseless and hate-based murder for what it is."

"According to a statement from the police chief this morning, Gates has been fired and a criminal investigation is underway, but on a more personal note—what about the officer who assaulted you? Are you also calling for the firing of Sergeant Johnnie Draco, who clearly can be seen forcing you to the ground in several of the videos? Many of the demonstrators think he should have also been fired. Should Draco face disciplinary action as well?"

"Sergeant Draco," she began, hesitant, "is part of a police force that has a long history of conflict with communities of color, and specifically the African American community, where thousands are brutally beaten and murdered every year. For the record, I'm not concerned about what happened to me personally that night. I'm no worse for the wear. It's bad enough that across America, the police are killing our teens, our men and women. But to kill an unborn child! Where's the humanity? You'd think that after all the media focus, the demonstrations and all the speeches, things would be getting better. But as you can see, they're getting worse!"

The next guest on the show needed little introduction in the current Bay Area television market mood, and yet he seemed little more than a side-kick in the crowded Green Room, where curious show guests peeked through the mass of bodies, trying to steal a look at the phenomenon the media had dubbed, "The Eighth Wonder of the World."

Though she was only three feet tall and weighed little more than one hundred pounds, she exerted a palpable presence whenever she was in a room. Seated on one of the couches while sipping a mineral water, she was at ease before the bustling throng of ASL translators, reporters, journalists and cameras. She had been a celebrity for years.

"Alberta!" one reporter called out. "Are you excited about taking your first transcontinental flight to Stockholm? Do you know how far you'll be traveling?"

Kendrick translated the answer as she nodded and began signing.

"Alberta says, 'It is not my first time to go oversees on a jet. I adventured to Tokyo in Japan when I was younger. Stockholm is in Sweden. Sweden is in Europe. The Internet chick says that Stockholm is 5,350 miles from here.'"

After a spattering of nervous laughter and applause, Kendrick acknowledged a second reporter, who wore a stylish business skirt suit.

"Alberta, it's good to finally meet you. Do you understand the significance of who and what you are? You are an ambassador for an entire species! And do you know why you are going to Stockholm?"

She looked toward Kendrick.

"I'm sorry," the reporter followed-up, "that was two questions, wasn't it? Maybe it was a bit complex…"

But the chimpanzee began answering before the blond could complete her sentence.

"Alberta says, 'too lippy, lippy. Alberta is not an ambassador. Alberta is not a chimp. Alberta is a person.' She says the reason she is going to Sweden is to help Kendrick for Kendrick to get money and a medal from a man who makes gunpowder. She will speak with the researchers in Stockholm."

The reporter attempted a follow-up, but another journalist was already speaking.

"Do you have a boyfriend, Alberta?"

"Alberta says, 'Cool your foot!' and she asks, 'Does pervert reporter have a boyfriend?'"

The reporters seemed put-off and uncomfortable with her flippant answers, but that did not hinder an older man from asking a final question.

"Do you really feel you are a person? Do you feel free? Do you ever want to go back to Africa?"

The chimpanzee wagged her head, seeming angry.

"Alberta says, 'Is reporter free? Why is reporter a person?' She says, 'Alberta was born in San Antonio. Alberta has never been to Africa. Does reporter want to go to Africa, to be with his own kind?'"

Kendrick smiled toward the reporter.

"Obviously, she's heard that question too many times. She's a little tired and anxious. No more questions for now."

He nodded toward the guard.

"A little privacy, please?"

As a guest of the show, Natsumi was allowed to remain as spectators filtered out the small room. Seated on the couch across from the chimpanzee, she smiled at Kendrick.

"I know how she feels. Sometimes reporters can ask the most asinine questions!"

"Yeah, reporters..." he nodded. "I have to deal with them, but I hate em!"

"Careful," she scolded. "My mother was a reporter."

"Really? In San Francisco? What's her name?"

"Kiyomi Yamakita. She worked for *The Chronicle*."

"Yep. I know who she is. Real feisty reputation. Took shit from no one."

"That's my mom," she laughed.

"And you're a civil rights lawyer—some kinda community leader?" he asked. "Are you as feisty as your mom?"

"Worse! I get it from both my black and Asian sides. Thank God for religion!"

Kendrick contemplated a moment as he glanced at Natsumi's pretty face and pronounced features. He could see the Japanese influence around her eyes, but otherwise she seemed like black. She had an athletic body and carried herself in a comfortable, self-assured manner.

"I saw the video, and I saw you on the show earlier. Why'd you cut that Draco asshole any slack?"

"Who?"

"The guy who beat you up, the cop who rough-handled you. I think it's punk-ass for any man to lay hands on a woman. Why didn't you demand to have him fired?"

"What good what that have done?" she shrugged. "The problem's bigger than him. Gotta keep my eyes on the prize."

"And what's that?"

"On winning by being more disciplined."

Alberta chattered to get Kendrick's attention and signed something toward him.

"What did she say?" Natsumi asked.

"She said 'black girl rock.' She obviously likes you."

****

"Look at the bright side. It could have been worse," Draco consoled.

"What do you mean 'it could have been worse'? It was a disaster! That interview aired on stations across the country! Now they're accusing one of our officers of a hate crime, of murdering an unborn child! How did you let that happen?"

Oakland Police Chief Charlene Fong huffed as she tapped her closely-cropped, gel-covered fingernails on the mahogany desk. She was avoiding calls from the Mayor and reporters.

"Do you know how close I came to firing you? The Mayor wanted you both gone. It was the optics: two white cops, beating up a pregnant Indian woman and a female black civil rights leader… before all Hell broke loose. I told you to maintain order, but no violence. We're under federal oversight, so the eyes of the whole world are on us."

"It wasn't us," he countered, "and it wasn't Natsumi Mitchell and Our Lives Matter. Someone else is pullin the strings, stirrin up all this craziness. They're tryin to control the narrative."

"Who is it? You know who they are?"

"I know some of the agents, the front people, but the real instigators are sittin back somewhere, spendin money across the board, flooding the inner cities with guns, payin off players to do their bidding. The stakes are high, but they're definitely one-percenters."

Draco and Chief Fong were unlikely allies, thrown together by chance. In the mid-1960s, Charlene's mother worked for Johnnie's grandfather in documentation during the Black Panther investigation. Since that time, the families shared a bond, which was cemented when Johnnie's brother married Charlene's sister.

"Sounds a little like an Occupy Movement conspiracy theory," she sighed. "Who says it isn't just local troublemakers or gang members who see the protests as an opportunity to loot, act out and make names for themselves?"

"Doesn't it strike you as odd that the same thing happens at every major protest, regardless of the city? East Coast, West Coast, North, South—in the redneck middle of the country? I'm not one for conspiracy theories, but this is just too easy! And no one can see it?"

"See what?" she asked.

"Two years ago in July, I was getting off work when I see this car with a driver who was obviously drunk out of his mind. I pull him over, ready to arrest him, when he tells me he's this big muckety-muck who's just come back from some secret meeting at the Bohemian Grove, up past Sonoma."

"Right..." she groaned.

"I didn't believe him either, so he starts showin me these pictures of himself with presidents, with all these politicians I've seen only in newspapers and on TV—and billionaire businessmen. He gives me a wad of cash and I ended up gettin him a room at the Hyatt Union Square San Francisco to let him sleep it off."

"Okay," she said. "You got my attention. Why haven't you told me this before?"

"So I stay there with him, and it's the middle of the night, and he starts talkin, tellin me he's plannin this huge race war for America. First the blacks, then the Latinos and all the rest against the government, against white people."

"That could never happen," she sighed.

"Look around. It's already happening. He said his group learned hard lessons durin the civil rights movement. King was too smart, he said, but there's no one like King out there now, and the integrity of the black family, church and community is nothin today like it was in the 60s. With Martin Luther King, white people joined the movement because the movement aspired to noble causes: social responsibility, non-violent protests, civil disobedience—that kinda of thing. White liberals couldn't wait to get on board."

Draco paused, glancing over at Charlene.

"But if it's possible turn the protests reliably violent, with the violence directed by blacks at white people, white businesses and the white establishment—then the movement will get no support from loyal white liberals. Instead, even the whites who are sympathetic to 'all that is black' will reject the movement.

"He says, 'As long as we can make their protests violent and the media is on board, then their movement can never grow past blackness, and it'll never gain the support of non-blacks.'"

"I can't believe anyone would scheme up something like that," she said, incredulous, "but it still doesn't get us to a race war."

"The frustration in the black community is growing with each incident, and the police are being subtly encouraged to keep on killing, while judges and juries are encouraged to keep on excusing and acquitting the killers. Eventually, the pressure-cooker will explode. It's only a matter of time and money. In the end, this frustration will transform to an all-out race war, and the one-percenters win."

"What does anyone gain from a race war?" she asked.

It was the first time that Draco had shared the story with any outside the Loverboy brotherhood.

"He explained that racism must be taught and instilled in the youth because it's generational. Every generation needs a hate event—a war, a movement, a massacre, a major injustice that'll carry the hate another 20 or 30 years. The scars from a bloody race war will insure racism for the next generation."

"That's anti-American!" Charlene scowled. "It goes against everything this country stands for."

"What they really want is a culture war, disguised as a race war," Draco continued. "With the poor masses distracted by manufactured hate and violence, the rich will only get richer, he said. Called himself a patriot. They want to take America back—make it a great country again. I didn't know who he was back then, but he told me his name."

"Who is he? Have I heard of him?"

"Everyone's heard of him, but no one would ever believe it."

****

"Now it's just you and me, Padmi. We haven't really talked. What's going on with you?"

Natsumi had driven to her best friend's Cupertino two-story home after Padmi stopped returning calls, emails and text messages. It was not like her to drop out of sight.

"Kinjal didn't seem like he even wanted to let me in. I've been worried about you, girl. What's going on?"

"I can't get past it," Padmi wept as she closed the bedroom door. "Kinjal and his mother—they will never let me forget. The baby was his son and her grandson."

The women embraced, standing at the center of the room as Padmi released.

"I don't know what I was thinking! You told me not to go. I was so stupid and irresponsible! It was supposed to be safe. What happened? Who were those other guys and where was Demetrius? Everything was fine until they showed up. I've lost my baby! It's my fault. I just want to be dead!"

Natsumi stroked her friend's face, wiping away the tears.

"No, Padmi. You have to stop talking like that. It wasn't your fault."

"Tell that to my mother-in-law! Tell that to Kinjal. He warned me not to go, and I didn't listen. They both hate me!"

"No!" Natsumi protested. "Kinjal loves you. He's just hurt. You've both lost something. We've all lost something. Remember the *Prakriti-Parināma Vāda*. Your family's been injured, but you have love for each other. You'll get through this."

She guided Padmi to the bed and helped her sit.

"Physically, how do you feel?"

"Physically, I want to die!"

"No, you don't. Have you eaten anything? I brought you lentil soup. I left some with Kinjal downstairs. Please eat."

Thirty minutes later, Padmi strained to muster a smile.

"Thank you, Sumi. I guess I needed to eat."

"You've been through an ordeal," Natsumi insisted. "You do know they fired that bastard Gates. The DA's already begun criminal proceedings. He's going to lose everything he owns and he's going to prison."

Padmi bowed her head.

"It doesn't change anything for my family." She nodded, contemplating. After a minute, she glanced up. "I saw you on television this morning. You were good, of course. You were fired-up, but you let the other cop off too easy—Draco, that asshole who screamed at us and started the violence by assaulting you. It's not like you to cut bastards like him any slack. What happened?"

"Well, it was more important that my best friend was being attacked. We haven't talked since our eyes met when you were on the ground—I'll always remember that moment. It's not about me. Justice has always been a long, uphill struggle, so we have to choose our battles."

As evidence that Padmi was feeling better, she strayed onto another subject.

"Did you see the monkey when you were there, at the studio?"

"You mean the chimp, Alberta? Yes, I got to meet her. She's just a phenomenally intelligent... person, I guess—enough to understand the nuances of sarcasm. I like her!"

"But I'm sure you were more interested in her handler or whatever he is. What is his name? Kendrick? A doctor! He's very handsome."

"Handsome?" Natsumi smiled. "I hardly noticed. I was too captivated by Alberta. I sensed a strange sista-girl connection between us."

"I'm sure you did..." Padmi teased her friend, "and that connection is a good-looking man by the name of Dr. Kendrick Vesey."

Chapter 4

They arrived at Stockholm Airport in the province of Uppland at 2:15 p.m., after having spent fifteen hours traveling. They laid-over in London for two hours forty minutes before the two and a half-hour hop to Stockholm aboard a Boing 767 twin-engine airliner. Alberta was unsettled after the flight, while Jennifer was visibly upset... and drunk.

"You sat next to her the whole way. You walk with her now! Leave me alone! I'm so mad at you right now that I might not even go to the ceremony tomorrow night!"

On hearing her words, Alberta glanced over, giving Jennifer the "talk to the hand" sign.

"She's just a stupid monkey! She's a disgusting animal! She probably had fleas and all kinds of other filthy diseases and parasites. And look at her— just nasty! Her stuff's all swollen up and red back there. She's going to bleed all over the place! A monkey on her period? Really, Kendrick?"

He shook his head.

"She's in estrus, and I'll admit it couldn't have come at a worse time, but she's wearing a dress to cover it. You know how she gets. Can we all please just try to get along, at least for the sake of this award? This is a big deal, coming here and doing this!"

"The hotel's really going to give a human room to her in that condition? Bleeding from her junk? She belongs in a kennel, in a cage, a zoo!"

"Jennifer, please, for me? For all we've been through? Can you please just support me on this one? Just for this one week. I promise things will be different when we get back home. I know I've neglected you this last month, but would you please just cut me a little slack and help me get through this? This is the Nobel Prize, for God's sake, and it would mean so much to me if I knew you were on my side, at my side."

"But I'm not at your side. She is. She's always at your side. There's no room for me in this three-sided relationship. You've made that abundantly clear the past few weeks. I'm just the dumb human. Whatever power she has over you, it's enough to always keep me off to the side."

"Tomorrow will be one of the most important days of our lives, Jennifer... and Alberta's. Can you two please try to get along, for me? I care about both of you, Alberta, but I love Jennifer. Jennifer, you will be my wife, my partner in life. Alberta's going to be hormonal. She won't be in control of her emotions. Can you just try to be the bigger person?"

Jennifer sighed, sarcasm flavoring her tone.

"Person? Please! If there was no such thing as bad luck, you wouldn't have any luck at all, Kendrick. Your monkey and I are both hormonal. My period started just this morning!"

****

Draco looked up from the digital notebook on the table.

"It's going to get worse before it gets better. I got you coffee. Dark brew, black."

Natsumi's eyes scanned the bustling Eighth Street coffee shop before she nodded and sat.

"What's going to get worse?"

"Cops killing black men, black men killing cops."

"Don't even try to equate those two," she sighed. "Black men don't kill cops. They get beaten or killed *by* cops—who get away with it, and no, it's not getting better."

She opened the lid to her coffee and blew slight ripples across the steaming surface.

"So why did you want me to meet you?"

"Because I know what they're doing."

"What who's doing?"

"The people behind all this, the ones who'll never tolerate organized resistance… like Our Lives Matter."

Natsumi studied Johnnie Draco's face, still unconvinced of his sincerity.

"Who's behind all this? Who would benefit from racial inequality? Who'd benefit from police killing unarmed black men on the streets?"

"You mean you really don't already see it?" Draco asked.

"See what?"

"They don't want racial harmony, because if that happened, then most whites and blacks in this country, mostly struggling families—they'd be on the same side of issues, because they'd be facing the same challenges that have more to do with economic inequality, with pay inequality."

"Okay, so who's 'they,' definitively?"

"It'll sound like it's a conspiracy theory, but they're the one-percenters—following a leader—the same one-percenters who tried to discredit Dr. King's movement. I've heard their strategy"

"Strategy?"

"Dr. King was a smart man. He out-thought them, and they learned from it. He beat them, so they tried to smear him, destroy him. They killed him in the end, but he still won. They made him a martyr. They couldn't help themselves."

He looked up into her eyes.

"And you don't think they know who you are, Natsumi? You don't think they're going to try to destroy you?"

"It's crossed my mind," she nodded. "It's why I have to be careful about trusting people like you."

"Oh, it's not me you have to worry about. These people would think nothing of killing you to keep you from leading a people's movement."

"Please explain."

"With Dr. King, the one-percenters blew it because they didn't believe in the decency of ordinary white people in America. When King borrowed from Gandhi and aspired to noble ideals, his non-violent protests—the decent white people of America went all out for him. They supported his movement, risking their lives and reputations. They were even willing to die for his cause. I understand because I still believe in the decency of people, black, white and everyone else."

"Many of our supporters are white and everyone else," she asserted.

"But these one-percenters learned from the King experience. They know many white people will embrace a movement that aspires to a noble cause, so the only way to disincline these white people is to tarnish the movement and its leaders—especially since OLM's got no one on the level of a Dr. King."

She leaned in, lowering her voice.

"And that's why you said someone's paying these agitators to come in and turn things violent? These people are behind the burning and looting?"

"Think about it," he insisted. "For these billionaires, how much would they have to pay some local gang leader to make sure that many well-meaning white protesters get injured by the same blacks who are getting on TV making these blatantly racist and hate-filled remarks? How much do you think they would have to coax their local and national media cronies to package and replay those racist remarks *ad nauseam*? They're billionaires in league. What do you think they're trying to accomplish?"

"That's happening," she acknowledged. "It's exactly what we suspected."

"They want to turn decent white Americans against Our Lives Matter to strangle your movement before it can grow. They're proud of the irony: when they brand your movement as racist and anti-white, they can have the final laugh at those who remember Dr. King."

Still struggling with skepticism, Natsumi conceded.

"I imagine you're telling me all this because you have a plan?"

"A partial plan. I think the man behind this made a mistake a couple weeks ago."

"I'm listening…"

"Do you remember the cop who was shot in the head in Memphis two weeks ago?"

"Of course! They tried to blame it on our 'rhetoric,' which made no sense. None of us even knew the shooter. He was never with us."

"We think the man we're after paid that gang member to do it and promised something for the shooter's family. Everything he did and said after he did it was all according to their script, and then they killed him. Since then, race relations have gotten worse, with increased polarization on both sides. It's easy to manipulate people, especially when it comes to racial division."

Both sat for a moment in silence, thinking.

"So they're making the cops believe they're under attack by black people and our movement?"

"And they're trying to convince black people that all law enforcement is out to kill them—that there are no good cops."

"Almost makes sense," she sighed. "And this person ordered the murder or that cop, that 'family man,' to discredit our movement?"

"Basically, yes, though we're still working on discovering the details. From there and with some help, maybe we can expose their tactics and bring down some of the other players involved. That's why I need a smart lawyer. That's why I wanted to meet with you today."

****

At the urging of Dr. Hadassa Sörensson, professor of personality psychology and animal personality psychology at Stockholm University, the chairperson of the zoology department invited Kendrick and Alberta to an early morning forum convened by an international panel of cognitive scientists and animal behaviorists as a beginning to the day's events. Alberta was uncharacteristically nervous, put off by the heavily-accented English during her introduction by the doctor.

Jennifer complained about convenient "stomach problems" and begged off going at the last moment. After checking into their rooms at 4 p.m., they slept until three in the morning, awaking at the equivalent of 7 p.m. in San Francisco, considering the nine-hour time difference. Thus the eight o'clock early morning forum felt more like 11 p.m. By the time the questions began, Alberta had become irritable.

"Are all chimps persons?"

Alberta frowned, wagging her head.

"This is not an intelligent question. Alberta can ask, are all humans persons?"

"I say yes," the Japanese professor from Kyoto answered in American Sign Language.

"Mi say no," the chimp countered, "because some animal are persons, and some humans who human laws call 'persons' are really animals. If human laws watch—observes humans and animals for one day, and if human law listens to—understands what humans and animals do, then human law will know who are 'real persons.'"

"What is her IQ, Dr. Vesey? Has she taken a human IQ test?"

"Yes, but we don't believe the test is a good indicator in terms of real world decision-making, though she tested at 131."

Another esteemed doctor, an Englishman in the front row, rose to pose a question, enunciating each syllable in an exaggerated manner.

"First of all, I am honored to meet you, Alberta. I have read much about you, and I believe you are quite a remarkable individual, or person. I would be fascinated to learn of your interaction with other chimpanzees, but I'm begging the question here. Have you in fact interacted with others of your kind, and what is your estimation of their intelligence? Are there any others like you out there that perhaps we have not discovered yet? Other chimp persons?"

Alberta bared her teeth in a passive-aggressive display.

"Interaction to you means 'Alberta looking at other chimp in the lab,' I think you mean?"

Kendrick hated having to translate from ASL to English, especially in academic environments, because it meant reconstructing sentences and reworking expressions in standard English syntax. He was accustomed to a more literal word-for-word translation, which to him seemed more practical. Alberta had her own language, her own way of speaking. He did not want to demean her by making her sound too human.

Many researchers and colleagues, however, complained that his literal translation diminished Alberta's perceived intelligence and made her sound like a mentally-challenged child. Kendrick took several ASL translation courses and planned on retaining a professional translator for high-profile events, but he'd been too busy to follow through. Feeling self-conscious, he abandoned his efforts and defaulted to literal translation.

"Alberta have seen other chimp, but mi cannot talk to other chimp if other chimp do not know ASL. Mi cannot not talk to human if human do not know ASL. If doctor want Alberta to say chimp and human who do not know ASL is not intelligent, not person—then mi conclude that doctor is not intelligent. Mi believe other chimp is intelligent. Doctor is human. Doctor should find other chimp in lab. Mi have no lab to understand other chimp."

"They tell us you have an extraordinary affinity for math," a subtly-shrouded Dr. al-Qahtani began. "What is the square root of 144? Do you know that?"

"That is not math. That is memory. Answer is half of half of 48. Question by doctor is not good. Alberta have question for doctor."

"Oh really?" the doctor asked, surprised, her face flushed. "Please, proceed."

"For integer n greater than two, the equation $an + bn = cn$ have no whole number solution. Can you prove?"

"That's *Fermat's Last Theorem*," the doctor answered, astonished, "but you do have an Einstein brain. That problem has stumped the greatest minds in logic and was proven only after 358 years, using a recent concept called the Taniyama-Shimura conjecture. How would you know that?"

"Mi understand math. Mi understand many thing human do not understand. To human, chimp is not intelligent, but mi understand. Alberta is person."

"I've read that you love the violin and you're a big fan of Mozart," another doctor asked. "Are you aware that Einstein felt inspired by Mozart, and he played the violin to relax and when he became stuck in his thinking process?"

"Mi never meet Einstein," Alberta answered. "Him is dead—He's dead."

"Well, don't you think that's ironic?" the doctor continued. "Are your habits similar? Do you listen to Mozart or the violin to help you think?"

"Mi like Mozart. Him music help me think. Violin music. Him dead."

Another doctor, an American, rose next.

"Dr. Vesey—I'm surprised you didn't bring a professional translator. You're butchering her responses. You should apologize to your audience."

Kendrick knew the man—Dr. David Jacobs, who was provocative and discourteous by nature. Ignoring threat of Kendrick's glare, he continued.

"Alberta, I assume you understand what 'personhood' means under United States law—especially the part about 'persons' carrying out social duties and responsibilities. Based on that definition, you are *not* a person. Would you be willing to submit to a series of scientific laboratory experiments so we could understand how your brain works? Call it the beginning of 'social responsibility.' It might lead to eventual personhood."

Alberta's reaction was immediate and angry. First the middle finger and then a series of nonsensical rants, gestures and facial threats and expressions. Jacobs looked toward Kendrick.

"What is she saying? Do you understand, Dr. Vesey?"

"That was a very inappropriate question, Dr. Jacobs!" Kendrick snapped back. "You understand ASL, so you of all people know what she's saying. You've obviously upset her! You're an idiot, doctor!"

He addressed the group in the auditorium.

"Look, we have a long day ahead, so we have to pace ourselves. Thank you all for having us. We'll put the money you've given us to good use."

Still seething, his eyes beamed on Jacobs.

"Questions like yours have no place in Stockholm this weekend!"

He glanced toward the event's host.

"Dr. Sörensson, I don't want Dr. Jacobs present at any of our other presentations or events. Please make sure everyone understands that. We're just trying to get through the day without a major incident."

Chapter 5

Struggling to balance the responsibility of a leadership role in a nationwide movement against her demanding job as an associate civil rights attorney with Reed and Wilke in San Francisco, Natsumi Mitchell kept odd hours. Her typical day involved a 5 a.m. alarm, a 30-minute workout at the gym in her building, an hour-long conference call with Our Lives Matter organizers and a 45-minute drive from her Claremont condo in Oakland to the JPMorgan Chase Building on Mission Street in San Francisco. She typically arrived at the office at 8:30 for the morning meeting with the firm's partners.

Over seven decades, Reed and Wilke had garnered a national reputation working with organizations and individuals championing civil rights. During 1953-1958, Oscar Reed and Trevor Wilke, among the first law school graduates from the Berkeley School of Law at the new Boalt Hall, worked with local organizers in many cities and neighborhoods of Mississippi, Alabama, Tennessee, Georgia and South Carolina.

From their time as law clerk volunteers in a famous Topeka case in 1954, to their work on the Emmett Till trial and the Montgomery Bus Boycott, both in 1955, to their work with CORE (Congress of Racial Equality) involving early tests of the Supreme Court's 1946 decision in the Irene Morgan case, which declared segregated seating of interstate passengers unconstitutional, both men—Reed was a Negro and Wilke was white—dedicated (and often risked) their lives in a shared quest to confront and defeat racial injustice. They opened a law office together on Telegraph Avenue in Berkeley during 1960.

Both had sons, Oscar Reed Jr., along with Theodore and Eric Wilke. All three boys became lawyers and took up the grim fight, which ranged from the Jobs and Freedom March on Washington in 1963 to the Selma protests in 1965 to the 1966 trial of the conspirators in the murders of three civil rights workers in Philadelphia, Mississippi. Returning to California in 1967, they joined their fathers in Berkeley and expanded the firm. Of the families' grandchildren, four were currently partners at the modest law office in San Francisco's financial district, led by Marybeth Wilke, the managing partner.

When Marybeth interviewed her four years earlier, Natsumi was a recent graduate from the UC Davis School of Law at King Hall, specializing in two areas: human rights and social justice law, and criminal defense. Her aunt, Destiny Mitchell, encouraged her to become a prosecutor, but Natsumi was passionate about helping the underprivileged and underrepresented. Thus she was a natural fit at the firm.

During her first two years at Reed and Wilke, she assisted other attorneys in various cases, travelling across the country to work on cases involving discrimination in housing and employment, criminal defense, civil rights violations, police misconduct, sexual harassment, veterans' concerns and LGBT issues. Over time, however, her focus narrowed to cases involving police killings of unarmed civilians.

As unrest about killing after killing grew within the black community, Natsumi, who held idealistic notions about the 1960s-civil rights struggle, sought to help organize a movement that could "rise to the noble height of opposing the unjust system while loving the perpetrators of the system... thereby enlisting "all men and women of good will in the struggle for equality." A gifted orator, she was one of the key organizers of the Our Lives Matter movement.

She typically finished work at the office by 6:30 p.m., but she had relented and taken two phone calls that delayed her departure from the office until 9:00. Exiting the elevator in the downstairs parking lot, she fingered her phone's keypad as she studied the suspicious man standing next to her car. She did not want to automatically judge him by his appearance: black male, probably mid-twenties, large and muscular, tattoos, braided hair, dark glasses, sagging pants and leaning against her BMW. Yet she was by no means naïve or overly-trusting. Her fingers moved from the keypad to the trigger of the pepper spray she always carried in her pocket.

"Excuse me, but you're on my car."

He stood, turning toward her, extending his arms outward.

"Well, excuse the hell outta me, Miss Thang. This yo car?"

She stopped advancing, prepared to launch the capsicum-laced attack.

"What are you doing down here? If you don't leave, I'll call the guard."

"Really?" he laughed. "You? All on the TV, tellin folks how bad the police are, how they be beatin up niggas and shootin niggas fa no reason? You wanna call the popo on me fa no reason, so they can beat my ass or merk me? Must be cuz I'm black!"

She walked around to the other side of the car, putting the girth of the vehicle between her and the man.

"What do you want? If you think you're scaring me, you're not. You want to rob me? I'll give you my purse, wallet and credit cards. You want my car? I'll hand you my keys. You want to rape me? It'll be the worst decision you'll ever make in your sorry ass life! Now get out of my way and move away from my car, because I have things to do."

He stared for a moment, and then he smiled, shaking his head.

"Rape you? Sorry. You ain't my style, Miss Mitchell. Naw, I got badder bitches than you all over the country, and smarter too. I came ta give you a message."

"A message from who?"

"A message fa your own good. Ya'll need ta quit. Ya'll need ta stop all that shit!"

"What shit?" she insisted.

"That Our Lives Matter shit! Causin problems for folks, powerful folks and folks like me… startin up all that fuss and trouble. Ya'll need ta stop before things start gettin real messy round here. The same folks you're out ta get—they gonna turn around and get you. By that time, they'll make sure everyone else hates your asses—politicians, police, black, white, brown, liberals, conservatives, everybody!"

Analyzing the young man's demeanor and words, Natsumi grew suspicious of the peculiar circumstances. He looked and talked like a gangbanger, but there was something else going on. His voice, his word choice and the veiled threat he posed—it was someone *else's* agenda. Reflecting on her last conversation with Draco, she began a new line of questioning.

"Did someone pay you to tell me that, or did you come to do it simply because you care? Who's paying you?"

"Ain't nobody payin me," he laughed. "I'm just workin with some folks who, just like me, like the way things are headed now with race relations—toward a race war and a real revolution."

"You could pull up your pants, stop sagging and maybe speak English—that would be the start of a real revolution," she said, growing bolder. "Look, whoever you are, you're entitled to your opinion. I get it. You're fine with the police using excessive force, beating up or killing your friends and family—or maybe even you if you run across a bad one. You're fine with that! To you, it's okay for cops to kill hundreds of unarmed men each year for no other reason than the color of their skin? That's fine with you?"

"That ain't the point," he sighed. "I'm about changin minds, changing the whole system. Our Lives Matter—you're just a buncha naïve, idealistic bitches over there who don't understand how the system really works. Protestin is therapy ta make you feel better about leavin your race behind, ta make ya feel like you're doin something noble, but you make things worse."

"You don't know what you're talking about," she argued.

"America's criminal justice system is about turnin black men inta slave-felons, where prisons are the new plantations," he insisted. "Black men on parole ain't got legal rights or equal protection under the law. Real change is gonna come only when the situation gets much worse, when the system breaks—not from you and your naïve friends—startin up all those marches and protests, makin your damn pointless demands—all so you can pat yourselves on the back."

"It's called a movement."

"Whatever. Ya'll gotta stop all that, or there will be consequences—fa you and fa anyone else involved in yo shit. I'm tellin ya that fa yo own good. Serious bidness."

"Sounds like a threat to me," she chided., "and I am an officer of the court."

"Call it what you wanna call it. I'd call it a warnin."

"Well then, I think you should stop being coy. Come out with it. If I don't stop doing what I'm doing, which I won't, and Our Lives Matter continues in our efforts… what's going to happen then?"

When he started walking around to her side of the car, she thought to flee, but she held her ground, gripping the spray in her hand.

"People are gonna start dyin… at yo protests, at yo rallies, wherever. First white folks—the same liberal white folks who are responsible fa makin any movement in this country succeed or fail."

"What kind of gang member talks like you? What kind of gang member thinks like you? Why would a gang member even care about what we do… to the point of murdering innocent people who're trying to help? You're obviously someone's bitch!"

Removing the pepper spray from her pocket, she was certain he was going to slap her when he raised his hand, but he just sighed and smiled, managing his temper.

"Here's what's gonna happen: when these white folks start dyin, the niggas doin the shootin are gonna say they're a part of you and your movement. They'll be 'Our Lives Matter' niggas, and they'll claim ta be speaking for your movement. So you can't win, Miss Mitchell. You're better off just slowin it down so you can cut yo'self a side deal with some powerful folks who can get cha a few of the things ya want. I can make that deal fa ya."

"That's called 'sellin out.'"

"Nah, it's called bein pragmatic, settlin. You're a lawyer. Ya know how it works."

"No, I'm not that kind of lawyer, and I'm not a sell-out!"

Fear abated, she walked toward him.

"You know, it's selfish people like you who made sure black people were enslaved as long as they were, and why we continue to be enslaved—you're callous collaborators who sell out your race for money, betray family your community for a bribe, all to do the bidding of the Massa."

Fearing he had revealed too much, he riffed freestyle, off-script.

"I don't see it like that. It ain't about bein black. It's about winnin. That's all that matters. I'm an anarchist! Change'll come only when there's blood runnin in the streets. If ya choose ta ignore ma warnin, then the first blood spilled in the revolution will be from your people, at your peaceful protests!"

As he turned to leave, she really wanted to shoot him with the spray, if only for her own satisfaction, but he called a comment back as he walked away.

"So once this shit get turnt up and the bullets start flyin, Miss Mitchell, don't be surprised if there ain't one of em with yo name on it!"

****

On the day following the Nobel presentation, Jean-Paul Bernadotte, a wealthy patron of the university who was fascinated with Alberta, invited Kendrick and Jennifer, along with five influential friends, on a tour of the Nobel museum and to dinner in Gamla Stan, the Old Town of Stockholm. While Jean-Paul's invitation did not extend to Alberta, he made a special request of Kendrick for an introduction to the chimp and an opportunity to ask her three questions in private, assisted by his own ASL translator.

Kendrick initially balked, but he relented after Jean-Paul assured him the questions would take less than ten minutes and they would in no way upset or offend the chimp. The septuagenarian also offered a donation to the foundation responsible for documentary work with Alberta and presented Jennifer with a ruby and emerald tennis bracelet. Beaming, Jennifer was relieved to know Jean-Paul wasn't "inviting the monkey out to dinner with us."

By all accounts, the restaurant was quaint though small, with a seating capacity for only fourteen guests, along with four places at the kitchen counter. In the most recent Michelin guide, the establishment had received its third star and ranked number twenty of the world's fiftieth best restaurants. Though Kendrick was well-travelled and had dined at many restaurants, the Stockholm experience was somewhat intimidating, and all the more for Jennifer, who began immediately with the wine and kept attentive servers busy refilling her glasses.

The dinner consisted of seventeen courses, beginning with a prologue, comprised of six bite-sized *amuses bouches*, including a pig's head crackling, filled with Vendace roe and chopped apples, a blood pancake with *foie gras*, and beef tartare with crispy lichens. Yet for all the work and careful preparation involved in crafting the selection, Jennifer whispered complaints to Kendrick, describing many of the culinary components as "gross," sending the unique creations on the marble stones back to the kitchen, untouched.

Despite Kendrick's pleas of encouragement for Jennifer to eat, she refused, choosing to swill the *Puligny-Montrachet Premier Cru Les Perrières* instead. After her fifth glass of wine with no food in her stomach, she began to act out, speaking loud and slurring her words. Kendrick sought containment, but for every attempt he made at reining in her behavior, she became more insecure and irrational. By the fourth course of Chapter 1, it was clear he would have to take her back to the hotel to put her to bed.

After apologizing to Jean-Paul and guests, he asked the *maître d'* to arrange for a short cab ride back to the hotel on Hornsgatan in downtown Stockholm. Embarrassed and frustrated, he complained to Jennifer that she was selfish and had ruined the trip. Yet instead of showing the least bit of contrition, she became uncharacteristically angry, insisting everything was Alberta's fault... and then his fault... "for loving Alberta more!"

Their argument in the hotel lobby was loud enough to draw the attention of security, who reacting to Jennifer's screaming and slurred voice, urged Kendrick to get her upstairs.

"Don't you dare touch me, you bastard!"

"What is wrong with you, Jen? This isn't like you! You need help."

"Not from you, I don't. Go help your bitch monkey! I'm sure she misses you!"

After the elevator door closed with Kendrick and Jennifer inside, she began crying, her voice screeching.

"Why, Kendrick? Why did you do this to me!"

"Do what, Baby? I'm not doing anything to you!"

She slapped him across the face.

"You and that damned monkey are making me crazy! This isn't fair! You were supposed to love me!"

"You're outta control, Jen. Calm down. I do love you."

This time, she punched him on the side of the head, right against his left ear. Surprised by the blow, he grabbed her wrists while at the same time turning her body toward his, her back toward his chest, wrapping her in his arms. In response, she stomped her stiletto heel into his foot, causing him to release her. Turning, she kneed him in the crotch, and he responded in reflex by pushing her, sending her crashing into the elevator wall, where she hit her head and collapsed to the floor, seeming unconscious.

When the elevator door opened on their floor with hotel guests waiting outside, he was kneeling on the floor, trying to awaken her, but she seemed dead to his touch.

"Jen! Jen, please! Please know I love you. Wake up. Let's just get back to our room!"

Despite his incessant and anxious prodding, he could not revive her, so he finally thought to drag her from the elevator and attempt to carry her back to the reserved suite. There was a woman outside the elevator, however, who followed him as he dragged then carried her inert body. Suspicious, she alerted the hotel front desk. When security personnel arrived, Kendrick was very near the door to their room, with Jennifer in his arms.

Noting the bruise on her forehead, security agents questioned him about events that transpired in the elevator. Defensive, he explained that his fiancée was out of control and that she had attacked him, and that his reaction to being kneed in the crotch was to push her away. As a result, she had accidentally bumped her head, and because she was so intoxicated, she passed out. Hotel security took a report and encouraged him to get her an icepack for the bruise on her forehead and get her to bed.

On the following morning, Jennifer arose, completely unaware of the events of the past night. When Kendrick reminded her about her behavior at the restaurant, she remembered few details and apologized profusely, promising to get help to control her recent problem with drinking. They had breakfast in the room that morning, taking the occasion to hash out problems they hadn't dealt with for the past two years.

While Jennifer admitted and accepted her animosity toward Alberta and tried to explain it, Kendrick did his best to listen, refraining from making excuses as he tried to put himself in her place, as he tried to understand how she, as a sensitive, vulnerable woman, felt in the situation. She had, after all, found herself in the unenviable position of feeling second-place to the ape. Yet her problem wasn't just with Kendrick. Everyone else asked him about Alberta before showing Jennifer the least bit of consideration.

"It doesn't help that she hates me and does things intentionally to piss me off!"

"Does she?"

"It's even worse when you don't notice her doing it."

"Okay, I will try to pay more attention. I'm sorry. You have to know that I love you more than anything. To me, you're second to no one, and I plan on spending the rest of my life making sure you know that."

She cringed in pain as he leaned toward her to kiss her, the wound on her lip cracking when she smiled and tried to pucker.

"Ow! My lip and my forehead? How did this happen?"

"You, um, you ran into the elevator wall and passed out."

"I did? I'm so embarrassed! Did anyone see me?"

"Nope. No one saw what happened in the elevator."

"Good! I'm sure I look like a hot mess, but it's probably nothing I can't fix with a little make-up."

She sprung from the bed, going directly to the bathroom mirror.

"Wow! I must've hit that wall pretty hard. This is a serious bruise here."

"Sorry about that. Does it hurt? You should probably take some ibuprofen for the swelling."

He went for her purse and removed her pill caddy, where he knew she kept her daily vitamins and medications. Upon opening it, he recognized the bottle of perfume, the powder case, the vitamins, supplements and the Advil, but there was a compartment with white oval pills that he recognized as cimetidine. *That explained her recent stomach problems!*

"Are you okay? You never told me you were taking Tagamet. Is there something I should know?"

"Please!" she insisted, taking the caddy from his hands, "It's just nerves. You know how worked up I get about things, especially with the wedding. I'm actually lactating because of the drug, but that's not something *you* would ever notice."

"I'm sorry," he conceded, wagging his head. "I'm sure you're completely stressed out trying to plan our wedding, and I know I haven't been much help. Did Dr. Truong prescribe the Tagamet? Did she do a medical work-up on you?"

"Nope. I told her I was having stomach problems and she did me a favor. My stomach problem's getting better. This weekend, it's just been 'no-romance' Auntie Flo."

"Well, did Dr. Truong tell you that you shouldn't be drinking alcohol when you're taking that? It explains why you're getting so drunk. Did you know that cimetidine impairs the body's ability to break down alcohol? You shouldn't be drinking, period, when you're taking Tagamet. That explains last night."

"Was I bad?" she cringed. "Did I do something to embarrass myself... or you?"

"We had to leave in the middle of dinner, but you weren't feeling the menu, and come to think of it, neither was I. I'm sure they all thought you were a drunk."

"I'm sorry," she said, stroking his face. "I've been feeling really sick for the past month. I know how much this trip meant to you. I'm sorry I get so pissed off about her. I'd rather be suspicious of you cheating on me with another woman, but she's a freakin ape! Sometimes it just feels like you put her first. I should be first with you, Baby. I'm your fiancée."

"She's not first with me. She could never be," he insisted. "She's an animal. She's just a project, and when we get back to San Francisco, I'll make sure both of you understand that. I'll make sure the world understands that. Now please, do this for me: if you're going to take the Tagamet, promise me that you won't drink alcohol with it. I saw the blood when you threw up at Zocalo in Sacramento. Tagamet or alcohol, but not both! Can you promise me that?"

"Okay," she sighed, "I'll slow down on the alcohol until my stomach problems get better. If you're really gonna put me first from now on, I'm sure I'll be fine from here on out. I promise."

Chapter 6

"Stockholm mi not like! Mi hate Dr. Jacob. Dr. Jacob want to put Alberta in cage. Dr. Jacob only skinny man. Alberta hurt Dr. Jacob! Alberta kill Dr. Jacob when no one see!"

"Stop with that bad talk, Alberta!" Kendrick insisted. "That's not Alberta! Hurting someone is bad! Killing is even more bad. If Alberta is bad, humans will put Alberta in cage. If humans are bad, then humans will put bad humans in cage. But Alberta's cage will come more fast. Alberta cage will be more bad."

"Dr. Jacob—him is bad man. Him is Anansi," Alberta signed. "Dr. Jacob break law. Him put Alberta in cage, experiment on Alberta brain. If Dr. Jacob come to put Alberta in cage, Alberta kill Dr. Jacob. Killing him not hard. Mi break him head! Mi gonna blood him up!"

"Again, stop with that! Kendrick does not want Alberta in a cage, and neither does Davis Franklin. Alberta is not listening to Kendrick. Listen now, Alberta!"

"Mi no lie. Dr. Jacob come close to Alberta, mi break him head, rip him face and bite off him balls!"

She imitated the action of biting something.

"Then Dr. Jacob talk like woman," she signed, imitating a woman's voice.

On their last day in Stockholm, Kendrick sat in the hotel room with Alberta, trying to explain the significance of the trip. He explained why so many scientists and animal behaviorists had converged on Stockholm to get a glimpse of her to posit questions and evaluate her responses, but she was always ahead of the simple-minded researchers with their idiotic questions.

"Other doctor is not smart, but other doctor is not bad. Dr. Bernadotte is smart man. Mi like Dr. Bernadotte."

"What did you two talk about?" Kendrick asked, no longer signing. "He said he had three questions for you?"

"Question is him secret. Mi no tell question. Mi no tell secret. Kendrick too nuff!"

"So now you're keeping secrets from me?"

"Mi like secret. Secret help Alberta, help Alberta fight Dr. Jacob. Mi hate bad human!"

"That's dangerous talk, Alberta," he warned. "I've told you that before. Hate is unproductive, and you have no reason to hate anyone."

"Dr. Jacob put Alberta in lab cage, lock door, eat key. Dr. Jacob cut Alberta brain. Him clone Alberta. Him kill Alberta!"

"No one is putting you in a cage, and no one will ever experiment on your brain. You will have rights and protections. No one will be able to do anything to you without your consent."

"Mi no consent."

"That's good, but for humans, with rights come social responsibility. You have to benefit society and do no harm. That means you can't hurt another person, even persons you hate. If you do that, humans will consider you a danger, and they really will put you in a cage, where neither I nor Davis Franklin can help you. Do you understand that?"

"Mi no understand, no. Human hurt human sometime! On news, in court, on TV!"

"And the humans who hurt others get locked up, in prisons, which are really just human cages."

"At prison, human kill human. Mi see on TV. Human law make prison give bad human bad drug that make bad human die."

"I think you're watching too much television, but we've gone over this before," he sighed. "Sometimes prisons do kill bad humans in America and other places. I don't agree with it, but it happens. It's all political, which means it's very complicated, and it usually doesn't make logical sense."

"Dr. Jacob, him is bad human. Dr. Jacob kill Alberta—Dr. Jacob go to prison?"

"He will if he breaks human law. Do you remember our discussion about morality?"

"Morality mean good and bad," she nodded. "Moral mean good."

"Yes, and do you remember when we talked about intent, which involves knowing what you are going to do and knowing the consequences of your actions?"

"That is *Mens rea* requirement in law. Mi read many time in book."

"Right, and that means that as a person, if you do something bad, and you know beforehand what you are doing and its consequences, human law will hold you responsible and punish you. It's a matter of perceiving guilt. You do understand that hurting another person, except to defend your life, is bad? You understand that?"

"Mi understand *Mens rea* is about 'bad thought.' Dr. Jacob, him think about how to hurt Alberta. Him have *Mens rea*. Mi have to kill Dr. Jacob!"

"No, he has done nothing to threaten your life."

"Dr. Jacob think him want to kill Alberta. Alberta not safe from him thought. Him thought mean bad for Alberta."

"But you can't punish or hurt a person because of their thoughts, Alberta. Persons are free to think what they want to think, however bad those thoughts might be. It's only when they act on those thoughts that they break human laws and are punished, and human law does not allow persons to punish other persons. Human law has a system to punish those who break human laws."

"It is 'political,' right?" she signed.

"I guess you could say that," he laughed. "But that's not to say it's a good thing to dwell on bad thoughts. Very often, those who dwell on bad will end up doing something bad one day. No more bad thoughts, okay? No more thoughts about killing Dr. Jacobs, do you understand? Remember—cock *mouth* kill cock!"

"Mi understand," she nodded. "What make human so special? Chimp is Pan and Human is Homo. Human say Homo is special."

"We share 98.8 percent of the same DNA, so we're both special."

"No! she gestured, shaking her head. "Only some Homo is special—white Homo with money like Davis Franklin. Other Homo is same as Chimp."

"Good point, but it's late, and we take the iron bird back to San Francisco in the morning," he said checking his watch as he rose. "Did you say your prayers tonight?"

"Mi no pray no more to Jah Jah."

"Why?"

"Jah Jah no love ape," she signed, shaking her head in the negative.

"Of course Jah Jah love ape. Him make ape and human, and him make Alberta special, more special than most human."

"Jah Jah is human, or Jah Jah is ape?"

"Neither. God is God. God is love. Him love both human and ape."

"Him not love ape. Him put ape in cage, ape in zoo. Not right. Human kill ape. Ape not kill human. Human kill ape, not love ape. Some bad human eat ape. God not love ape. Jah Jah not love Alberta."

"Oh please! Come on, Alberta. You really need to lighten up. Bos out! Of *course* God love ape. Sometimes, it just takes a little time for the world to change, and you are part of that change. You've read enough about human history. You just gotta be patient. You'll see."

He smiled as he unzipped his leather carry pouch.

"But enough about all that. I know just what you need…"

Turning away, he withdrew the tiny plastic Ziploc baggie, and then he turned back toward her.

"*Ganja far da head!* Just a little, just a little toke, and you'll forget all those negative thoughts, Alberta. You be feelin Jah Jah love in no time!"

****

Natsumi convened the discussion in the meeting room of Reed and Wilke's downtown San Francisco office, where she along with her cousin, Lyndsey Mitchell-Ettinger, Queen Shabaz, Demetrius Berry, Heather McKinney, Padmi Ravi and other leaders of the Our Lives Matter movement sat around the long table, discussing concerns related to the upcoming week.

The others in the room were riveted as Natsumi shared details of her encounter with the young man in the downstairs parking lot and the nature of his threats. Our Lives Matter had already organized a security detail for scheduled events, and leaders were vigilant about crowd control and screening potentially violent motives and divisive language in protesters.

More than that, leaders were skeptical about many of the "overly-zealous" and "overly-helpful" volunteers who sought inclusion in the groups' inner circle. Demetrius, who chaired the committee for security, sometimes seemed paranoid about a looming "existential threat" posed by the government and rich racists.

"Who do you think put him up to talkin ta ya?" Demetrius asked. "My guess is the FBI. They have a history of employin those exact same tactics—killin off white people and blamin the movement."

"How exactly did he say it, Natsumi?" Heather asked. "Did he say he was a gang member and the gang was going to kill people in Oakland, or was he suggesting something on a more national level?"

"He wasn't that specific," Natsumi answered, "but when he said it would happen at our rallies and protests, it didn't seem like just the Bay. He seemed to be saying 'wherever we go.'"

Most of the group leaders respected Lyndsey's advice and opinions. Older than most in the room, she chaired the progressive Aegis Foundation and was the adopted daughter of women's advocate, former presidential adviser and U.S. Senator, Destiny Mitchell.

"Well, we have to tell someone about this," Lyndsey opined, "if only to cover our asses. The question is: how do we share this without inviting someone else to adopt a similar strategy?"

"Definitely no one in the media!" Demetrius insisted. "And I don't trust anyone at the FBI either. They've been tryin to discredit us and undermine us since day one."

In the silence of contemplation, Padmi cleared her throat.

"Your mother's well-connected, Lyndsey, and she has experience at this kind of thing if she's not too busy. Maybe we could ask the senator to make some phone calls, get us some extra protection and expertise?"

"That would be my call to make," Demetrius answered, "and we don't need to call anyone else in right now. My team controls the perimeter at all events, and we check every single person who comes in. Besides, gangbangers don't protest. We'll be watchin for em. If anyone seems suspicious, we pat em down. Invitin someone else in would only confuse things and make us more vulnerable. You all need to trust me on that."

"What about your mother, Natsumi?" Queen asked. "I'm sure we could trust her. Isn't she on the editorial board of *The Chronicle*? We could tell her about your encounter, and maybe she could get some reporter she trusts to investigate the threat and maybe find out who this guy's working for?"

"I…" Natsumi stammered. "I would kinda like to leave my mother out of this. We haven't been on the best of terms lately. Besides, this is my thing. And for those of you with Japanese mothers, you already know. My mother has this tendency to take things over."

"Natsumi's right," Demetrius interrupted, nodding emphatically. "We don't need anyone else. It was a threat and it was appropriate for her to tell us about it. Now we just have to be ready for it."

"Lighten up, Demetrius," Queen answered. "Stop playin the 'conspiracy brotha' role. This is serious."

"Who says I'm not serious?"

"*If* we can be ready for it," Heather continued, ignoring him. "We're obviously in someone's crosshairs, someone powerful, so we might be dealing with a level of sophistication that we haven't seen thus far. No offense, Demetrius, but at some point, it's going to be too big a job for you."

"No offense taken, Miss White Privilege, but we're not even close to that point. I'll let you know when I need help, so you all need to stop meddlin with something that's already workin and just do your own jobs."

"That brings us to our next order of business," Natsumi announced, annoyed by Demetrius' defensive posture. "As I mentioned at our last meeting, I have been engaged in unsolicited dialogue with an officer on the Oakland Police Department who wants to help the movement. Being the police are usually on the other side, I was initially skeptical of his motives, but Padmi and I have interviewed him on several occasions. We've vetted his background, information and claims, and we feel he has something to say that the leadership should hear."

"A cop who wants to help us?" Queen asked. "So why would a cop betray his own to do that? We know they'd kill us all if they could get away with it. Skeptical is an understatement!"

"We know first-hand the lies and deception the cops are capable of," Heather echoed. "I'd find it hard to trust anything he could tell us. My opinion."

"This cop you been secretly talkin to—is he black or white?" Demetrius demanded.

"What difference does it make?" Natsumi sighed.

"He's a cop, and I would never trust a black cop, or a Latino or Asian. Black cops are the worst, but I would trust a white cop even less. They're the enemy, and they're the biggest reason this movement was necessary in the first place. They execute us in the streets and lie to get away with murder, and they can only do that by closin ranks, sayin whatever they can get away with to protect each other…"

"One word: Chicago!" another organizer interjected.

"When you tell us you got a cop who wants ta go against alla that and help us," Demetrius continued, "it goes against my good sense and judgment to believe it, especially if the cop in question a part of the white supremacist 'blue blood pig' culture."

"He's waiting in the lobby downstairs," Natsumi maintained. "Are you telling me you don't even want to hear what he has to say?"

"Hell ta the 'no'!" one of the other members yelled out.

"Why? Because he's white?" Lyndsey asked. "Do you realize how that sounds to me and the other members here who are white? When I signed on, it wasn't to sit here and listen to all this divisive language. I believe in Our Lives Matter because 'justice' matters, for all. Once again, Demetrius, you're trying to take us somewhere that this group doesn't need to go."

"Well, this cop's here, and he's been waiting," Queen amended. "We might as well hear him out."

Natsumi scanned the faces at the table, measuring the timbre in the room before beginning a summary statement.

"Let me remind all of you of a quote from Dr. King that we read on the first night we came together and decided to do this. He wrote, *by nonviolent resistance, the Negro can also enlist all men of goodwill in his struggle for equality. The problem is not a purely racial one, with Negroes set against whites. In the end, it is not a struggle between people at all, but a tension between justice and injustice. Nonviolent resistance is not aimed against oppressors, but against oppression. Under its banner, consciences – not racial groups, are enlisted,* so let us never forget why we came into existence in the first place."

She lifted the phone receiver, calling down to the security desk.

"We're ready. Can you escort Sergeant Draco on up?"

****

When the jumbo jet encountered turbulence mid-way across the Atlantic Ocean, the captain's soothing voice spoke on the intercom, encouraging passengers to refasten seat belts until the flight became more stable.

"I can't believe this experience is almost over. I, for one, can't wait to get back to life at home! As soon as we get back, I'm going to get me one of those big, gooey Neapolitan pizzas at that place on 11th. They're the best! And I will start helping you plan our wedding, whatever you tell me to do. That's the big event from here on!"

Kendrick sat in seat 3B in first-class, with Alberta, attention keenly focused on the video device in front of her, seated in 3A, the window seat, with Jennifer just across the aisle. While boarding, many of the passengers were fascinated upon seeing the ape seated in the cabin, since some had followed her story in the newspapers, on television and on the Internet. The French couple in the seats directly in front of Kendrick continually looked back at the ape and tried to initiate small conversation.

All the attention directed toward Alberta annoyed Jennifer, as usual. She did not want to sit anywhere near the chimp and sought to make Kendrick choose between sitting either next to her or Alberta, in different rows. Practically begging, he persuaded her to take seat 3C, across the aisle from him, by promising a Rodeo Drive shopping trip in the upcoming week. Jennifer sat three feet to his right, uncomfortable, refusing even to look over at Alberta.

"She stinks! You can't smell that?" Jennifer complained, spraying perfume. "I need a drink to endure it!"

"No drink. You just took a Tagamet fifteen minutes ago."

"And it isn't working!" she snapped. "I swear, between her smell, the turbulence and the Tagamet, I'm going to lose my lunch all over everybody within minutes! Just get me a drink!"

She signaled one of the flight attendants.

"Double martini, please. Bombay Sapphire."

"No drink!" he interrupted. "She's on medication. She can't have anything."

Jennifer crossed her arms, angry.

"You jerk! Let me tell you something—when that seatbelt light goes off, I'm going to the restroom where I'm going to force myself to purge those damn pills, and when I come back, I'm having me a stiff drink."

Kendrick looked over toward Alberta after Jennifer left.

"What are you watching there?" he asked, craning his neck. "*Planet of the Apes?* Again? Are you serious?"

"Movie ape is not smart," she signed. "Talking not make ape smart."

"Movie ape is not ape," he responded. "Man make movie, but man no understand ape."

"Jah Jah understand ape. Him not make ape smart."

"Jah Jah make Alberta," Kendrick said. "Jah Jah make Alberta smart. Alberta not ape?"

He smiled, speaking rather than sighing.

"Now, are you watching that movie so you can someday take over the world? Or maybe you have a crush on Caesar?"

Alberta had not only practiced, but she had perfected the ghetto eye roll.

"*Cette histoire, monsieur!*" the man in front of Kendrick insisted. "*Il faut que vous regardez ce reportage… en anglais, si vous n'apprenez pas Francais!*"

He motioned for Kendrick to take the iPad device from his hand, which Kendrick did with a natural reluctance. When he looked down at the screen, his expression was transformed to one of horror. There he was, with Jennifer in the hotel lobby. She was screaming at him and then he screamed at her (though he did not remember screaming). The French reporter's narrative continued as the screen cut to the scene inside the elevator.

The camera was positioned so that only the upper portions of their bodies were clearly visible, and there she was, screaming again. There was no audio as she continued and he responded. There was a glitch in the video as time obviously jumped forward. He saw himself cringe when she grabbed his crotch, and then, for no obvious reason, he pushed her, sending her slamming into the wall where she hit her head and collapsed to the floor. But the camera didn't show that he had pushed her in an instant reaction to her kneeing him in the crotch. *He never noticed the camera!*

The broadcast was in French, so he did not understand what the reporter was saying, but her voice carried a condemnatory tone, confirmed by comments in English from the women on *The View*.

"You just never can tell," one host commented. "Highly-educated, good-looking, promising career as a research doctor and even a Nobel Prize! Abuse has many faces. It's a damn shame!"

Jennifer plopped down in the seat just as the story came to an end.
"What's that?"
He closed the app, nervously passing the device back to the Frenchman.
"Nothing! He was showing me a story, that's all. Are you okay?"
"Never felt better!" she announced. "I'm ready for my double martini!"
He closed his eyes briefly to build resolve, and then he took her hand.
"Baby, I've never asked you to do anything 'just for me,' but I need to ask you to not have that drink. It wouldn't be a good thing right now."
"Why? What are you talking about? I want a drink."
"Listen, I have a feeling things are going to get a little crazy in the next few days, so I need to make sure you're ready for it."
"What does that have to do with me ordering a drink?"
"I need to tell you what really happened in that elevator that night—something that will probably change everything."

Chapter 7

The space was silent as Draco entered, glanced toward Natsumi for a tiny clue about the immediate climate of the room and sat, bowing his head. He stared down at white knuckles. She had warned him that he would not be trusted by anyone and about a level of animosity his presence would invite. He knew who Lyndsey Mitchell-Ettinger was, who Padmi Ravi was and he recognized a few other faces in the room from television reports and viral Internet videos.

But he definitely knew Demetrius Berry, as tempers between the two had flared in verbal exchanges at protest events over the last few months. To Johnnie Draco, Demetrius represented everything he resented about the black/brown protesting. Rather than being based on so-called justice or goodwill, it was an excuse for some blacks to vent hatred and resentment, to complain and to put white people constantly on the defensive.

To Demetrius, Draco was a willing and integral part of a system that, at its core, was designed to intimidate, oppress, institutionalize, abuse, enslave and murder black males in particular, a system where corporate rights trumped human rights. Demetrius was comfortable with the hatred he felt toward such an evil and unjust structure, based on white supremacy, and the resentment he felt for whites who called for an end to political correctness.

Political correctness, after all, was frowned on by the whites who referred to blacks as 'niggers' and the ones who told 'nigger jokes' and made racist statements. It condemned those who sought to discriminate and deny constitutional rights to blacks and other minorities. It held the cops accountable when they brutalized and shot black men in the streets, lied for each other and tried to get away with it. It discouraged lynch mob mentality. It supported the First Amendment: the right to freedom of speech, assembly and petition.

To Demetrius, doing away with political correctness meant going back to the way things were in the 1950s—when America was truly "great," for white people only. Doing away with political correctness meant restoring the right to be unapologetically racist and the right to discriminate and to dominate by intimidation, unfairness and slavery through the criminal justice system. Thus he and Sergeant Johnnie Draco could not have been more opposed. The collision was inevitable.

"I *know* you!" Demetrius sneered. "You're the asshole cop who won't even recognize our petitions when they're signed by a judge. You refuse to do your job, which is to follow the rule of law. Why? Because you're a bigot, that's why!"

He called an aside to the group, loud enough to embarrass Natsumi.

"And this is who she brings in? The cop who caused the death of Padmi's baby?"

"Listen, Demetrius!" Natsumi interjected immediately, bristling with anger. "Officer Draco is my guest before the group tonight because I believe he has something important to share with OLM. If you want to question my judgment and disrespect my guest, then you can leave right now. I'll show you respect as long as you show me respect. I try to be professional, but I think you got me twisted!"

She regretted losing her temper, but she knew she had to maintain order.

"That being said, are you going to stay or are you going to go? Your choice. Make it now."

Demetrius raised his hands, resigning.

"I'm in check. I need to be here for this."

"Check it fo you wreck it."

She turned toward the group.

"For the record, Officer Draco was present on the night that Padmi lost her baby, and yes, he refused to recognize our petition to protest that night, so I was naturally skeptical when he approached me and apologized, condemning the officer who tasered her. I thought he was just trying to save his job."

Her eyes scanned the room, surveying the faces to see who was still with her. She nodded, comfortable.

"But then he told me a story and a theory about what he sees as a plot against us. He said he wanted to help."

"Why?" Demetrius demanded. "Why would he want to help us?"

"Why not?" Draco interrupted. "I want to help because, contrary to what you believe, I'm a decent human being."

"Bullshit!"

"Easy for you to say," Draco countered. "I came over here, knowing it wouldn't be easy for me. I knew most of you wouldn't trust me, but I came anyway. I have trust issues too, so you definitely weren't my first choice."

"Trust?" Lyndsey asked.

"Where do I start? Well first, you need to know that my presence here is not a betrayal to my brothers on the force. I'm a cop first, so my loyalty is to cops. Just so we're clear on that."

"Even the bad cops?" Queen asked.

"I don't judge fellow cops or anybody unless they break laws or dishonor the badge, and even then they're subject to the rule of law. I have never lied to cover wrongdoing by anyone."

"Do you believe in what Our Lives Matter stands for?" Heather chimed in.

"Do I believe in what you people do? In essence, yes, but I don't support your 'in your face' tactics, and I think you irrationally go after cops who don't deserve it. You go out of your way to ruin the lives of innocent people who are only trying to help."

"Bullshit!" Demetrius interrupted. "Innocent? By beatin down and shootin unarmed black men and claimin you feel so threatened? By plantin weapons and lyin for each other? By coverin up hundreds of murders? History shows you can't intimidate black people, but we feel threatened every time we see one of you."

"Sure, there are some cops and probably entire departments that need some manner of diversity training," Draco nodded, "but by and large, most of us don't deserve the negative reputation you've trying to create. You're turning your entire community and other communities against us, which makes it harder for all sides. You make things worse."

"And the alternative is what?" Lyndsey countered. "Inaction when unarmed black men are being gunned down in the streets every day by cops all across the country, by cops who lie to get away with it because they can in a flawed criminal justice system that enslaves black men? Are we supposed to wait for people like you, cops loyal to their brethren, to fix it? People like you make things worse because you don't see the need for change. Sorry, but you're not the ones dying out there."

"I agree, Lyndsey, but those issues will not be resolved tonight," Natsumi insisted, asserting her influence as chair of the meeting. "Sergeant Draco is here for a very specific purpose, and I think we should hear that."

She turned toward the officer.

"You said you needed our help and you wanted to talk. Now you have your chance."

"Thank you, Ms. Mitchell, and I'll start with general information about why I am here, which I think will help some of you realize that we're natural allies. Please understand: I don't want to see unarmed black men killed any more than you do. I don't want to see anyone killed, no matter what race or what job they have.

"I told Ms. Mitchell on the first time we met that there are people hell-bent on turning everyone against your movement. I disagree with your methods, but these people have an agenda. They want to destroy you, and they have the resources and hate to do it."

"And how do we know they didn't send you to help them to do exactly that?" Demetrius asked.

"Because I have skin in the game. I'm risking everything, including my life, by being here. I have information about a group that has been paying street gangs to disrupt your protests in order to discourage diversity in your movement—so they can pit black against white. It hasn't worked, so they are taking more drastic measures. If they can't stop you, they'll kill or otherwise neutralize your leaders.

"And these aren't cops, but they're using cops and they're using your own people to control the narrative. I'm sure you all mean well, but you have no idea what you're up against."

"But apparently you do," Demetrius sighed. "So why don't you tell us?"

"All this talk of race wars back in the seventies—that was real," Draco answered. "It's what these people have wanted all along, only this time it'll start with the blacks against the cops, and everyone else will get dragged in. I'm a cop, so I care about that. You don't believe me—take a look at firearm sales over the last two months. They're off the charts. Everyone's stocking up, especially in inner city neighborhoods. A lot of cops and a lot of blacks will die, which is fine by them, because neither of us matter. In the end, it will be a culture war, with everyone hating and distrusting everyone else.

"But their problem with you is that your movement is multi-racial, like Dr. King's movement. They've learned from that lesson. They won't underestimate you like they did him. They have to discourage whites and others from joining you."

"Who's this 'they'?" a woman at the table asked.

"I don't know exactly who 'they' are," he answered, "but I know what they are."

"What's that?"

"They're rich."

"So why do you need us?" Heather wondered aloud.

"Because you're the only thing standing between them and racial chaos as far as I see it. Our Lives Matter is our only hope."

"And you have a plan?" Queen asked.

"They have a vulnerability," Draco answered, "and it's a big one. I have something on one of them, something huge. I just need to figure out how I'm going to use it. I'm working with a few cops across the country who I know I can trust, so I'm looking to find someone in your group who I can trust. It's dangerous business, so I'll understand if no one wants to help me. Any volunteers?"

****

Jennifer stared into Kendrick's eyes as the jet's tires squealed down on the runway, a sense of terror evident in them.

"I'm not sure about this, papi. You didn't tell me things got physical on the elevator, and it was all on tape. I don't know if I can do this. Who's gonna be out there?"

"I don't know, but we have to expect the best and prepare for the worst. By now, it's an international news story. I think the best thing, if there's anyone out there, is for us to just bow our heads and to not comment. We shouldn't even react if they ask questions. I'll call a lawyer as soon as we get home."

Even though they were in first-class, they were last to leave the cabin, as getting Alberta up and into the aisle took extra time and maneuvering.

Kendrick thought to leave the jet by the rear exit to the tarmac, which was available, but having Alberta along rendered the option untenable. He would just face the music.

"Good luck, Mr. Vesey," one of the flight attendants called as he exited. "I saw the news. I know that's not you."

The walk down the ramp to the terminal was mostly silent, with Alberta uttering intermittent complaints about her tired feet. Kendrick figured there would be no reporters in the security area, so he braced himself as he stepped onto the escalator, headed toward the baggage claim area. The scene below was surreal, packed with photographers flashing cameras and reporters, who began yelling questions as soon as they recognized the group.

"Miss Alvarez, will you be pressing criminal assault charges?"

"Are you calling off the wedding, Miss Alvarez?"

"How long has Mr. Vesey been abusing you? Are you afraid of him?"

"Does he abuse his monkey too?"

Jennifer pulled her jacket over her head to obscure her face, holding her palm forward to indicate that she was not answering any questions. There were more than twenty reporters in the baggage area, accompanied by a dozen camera persons and a crowd of nosy observers.

"Mr. Vesey! Now that you are a proven violent abuser of women, will you be resigning from your job at UC Berkeley?"

"Will you now forfeit your recent Nobel Prize?"

"Will you be turning yourself in to the local police?"

Fortunately, a group of private security guards arrived to shield the group from the questions, and none too soon. The leader identified himself as an employee of Davis Franklin, Alberta's billionaire benefactor, and instructed Kendrick and Jennifer to follow a protective escort to the Hummer outside the airport doors. A second group of guards took Alberta and retrieved the luggage.

Davis Franklin waited patiently inside the Hummer, his mood anxious.

"Okay, what really happened inside that elevator?"

Kendrick swallowed trepidation, wagging his head.

"I'm not making any excuses. Cameras don't lie, but they don't begin to tell what actually happened."

"I'm listening."

"It's no excuse, but Jenny was drunk..."

"I was drunk," she interrupted. "I really was."

"My God, Jennifer!" Davis whispered, examining her face. "You don't look well. That happened in the elevator?"

"I had to get her away from the restaurant," Kendrick continued, "and I was just trying to get her back to the room. I had no idea she was taking Tagamet for her stomach, which only made things worse, which made her even more drunk and more argumentative."

"It was me, Mr. Franklin," she insisted, "it really was!"

"But we're in the elevator, and she punches me, but somehow the cameras didn't get that. She grabbed me in the crotch, and then she kneed me down there, and all the cameras caught was the moment when I reacted, which I shouldn't have done. It was reflex—not that that makes it any more appropriate, but what does a guy do? I didn't mean it, but yeah, I pushed her and she hit her head, but I didn't push her hard. The camera made it look worse than it was. I think she passed out more from the alcohol than from any injury. She drank almost two bottles of wine by herself at the restaurant."

He paused, realizing he sounded defensive.

"What's going on? Is it bad?"

"It's pretty bad," Davis nodded. "They're calling for your head. Everyone is."

"But I'm just getting back! No one's given me a chance to explain! No one's heard my side."

"I'm not sure that will matter," Davis answered. "We're going to have to get you a lawyer and a public relations expert. I know someone in San Francisco."

"And Alberta?"

"She'll be going back to the house in Oakland," Davis answered. "But for the short-term, it's probably best that you're not there. Go back to your apartment. Spend some time with Jennifer. You two probably need some alone time anyway, to get your story straight."

"No Davis, you can't do this! Alberta won't understand. Just let me just go by to explain what's going on to her. She needs me!"

Kendrick sat the rest of the ride in silence, clinging to Jennifer's limp hand. When the Hummer arrived at his apartment, the reporters, shouting questions, were already there. Clearing a path to the door, the guards escorted the shrouded couple into the building.

****

Dr. David Jacobs had returned to the U.S. a day earlier to attend the Annual Symposium on Nonhuman Primate Models for AIDS in Portland, sponsored by The Oregon National Primate Research Center (ONPRC). As an internationally-recognized primate neurologist at the California National Primate Research Center (CNPRC) in California, he was an esteemed lecturer at such events. The CNPRC was an Organized Research Unit of the University of California, Davis and part of the National Primate Research Centers Program at the National Institutes of Health.

As a faculty representative to the Regents of the University of California, Dr. Jacobs had spent considerable time and effort at securing funding for animal research centers at universities throughout the state, with a special interest on primate research. The successes of the research included the drug tenofovir, which made it possible for HIV-infected mothers to give birth to HIV-free infants and for HIV-infected people to live long and healthy lives, therapies for Alzheimer patients (including reversal of damage), tissue engineering approaches to regenerate kidneys and other remarkable discoveries.

Before coming to UC Davis, Jacobs worked at the Southwest Foundation for Biomedical Research Primate Research Center in San Antonio, one of the few remaining research centers in the country to work with chimpanzees. When he arrived at SFBRPRC, Alberta was still an infant, and ironically, it was his written dissertation about the young chimp and her unique brain that caught billionaire Davis Franklin's attention.

Davis was fascinated by the implications contained in Jacobs' obscure analysis and report. He immediately contacted a lawyer who knew one of the key executives of the private company with the proposition of a major research donation and an offer to purchase female #17 at SFBRPRC. Unaware of the Jacobs' ranting and boasting about precocious little *Kipekee*, the Board summarily approved the sale.

So the next morning when Jacobs arrived at the lab, he went to begin work with his precious little chimp—only to find her missing. Outraged, he learned of the sale and protested passionately, but according to the contract that Davis instructed lawyers to draft, the sale was irrevocable. As a result, Jacobs' protests fell on deaf and impatient ears. According to state law, all property was held in SFBRPRC's name. Despite her remarkable nature and the potential for study and advancement, the Board had the right to sell her.

Jacobs felt cheated and betrayed, so he immediately left Texas for California, mildly obsessed, following the chimp. Over time, he arranged to meet with Davis Franklin to sell himself as Alberta's best caretaker, but the businessman put him through a vetting process, along with four others, and he ultimately chose UC Berkeley professor Kendrick Vesey for the job.

Jacobs, however, believed that Franklin had erred in judgment and that Vesey was too undisciplined and unstable to be trusted with such a valuable subject. Beyond that, *Vesey simply did not have the intellectual acumen to realize just how profound Alberta was in terms of scientific discovery.* Jacobs took a job at the California National Primate Research Center in order to remain close, but he had never abandoned hope.

Alberta, after all, should have been Jacobs' ticket to wealth and fame. His papers would have been revolutionary, there would have been book deals, and he would have tripled his professors' salary as a coveted lecturer, with Alberta at his side. But his greatest fame would have come from the revelations that only he could share about her unique brain and how he alone had helped it to develop.

Her language abilities were nothing short of remarkable, while her brain had a profound capacity for abstract mathematics and logic. The professor, who had struggled financially after his divorce, should have already been rich, with a Nobel Prize to boot. Without him, after all, Alberta would have been just another research ape headed for a sanctuary.

He was seated with a colleague in a Portland bistro on Harbor Way when he looked up at the television and saw the report.

"Can you turn that up, please?"

Continuing coverage of the scandal that has rocked last week's Nobel Prize Awards... according to videotaped recordings from a hotel elevator, UC Berkeley professor Kendrick Vesey can be seen lashing out at fiancée Jennifer Alvarez and striking her, sending her crashing into the elevator wall – an impact so violent that she was rendered unconscious. More on the story from Channel 7 reporter, Fatima Kanouch...

"Couldn't have happened to a nicer guy..."

"I take it you're being facetious?" breakfast mate Oswald asked, looking up from the lobster Benedict.

"Can't stand the guy! I've met his fiancée. She's a pretty decent for a girl whose parents are illegals, but that Vesey moron should have never got Alberta in the first place. I know what she's capable of. In fact, I think she's smarter than he is."

So far, the couple has avoided reporters and questions, though it seems on yesterday, Jennifer Alvarez took to the Internet to post a terse Facebook message, which read: The tape is misleading. I was the aggressor. I was hitting Kendrick, and he reacted defensively. He has never laid a hand on me. He's a sweet man. This entire ordeal has been blown way out of proportion. Please stop judging us!

"What did he expect? Look who he's with?" Oswald responded. "And what is he? Jamaican? Neither of them are exactly Americans. That's precisely why we're losing ground to everyone else."

And now the calls for his resignation from the University of Berkeley... and the beginnings of an effort to pressure the Nobel Committee to revoke his award... and possible criminal charges by the authorities in Stockholm... What a difference a little camera makes!

"Looks like he's going down," Oswald concluded, resuming his meal. "So what happens to Alberta if this Vesey guy's out of the picture?"

Dr. Jacobs smiled, thinking.

"Now that's what I'd like to know."

Chapter 8

"Kendrick come to see Alberta soon. Who with Alberta? Roland?"

"Roland with Alberta. Mi no happy. Mi watch news on television."

"Yes, Kendrick see a little trouble. No worry, Alberta. Kendrick is fine."

Kendrick adjusted the camera so that she could see more of the room. Alberta had been Skyping him all morning, but he did not answer because he had been busy writing a statement to counter all the mean-spirited misinformation about him on the television news and the Internet. After her messages became more urgent and desperate, however, he realized she deserved answers. He motioned about the apartment.

"See! Everything is fine. Kendrick fine."

"Where is Jennifer?"

"Jennifer is sleep, she no feel good. Kendrick write letter to explain to human."

The chimp made a face and rolled her head.

"Jennifer, her Tekeisha! Jennifer rum-head, her have bad mind, make trouble all the time!"

"Stop, Alberta!" Kendrick interrupted, speaking aloud. "Jennifer is my fiancée. I love her. I wish you would like her too, because she's going to be my wife. She's not going away, so you might as well get used to it, and we'll all be better off if you start showing her a little respect."

"Jennifer hate Alberta!"

"She does not hate you, Alberta! She's a little jealous. She thinks you're getting more attention than she is, which is not true! I love Jennifer."

"Jennifer, her silly bitch!"

"Stop, Alberta!" he shouted, losing his temper. "When a man marries a woman, that woman is *number one* with him. I like you, but you are my work—my project. You need to understand that Jennifer will be number one with me, and that's that—and if you can't handle that fact, Kendrick will go away, always. You'll live with Roland, always."

Alberta immediately made her pout face and softly barked to herself, her feelings hurt, while Kendrick studied her expression on the computer screen.

"Look, I'm sorry, Alberta. I'm under immense pressure right now, and the last thing I need is you sniping at Jennifer today. She's not feeling well. Have you been watching the news?"

"Yes," she nodded. "Kendrick hurt Jennifer. Pow-pow!" she signed, imitating the blows, punching the air, "in elevator."

"Today for me, tomorrow for you," he warned. "It didn't happen the way they've been showing it. That tape had to be edited somehow. Someone did that to me. I just don't get it!"

"Kendrick no hurt Jennifer? Camera lie? Kendrick no hit Jennifer? I ask to know."

"I pushed her. I did not hit her. She was hitting me, so I was defending myself. I just pushed her away from me."

"Human on TV say Kendrick, say him is bad man. Him bunk Jennifer head. Pow!'"

"No more news for you. I mean it!" he half-laughed. "The news lies. You can't trust what you hear on the news. They all have an agenda, and it's never the truth anymore! Stop watching that fake news!"

"Mi watch *Planet of the Apes?*"

"Yeah, watch *Planet of the Apes*. It's about as real as the news!"

The Skype conversation continued for another ten minutes as Kendrick assured Alberta that he would come for her as soon as he cleared up the misunderstanding about what happened in the elevator. He told her he expected her to complete all the schoolwork assigned for the week by Friday. Then he called Roland an insisted that she should not be allowed to watch any news story about the incident, or was not to watch any stories that were about her.

"Bless up, Alberta."

She signed a response and extended her palm.

As Kendrick reread the letter that he had drafted to the chancellor, he considered whether or not a response was even in order. The incident in the elevator had zero to do with his job at the university, and the video certainly wasn't a conviction, except in the court of public opinion, if even that. It was just unfortunate! *He should have never let her drink so much!* And shoving her while they were in the elevator—he should have never lost his temper!

Kendrick Vesey @kenVeseyjam   11/25
The media got it all wrong! It's fake news. Don't judge me without the facts.
Explanation forthcoming #elevatorcamerawhack

He regretted sending out the tweet. *Probably better to let things just blow over!* He had drafted another letter as a public statement, explanation and refutation to the accusations being made about him in the media and on the Internet, but after re-reading it, he thought it might make people think he was trying to excuse bad behavior.

His mother called as he was finishing, scolding him for not showing more love and concern for Jennifer and warning him, "tere is somethin very bad in dat monkey!" Hardly able to get a word in edgewise, he tried to explain how exceptional Alberta was—not just as an ape, but as a person.

"You remember that story I told ja about the monkeys savin the fish?" his mother asked.

"What story?"

"It's ma granmama story, Ricky, from Africa. It go like this: The rainy season come that one year, and it was the strongest ever, and da river floodin all over its banks. There was floods everywhere, and the animals was all running up inta the hills. The floods come so fast that many drowned, cept the monkeys, cuz they could climb high up in the tree. So sittin up there, some smart monkey looked down on the water ta where da fish was swimming and flippin out there in the wata. Oh, them fish was partyin, havin a wild time! while everyone else was knocked down by the flood, some floatin in the wata, dead as dirt."

"I think I have heard this story," Kendrick sighed. "Please don't do this now."

"Lemme finish, Ricky! So one of them so smart monkeys saw the fish swimmin and said ta his friend:

'Look down, mon. Look at them poor creatures there. They sho gonna drown. See how them struggle in that water?'

'Ya mon,' that other monkey say. 'Too bad! They was lazy and slept late, and they couldn't go ta da hills cuz them got no legs. How can we save em?'

'Well, we gotta do somethin!' his friend said. 'I got it! Let's just ease up ta da edge of da flood ta where the water ain't too deep, and we can get them guys outta there.'

"So that's what them monkeys did. They started catching all them fish, even though them fish didn't wanna be caught! One by one, they brought em out of the water and put em on the dry land. So before long, there was a big ol pile of fish, lyin on the grass, no one movin—not even one!

Then one of the monkeys say, 'See that? They was just tired, that's all, but we saved em, and now they just sleepin and restin up. If we wasn't so smart, mon, all them poor people without legs woulda drowned!'

"So the other monkey, him say, 'When we was tryin ta catch em, they was tryin to escape from us cuz them not understand how truly good and smart we was. But when they wake up, them gonna be so happy cuz we saved them lives!'"

Kendrick always tried to be patient when his dementia-challenged mother launched into one of her stories, but the pressure and criticism had made him a little irritable. He did not mean to snap, but he was the first to notice his angry, antagonistic tone.

"That's a ridiculous story. What does it have to do with me?"

"Sometimes smart ain't all that smart. Ya listen ta the gray hair, boy," she scolded. "Wife better than monkey. Sometimes ya gotta leave nature be. Monkey be monkey. By savin them fish, they killed them fish. Somethin ta tink about."

"I'm a scientist, Mama," he complained. "We can't leave nature be. If we did, there'd be no science."

"There was science before you came about, and there will be science after you been long gone. Ya need ta start tinkin about what's really important in life," she countered. "Makes me sad ta have such a 'smart' son. So how is Jennifer? How is my favorite future daughter-in-law?"

"She's sleeping, resting up—like them fish."

"Well, wake that fish up. Tell her I need ta talk ta her about the weddin, the table settins. I just gotta axe her somethin rite quick."

"How about if I just take a message?" he asked.

"No, I need ta talk ta her! This woman business. I'm still yo mama! You get her up now, child!"

Feeling like a little boy again, he rose, sighing as he headed for the bedroom.

"Ricky?" his mother called through the phone after two minutes, and then again after three. "Ricky, are ya there? I know you didn't just leave me hangin on this phone!"

A minute later, Kendrick rushed from the room, wide eyes, face flushed, breathing hard, his movements jerky. Panic had transformed his demeanor. When he spoke on the phone, the pitch of his voice was muffled and elevated.

"Mama! Mommy! I can't wake her up! I don't know what's wrong! Jennifer! I gotta go! I gotta call 9-1-1!"

****

Jennifer Alvarez was at the hospital in the Intensive Care Unit, in a medically-induced coma. Kendrick Vesey had found his fiancée unresponsive in his home and called for an ambulance. In a desperate phone call, he explained that he could not awaken her and that her breathing was shallow. He said her face seemed yellowish and there was blood in her mouth.

Ten minutes later, the paramedics arrived, checked her temperature and stats, administered pressurized oxygen to stabilize breathing and began an IV with plasma expanders and vasopressors to treat perceived hypotension, or abnormally low blood pressure. While the attendant paramedic was busy working to make Jennifer ready for transport, the "second" began with questions.

"How long has she been like this?"

"I don't know!" Kendrick yelled, anxious. "I checked on her about forty-five minutes ago, and I thought she was just sleeping. She's thrown up blood before though."

"I'm not a doctor," the young man explained, "but if I had to guess, I'd say it was something she ingested. Has she eaten anything today?"

"Not that I know of. She's been having stomach problems lately. I know she was taking Tagamet for whatever it was. Is she going to be okay?"

"That I definitely do not know, but it would be helpful to us if you could make some notes about what she's done over the last twenty-four hours: what she's eaten, what medicines she's taken, and definitely the name of her doctor, and share those with the attendant doctor at the hospital."

"Am I allowed to ride in the ambulance with her?" Kendrick asked, following as the paramedic made ready to leave.

"Are you her husband?"

"I'm her fiancée. We're getting married next month."

"Then of course you can. Come on."

By the time Kendrick and the second got out the door, however they faced a surge of reporters and cameras, blocking the sidewalk and their path to the emergency vehicle.

"Dr. Vesey! The woman in the ambulance? Is that Jennifer Alvarez, the same Jennifer Alvarez who you assaulted in the Stockholm hotel?"

Kendrick raised the notebook in his hands to block pictures from the cameras as he turned away, determined not to comment.

"Get out of our way! You're trespassing."

"Why the ambulance?" another reporter called. "What's happened to Ms. Alvarez? Was this another violent episode? Was this your doing?"

"The world is watching and listening, Dr. Vesey," a third reporter added in a condescending tone. "You just won a Nobel Prize. We're not going to stop until we have some answers. What happened to Ms. Alvarez in your apartment?"

Inside the ambulance, Kendrick looked down on Jennifer and began to sob, quietly at first, before the emotion of the moment consumed his gut, causing him to groan. The world around him faded until he could only see her strained expression as she struggled to breathe. Time seemed to cease as the sounds of the instruments and the paramedics' causal banter blended into the fading numbness of his mind.

He met Jennifer Alvarez two years earlier at a media function at Mezzanine in Central Market/SOMA, two blocks from the Moscone Convention Center. As administrator for the Mission Flowers Project, she had brought a group of nineteen Latino middle school girls to a three-day technology career workshop that culminated in speeches by industry leaders, which included Kendrick as one of the orators.

The flirtation was instantaneous, since both had recently become single and neither was seeking a relationship. Over three months, however, a genuine friendship grew, and though both resisted, a deepening affection followed. It began with intense nighttime phone conversations, often lingering until sunrise, during which they shared their histories and hopes, doubts and disappointments—their hearts and their very souls.

Kendrick loved Jennifer's passion and ambitions for the girls, most of them from disadvantaged backgrounds, and many of them first-generation immigrants. Kendrick and Jennifer were themselves immigrants, so both understood the importance of the opportunity existing in education for the girls, especially in technical fields. They had determined they would adopt two disadvantaged immigrant children after they were married, and depending on results, perhaps one or two more.

The relationship had its trials, most resulting from busy work schedules, but the greatest challenge involved the obvious rivalry between Jennifer and Alberta, which had grown to unnecessary and unhealthy proportions. Though Kendrick had worked closely with Alberta for over seven years, he explained to the chimp that he would have less time to spend with her after he got married. At the same time, he told Jennifer that suddenly abandoning Alberta would cause the chimp irreparable harm and would represent a betrayal to Davis Franklin, her wealthy patron. He encouraged the need for patience and time for transition from both sides.

But Jennifer's behavior had changed profoundly over the last month and a half. While she had always enjoyed a good cocktail or a glass or two of wine, she had been drinking to extreme intoxication over the last month, which only exaggerated her insecurity about Alberta and her anger toward Kendrick. The incident at the restaurant and hotel in Stockholm was highly irregular though not unexpected, given her behavior in several incidents leading up to the trip.

She took a leave of absence from her job so she could finalize the wedding in Jamaica, get married and travel with Kendrick to Belize for the honeymoon. The couple had already made a downpayment on a high-rise condo at Millennium Tower in San Francisco and had booked a second wedding reception at the Top of the Mark, located on the 19th floor of the Mark Hopkins Hotel on the pinnacle of Nob Hill. They had planned for a good life.

As Kendrick knelt next to her prostrate body on the gurney, clutching her clammy hand, he struggled to understand how things had gone so wrong so fast. The days since their return were horrible, with various media personalities constantly calling with insulting and intrusive questions, the public dissection of their lives, the insinuations and innuendo and the name calling. Jennifer had been described as a sloppy, irresponsible drunk on the Internet, while several commentators labeled him as a cruel narcissist and misogynistic abuser.

When he brought Jennifer a mug of beef bone broth and kimchee an hour before his mother called, she seemed a bit groggy, but she had always been difficult to wake from sleep. However, when he went in to wake her for his mother's inquiry, he noticed the distinct blood-tinged saliva trailing over her lip onto the pillow and that her breathing was shallow. He called her name, shaking her and patting her cheeks, but she would not respond to anything he tried. Panicked thoughts running through his mind, he had called 9-1-1. The very next call was to Davis Franklin.

"Can you tell what's wrong with her?" he asked the paramedic. "Is she going to be all right?"

"There is no way of knowing," he answered. "We're just trying to stabilize her until we can get her to the ER. Could be a lot of things. As I understand, she had a recent head injury?"

"Yeah," Kendrick sighed, "not a serious injury, nothing that could have caused this. I know that."

"Her brain could be hemorrhaging. We just don't know enough right now."

Two minutes later, instruments indicated sudden cardiac arrest.

"What's going on?"

"Please move back, Mr. Vesey!" the paramedic demanded, springing forward. "Looks like her heart's failing. We have to begin CPR!"

****

Marybeth Wilke read over on a legal brief as she sat in the conference room, awaiting the arrival of one of the other partners and an associate. It had been a long day, with depositions all morning, a court appearance in the afternoon and an assessment/consultant role at a news conference in the early evening. The news conference, convened by a local broadcaster, was perhaps premature, as few facts had been established.

Scrolling through recent articles and broadcasts on her smart phone, Marybeth narrowed search parameters to a live-stream a second broadcast from a vigil being held at a community center in San Francisco's Mission District, where many friends of Jennifer Alvarez had congregated to pray for her and indict the "monster" who had caused her downfall and injuries. The group was led by a nationally-recognized women's rights activist, who made sure cameras were locked and loaded before she began.

"What has happened to Jennifer Alvarez over the last year is truly a tragedy, but it was clearly a preventable tragedy," a fiery Gabriella Medina insisted. "The truth is: we failed her! When her father spoke out last week, telling the world that Kendrick Vesey was not the wonderful man he pretended to be and we did not act, we failed Jennifer. When women's groups and a director at the Mission Flowers Project called on the Board of Regents for the University of California to fire Kendrick Vesey for beating a vulnerable, alcohol-compromised woman before the world, when I and others demanded that the Nobel Committee immediately disqualify that violent man and invalidate his award, and I received little support from anyone, you all failed Jennifer…"

As a camera panned the faces in the crowd of three hundred packed in the room, many responded with angry shouts, frustrated gestures and heated comments.

"And when, just three days ago, we saw the rest of tape from the lobby and in that elevator that night when he assaulted her, and then lied to cover it up, and then hid her out at his apartment to isolate her and control the situation, we all failed Jennifer!"

She paused to allow the loud crowd response to dissipate.

Having had watched enough of the sideshow, Marybeth ended the live-feed, shaking her head in frustration.

"Oh Lord! Now even the media in the Bay's gone to hell in a handbasket!"

Natsumi Mitchell arrived a few minutes later, attributing her tardiness to the traffic as she rechecked her watch. Devon Reed showed up shortly thereafter, confirming the traffic problem, while indicating that the Our Lives Matter group had blocked a major intersection in the city.

"And you didn't know about that, Natsumi?" Marybeth joked. "Rabble-rouser! Sit down, please, both of you."

After the lawyers sat, Marybeth wasted little time in getting to her point.

"I got a call late this afternoon from Davis Franklin. You both know how dear he is to us. So anyway, in case either of you have been under a rock all day, you'll know that Jennifer Alvarez, the fiancée of Dr. Kendrick Vesey—the guy with the smart chimp, Nobel Prize winner and Berkeley professor—Jennifer Alvarez is in ICU at San Francisco Memorial Hospital, and if you've been following the story, things have gotten a little dicey."

"Looks like he needs to hire a PR firm. It's a PR problem, not a legal problem, not yet," Devon shrugged. "I've been saying it all week."

"Mr. Franklin thinks it's more serious than that," Marybeth countered. "He thinks the sooner the better for lawyers being involved. He wants us in on this."

"Us?" Natsumi asked. "You can't mean me? I've got a full schedule."

"Definitely you, Natsumi, per his request, but you'll have Devon's assistance. Devon understands our firm's loyalty to Davis Franklin. The partners have talked about it and we agree, Natsumi: you're the perfect person for this… situation, if you will."

"But what about my existing case-load?" Natsumi protested. "And my other work?"

"We'll reassign your cases," Marybeth answered, "and as for the other work, Our Lives Matter—you're going to have to assume a lesser role in the movement. OLM is a highly-organized group, thanks to you. I'm sure there's someone else there who can step up and fill your shoes."

Natsumi seemed flabbergasted, barely able to construct a rebuttal.

"Fill my shoes? That's not the point and you both know that. I'm fully invested in this movement because I deeply care about what's happening to people in this country."

"We know you care," Devon responded, "and that is why we've supported your efforts all along. It's just that now you have to return the favor by supporting us in what we've been tasked to do. Apparently, Mr. Franklin wants our firm involved, and he specifically requested you. What else can we do?"

"Tell him I'm unavailable. Assign another lawyer?"

"We can't do that, Natsumi," Marybeth sighed. "As a firm, we've had a rough last couple of years. Davis Franklin has been good to us. He's contracted us for legal work, paid client expenses and donated to our various causes, including Our Lives Matter. And for all that, he has never asked us for anything, until now. Apparently, this Kendrick Vesey character is very important to him. Maybe it's the ape, but Franklin thinks you're the perfect person to handle the situation—in fact, the only person."

"That's very flattering," Natsumi groaned, "but why me? He doesn't even know me."

"He says Dr. Vesey mentioned your name specifically, and since you've been so high-profile lately, he linked you to this firm. How is it that you know Kendrick Vesey?"

"I don't," Natsumi answered. "I met him once in the Green Room at a television station. We barely even talked!"

"Then you must have made quite an impression," Devon interrupted, smiling. "You know the African saying, *the higher a monkey climbs a tree, the more of his black ass you gonna see!* It's the price of fame, Natsumi. Sorry."

"Is there any way I'm going to get out of this?" she asked. "Is there any argument I can make to change either of your minds, any deal I can cut with you here?"

"You already know the answer," Marybeth maintained. "The die was cast from the moment you walked in the door. We've already re-assigned your case-load, and you'll have two weeks to transition out of the Our Lives Matter movement."

An alert buzzed on Marybeth's phone. After reading the message, she took a deep breath, closed her eyes briefly and wagged her head.

"In the meantime, your new client is going to need all the help he can get. The story will be all over the news within the hour. I just received notice that Jennifer Alvarez… isn't going to make it."

Chapter 9

"You've done a commendable job, Colin, despite your obvious lack of success."

The older man glanced over at his much younger colleague as he turned a cigar before a cedar spill, watching the end as it began to burn.

"But it's a long day and a long battle. How's it going with getting someone on the inside? Is that working out for you?"

He hit the cigar, passing the spill to Colin, who smiled as he began preparing his own stogie.

"You're obviously a smart man, Mr. Luck, but you don't understand black folk."

"No, you underestimate me, Colin. I know the blacks and what motivates them. Most blacks are just like you and me. It's just that the criminals, gang bangers, drug dealers, sports figures, celebrities and thug activists like OLM get all the attention. Black leaders claim to be speaking for the blacks when all they're trying to do is line their own pockets, like you. Maybe one day the blacks will speak up for themselves, but it won't be today or any time soon."

Colin blew a cloud of smoke, sighing, savoring and brushing the dreadlock braids from his face.

"I get the feeling that some of them think they're already speaking up, and since no one wants to listen, they figure they're going to *make* people listen."

"Who? Jesse Jackson? Sharpton? Give me a break!"

"Natsumi Mitchell. She's going to be a real problem."

"Who? A problem for you, maybe. Whoever that is, she won't be a problem for me."

"Of course she will."

"Really? And why's that?"

"Because she understands you better than you understand her."

They were an unlikely pair: the 70-year-old white billionaire businessman and the 29-year-old black music producer-turned-entrepreneur. Colin Stein-Whitaker was not what he appeared to be. At six-foot-three and with a well-muscled physique, he was physically intimidating.

A mulatto with green eyes, he was a handsome and affable graduate from the Master's program at the Brown University School of Business, though his educational history and activity in Rhode Island was a well-kept, guarded secret. To many in the hip-hop underground world, he was Cyanide, a pants-sagging, chrome grill, tattooed, murder-talking wild-eyed rapper and underground music producer.

He had been raised in Jamestown in Newport County, Rhode Island, where his black father was a doctor and his white mother was a banker, financial adviser and heiress to a national mercantile manufacturing empire. Colin became fascinated with rap music and rap lifestyle as a teen, deciding that he wanted to ultimately dominate the industry and innovate. His conservative father, however, was strident in his objection to any endeavor that did not result in an advanced college degree, so only child Colin went to Brown and got his MBA under the threat of being unsupported, disinherited and disowned. As a result, he quietly resented his father.

Because he did not have the proper pedigree for a rap star, he took great pains to create a hard, raw persona, contriving a lurid backstory that cast him as an urchin, fathered by a pimp and born to a crack addict prostitute in Compton, California. He claimed his mother beat him every day of his life until she was murdered when he was seven years old. He was passed along by several abusive aunts and uncles until he hit the streets at thirteen and joined a gang, where he sold drugs and eventually amassed the money to invest in a rap studio.

Every time he re-told the story in verse, he embellished his hardship, street smarts and criminal exploits, eventually portraying himself as an abandoned cold-blooded killer who had taken the moniker, Cyanide, a name that loomed large in rap underground. He went through a daily routine that darkened his skin. Colin was obsessed with making money to prove himself smarter and blacker than his father. *Disinherited? Disowned? I never needed ya, bitch Nigga!*

After six years in Los Angeles, Colin had become a rap mogul and the ruler of a vast underground empire stretched across the globe. His music and fashionwear companies, through diversified investments, were worth well over two hundred million dollars. Concerned about being recognized and revealed, Colin rarely made public appearances and did not allow photographs. He hired a company to destroy or alter every image of him that ever existed, wherever possible. When promoting his company and products, he always sent someone in his stead, or he wore the mask of a ghost.

Justin Luck was acquainted with Colin's parents, and though they were not friends, he knew the family well enough to recognize Colin unmasked outside a local Los Angeles cable television show, promoting a hip-hop film as its executive producer. Luck thought the idea of Colin being this "Cyanide" character was hysterical, and he discreetly contacted the young entrepreneur for a meeting, under the veiled threat of exposure. However, over the course of a few conversations, he decided "the kid has spunk and smarts," taking him on as a business associate, of sorts.

"When do we start the next phase of this operation?" Luck asked.

"You been asleep?" Colin answered, blowing smoke. "I already told you. It's on already. I already got someone on the inside. It's a little shaky for the moment, but we'll see how it takes. We'll give it a little time. Besides that, I got five artists droppin albums this month—serious gangsta shit, all about the revolution, all about what they need ta do with those guns you been floodin inta their neighborhoods. The revolution's ready on my end."

"Hey, I'm a patient man, and I'm rich enough to give you the time you need, as long as we get necessary results."

Colin was smart enough to discern that he was only part of a larger plan.

"Okay Mr. Luck, aside from my revolution and your race war, we destroy Our Lives Matter from the inside out… so what? What's the purpose of that?"

"So they're no longer a problem," the older man answered, "so we can all get back to the business at hand, back to continuing division and racial animosity."

"Yeah, back to the business at hand—okay, but you're into banking and building big shit. How is that little movement in Oakland hurting your business or your war? I know how they hurt my cause, but how could they possibly hurt your business? You never told me that."

"Because it's my business, not yours," Luck snapped. "Look, this whole thing is bigger than you. You're an amateur. You just keep on making money and then you'll understand. Movements are bad things, with unpredictable and far-reaching consequences. I'd like to make the world a better place for everyone who deserves it, but I have to take care of the things I care about first."

"But I want a revolution while you want a race war. Of course ours is not a perfect union, which we both knew going in. We don't care about the same things."

"Money. We have money in common, Colin. We both care it. That's not to say I don't care about the blacks and black lives, but am I worried or upset when a thug gets gunned down in the street by a cop or some vigilante? Give me a break! I'm no more worried than I am when a black shoots another black in a gang fight, or when Mexican or Asian gangs wipe each other out. That's never going to end."

"You don't want it to end," Colin proffered.

"Why should I want it to end?" Luck answered. "They live in a different universe from me and you. Their reality and ours could not be more different, and they no more understand us than we understand them. They don't matter! When you are superior, simply be superior. It's a waste to concern yourself with lesser beings. When you understand that, Colin, you'll surpass your father and the so-called upper crust of America, and maybe even me, given you have advantages that were never available to me. Be what you are. Devour your heart now, before it destroys you…"

Luck looked over, and noting Colin's natural tendency to resist authority, he smiled.

"Or give in to your father, become your father."

"I'm in it for the thrill, Mr. Luck. I don't have a heart," Colin insisted, glaring over before stiffening his square jaw and blowing a cloud of smoke. "I ripped that out six years ago when I became Cyanide."

****

Per instructions from Davis Franklin, Kendrick sat trembling in a private room at the hospital, face in his hands, alone with his thoughts. Minutes earlier, he had watched panicked nurses call "code blue" before various personnel came running in from all directions. The attending doctor shouted that Jennifer had gone into cardiac arrest as he threw the sheets back and ripped open her gown.

"Defibrillator! Get it over here! Now!"

By that time, nurses were pushing Kendrick out the room.

"Okay! Clear!"

The jolt of electricity caused Jennifer's body to stiffen, bouncing four inches off the mattress before sinking back into the sheets. The electrical instruments indicated three weak heartbeats before stopping again.

"Clear!"

Again, the heavy jolt and the body rigor. The five nurses crowded around performed various tasks in between the resuscitation attempts, checking for a pulse, examining Jennifer's eyes and monitoring the electrocardiograph and other instruments. Unresponsive. A third attempt.

A large man from Davis Franklin's security detail pushed open the door, bowing his head nodding as the billionaire entered. Seated with hands still clasped over his face, Kendrick snapped his head up and rose, relieved to discern a supportive expression on his friend's face. The hug was brief and tentative.

"Any news, Ken? What are they saying?"

"She coded a few minutes ago," Kendrick sighed. "They put me out of the room. I don't know. I don't know what happened to her. It looks bad."

"I'm sorry. I saw her family out in the lobby. Apparently, her mother's having a hard time with all that's been going on. I think the hospital had to admit her to monitor her heart condition."

Davis walked to the door and opened it, peering outside.

"The halls of the hospital are crawling with reporters, and I saw three or four television crews out front: *Dateline*, *20/20*, *48 Hours* and local stations. Maybe there were more."

"This is all a nightmare!" Kendrick moaned, eyes puffy and narrowed, wagging his head. "How is this all happening? She was fine this morning. Something isn't right here!"

"You're not the only one thinking that, Ken. I heard a few theories on the way in, most of them suggesting that her sudden life-threatening condition has something to do with you."

"Me? No! Why would anyone say that? I'm the one who called the ambulance. Why would I do anything to my fiancée? We're getting married!"

Davis placed a hand on Kendrick's shoulder to calm him.

"I know that, Kendrick. I know you, but those reporters out there don't know you. They're looking for a sensational story. And the cops—they're just doing their job."

"Cops? What do you mean 'cops'?"

"There are a few detectives out there, or investigators. Whatever happens with Jennifer—even if she recovers, I'm sure they'll want to sit you down and ask you a few questions."

"They can ask whatever they want," Kendrick shot back, his irritation growing. "I have nothing to hide."

"I know you don't, but all the same, I've gone through measures to hire you a lawyer, an excellent criminal defense attorney."

"Criminal defense!" Kendrick shouted, incredulous. "I don't need a criminal defense attorney! I just need the doctors to do their job and help her recover. This is about Jennifer, not about me!"

The sound of the door caused both men to direct their attention to the doctor who entered, his expression guarded.

"Mr. Vesey, is it possible to have a word with you, alone?"

"Why? What's this about?"

"It's, it's a private matter."

"I'll leave," Davis offered.

"No!" Kendrick objected, nervous. "You are my friend, Davis. Whatever he has to tell me—I want you to stay." He looked back toward the doctor. "Whatever it is, just tell me. Tell it to me straight."

The doctor closed his eyes briefly and took a breath.

"We weren't able to *save* her. She's still on life support, which means her heart is beating and she's breathing by means of medical technology, but for all intents and purposes, Jennifer Alvarez is gone."

Suddenly weak in the knees, Kendrick nearly collapsed. Clutching his stomach, he strained to breathe, feeling as if someone had just punched him in the solar plexus.

"Her family wants her to remain on life support," the doctor continued, "but I told her older brother, Armando, who is speaking for the family, that Jennifer had an advance medical directive in place and that she had given you power of attorney, which we adhere to in such a matter. He objected, but the hospital is not the arbitrator of law. Legally, what happens next is your decision."

"No!" Kendrick contended, seated and bowed over. "Tell me you're lying! Tell me this isn't really happening!"

"Mr. Vesey, I realize this is a very difficult time for you. It's never easy for anyone, but take a few minutes to let it all sink in. Find your peace with it. If you have a faith, maybe you'll find your answers there. There's no rush, but when you decide what you want to do, just let us know. I'm sorry for your loss. We did everything we could to save her."

The room was silent for five minutes after the doctor left, save Kendrick's sporadic sobs and unintelligible, softly-spoken remarks in Jamaican patois. Seated across the room, Davis cleared his throat, and when he got Kendrick's attention, he spoke.

"I'm very sorry about Jennifer. You're understandably emotional, but this is a crucial time, which is why it would be best if you didn't speak with anyone about this matter until you've spoken with your lawyer. Do you understand what I'm saying?"

Kendrick nodded.

"I've made arrangements with the hospital to have you exit unseen to the roof, where you'll be transported by helicopter to a discreet location where your attorney will be waiting."

The man who entered the room with a large man from Davis's security detail was roughly Kendrick's height and build, and his face held an approximation to Kendrick's face.

"You're going to leave right now with Cecil here," Davis insisted, "and this man will remain in your place until you're safely away. It's only a matter of time before the reporters and the police understand exactly what's going on and converge. By that time, you'll already be speaking with Natsumi Mitchell, and she'll handle things from there."

"Natsumi Mitchell?"

"Your attorney and spokesperson. We'll leave it to her to deal with the madness that'll ensue when you end Jennifer's life support."

Natsumi Mitchell? Kendrick thought, remembering. *There is obviously more going on here than I understand.*

****

Because Natsumi had been called away on business, the Our Lives Matter meeting was rescheduled and reconvened in a conference room on the forty-eighth floor of the Transamerica Building in downtown San Francisco, at the intersection of Montgomery and Washington Street at Columbus. The office belonged to the *Aegis Foundation*, a women's advocacy organization founded by Allegra Benson, who was Lyndsey Mitchell-Ettinger's grandmother.

From its inception through its development and outreach over twelve years, the foundation had been in the hands of Destiny Mitchell, who adopted Lyndsey after her father murdered her mother and later committed suicide. Destiny was the prosecutor in the highly-publicized criminal trial, which resulted in a less than conclusive outcome, though the subsequent civil trial resulted in millions of dollars of damages that Allegra used to set up the foundation.

Destiny Mitchell ran the foundation for a dozen years before accepting a White House job as a domestic issues advisor to the President, though she resigned after only two years for unspecified reasons. When she departed San Francisco for Washington DC, she put Lyndsey, who had been her protégée, in charge of Aegis. Upon Destiny's return, Lyndsey offered to step down as director, but her mother had no desire to return to her old position, though she served as an advisor on the foundation's legal committee.

As Destiny's adopted daughter, Lyndsey and Natsumi grew up as family, though Lyndsey was nine years older and protective of her passionate cousin. She had joined the Our Lives Matter movement because she believed in its goals and purpose for existence. As the organization's executive committee members filed into the room, she couldn't help but wonder how the meeting would go without Natsumi at the gavel. Queen Shabaz called the meeting to order.

"I'm sure she already explained the situation to you, Lyndsey, but Natsumi phoned me this afternoon with an apology, along with the alarming news that she had been recently assigned a high-profile case, albeit against her wishes. The case'll render her unable to chair our meetings over the next two to three months. As a co-chairperson, she asked me to lead in her stead, while she would lend support as a regular member of the executive committee."

Seated across the conference table from Queen Shabaz were Demetrius Berry, Heather Kaplan, Padmi Ravi, Lyndsey Mitchell-Ettinger, Calvin King, Mia Melendez, Phi Truong and three other committee members. After Queen finished going over the meeting agenda, Demetrius signaled to make an inquiry.

"Okay, so Natsumi is basically gone for three months, right? You were her co-chair, and that means you're taking over for her, right? From an organizational point-of-view, it seems the next order of business is to determine who is going to be your co-chair."

"Your point is well taken, Demetrius" Queen nodded. "I suppose we'll have to vote in a new co-chair, at least for the time being. We'll open for a nomination."

"I think it should be me," Demetrius insisted. "Next to you and Natsumi, I have the most time and sacrifice in, and I'm probably the best person at this table security-wise. I realize all ya'll want nothin but women in leadership, but ya gotta give a brotha a chance every once in a while—or else you ain't no better than the rest of em out there."

"This isn't tokenism," Heather interjected, "and it's not about how much time anyone has in. When we did our by-laws, we said leadership would be elected by the majority of executive committee members present. I nominate Padmi. I think Natsumi would agree."

"Thank you, Heather," Padmi smiled, "but I was going to nominate Lyndsey."

"I'm afraid I would have to decline," Lyndsey interjected. "It would be an honor, but my schedule would not allow the required time. I was going to nominate Calvin."

"Calvin?" Demetrius sighed, perplexed. "Is someone going to nominate me?"

"We're looking for a person who could be a good leader," Mia answered, "but you're just too aggressive and arrogant, Demetrius. You come off too strong for some of us."

"Yeah, because you've all been programed by a system that can't handle the idea and reality of a strong black man, especially those of you who ain't black!"

"Now hold on, Demetrius!" Queen called out. "This committee is inclusive of everyone in our movement, regardless of race. It is more than a black thing, so for you to make it about that does not serve this committee well. In my opinion, you've already disqualified yourself for the position."

"I nominate Demetrius Berry," Calvin offered, nodding toward his friend.

"Very well," Queen answered. "We'll vote by secret ballot."

Heather Kaplan, as secretary, stood and passed out paper chits, making sure all members had pens for writing in a selection. After three minutes of silence, she collected the ballots and sat, tallying votes. Finally, she stood to make the announcement.

"With a grand total of five endorsements, Padmi Ravi will be our next co-chair."

The matter thus resolved, Queen proceeded down the agenda, taking up reports from the finance committee, operations committee, media committee, legal committee and security committee. After the reports and discussion, the executive committee's guests were invited in, one by one, beginning with a local activist seeking funds to provide bail for recently arrested protesters in jail. The executive committee's second guest discussed large crowd logistics and recommendations for future protests.

The executive committee's final guest, who had come upon Natsumi's insistence, was Sergeant Johnnie Draco of the Oakland Police department. During his last appearance, Draco warned that Our Lives Matter was in the crosshairs of a group of rich white men who wanted a race war in America.

Because the organization was multi-racial while advocating cooperation and judicial and economic equality, it threatened their aims and had to be destroyed.

Draco insisted the rogue one-percenters were a real threat, not only to OLM, but to its individual members. Yet he said the rich white men had a vulnerability.

"Are you going to share who these dangerous men are and what their vulnerability is?" Lyndsey asked.

"They're billionaires, and they own your politicians in Washington and at home, they've got government officials, federal agencies and media empires working for em—church leaders, people you trust, people you see every day. They're leading this country exactly where they want—into a race war."

"And who would benefit from that?" Heather piped in.

"The super-rich. They don't like where this country is headed, with African Americans, Latinos and Asians finally realizing they have enormous economic and political power—whites will be the minority in 2044—with Muslim countries, Israel, China and the rest of the world catching up, with political correctness, and what they hate most: the subject of income inequality."

"And how would a race war or revolution solve those problems?" Phi asked. "A race war would only divide America, making it weak and more vulnerable."

"These people aren't as loyal to America as they are to their profits," Draco responded. "A race war would change the national debate and the course of American history. By way of contrast, they fear unity because they have always profited on division, distrust and hate."

Demetrius wagged his head, disgusted.

"Sounds like you're off the deep end on one of those conspiracy theories to me."

"I'm sure you've seen it with Our Lives Matter," Draco countered. "'They've been coming after you guys since you started, and if you had to tell the story of your movement, I'm sure a lot of people would think you were making it up, that you're paranoid… unless you think it's all a coincidence, meaning the anti-protests, the negative news coverage, the conflicts with the cops, the gang members and white supremacists. They're all trying to destroy you."

"I get that," Queen nodded, "but a race war in America. It seems far-fetched."

"I halfway believe Draco," Mia continued. "Does anyone else think it's a coincidence that Natsumi suddenly got called away on some big case?"

"Research it yourself. The real conspiracy is the start of a race war in America," Draco asserted, "and it's been going on for years. Latinos and

Hispanics didn't even exist before 1970—they were considered Caucasian until the government decided it need another minority to compete with the blacks. But Latino's an invention, not a race. No one can even define the term—it's just another division, another way to pit one group against the next."

"That much is true," Padmi conceded.

"For Hispanics," Draco continued, "the next step is to pit them against each other, against Blacks, whatever that means, against Asians and Jews, and to pit everyone against Whites, whatever that means. It's all bullshit, and they're counting on idiots to buy in."

"So let's hear this out, Draco," Calvin concluded. "Who specifically is behind this, and what is their vulnerability?"

"Okay," Draco began, leaning forward, lowering his voice. "Do you remember the two cops who were killed in Indiana two months ago, in Gary, the next day after one of your protests there?"

"Yeah, they blamed us for it…" Heather answered, "Fox News and conservative radio."

"And do you remember the cop who was shot in Memphis last month?"

"They blamed that one on our 'rhetoric,'" Mia answered.

"Well, the truth is: in all these recent cop shootings, it's not you or your rhetoric. It's one of the players in the group I told you about. They're killing cops to radicalize the white racists in this country who are tired of political correctness, tired of suppressing their beliefs and resentments."

"I call bullshit again!" Demetrius snarled, incredulous.

"When the cops—some who are legitimately fearful—are quick to shoot when it's a black man or brown kid or innocent victim, when they take out their frustration on a helpless black woman in a jail cell—this same group, who own the judges, prosecutors and lawmakers—they make sure the cops aren't punished, which only increases the frustration in black and brown communities."

"If that's true, it's pure evil," Lyndsey lamented, "and when both sides reach critical mass, that will be the beginning of this race war?

"The race war has already begun. This revolution will be televised. The bullets are already flying. We'll be working against time to try and stop it."

"Back to the vulnerability you won't answer about," Queen redirected. "Given if what you're telling us is true, how do we exploit this vulnerability?"

"Well, there's the finger in my eye," Draco answered. "Someone gave the order to kill these cops—the same someone who needs good cops to die to fuel the race war. We've got evidence about the man behind it, but we can trust going public with it. I just made detective, and I've got a few other detectives I trust across the country working with me. I need someone from your movement to work with us to slow things down on both sides, to de-escalate hostilities while we still can."

"Let's be specific, Sergeant Draco," Queen demanded. "What exactly do you need us to do?"

"I need someone to volunteer to work with us—someone who knows up front that if we fail, we're probably going to die, and we'll be exposing our families to grave danger. We can't do it on one side alone. Let's see if anyone in your movement really believes 'our lives' really matter. You can take some time to figure it out, but let me know.

"No need!" Demetrius called out.

"Excuse me!" Queen objected. "That's not your call to make, Demetrius."

"Of course it's my call to make!" he snapped. "I don't trust this bastard, but he asked for one of us to work with him in this dangerous situation. I'm volunteerin. That someone is gonna be me!"

Chapter 10

"Good to see you again, Mr. Vesey," Natsumi said in a professional tone. "We met before, briefly, at the television studio under vastly different circumstances." She motioned toward the woman at her left. "This is Miriam Wilke. She works PR for the firm. Can we all sit down, please?"

Natsumi had phoned Kendrick early that morning to schedule the late afternoon meeting at her new office suite. Two days earlier, she had re-located to a new project on Market Street that Davis Franklin had recently purchased and renovated. Franklin insisted on a private, guarded space for Natsumi, separate from the Reed and Wilke offices, to better control unwelcome intrusions and interference by reporters, investigators and activists.

"Mr. Franklin called right before you walked in the door, Kendrick. I understand doctors are saying your fiancée, Ms. Alvarez, is basically on life support, and they're waiting on *your* decision on when to pull the plug."

"I just came from the hospital," Kendrick answered. "Jennifer's mother's also there, admitted, in one of the rooms. She had a heart attack and she's not doing well. So I got into it with her brother, Armando, when I was there, and he's blaming me for everything."

Kendrick removed his jacket before sitting, exposing his torn shirt.

"How am I supposed to pull the plug on Jen? I'm thinking I'll just sign the responsibility over to the family. I should leave that responsibility to her brother."

"And create the perception that you don't care about her?" Miriam asked. "After she trusted you, after she put this life and death decision in your hands? You just want to throw your hands up in the air? Think, Kendrick! You have to think about everything you do right now. With stakes as high as they are and getting higher, any miscalculation on your part will definitely come back to bite you."

"But if I tell them to pull the plug, won't that be like I'm killing her? Won't they use that against me?"

"She's already dead," Miriam insisted. "You'll just be doing the merciful thing, the responsible thing. The doctors don't know the exact cause of death yet, but you have to fulfill your obligation in doing what she entrusted only you to do. Conferring that responsibility on anyone else would be a breach of trust and a break in character."

"Do you love her, Kendrick?" Natsumi asked.

"Of course I do! Why would you even ask me that?"

"We just need you to do what you would normally do for her, as her fiancé," Natsumi answered, "without the added calculation of what other people are going to say and do. Tell us: if none of this media circus was going on, if the Nobel Prize hadn't happened, and if you and Jennifer were just regular people and she was lying in that bed, what would you do?"

"I've already said my goodbye to her," he responded, his eyes swelling with tears. "She's gone. Under normal circumstances, I would pull the plug, or I would tell the doctors to pull the plug."

"Then pull the plug!" Miriam asserted, her voice breaking shrill. "To do anything else, to calculate any motivation beyond what is in your heart would be a mistake. If you haven't done anything wrong, then you have no other choice."

"But shouldn't I discuss it with her family? Her brother attacked me because he thought I was going to pull the plug—you know, because of her mother's condition. He thinks that if Jen goes, her mother won't be able to take it, and she'll die too."

"Jennifer gave you the power to decide what happens at this point," Miriam countered. "She didn't give it to her brother, and I am sure there's a reason for it. Kendrick, you have to realize you have a legion of reporters out there, representing billions of corporate dollars—hollow people who've sold their souls just to get anywhere close to a story like this.

"These are people who will parse, analyze and even make up lurid stories. They'll lie to sell news. That's who we'll be up against. If you relinquish your legal right and the PR advantage to her family or her brother, then we'll lose control of the narrative. At that point, the media, not you, not the family—will wrest control of the story from there. You have to decide, Kendrick, and you better be prepared to fight the media trolls from that moment on."

Natsumi, while listening, had readied her laptop, prepared to take notes.

"Why don't we begin by hearing your side of the story, Kendrick? What happened in that elevator? And is there any way the injuries she sustained in that altercation could have led to her inexplicable death?"

"The story is exactly as I explained it," he answered, confident. "Nothing that happened in the elevator could have killed her. Nothing I did could have resulted in her to being in a coma like she is. I was there: she kneed me in the nuts and I reacted, and she did hit her head, but I was looking right at her. The bump on her head wasn't life-threatening. She was fine until yesterday! I swear."

"And has there been any physical violence or any other altercation since that night in the elevator?" Natsumi asked.

"No, no. Nothing at all!"

"No history of physical violence before?" Natsumi continued. "No police record, no neighbor complaints? You can't hide it."

"Never!" he answered. "We're not like that. We've never been violent, and she's never been like she was in the elevator that night. I swear it was the medication she was taking."

"Medication?" Miriam asked. "Prescription medication, or was it drugs? Was she an addict?"

"No! She was just taking Tagamet for her stomach, and when she was drinking alcohol with it, she sometimes got a little out of control."

"She was an alcoholic?" Miriam asked, her voice insistent.

"No. She would maybe have a glass or two of wine after a long day of work, but that was it. She was different over the last month, but I'm sure it wasn't drug or alcohol addiction. She wasn't like that. Maybe it was the pressure from our upcoming wedding..."

"She was taking prescription medicine?" Natsumi asked. "Was she under a physician's care?"

"Not directly. I think she called her doctor and asked for the Tagamet, as a favor. She was a long-time patient."

"What was her health condition?" Natsumi continued, seeming perplexed. "Why did she need the Tagamet?"

"I—she'd been sick for over a month. Her stomach was upset a lot, and there was blood," he answered, "maybe because she was nervous about the wedding in Jamaica?"

"How big a wedding? How many guests?"

"I don't know. Maybe between eighty and a hundred. It'll be an exclusive event in Negril."

"A hundred guests?" Natsumi scoffed. "Wasn't Jennifer a seasoned administrator for a program that handled hundreds of girls—many of those from at-risk environments? She staged much larger events in Central and South America as a regular part of her job. You're saying she was losing it over a private wedding with maybe a hundred guests? That makes no sense. Are you guessing about the Tagamet?"

"Well, yes. I guess so."

"I'll need the name of her doctor. And it will be helpful if you can find her daily planner or calendar, a journal or any other written schedule where she might have made notes to herself or recorded her activities? As busy as she was, I imagine she had something like that. Do you have access to her laptop?"

"Yes, yes," he nodded. "I'll make sure you have all those things."

"Did you notice any changes in her behavior in the twenty-four hours leading to the moment you discovered her non-responsive?"

"No," he answered, "nothing, other than that she was sleeping a lot. I thought it was jet lag or stress."

Natsumi looked up from the computer.

"Of course, you know that after you pull the plug, there will be an autopsy, and if anything comes up irregular, as in foul play or murder, then you'll be the primary suspect? With all the press that's already going on, the

DA and detectives will do everything in their power to make you look guilty and put you away for murder."

"But I didn't do anything! I loved Jennifer. Doesn't that matter?"

"You should know better than that," Miriam sneered. "In high-profile case these days, you're guilty until proven innocent."

"The courts have never expressly held that discovery at or before the preliminary is unavailable," Natsumi remarked, "but based on what I know about judges here in San Francisco, the more we discover early on, the less we'll have to share. I'll also need a copy of her most recent medical records, if you can get them. Since you're her power of attorney, make sure you order those before giving the order to remove life support."

"Okay," Kendrick nodded, "I can do that."

"And once it's done, do not discuss details involving Jennifer or yourself with anyone but Miriam and myself, do you understand? Not a word—not to a friend, not even to a family member!"

"I got it."

"I'll begin by writing a public statement from you," Miriam added, "expressing your profound grief for the loss of your fiancée and your appreciation for all the love and support the both of you received from friends and family. You will be the first to demand answers about why she fell ill and died. You'll be the first to ask the medical examiner to begin an investigation."

"Okay," he nodded, "but what about her family? What about her mother?"

"Look Kendrick—the press, the DA, the police, her family—they'll all be coming for you," Miriam warned. "Forget her family. You need to focus on covering your own ass!"

****

Impatient, Alberta switched to a different news channel at every commercial break in an effort to follow the breaking story: *Jennifer Alvarez, Dead at 31*. At 2:00 a.m. PST, doctors removed life support from Jennifer, who was pronounced dead at 2:08. The scene at the hospital was chaotic, with Jennifer's family members shrieking and weeping and video footage of her brother blaming Kendrick for his sister's "murder."

And worse, news came at 2:22 a.m. that Jennifer's mother, Teresa, had succumbed within minutes after hearing that her daughter had died. It was a double tragedy for the family and a story that would run and gain momentum throughout the day.

"What are you watching, Alberta?" Roland scolded, tugging the remote from her hand. "You know you shouldn't be watching that. Kendrick said 'no news for you!' What are you doing up so early?"

"Mi no can sleep," she signed. "Jennifer dead. Jennifer mother dead. Mi no talk to Kendrick for three days. Alberta no sleep before Alberta talk to Kendrick."

Roland, still in his pajamas, cut off the television and plopped onto the couch, extending his legs. Lazy, he spoke rather than signing.

"Jennifer's dead? You never liked her anyway. I'm sure you won't be any losing sleep over that."

"Jennifer brother, him is bad man. Him name is Armando. Armando hate Kendrick. Alberta need to see Kendrick. Alberta worry too much. Kendrick no kill Jennifer!"

"No, he didn't. You're right. No motive there," Roland asserted. "Kendrick loved Jennifer. Why would he kill her? They were going to be married. Once they investigate, it will become obvious. Humans do not kill other humans unless there is a motive."

"Explain 'motive'," Alberta signed.

"I'll try," Roland sighed. "Okay, a motive is a reason, and while there is not usually a good reason why one human should kill another human, most humans kill because they have a reason or invent a reason why they believe they have to kill, for profit, for hate or revenge, or for some advantage. But there are a few who kill just because they are evil, and none of the above applies to Kendrick."

"Why above? Above what?" she responded, confused. "Hate is motive?"

"Yes, hate is a powerful motive. For that reason, when someone is killed or murdered, one of the first questions humans ask is, 'did the murdered person have any enemies?' and 'who would want that person dead?'"

"Explain 'murder' for human killing human."

"Wow!" Roland laughed. "I'm barely awake and you want a civics lesson? Okay, murder is when one person decides they want to kill another person and they make a plan to do it, and then they actually *kill* that other person, knowing in advance that they are going to kill that other person."

"Human decide and plan to kill and kill every day. Human fight war. Human hunt to kill. Human kill lion. Human kill ape. That is murder?"

"No. Murder does not apply to animals. It only applies to humans, to persons."

"'Person,' or 'human?'"

"I'm not sure. I don't know it the definition makes that distinction."

Alberta's face showed confusion and concern. She mumbled something to herself before continuing.

"Human kill Alberta—that is murder?"

Her face's confusion immediately migrated to his.

"Well, I don't know. I mean, I think you're a person, legally. I don't know. There's never been a situation like this before, as far as I know. I supposed it would be up to the courts and finally up to a judge, maybe the U.S. Supreme Court."

"Person is not human?"

"Humans are persons, and persons are humans, but it's more complicated than that. You're the beginning of something new, Alberta. You're the only one like you. You are a person who is not a human, an almost-legal nonhuman person. I'm sure they would have to make a new law just because of you."

"Maybe there is more chimp smart like Alberta? Maybe Alberta is not only smart chimp. How Roland know?"

"I don't know," Roland confessed, removing his glasses to massage his eyelids. "Maybe there are other chimps who are unusually intelligent like you, and maybe there's a chimp out there somewhere who is even smarter than you are, but no one would ever know it. That's because you're the only chimp who can talk to us. You're the only chimp who understands and accepts human societal norms. You've read our books, studied our history and argued our philosophies. Besides that, you're a math genius. Believe me, there aren't many humans smarter than you."

"Alberta kill human—that is murder?"

Roland sat forward, a little alarmed.

"Again, I don't know for sure. That would be up to the courts. I'm not a lawyer, but let's look it up."

He held the smart phone close to his mouth.

"Siri, what is the legal definition of murder?"

The voice on the phone answered immediately.

"Murder means *the unlawful premeditated killing of one human being by another.*"

"Human being?" Roland said aloud as he typed a few words on the phone keypad. "Murder… it says here that premeditated murder is the crime of wrongfully and intentionally causing the death of another human being after rationally considering the timing or method of doing so to either increase the likelihood of success or to evade detection or apprehension.

"Based on that, I still don't know the answer in your specific case, Alberta. If someone killed you, would it be murder? I don't know. If you killed a human, would that be murder? You are not a human being. I don't know that either. It seems likely, but I suppose it would come down a judge determining whether or not you are capable of premeditation."

An hour later, in one of the developing stories about the life of Jennifer Alvarez, CNN highlighted a biographical feature about Kendrick, beginning with his childhood in Jamaica and focusing on his education at the University of Chicago, his early primate language work at the New York Academy of Sciences, his work at the University of Berkeley and his Nobel Prize. During a story segment that featured his work with Alberta, several other specialists on nonhuman primate languages were interviewed for relevant comments. Alberta bristled with panic and rage at the very sight of Dr. David Jacobs.

"What nobody realizes is I'm the one who discovered Alberta in the first place," Jacobs scoffed. "I discovered her and unlocked her brain. From the day she was born, she was my special project, until SFBR pulled the rug out from under me. They never told Davis Franklin about us or about the trauma they caused by allowing us to be separated. Alberta had a special bond with me from the very beginning."

He paused to wipe the moisture from his eyes.

"What I'm hearing about Kendrick Vesey is unsettling, but only because I care about Alberta's welfare and her future. If he did what Jennifer Alvarez's family and the DA are accusing him of doing, then he is not in any way a person who should exert an influence in Alberta's life. I only hope that Davis Franklin will finally recognize my contribution and allow me again to be a part of her life. Alberta and I are family."

"Jacob is not family! Alberta see Jacob, Alberta murder Jacob!" she signed vigorously.

"No!" Roland reproached. "Alberta should never talk like that! You don't mean that!"

"Premeditation!" she finger-spelled. "Alberta can murder!"

****

He asked the priest to let him know when the last of the crowd was gone so that he could have a moment alone with her. His knees weakened as he walked through the door, making him swoon, making him struggle to keep from passing out. There she was… in a casket, her body still—forever still. As he approached, she seemed noticeably smaller, and the expression on her face was one that had never shone there before. Her complexion was pallid.

He reached out a hand to grasp her shoulder, which felt cold and hard, so unlike the soft, tender shoulders he used to caress and massage. The moist, supple skin of her once-kissable neck seemed shriveled, and the outlines of her mouth, beyond the lipstick, were blue. He knew the autopsy required the medical examiner to saw open her skull to remove her brain. As a result, the doctor had pulled and stretched her face in so many directions that the mortician, despite having an album full of pictures, could not restore her rightful semblance.

Leaning over the casket, he neared her face and kissed her on cold, stiff lips, remembering how, on every other occasion, how velvety and warm they had been. His tears fell onto her face, soaking into the make-up.

"For the love of God! Why?"

He said a prayer, relinquishing his connection to the body that lay before him, realizing the body had no more connection to Jennifer, or to him. It was just a vessel she used to inhabit, an evanescent, mortal place she had departed, never to return. And yet as he felt a portion of her spirit dwelling in his own heaving chest, breathing as he breathed, he knew she would remain with him.

"I'm sorry, baby," he cried, clasping his hands, gazing upward. "I believe in God, but I don't understand how he could have let this happen. Not *you*! I begged and bargained to take your place. Even if there is a reason, Jen, I will never accept it. God has broken my heart forever."

"Dr. Vesey," a voice from behind interrupted, "it seems you made it after all. I think most people would find it a little suspicious that you didn't even have the respect to attend your fiancée's wake."

Kendrick turned, already certain about who owned the voice causing such irritation.

"Dr. Jacobs, you caught me at a bad moment, so this is a warning: I'm exactly one sarcastic remark away from kicking your sorry ass—right up in this place, so choose your words carefully."

"I only came to offer my condolences. I knew you'd be here, and I knew with all the crazy press around the murder—I mean the *death* of Jennifer Alvarez—that you couldn't well afford to be here with the family who blames you… and all the reporters. Beyond that, I came here to attempt to bury the hatchet with you."

"Where?" Kendrick responded, his voice mocking, "In my back? Maybe my skull?"

"Listen Kendrick," Jacobs insisted, raising his hands in a symbol of submission, "I realize we got off to a bad start. I think I blamed you out of frustration, or maybe jealousy, but you do realize I'm the one who discovered Alberta. I'm the one who had the insight to understand how very special she was. And to have that taken from me overnight, well…"

Jacobs came a step closer.

"I've been divorced three times. I don't have a wife or a single kid who cares about anything other than the money I don't have. Alberta, for those three years, was like a daughter to me. I was thinking that that, in light of your recent loss, maybe you might understand just how devastated I was when Alberta was so suddenly ripped out of my life."

"I had nothing to do with that," Kendrick answered, his demeanor remaining skeptical.

"I know you didn't. That's why I overreacted and blamed you. I was wrong. I just hope that now we can turn the page, starting with today. I am very sorry for your loss. I'm sure you loved Jennifer Alvarez very much."

Kendrick was unmoved.

"You have to know that Alberta completely hates you, and for that reason, I would never let you see her. I fear she would kill you on sight—

something that would risk her pending legal status. The mention of your name brings out the animal in her. She would tear you apart, limb from limb, and that would be bad for both of you."

"I don't know what you've taught her, doctor," Jacobs responded, "but I taught her to be loving and compassionate. I took painstaking efforts to imbue her with a sense of morality, and personal duty and responsibility. The Alberta I raised and knew was gentle and caring and would never think of harming anyone. I taught her love."

"You knew Alberta when she was under three years old, Jacobs—an infant by any measure—but I'm guessing her memory of that early period was not positive. She's grown up now, and because she is so intelligent, her sense of morality, like ours, is often beset by things that are contradictory, things that don't fit into anyone's plan for her. She has real feelings, doctor, and she does not like you."

"I would like to see Alberta," Jacobs explained, "and I know that can't happen unless you sanction it. Even with all this bad press, Davis Franklin still believes in you and would never allow such a meeting unless you told him it was a good thing for her."

"Really?" Kendrick asked.

"And you'd have to explain it to Alberta as well. You'd have to tell her that I'm the one who discovered her—that I was the one who made her special, and without me she would just be an ordinary chimp in some exhibit or animal park or zoo. You have to convince her of that."

"You're delusional, Jacobs. I'm grieving! Leave me the hell alone. She's got good instincts. It's why she never trusted you."

"You and Davis Franklin turned *Kipekee* against me," Jacobs scowled. "You two are making money off her, when I'm the one who found her. I made her what she is. I'm broke because of you. I deserve something for discovering her!"

Sensing resolve on Kendrick's angry face, Jacobs backed, turned and receded a few paces to a safe distance.

"I came here to issue you a warning, Vesey. You're going to prison, and Alberta will eventually come back to me anyway. All this legal nonhuman person talk is nonsense."

"Nonsense?"

"Yes! Where does it lead anyone?" Jacobs scoffed. "What if you gave Alberta and other nonhuman animals legal status? What would that mean? What would it mean if they became so-called 'persons'? What would their rights be? Would they have the same rights as humans?"

"That would be for the courts to decide," Kendrick answered. "Right now, she meets the scientific and societal criteria for a legal person. We've demonstrated that she possesses continuous consciousness over time and we've documented she's capable of framing representations about the world, formulating plans and acting on them. How is that any different from any human with legal rights?"

"Because she's an ape! She's an animal, that's how. The courts have said it: in order to have rights, chimpanzees need to carry out societal 'duties and responsibilities,' which you can't prove. Even if Davis Franklin succeeds at making even some animals equal to humans, where would it lead? Imagine living in a country where humans could be sued in court by a chimp, a pig a dolphin or an elephant. And what exactly would the legal status of these animals be? Would they be allowed to become U.S. citizens? Maybe you'd let them vote in elections somewhere along the line? Would they have the right to marry humans?"

"That would be up the courts. Alberta's a cognitively complex individual. Do you think she should be given no more consideration or legal protection than any ordinary pet? No more or a right to justice or legal protection than a dog, a cat, a canary, or maybe a goldfish?"

"Of course not! Chimps should never have protective rights! You think she should be treated equal to a human?"

"To a person—she should be treated as a person," Kendrick insisted. "There's got to be some middle ground. You want to put her in a cell and experiment on her brain. How cruel is that, knowing she understands social responsibility, the world and relationships in it like you and I do, if not better? She doesn't the deserve the dignity of personhood and the legal rights that accompany it?"

"It's a dangerous precedent, and you have no idea where it might lead us all."

"Oh," Kendrick sighed, "you mean like in early America, when women weren't considered 'persons,' or when the legal status of black slaves was 'real estate' or chattel property? You mean like when black people weren't citizens, when they were only considered 3/5ths of a person, when they couldn't vote or run for office, couldn't own property or sit on juries…"

"Only a liberal like you, Vesey, would have the gall to think it's okay to compare chimpanzees and other animals to black people and the black experience in America! If you go on record saying something so stupid, the blacks in this country will kick your arrogant ass back to Jamaica in a New York minute. My black friends won't have any of that talk from you!"

"That's not what I meant," Kendrick protested. "I wasn't comparing chimpanzees to black…"

"Let's just get to the point, Vesey: humans are humans and animals are animals—that's how God intended it. He put all the animals under the subjection of man. They were never meant to be our equals and never had any status under the Law. If God made Alberta different, it was so that we could learn something to better ourselves by studying her unique brain.

You're too politically correct to see it, and you're going to prison for murder because you're anti-progress and you got in the way!"

Chapter 11

The court-enforceable settlement agreement brought sweeping changes in training for recruits and seasoned officers, in developing programs to identify and support troubled officers, in updating technology and data management practices, and it brought in an independent federal monitor to ensure that the goals of the decree were met. The settlement was not an admission or evidence of liability, nor was it an admission by the city, police department, or its officers and employees that they had engaged in unconstitutional, illegal or otherwise improper activities or conduct.

In the country's Midwest, Cleveland was not the only city that, resulting from incidents, patterns and practice, found itself under the oversight of a U.S. District Judge working on behalf of the Department of Justice. Eighteen months earlier, the city had been the site of major protests that generated global media coverage concerning the police shooting of an unarmed 13-year-old black youth.

The officers, responding to a 911 operator's call about "a violent black gang member brandishing a gun and threatening people," had rushed to the scene, overwhelmed by adrenaline, conditioning and animus. Within fifteen seconds of their arrival, the frightened and confused youth's undernourished, scrawny body was riddled with 21 bullets from four police guns—one obliterating a right hand held out in a feeble protest. The reported "gun" turned out to be a cheap cell phone.

The source of the 911 call was an 85-year-old white woman, Clara Belle McCain, originally from Mississippi, who was paranoid about the influx of black families in her developing neighborhood. To her, all black men were drug dealers and pimps, all black women and girls were prostitutes and drug addicts, while all black boys were gang members or thugs. She was certain the boy had a gun in his hand, and when confronted about the consequences of her mendacious claim to the operator, she said the boy "probably did something to deserve it. If he hadn't already, he was certainly going to get around to it!"

Our Lives Matter organized angry though peaceful protests in the city, calling for charges against the officers, who began shooting seconds after they arrived. Natsumi had taken to the national airwaves, castigating the police department, the mayor's office and local media. The protests proved effective, focusing the country's attention on Cleveland, while enlisting the support of people of all races who could no longer deny the inequality of justice afforded blacks in America's cities, large and small.

When the volume of protests reached levels that the federal government could no longer ignore, the Department of Justice, under the direction of the Attorney General, launched an investigation into a long-term pattern of excessive force by the Cleveland Division of Police officers. The investigation ended in a settlement between the CDP and the DOJ, as well as the enforcement of a consent decree purposed to reform the division.

Despite the consent decree and a federal monitor, ongoing tensions continued to persist between law enforcement and the African American community. Many of the police officers resented the federal government oversight, blaming black communities for a high crime rate and a culture of violence (attributed to rap music lyrics) that left officers no choice other than to meet force with force. The African American community, notwithstanding, was certain that the police would find ways to circumvent reform (disabling vehicle and body cameras, falsifying reports, planting or destroying evidence, etc.) and to bamboozle the monitor, "who was on the cops' side anyway."

Three months later, some ne'er-do-well firebombed the home of Clara Belle McCain, the old woman who had lied about the boy having a gun. Unharmed but afraid for her life, the octogenarian immediately abandoned her home and moved to Atlanta to live with her sister, blaming "immoral, out-of-control blacks and the Our Lives Matter movement."

One month after the firebombing, a white Cleveland police officer, Brian Hitchcock, was lured into an elaborate trap in a dangerous neighborhood and shot in the head, apparently by black gang members. Again, police believed that if not for Our Lives Matter and its activism that incited irrational and undeserved anger toward the police, their colleague would have still been alive. One week later, a group of blacks allegedly murdered a second Cleveland cop, Jackson Bryant, while he was responding to a liquor store robbery. Perpetrators shot a second cop, his partner, in the leg.

Around the city during that same month, police officers shot and killed four gang members in separate incidents, while receiving tacit support and justification from the mayor, Internal Affairs, the local media and the federal monitor, who rationalized the heightened lethal response had resulted from a premeditated and organized campaign by some in the community who wanted to murder police officers. Racial tensions were at a tipping point in the city of Cleveland.

****

Johnny Draco arrived at Cleveland Hopkins International Airport (CLE) exactly one week after the Bryant murder, quietly shadowed by Demetrius Berry, an Our Lives Matter executive committee member. Demetrius had volunteered to help the officer investigate a notion that recent events in Cleveland were the opening volley in a nefarious plot that wealthy players hoped would culminate in a race war in America, first pitting blacks against the law enforcement and expanding to racial and cultural divides.

The wealthy and powerful business interests behind the alleged plot, according to Draco, had spent vast sums in a war against "political correctness," which by definition was "language, policies, or measures that were intended not to offend or disadvantage any particular group of people in society."

The onus of "political correctness" had alienated many "traditional" Americans, whom society had punished, ostracized and disenfranchised over three decades for speaking their minds. To these interests, these patriotic "real Americans" occasionally used words like "niggers, kikes, ragheads, jihadis, japs, chinks, gooks, wetbacks or fags" to describe troublemakers, and they were not always overly-concerned with being nice about it. They were honest about the nation's problems and unafraid to name instigators, even if doing so seemed offensive or mean. They were brave enough to stand up to all the minorities, special interests and identity groups that had taken over America.

Indeed, there could be no race war without first dispensing with political correctness and the compromises it demanded on traditional American values. Over the last two decades, beginning with media and the way its affiliates promulgated what was newsworthy, political correctness, a liberal impediment, was in the crosshairs. The proliferation of social media on the Internet, with added emphasis on First Amendment rights, had reduced "political correctness" to a pejorative term.

When Draco left the baggage claim area and took a bus to the consolidated rental car facility off the airport grounds, Demetrius was right behind him. And when he drove into the parking lot of the roadside hotel off Euclid Avenue and headed up for the room, Demetrius remained in his rented vehicle, awaiting call instructions to come up.

"Okay Demetrius, Room 206. We're waiting for you."

"Now hold on!" the younger man protested. "I said I would help you, but I didn't say I was stupid. What's to say ya'll ain't just lurin me up there as part of a trap, when your plan really is ta torture me, ta get me to give up all our secrets? Or maybe kill me. Who's all up there?"

"Natsumi Mitchell already told me that you're not part of the operations detail. You don't *know* any secrets. You volunteered for this. Are you going to do it or not?"

"I'll be right up," Demetrius conceded, his voice trailing, his heart sinking.

"Grow some balls and get up here!"

Despite the nature of the meeting, the atmosphere in Room 206 was casual and friendly. It was mostly white guys, but there was one black guy and one Latino guy, probably Mexican. They all looked like cops, with "high and tight" haircuts, indicative of their U.S. military backgrounds, although two of the white men were bald. Five of the men sat around a table on the right side of the room, while the other two occupied chocolate-brown leather armchairs, scooted in close in to join the circle.

Draco, seated at the table, motioned toward Demetrius, though he did not bother to stand.

"Gentlemen, this is the Our Lives Matter executive committee member I told you about. Demetrius Berry—these are my friends. On my left is Sergeant McCarthy with the Boston Police Department. On my right is Detective Snow from Chicago, and that's Inspector Williams from Philadelphia. And next to him is Detective Gutierrez from LA. Right out front there, you got Lieutenant Dunleavy from Dallas. We've got almost all the Loverboy Elites here. And last, but not least, you got our host this evening—at least he's payin for all the food and drinks tonight—Sergeant Collins from right here in Cleveland. Our New York and Miami associates couldn't make it."

"It's nice to meet you all," Demetrius nodded.

"We're on a mission to save our country," Draco continued, "because judging from what's already happened here in Cleveland, the race war has already begun."

"Mr. Berry?" Snow asked. "Without making any assumptions on our part, what is your degree of influence in the Our Lives Matter movement? Beyond security, which you seem to be doing well, do you have a role in decision-making for the group?"

"I'm on the executive committee," he answered, "so there are no decisions or planned protests that happen there without my knowledge or input."

"Excellent," Williams responded. "So you will be a key component in our effort to stop this war?"

"War?" Demetrius asked. "I still have a hard time believing we could actually have a race war in this country. It sounds like a conspiracy theory to me."

"Oh, we're closer to it than you think," Dunleavy warned. "All of us— we represent law enforcement in America's major cities. We see it happening, and for us, it's not so subtle. Someone's dropping a shitload of illegal guns in the inner-city neighborhoods all across the country, like over 100,000 weapons. I know your group does extrapolations, so you understand that just last year, 700 blacks were killed by law enforcement, and we know that number will be much higher this year."

"When you add in the Latino statistic—because for law enforcement, there is no difference between black and brown in the big cities—that's another 340," Gutierrez commented. "In all, that's the equivalent 28 platoons, maybe ten companies or an entire regiment. It's a war."

"My friends call it a race war," McCarthy added, "but I would say is it's more a culture war, because, as quiet as it's kept, police kill far more white people in this country—poor white people—but only because the country is majority white. It's not in the same proportion. When you add in the poor whites, it's definitely a culture war, manipulation on a national scale."

"The problem with calling it a culture war," Draco countered, "is that a culture war would involve black, brown, immigrant and white working together, taking on the one-percenters or whoever's behind this. The instigators we're up against will only win when it's white versus black, black and white versus brown, brown versus immigrant, black versus black, and so on. They win by dividing the people, by dividing the country. Their continued dominance depends on it."

"What is it ya'll need me to do?" Demetrius asked.

"What we like about Our Lives Matter," Snow answered, "is that the movement is multi-cultural—it's inclusive, as it considers black, brown, white, Asian, East Indians—they're black or brown, LGBT, middle-class and poor. It's everybody. It's about building bridges between communities rather than walls. We believe that by working with your movement, we can win the war on a different front, which is unity."

"As cops," Draco interrupted, "our lives matter too, so our relationship with all the other groups doesn't have to be hostile or antagonistic. It would be better if we all take up the fight to show our country and the world the power of people working together."

"I'm still confused," Demetrius continued. "What do you all need me to do?"

"Represent us, our interests, our concerns at your OLM meetings and press events," Draco answered. "Instead of calling us out on every unfortunate encounter or misunderstanding, work with us instead. Help us work better with your communities. It's the only way we'll win this war."

"And what about the cop-killings in Gary and Memphis you told us about?" Demetrius asked.

"That's another whole deal," Draco answered, "our ace-in-the-hole for the end game. As I shared with you earlier, we know that gang members killed officers Hitchcock and Bryant here in Cleveland, but there was someone else behind those murders. We know someone paid the gang members who did it, provided tactical support and helped them plan the killings. Maybe there was some collusion by corrupt cops, but we know there's someone big at the top, a wealthy boss who could be held accountable."

"They weren't random cop-killings here by any measure," Collins from Cleveland continued. "Hitchcock must have been one of the most beloved officers in the department. He was a fourth-generation cop from a big cop family. And Bryant, the chief's nephew—those thugs later broke into his house and raped his wife in front of his kids. It's a volatile situation here. Officers feel they have to defend themselves. It's gonna be one bloody summer."

"Who's behind all this?" Demetrius asked, still standing.

"When I went before your group," Draco answered, "I was not at liberty to begin an interrogation. This is our operation. We won't be telling you anything more than you need to know. Our plan is to find ways we can work together, and that's the only reason I brought you here."

Demetrius started to voice a pissed-off, "street" response, but he thought better of it.

"Okay. That's fair. So how can we work together going forward?"

****

Autopsy results contradicted claims by Jennifer Alvarez's family that her death was from result of the blunt force trauma she suffered in the Stockholm elevator. In fact, the medical examiner indicated surprise that her brain was healthy and undamaged. The bruise on her forehead had faded, making it difficult to discern. In a public statement, Dr. Singh determined the cause of death as "unknown, pending blood and tissue toxicology results," and said it could take weeks before those results revealed how Ms. Alvarez died.

In the meantime, local authorities, who could not help reacting to persistent stories and theories advanced by the media and on the Internet, were investigating the suspicious circumstances of her death. On the day after the funeral, one of the detectives phoned Kendrick, asking him to come down to the station to answer a few questions that might be helpful in terms of clearing the matter up.

When Kendrick arrived alone at the station for the interview, a smiling detective, Inspector Dana Murphy, greeted him, offering a cup of coffee before conducting him to a small, windowless room. After opening a folder and placing it on the table, she pulled up a report on her iPad and turned on another small media device, placing it on the table. Kendrick's eyes scanned the corner of the room, spotting a small camera.

"Despite the sad circumstances, how are you today, Mr. Vesey?"

"How am I? I'm concerned about your real motivation for calling me here. You tryin ta bait me up?"

"Just thought it would be good to talk," Dana answered, shrugging. "There are a lot of wild theories and stories flying around out there about the circumstances of Ms. Alvarez's suspicious death—as I'm sure you're aware."

"I've heard a few," he nodded. "Are you going to question me?"

"I just thought we'd talk…"

"Well, let me ask you this, Inspector Murphy. Are you taping me? Is that camera on?"

The sheepish detective glanced up toward the camera.

"Well, yes. It's a fairly standard practice for our interviews."

"That's what my lawyer said," Kendrick responded, "but she said you are supposed to read me my Miranda rights before questioning me."

"I have not actually asked you any questions yet," Murphy countered.

"She said you would tell me that too."

"O… kay. You have a lawyer?"

"Natsumi Mitchell. She's on her way down."

Natsumi was all business when she arrived, unwilling to smile and brushing past formalities as she settled into the seat across the table from the detective.

"Is this a criminal investigation?" she asked. "You've compelled my client to come down here for an interview, so let's get on with it. You have questions?"

Flustered and self-conscious, Dana glanced up at the camera again.

"To answer your question, Ms. Mitchell, this is not a criminal investigation, as you well know. The medical examiner so far has ruled the cause of death as 'unknown.'"

"Then let's get to the point here, Inspector Murphy," Natsumi countered. "It's no secret that the San Francisco Police Department and the rest of the world believe that Ms. Alvarez died under suspicious circumstances, and that video from Stockholm with that doctored-up 'violent' elevator episode got over twenty million views in the first week. Three other related videos have gone viral just this past week. Again, what are your questions?"

"Well, Mr. Vesey, would you like to tell me about what happened on December 17th, the day you found Ms. Alvarez unresponsive at your apartment?"

He glanced over at Natsumi, who nodded.

"For the record, Jennifer was staying with me because of all the madness and crazy media after we got back from Stockholm. That in itself should be illegal. We were physically assaulted by one reporter who just wouldn't leave us alone. Jen was already stressed out about our wedding, so this was like pouring the petrol on the flames. She was sleeping a lot, and I was trying to take care of her, trying to insulate her from the people and things that were stressing her out."

"Did that include her family?" the detective asked.

"Yes, it did—mostly her brother, Armando. Armando was making things worse because he wanted to assume her missing father's role. He was against me from the beginning. He wanted her to marry a Mexican guy, a friend of his."

"Armando says you were holding her at your apartment against her will," Murphy countered, "that there has been a history of violence and abuse since the beginning. He says she was terrified of you and your explosive temper—the same temper the cameras in Stockholm apparently captured."

"That's a bald-faced lie, Inspector. There has never been any violence. That incident in Stockholm was just the critical point in a pattern of behavior from her that was getting worse. She was stressed out, so she was taking medication… while still drinking. She had become verbally abusive and had gotten a little physical on occasion, but that was never her nature. It was never us as a couple."

"The medical examiner has completed the autopsy," Murphy continued, "and she's sent toxicology samples to the labs for analysis. Do you believe there is any reason that the results might come back indicating foul play?"

"No, Inspector, because there was no foul play."

"Were you, in any way, involved in an effort to poison your fiancée?"

"No," he sighed. "Why would I do that? We were going to be married… and have kids."

"Did the two of you recently take out substantial insurance policies, naming each other as beneficiaries? A million for you if she died, and two million for her if you died?"

"Yes, it's the responsible thing to do when you're getting married. We were basically insuring each other's income."

"A million dollars is a lot of money, Mr. Vesey. Do you see how some might see motive in that? Her death will potentially make you a rich man."

"I'm going to stop you right there, Inspector Murphy," Natsumi interrupted. "It's obvious where you're going with this line of questioning, so if there's nothing else, we're leaving."

"Hold on, Ms. Mitchell," Kendrick countered, seething, "I want to answer that. I don't need money that bad. I'm pretty much set for life, so for you or anyone else to impugn my character and assign monetary false motives makes me angry. I've seen this happen to black men before, once they get a little fame, but I'm not going to let you do it to me."

"I'm not trying to do anything to you, Mr. Vesey," Murphy responded. "I'm just trying to figure out what happened, just trying to figure out why this healthy young woman just suddenly died. If the toxicology reports come back indicating poisoning or foul play and you claim that you are not guilty of harming your fiancée, can you think of anyone else, some other person, who might have wanted Jennifer Alvarez dead?"

He stood, offended at the insinuation.

"You're right, Ms. Mitchell. This interview is over."

He glanced toward the camera and back to the inspector.

"I already know who you've been talking to. Thanks for the warning."

Chapter 12

Tyler North came as a guest, so no one suspected that the frail, oily-haired young man with a bad complexion was not there for the funeral. In fact, he had never met the deceased, though he read about the dead teenager in the newspapers and watched the biased stories about him on television and the Internet.

At 17, Shalamar Jones was typical for his Overtown neighborhood, which was just northwest of downtown in Miami-Dade County. He liked sports, girls and rap music, and he sometimes hung out with two cousins, Aristide and Étienne, who were actively involved in the Zoe Pound (mostly Haitian) gang. His father, Bertrand, had been murdered in Evansville, Indiana, when Shalamar was only seven years old, and though Bertrand never lived with Lisa Jones, he visited his son two or three times a month, providing a scant role model and financial support.

Three weeks earlier, Aristide and Étienne were arrested in connection with a cop-killing in nearby Coconut Grove, in the southwest section of the city. Fourteen days later, Coconut Grove police from the northeast encountered Shalamar at a basketball court in Peacock Park, and in what many witnesses saw as an act of retaliation, began harassing and then beating the young man. According to one bystander, "as soon as the kid raised a hand to defend imself, the cops straight-up shot im dead."

The black communities of Overtown and Coconut Grove staged protests in the days after the shooting, calling for police accountability, and Our Lives Matter was there, organizing, preparing a list of demands and articulating local concerns to the national media.

"Will there ever be any justice for us? Will our black communities ever matter?" OLM spokesperson Calvin King offered. "How many times have we been here? Today it's Coconut Grove, but yesterday it was Chicago, and tomorrow it will be another city. And it's always the same story: Cop kills unarmed black or brown person; cop claims he acted because he feared for his life, though scores of witnesses say otherwise; then there's a mock investigation, with false claims of concern for the family and community. It's the same story, played out hundreds of times each year, all with different victims, but the ending is always the same: the cops who murder black and brown men just get to walk away free."

According to one of Shalamar's neighbors, law enforcement officers had been stalking the teenager for days and were seeking an opportunity for confrontation and retaliation. "It was a deliberate act, an outright murder," he asserted.

In the days before the funeral, perhaps a thousand protesters had converged on Overtown from surrounding cities in Florida, Georgia and Alabama for three days of marches and protests, culminating in a keynote speech by Calvin King before The Greater Bethel AME Church on northwest 8th.

"The police and the press were quick to point out that Shalamar was no angel," Calvin eulogized, "that there was a petty shoplifting incident when he was thirteen, and that he was suspended from school in tenth grade for three days for a little marijuana in his pocket. But who among us, black, white or different shades of brown can say they are raising or have raised perfect children. In fact, the only father who can say he has angels for children is Almighty God himself. God loves all his children from charcoal black to pasty white, and you can best believe he loved Shalamar.

"In Overtown, Our Lives Matter will continue to work with the community and all those who mourn and fight to see that there is justice for the police-instigated murder of Shalamar Jones, and we know that while man's justice is sometimes slow and unfair, God's judgment is right and unassailable, that he will give trouble and suffering to everyone who does evil, whether they be police, judges and your even high and mighty elected officials. God judges everyone the same. It doesn't matter who they are."

Because the funeral took place on a Monday afternoon, overcast and hot, many of the protesters had left the area. The service was attended by no more than two hundred persons at Greater Bethel AME, though the press was there. As family and friends exited the church, a few stopped to provide interviews for reporters calling questions from behind cameras and bright lights.

Nervous, Tyler rode to the gravesite burial with a black family he did not know, considering twice that he would abandon the plan. He remembered how a professor explained cognitive dissonance to the class during his freshman year of college, which he remembered exactly: the state of having inconsistent thoughts, beliefs, or attitudes, especially as relating to behavioral decisions and attitude change.

He didn't always hate black people. Though his father screamed the occasional N-word, usually during football and basketball games, and he would repeat a rare racist joke, neither he nor his second wife ever taught Tyler to resent the blacks. No, that was done in his college fraternity, where he was recruited by an attractive undergrad coed to join a white supremacy meet-up, and while he joined for the potential sex, he never initially believed in the hate and slander, not until he eventually became a convert, a soldier.

Tyler understood how brainwashing worked, and he recognized the obvious tactics they were using on him, but he was at a point in his life where he just didn't care. Were the blacks lazy, unclean and innately less intelligent, a sub-species? He knew better. From the seventh to the tenth grades, his best friend, Darnell, was a black guy. Darnell got a scholarship out of high school to Columbia in New York, though it may have been affirmative action, but he knew Darnell really was a smart black guy, the equal or better of any white guy he knew.

Ever since the former president was elected, however, it seemed the blacks and browns were really just rubbing it in, and white people like Tyler seemed to be getting left behind. The blacks and others had taken over the system and had begun discriminating against whites, especially white males. Tyler had actually voted for the last president, but it seemed *the minorities were making everything about race and gay rights. Political correctness was ruining the country!*

After final remarks, the minister said a prayer and guests filed past between the casket and the family, offering condolences. Tyler walked along patiently until he was directly across from her.

"Are you Shalamar's mother?"

"Yes."

No one saw the gun until Tyler whipped it out of the waistband at his back. He hesitated in the last instant, remembering his parents and the life he used to love, clinging to the final remnants of self-love and self-respect left as they faded. Even if he wanted to turn back at that moment, he couldn't have. Everyone saw the gun pointed in the face of Lisa Jones, the deceased's mother, her grief transformed to abject horror. The die was cast. Closing his eyes, he squeezed the trigger.

Blood spattered everywhere, spraying a crimson streak across the terrified face of the child in her lap, on family members at either side, on his jacket sleeve, pants, front and face, which was contorted by shock and fear. A sense of mania took over so that he was no longer in control of his own thoughts. It all seemed automatic: every move, every action. He could hear the words of the man who trained him, who conditioned him for the moment.

Kill them! Kill them all, brave soldier! Save your country! You're a hero! It doesn't matter. They ain't even humans!

Pivoting, he re-aimed at another black and fired, and then at a third. To Tyler, time had slowed to a crawl. He watched the bullets explode from the barrel and marveled at the eyes of his victims, the vacuum sucking them deep into the sockets as the brain exploded from the back of their skulls. Yet his hand became less steady after the first three so that he missed the next two shots. He caught a teenaged girl in the back with the sixth and missed the next two as pandemonium spread. He missed with the ninth and hit a cameraman, who tried to rush him, with the tenth.

He wasn't sure of the count when he spotted Calvin King, the Our Lives Matter spokesman he despised, cringing on the ground, on the other side of the casket. Mind focused, he walked quickly over, and placing the barrel on the back of the man's head, he pulled the trigger.

Click!

He was out of bullets. To Tyler, the click seemed even louder than the gunshots. It reverberated in his mind, rippling outward as angry black figures rushed in, like dark, terrible demons. He saw the fists flying toward his face and several of his cracked teeth career out in a jagged spray of blood, but he felt nothing. At that moment, he was immune to reality. He felt the sensation of his own bones giving way under trauma or pressure, though without pain. The last image he remembered was a ballpoint pen, headed directly for his left eye before *squish!* and goo oozing, and then there was nothing.

He awoke in a hospital bed with both legs and an arm in traction. As far as he could tell, his left eye was gone and he could not feel his legs. One of the armed guards standing at the door, a black man, seemed to sigh in disgust when he saw Tyler try to stir. Leaning over, the black guard whispered something mocking to the white guard, who laughed. Only then, Tyler felt sorry and ashamed about what he had done, but there was no use in expressing it. No one would ever understand.

****

Alberta was working a chemistry problem in thermodynamics when Kendrick finally arrived, so she was annoyed and conflicted, annoyed that he was two hours late and was breaking her concentration. Yet she felt conflicted because, while she as happy to see him after so much time, she was anxious that they had not talked about Jennifer. She rushed to the door, wrapping her arms around his waist.

"It's good to see you too, Alberta… Where's Roland?"

"Roland is sleep. Fool sleep like dead, but Master is awake—him live forever."

"From Gautama Buddha. We read that when you were twelve, though sleep is not an entirely bad thing. It refreshes the soul they say."

Alberta clung to him again, refusing to let go.

"I'm sorry for putting you through all this, Alberta. Do you understand what's going on?"

"Jennifer, her is dead. Jennifer family call Kendrick bad man. Human on news call Kendrick bad man."

"That doesn't mean anything," he answered. "Humans are a mess sometimes. They don't care about the truth. They only want what they want, and usually that has to do with money."

"Human law punish Kendrick? Why human hate Kendrick? Because him is black? Kendrick not kill Jennifer."

"Of course not," he said. "But it doesn't matter to them, and I mean the media—the human news faces. They want a juicy story, never the truth."

"Kendrick know truth?"

"What truth?" he asked.

"Kendrick know why Jennifer die? I ask to know."

He thought to himself a moment.

"Well, I guess, 'no' is the only answer I can give, but Kendrick know Kendrick not kill Jennifer."

"Mi know Kendrick not kill Jennifer. Kendrick is good man."

She hugged him again.

"Alberta miss Kendrick. Kendrick never call Alberta. Long time. Mi sad. Mi worry mi never see Kendrick again."

"Oh please!" he laughed. "Kendrick ain't goin nowhere. I'll deal with this craziness and things will be back to normal in no time. I promise. If someone killed Jennifer, it wasn't me."

"Alberta love Kendrick."

He rubbed the top of her head.

"And Kendrick love Alberta. We'll get through this. You'll see."

"If human try to hurt Kendrick, mi kill human!"

He backed away, sighed and took her chin in his hand.

"Well, first of all, I can take care of myself. And second, as of today, Alberta can never talk like that again, to anyone. It's bad for Kendrick and for Alberta. Alberta must not ever talk about killing again, even in hyperbole, to show you care about me. It's dangerous! If Alberta talk to human about killing after today, bad humans will take Alberta away, and Alberta will never see Kendrick again. Do you understand? That's what they want, what some bad human wants."

Glancing briefly down at her work, Alberta thought for a moment, made a pout face and nodded vigorously.

"Alberta miss Kendrick," she signed. "Kendrick miss Jennifer?"

"Of course I do," he answered. "I'm grieving. We talked about it, you remember—when Alberta mother die? Remember?"

She used her right hand to rub her chest.

"Heart is breaking… big hurt."

She patted her eyes.

"Crying, mi cry… tears."

"That's exactly how I feel right now, Alberta, but it's worse than that because I have to deal with all these insinuations that I'm somehow responsible."

"Insinuation?" she finger-signed.

"An insinuation is a poisonous snake that bites and moves away. The venom is slow, but it can kill even after you think you survived."

"A snake?" she asked, confused.

"It's a metaphor. Some humans are like snakes, where their words are like poison. They kill you slowly, over time, by what they say or do."

"A snake kill Jennifer?" she asked.

"Maybe she died of natural causes," he nodded, "but if not, then yes, somewhere there's a snake, and it's not me."

"Snake is person?" Alberta asked.

"Yes, when a snake is not snake, snake is a human person."

He studied her reaction and the expression on her face as she struggled to assimilate meaning from his words.

"Satan is a snake, and Satan is a person," she signed.

"Enough about that! How have you been, Alberta?"

Over the course of the next thirty minutes, she told him that she had finished one online advanced College Calculus course and another class in European history at the University of Pennsylvania. In her spare time, she was systematically working through Purdue University Michael Golomb's eighteen math challenges, listed as his *Problem of the Week*, at the rate of one every four days.

She had also been following the domestic and international news, though she admitted an obsession with pursuing every print, video and Internet story related to the death of Jennifer Alvarez and the precipitant investigation. She wanted to help Kendrick so that he could spend more time with her, but she did not know how.

"Who help Kendrick if Alberta not help?" she asked.

"I have a lawyer for that," he answered. "Her name is Natsumi Mitchell. I think you met her once, in a green room before we did a show on television."

"A lawyer is friend to criminal, and Kendrick is criminal?"

"No, I'm no criminal."

"Yes, Kendrick criminal. Why Kendrick need lawyer?"

"A lawyer is also the friend of good people, no criminal. Lawyers also protect good humans from bad humans."

"Lawyer go to court?" she asked. "Court is with judge?"

"Yes, and the judge or an assigned jury determines guilt or innocence."

"But how judge know?" she asked. "Some judge is stupid human. Smart human trick stupid human many time. Human lie."

"That's why most of the time it goes to a jury," Kendrick answered, returning to ASL. "Twelve human. One smart human can trick one stupid human, but too hard for one human to trick twelve stupid human. Every dawg have him day and every puss him four o'clock."

Alberta thought for a moment.

"I remember Natsumi Mitchell. Mi see her on TV. Natsumi is smart human. Her talk and taste her tongue. Kendrick think Natsumi is pretty human?"

"Well, I haven't really considered her in that way. She's a professional, but yes, I suppose she's pretty. You saw her."

"Jennifer dead. Kendrick will marry Natsumi?"

"No, no. Stop," he said, wagging his head. "It doesn't work like that. Humans just don't hook up like that. Marriage is a major, lifelong commitment, and while some humans may base it on looks, most are looking for compatibility. Serious persons seek someone for the long-term, and prettiness does not last."

"If Kendrick want not pretty only, what Kendrick want?"

"Kendrick wants a friend, a partner, someone with shared dreams and shared ambitions."

"A person?"

"Of course. Someone you see yourself growing old with, someone who will always be there for you, no matter what, come Hell or high water."

Alberta smiled and kissed his hand.

"Natsumi lawyer? Her help you?"

"Kendrick not know Alberta. Davis Franklin pay Natsumi her to help mi. Her just doing her job. When her help mi, her help herself. Natsumi not love Kendrick and Kendrick not love Natsumi. Mi—mi not marry Natsumi Mitchell. Kendrick still love Jennifer, but Jennifer is dead. Kendrick marry no one."

He was silent for a moment as a tear trailed down his cheek. Looking over at Alberta, he tried to lighten the mood.

"It's great to see you, Alberta. Did you have coffee yet?"

"No," she signed. "When mi know Kendrick come, mi wait for Kendrick. Mi make coffee for Kendrick and Alberta."

Fifteen minutes later, Kendrick smiled and looked across the table into the chimp's eyes over coffee.

"Speaking of Natsumi Mitchell... She wants to come over here to interview you."

"Mi? Why her want to interview mi?"

"Well, depending on what comes back from the medical examiner, there's a chance I might be arrested under the suspicion of murder. Natsumi says she needs to interview every person who might have information that will help me, especially persons who know me and have spent time around me and Jennifer."

"Natsumi think Alberta is person?"

"Of course she does, because legally, that's what you'll be."

"And court, and judge," she signed. "Judge in court think Alberta is person?"

Kendrick paused, thinking.

"I, I can't say for sure, but it would make sense. When you're legally a person, any judge would have to recognize that."

"Testify mean 'talk under oath,'" she continued. "Alberta testify in court? Alberta testify for judge?"

"Wait!" Kendrick laughed. "I think we're getting a little ahead of ourselves. At this point, no one knows exactly why Jennifer is dead, and here you've already got me arrested and on trial. All I said was that Natsumi Mitchell wants to interview you for background. Let's just take this one step at a time."

****

The plan was to meet in Los Angeles, but Justin Luck's busy schedule did not allow for a West Coast trip. They opted instead for a Skype call, and though 3,000 miles apart, they smoked cigars together, as was their custom.

"Did you get all the inside shit on Overtown, Colin?" Mr. Luck asked, straining to hold in the smoke before exhaling.

"Oh yeah!" the younger man answered. "I don't know who was handling the kid, North, but whoever it was, they did a number on him. I can only guess it was your people. I was there, keeping a safe distance, but he was a beast. I've never seen anything like it, so cold and hard. He shot the mother in the face at point-blank range. Then he smoked one of the kids—little girl had to be about eight years old."

"Sick bastard," Luck sighed. "You know I don't like that stuff. I think we could do without that sick stuff."

"I saw his eyes," Colin continued. "He was in some other place. I don't think he even knew what he was doin after the first shot was off. He reverted to the training. Props ta whoever made him like that. It's some sick-ass shit!"

"We are at the start of a war," the older man shrugged. "I don't like it, but I suppose it had to be done. How many dead?"

"Five dead, eleven injured, mostly tryin to get away."

"Think it'll light a fire?" Luck asked.

"Already has," Colin answered. "There are protesters in the streets in almost every major city. The anger level in black neighborhoods is through the roof. They're not just blamin the cops anymore. They're gettin suspicious about all white people."

"Then it's working. What about on the other side?"

"Mr. Luck, these people you've hired—they're ruthless as all hell. They've got somethin diabolical planned for the white community as well. They won't tell me what it is ta keep us outta the mix, but believe me, it'll be huge. Revolution time."

"I hate that we have to do this," Luck said, wagging his head. "I don't want to know. Don't even tell me what it is when it happens."

He glanced down, reading a newspaper headline.

"What about this Calvin King idiot from Our Lives Matter? He was speaking there. Looks like he was pretty shaken up?"

"He literally crapped his pants," Colin answered. "One click, one more bullet… woulda been a cap in his head. He's in some kinda looney bin still pissin all over himself. Rumor is he's outta the movement for good."

"And what about your man on the inside?"

"They'd never expect it. He's in place, and they completely trust him. He just waitin on us and whatever his orders are, but he wants ta be paid. He wants some kinda advance… in case things get crazy."

"Tell him 'no,'" Luck snapped. "Tell him hell no! He's going to have to give me something to prove his loyalty. Tell em he's in when he gives me Natsumi Mitchell. He's got to help us cut the head off the snake."

Chapter 13

The toxicology results came back sooner than expected. Medical examiner Medha Singh was thorough, and her findings were conclusive. Jennifer Alvarez had died from chronic cyanide poisoning, with tests indicating that the exposure had been over time, "perhaps in the last 30-45 days." Cyanide poisoning is a form of histotoxic hypoxia, which renders the cells in organisms unable to use oxygen, primarily through the inhibition of cytochrome c oxidase. Cyanide's mechanism of action blocks aerobic metabolism, so that affected cells quickly starve for oxygen and die, and no amount of supplemental oxygen can overcome the deficit in these cells.

While Dr. Singh's written narrative indicated chronic exposure, she concluded that the decedent's death was a product of sudden acute exposure. An examination of Jennifer's stomach contents suggested that the poison had not been ingested. Rather, it had been inhaled, as there was ground-glass attenuation apparent in both lung fields, along with inflammation indicative of exposure to cyanide. Renal failure was also apparent.

According to the doctor, such exposure would be consistent with smoke inhalation, since cyanide is the product of the combustion of common materials. Substrates for hydrogen cyanide are natural and synthetic substances containing carbon and nitrogen, such as wool, silk, cotton, paper, some plastics and other polymers. And yet the concentration in alveoli and the degree of saturation in tissues was more consistent with a mist.

The doctor noted that her skin, in various areas, was lightly-coated with a thin layer of cyanide residue, which could have been the result of exposure to cyanide-laced smoke, but the degree of saturation indicated a more direct exposure, where the substance had also entered the body through the skin, constituting the prevalent chronic exposure. At some point, however, Jennifer had inhaled a sufficient amount of cyanide in aerosol form to bring on symptoms and death.

For detectives investigating the case, the doctor's report did not support a theory that Kendrick Vesey, in an effort to allay an investigation into the alleged long-term abuse and cruelty toward his fiancée, had laced her food or drink with a cyanide compound to murder her. The chronic nature of the poisoning, which stretched back at least 30 days, obviously pre-dated the Stockholm elevator incident.

Armando Alvarez, the decedent's brother, however, continued to advance the narrative in the media that Kendrick wanted Jennifer dead all along, for the insurance money and because she would not let him manipulate her. He called Kendrick "a control freak who wanted to mold her or destroy her." Armando insisted that if his sister's death was ruled a homicide, there was no one else on the planet who would have wanted her dead. "Everyone else loved her… in a healthy way."

Inspector Dana Murphy remained unconvinced, though she felt pressure from her superiors at the San Francisco Police Department to focus the investigation on Kendrick and his actions over the previous month. One of her up-line supervisors, Commander Tom Brady, seemed dead-set on establishing a case against the Berkeley professor, and while Dana knew there was no relationship between the two, she sensed an odd animus from the commander.

The problem was motive. Why would Kendrick Vesey want to murder his fiancée? The money motive was specious at best. Apparently, Kendrick was in the pocket of software engineering giant Davis Franklin, who not only supported and trusted the talented doctor, but he had proven generous over time, providing facilities and resources carte blanche upon request. In addition, recently Dr. Vesey had been awarded US $1.4 million from the Nobel Foundation for his work with Alberta, though he donated it to a charity purposed to preserve the world's great apes and advance the rights and protections of nonhuman persons. He could have kept the money, but he didn't.

Something was off about this homicide being portrayed as a murder. There was Kendrick's lack of motive, though he had the opportunity. Also, there was the issue of un-prescribed medication, the Tagamet, to relieve stress or nervousness in a woman for whom multi-tasking huge people-involved responsibilities was an everyday activity.

It did not add up. And though the interview with Kendrick was brief and obstructed by his lawyer, Dana's gut said he didn't do it… if she was in fact murdered.

She phoned him three times before finally getting a response.

"Kendrick? I was beginning to think you were avoiding me."

"Just busy… and dealing with it. What is it now?"

"We're going to need to talk again," she answered. "By now, you must know that the toxicology reports are in, and you know Jennifer Alvarez was killed by someone. She was poisoned—cyanide poisoning."

"I heard that. I just don't understand it."

"It's not so hard to understand. Someone killed your fiancée. It was either you or someone else, and the list for those with motive and opportunity is scant, believe me."

"This whole deal is whack-whack."

"Will you have time to talk to me today," she asked, "with or without your lawyer?"

"I'll let my lawyer decide that," he answered. "I think you're trying to put all this on me."

"I realize you won't believe me, Kendrick, but I'm not. I'm just trying to bring the killer of Jennifer Alvarez to justice. If you're really innocent, I think you'd want to help me do that."

"I am innocent," he answered, "but I just don't trust you. You're part of the problem. All you guys wanna do is make a name for yourselves, at my expense, at Jen's expense. You didn't know Jennifer, so you don't care about her. The thing is, I have always cared about her, and I'm not gonna let you exploit her and make your careers off her death."

"Jennifer did not die of natural causes, Kendrick! Someone killed her, maybe murdered her. The medical examiner confirmed it. Don't you care about that?"

"Murdered?" he pronounced, emotion overwhelming his eyes. "That makes no sense. She was with me the whole time. I was taking care of her. How could anyone murder her?"

He stopped speaking, suddenly concerned about creating legal liability.

"I don't know for sure," Inspector Murphy answered. "Why don't you just come to the station to meet with me? We'll go over everything. Between the two of us, maybe we'll figure it out."

"That's bull!" Kendrick objected. "If you've already got the medical examiner's report, you already have a theory about what you believe happened."

"No, Kendrick. Trust me," Dana urged. "You have me all wrong. I'm in the minority, but I for one think there's something more to what happened to your fiancée…"

Just then, someone pounded at Kendrick's door with an insistent, heavy fist.

"Kendrick Vesey!" a male voice shouted before pounding again.

"Right…" Kendrick said to the inspector before disconnecting the call.

Initially hesitant, he went to the door and opened it before two armed police officers with dark glasses forced themselves inside, presenting paperwork.

"Kendrick Vesey, we have a search warrant, issued by Judge Rosenthal from Superior Court, County of San Francisco, authorizing us to search the premises for property that constitutes evidence of the commission of a criminal offense. This includes all tangible and intangible property within your residence—everything here, including your computers and electronic records. Please stand aside."

Three smug detectives arrived a few minutes later to begin a systematic examination of the apartment, beginning with the bedroom where the paramedics' report described finding Jennifer's inert body.

"Wait! I have a lawyer," Kendrick threatened.

"And we have a search warrant, issued by a judge. If you didn't murder your fiancée, Mr. Vesey, then you have no reason to worry. Please step outside the door!"

****

Queen Shabaz, the acting chairperson for the OLM Executive Committee, called meeting to order at 7 p.m. In the first occasion to come together since the violent incident in Miami, members were interested in hearing from Calvin King, who had nearly been shot in the head by Tyler North in his killing rampage at the funeral of a black youth, slain by police.

Former chair Natsumi Mitchell was in attendance, along with Lindsey Alexander-Ettinger, Padmi Ravi, Demetrius Berry, Heather Kaplan, Mia Melendez, Phi Truong and Hector Alejandre. As usual, the meeting was convened in the conference room at the Reed Smith law offices, located in downtown San Francisco. All sat rapt as Calvin described the incident.

"Durin the final rites, for some strange reason I noticed that boy, that North boy. I looked right inta his eyes, and I noticed, right then, that there was no soul behind em. It was like some demonic presence was starin back at me, focusin on me. He had Satan's eyes. I swear my blood ran cold when I realized what I was up against. I just wanted ta finish and get away from there.

Calvin took a deep breath as he wiped the sweat and anxiety from his face.

"I watched him when he got up, oblivious ta everyone else around him when he walked right up to her and pulled that gun from the back of his waistband. He shot her in the face without hesitation. And then when he turned the gun on the little girl, I... I just couldn't watch that. I fell, my face ta the ground, prayin to the Lord, for sake of justice, for sake of decency, ta intervene.

"People were runnin all over the place, the gun was expodin, bullets were flyin, blood spatterin, and I was just layin there, prayin. Then all of a sudden, the shootin stopped, and right away, I knew he, or whatever was in him, was looking for me. Walkin past everyone else, he found me on the ground, on the other side of the coffin. That's when he pressed the barrel hard ta the back of my head. 'You can't win,' he said to me, and he pulled the trigger. When I heard that 'click,' it was the beginnin of a new life for me.

"The Lord saved me that day, because he caused it ta be that there was no bullet in the chamber. So the boy tried with the trigger again, and then again, but his scheme had been blocked by the Lord. Once everyone knew he was outta bullets, they all jumped on him, poundin im, and they showed im no mercy—just like he didn't show no one else any mercy. I was surprised he survived with what little life they left im. I suppose God kept im alive so he could answer for his deeds in this world before he goes ta the next."

Silence dominated the room as listeners absorbed the horror of the story. After a while, OLM chairperson Queen, feeling pressed to respond, reached over and placed her palm over Calvin's clenched hands.

"We are all so sorry that you had to go through that, Calvin. You are not alone in your experience of tragedy, injustice and loss. When one feels it, we all feel it. I just never imagined how horrible people can be, but that's the reason I'll never quit. Some of us have to stand up and make a difference."

"Queen's right," Natsumi continued. "I don't know what it is. During Dr. King's movement, there were at least enough decent people, enough principled people who stood up for justice to make a difference. Where are those people today?"

"Oh, I know where they are—those 'used-to-be-decent' white people of the past," Demetrius answered. "They're at political rallies, spoutin hate and railin against 'political correctness,' which used to be called 'decency.' And the media gives them legitimacy by never callin them out on anything. The media helps em confirm that 'hate is great and white is right.' Decency is no longer a virtue among white people."

"It's not just white people, Demetrius," Heather differed, "it's everybody. I've seen it and heard it. For some blacks, it's okay to blame immigrants and hate Muslims, and some despise all white people. The problem is division. Someone is working hard to divide us against each other, make us all end up hating each other. You play right into that."

Something about the discussion spurred Lyndsey, who seldom shared her opinions, to interject.

"I didn't believe it before, but I'm beginning to think there's something more to Draco's race war conspiracy. After what we've seen these past few months, who can dispute it? When Charles Manson was advocating a race war, he said 'blackie never did anything without whitie showing him how.' Someone's not only trying to show black people how—they're instigating."

"I'm feelin that," Calvin interjected. "I think blacks and whites both are bein manipulated by someone else who's got somethin ta gain… with the Latinos, Asians and Muslims thrown in for good measure."

"According to Draco, that's exactly what's going on," Natsumi amended. "And for that reason, they've singled out our movement, because we are the few voices still speaking that advocate unity—all races working together. As long as we advocate for unity, we will be a threat to them and whatever they're up to."

"You met with Draco and his group in Cleveland," Hector directed toward Demetrius. "As I understand, those guys are a bunch of cops who are tryin to diffuse the escalation of violence between minority communities and law enforcement. What did they say? Is this race war they're talkin bout for-reals?"

"They tried to convince me of it," Demetrius answered, "but I don't believe em. First, who would benefit from a race war? It's a convenient explanation that makes those cops key players, but it makes no sense. They're trying to create some kinda public paranoia about a race war that doesn't exist. The problem is white people—not all of em, but most white people. That decency you talk about, Natsumi, is long gone. You're speakin to an empty white audience today. Get over it."

"I don't believe that," Natsumi answered, "and your job wasn't to tell us what you think. You were supposed to facilitate coordination between us and them. If you're not up to the job, Demetrius, then we need to assign someone else tonight."

"It's hard to argue with him, Natsumi," Queen added, referring to her notes. "If there were enough decent people left, then what happened with Michael Brown? with Eric Garner? with Dontre Hamilton, John Crawford, Ezell Ford, Dante Parker, Tanisha Anderson, Akai Gurley, Tamir Rice, Rumain Brisbon, Jerame Reid, Tony Robinson, Phillip White, Eric Harris, Walter Scott, Laquan McDonald, Freddie Gray, Trayvon Martin and Alton Sterling. Do I need to name more? How much justice do black people see or get in any of those murders by cops and DAs?"

"I wouldn't blame the police any more that I would blame a spoiled kid from acting out," Padmi answered. "When you have puppet local DAs, looking to money and elections instead of justice, and the media, enslaved to profit, the notion of justice in America is a big joke to everyone but Americans. When a spoiled kid acts out, the problem is always the parents. The government and the media are to blame."

"When you met with Draco and his buddies in Cleveland," Mia asked Demetrius, "what did they say they want us to do?"

"They want us to work with them to stop the race war," he answered. "They think they can change things by bringin folks together, which is why they came to us in the first place."

"What does that actually mean?" Natsumi asked.

"It means we share information with them, and they share with us—but only the information they think is relevant. I know you don't care what I think, but I don't trust em," he insisted. "They said they'd have someone from their group at every one of our events from now on. They had someone in Miami, Calvin, but he couldn't act because he was out of his jurisdiction."

"You mean some cop could have saved lives and didn't?" Calvin asked.

"They're a secret order. They can't expose themselves, but yeah, he watched as that North kid killed people. They're after someone much further up the line."

"I don't know bout that," Calvin answered, "but my 'someone further up the line' is the Lord himself, and he's gonna set everything right. He saved me ta use me. So whatever he puts me ta from here on, I'll do. I am no longer afraid."

"Till the next fool starts shootin…" Demetrius said in an undertone purposed to elicit irony, since everyone on the committee knew that Calvin had soiled his pants during the incident. Members answered Demetrius with angry and disapproving glares.

"What about you, Natsumi?" Lyndsey asked. "It's good to have you here tonight, but it looks like you're going to have your hands full with that Kendrick Vesey matter. I take it you won't be at many of our events going forward?"

"I'll still try to make all the meetings," Natsumi answered, "but I'm probably sidelined from events and protests for the next year or so, depending on how things develop. My primary responsibility will be to my client."

"Did he *do* it?" Mia asked.

"Of course he did!" Hector answered. "He was already beatin her ass. That's documented, so it was only a mattera time before he went too far. He's the OJ of our generation."

"You *would* side with the Mexicans, Hector," Demetrius remarked.

Natsumi only shook her head, resisting the urge to comment.

"She can't talk about it," Phi, also an attorney, explained, "and it is not an appropriate matter to be discussed at our executive meeting."

"The chair concurs," Queen added.

"I get it," Heather nodded as she scrolled on her iPhone, "but I've been monitoring the local news. Natsumi, are you aware that the police got a search warrant and they're searching Kendrick's apartment as we speak?"

Natsumi took her phone from her purse and turned it on.

"I had no idea. Oh! He's calling me now. If there's nothing else, Padmi, I move to adjourn tonight's meeting. I've really gottta take this call."

****

Investigators Nick Jantzen and Tramaine Lee were in the second hour of the search when they began to realize there was little incriminating evidence to be found at the apartment. Aside from two soiled sanitary napkins in the bathroom trash bin, there was no blood to be found—not even in the drains. Undeterred, the detectives left no stone unturned. They pulled the sheets and pillow cases from the bedroom, along with combs, toothbrushes, razors, a pumice stone, medications and prescription drugs from the bathroom.

They took his iPad, his two computers, along with two terabyte external drives and 17 USB and 20 3½-inch floppy discs from his office. They also took his iPhone and the file contents of his desks. They searched his pockets, his closets and they ripped up corner sections of the carpet. They confiscated the books in his library, a locked security box and two cameras. However, they focused on items that they believed belonged to Jennifer.

Jantzen was white and Lee was black. The chief, after learning that OLM activist Natsumi Mitchell would be Vesey's attorney, thought it would be best if a black detective was involved, a politically-motivated decision, endorsed by the mayor and the attorney general for the state of California.

Simultaneously, another set of investigators were conducting a search of Jennifer's apartment, while a third set had gone over to search the Davis Franklin-owned house in the Oakland Hills, where both spent time together with Alberta.

"What do you guys think you're going to find?" Kendrick asked. "What are you looking for?"

"I don't know," Janzen answered, "just anything suspicious… anything out of the ordinary."

"Like a jug of cyanide? Good luck. I don't even keep aspirin. There's nothing here. Thanks for destroying my apartment, guys."

"You're the monkey man, right?" Jantzen asked. "You've got that monkey that supposed to be so smart…"

"Alberta's an ape, not a monkey, and yes, she's more intelligent than most of the humans I meet."

"Whatever. Was the monkey ever here? Did she ever come here to visit?"

"You don't have to answer that question," a female voice called out. "The investigator is here to execute a search warrant, not to conduct an interview."

Kendrick initially thought the voice belonged to Natsumi, but the timbre was off, a little deeper, with harsher vowels. When he turned, detective Dana Murphy stood there, her arms crossed.

"Do I have to remind you of the limits to your duties here, Jantzen? Are you purposely trying to open this investigation to liabilities? Leave Mr. Vesey to me. Continue with your search."

She smiled, trying to put Kendrick at ease.

"I'm sorry about all this. He was out-of-line, but of course you were savvy enough to decline to answer."

"Why are you here?" Kendrick asked.

"You just witnessed it," she answered, "all this testosterone on the premises. Jantzen and Lee are cowboys, trying to make names for themselves. They're the kind of cops who complicate any kind of investigation."

"They've been here for two hours, tearing up the place and taking my stuff. Isn't it supposed to be 'innocent until proven guilty'?"

"It is, Kendrick, but there's a woman dead, under questionable circumstances. The medical examiner concluded that she was poisoned, so someone must have done it, and so far, you are the only person who's had means, motive and opportunity. That's why the judge issued the warrant."

"Motive, really? I loved her. We were getting married."

"Well, yeah, but there's the insurance money…"

"That's ridiculous. I grew up poor in Jamaica. Greed is more ingrained in people raised in America. I have all I need."

"You might be right about that," Dana nodded, "but because a woman is dead, this is the natural and responsible process." She smiled again. "By the way, I've been reading up on Alberta. Quite a remarkable… person—that's what they're calling her, right?"

"She is. Until she's a 'legal' person, she's an 'autonomous being with a high level of emotional intelligence and cognition.'"

"Exactly how smart is she? Is she more intelligent than the average human?"

"It's complicated. If you're talking math and logic, she much more intelligent. She's learning history and sociology, though she struggles with the lack of logic in most human reasoning and interaction. She's just unique, but so far she doesn't completely understand 'humanness,' which is a far cry from humanity."

"How is she taking all of this? Does she understand what's going on?"

"We've limited her access to the media, which would only confuse her, but yes, she knows Jennifer is dead and that the media and police are engaged in an irrational effort to accuse and convict me."

"You know they're conducting a search at the Oakland Hills house and at Jennifer's apartment?"

"Yes," he nodded.

"Routine procedure. You know, Kendrick—I was outside the bathroom when Lee was inspecting it…"

"Okay…"

"Well, he found something a little odd that might need an explanation."

"What's that?"

"It was in a plastic bottle under the sink. It looked like water, you know—no color, but when one of the chemists took a closer look, she determined that it was dimethyl sulfoxide, more commonly known as DMSO, a solvent. You're under no obligation to answer, but at some time you might have to explain what it was doing under your sink."

Chapter 14

"Can you please keep the monkey out of the way?" investigator Sandra Ballesteros pleaded. "She scares me. Please just keep her away from me until we're able to finish here. She really creeps me out. No offense." She glanced toward the ape. "It's weird. Does she actually understand what I'm saying?"

Roland smiled, leaning in.

"More than you want to know," he said, looking over at Alberta, who signed a response. "She says you have well-fed bovine qualities—in her way—and she wants you to know that she is uninterested in you."

"Well that's good," Sandra sighed, the insult slowly sinking in. "Can you show me to Mr. Vesey's room? I'll begin there."

During the course of her search, Sandra tried her best to be neat though thorough, reclosing drawers, re-adjusting objects she had disturbed and placing confiscated items in bins with labels. She took numerous pictures in the bedroom and bathroom. Kneeling, she collected hair samples from the carpet and an empty prescription pill bottle from the waste bin.

Careful to make sure her latex glove-covered fingers did not smudge the bottle, she placed it in a plastic bag before reading the label: Jennifer M. Alvarez... Tagamet... Dr. Truong... *Do not drink alcohol while you are using Tagamet*. She also retrieved a soiled sanitary napkin.

"Your name is Roland Hughes? How long have you lived here?"

"I don't live here. I've just been filling in since Kendrick's been dealing with all this madness. I've been here a couple few weeks max."

"Are you staying in his room?"

"No, I stay in a guest room."

"Did Jennifer Alvarez ever spend the night here?"

"I wouldn't know. Maybe you should ask Alberta."

"The monkey?" Sandra asked, shocked. "She would understand that question?"

"Of course she would, but she's not a monkey. Monkeys have tails, apes have no tails—not so hard to remember."

Ten minutes later, Alberta sat at the kitchen table, annoyed, as the nervous investigator stood near the door, ten paces away, prepared to flee, though she held a notepad and a pen in trembling fingers. Roland was seated between the two, prepared to facilitate communication.

"Ask her if she ever witnessed a fight between Mr. Vesey and Ms. Alvarez..."

After a few seconds of interaction between Roland and Alberta, he answered.

"She says 'no,' she never saw them fight, but she watched a fight with them twice... one was um... Rocky Hendricks, for the world welterweight championship."

"She said all that?" Sandra asked, unconvinced.

"Oh, absolutely."

"Okay, well ask her if she remembers any arguments."

"I don't have to ask her, Detective," Roland laughed. "You can do that. She understands everything you're saying. I'm not here for her. I'm here for you, since you don't understand American Sign Language. I'm just her voice." He glanced over at the ape. "She says she remembers many arguments… on CNN, but she says Kendrick and Jennifer did not argue."

"Did you ever go in Kendrick's room?"

"No. Bedroom is for sleep. Mi have mi own bed."

"Did Jennifer spend the night often?"

"Two nights in two weeks, but sometimes less."

"Why did she come here?"

"Bedroom have door, but Jennifer no come for sleeping. Her come for sex."

"Oh!" Sandra gasped, embarrassed. "I didn't mean it like that. I meant that he has an apartment in San Francisco and so did she. I just wanted to know why would she need to come here?"

"Jennifer can answer, but Jennifer is dead."

Sandra glared toward Roland, unconvinced.

"She really said that?"

"Swear to God," he attested. "I'm an honest broker."

"Did you like Jennifer?" Sandra continued.

"Mi no love Jennifer, but mi no like you too."

"Are you glad she's gone?"

"Jennifer not gone, but she be with Jah Jah."

Roland spoke to the confusion on Sandra's face.

"Jah Jah—you know. She means 'God.'"

"God? Waitaminute! She…" Sandra turned toward Alberta. "You believe in God? You're a Christian?"

"Jah Jah be God. Mi know Jah Jah."

"But you can't be a Christian. You're a monkey. Christ did not die for your sins—that is, if you have the *capacity* to sin. You're an animal."

"And human is animal too."

"You don't have a soul."

The chimp bared her teeth and panted before signing.

"Alberta have more soul than most human. Mi have soul!"

"Hold on," Roland interrupted. "And this is me talking here, not Alberta. What does any of this have to do with your search warrant here? Are you trying to upset her?"

"No, oh no!" Sandra gushed. "This is just unreal. It caught me by surprise. I heard about her, but I had no idea she could communicate like this. She's a very smart monkey."

"Well, you got that much wrong," Roland insisted, glancing over at Alberta, who crossed her arms and stretched her face in a pout. "First, you've got to understand that she's an ape, not a monkey. Look at her—monkeys have tails and apes don't. It's a fairly easy distinction. She doesn't like being called a monkey any more that you'd want to be called a gorilla or Neanderthal."

"In that case," Sandra shrugged, wagging her head, "by all means let me apologize." She leaned forward to speak directly to the chimp. "I am sorry, Alberta, for calling you a monkey. I had no idea. I hope you'll forgive me."

"Alberta is chimp," Roland translated. "Only Jah Jah forgive. Woman too nuff!"

The search of Kendrick's room at the house produced little promise for items with evidentiary value. The room was clean and organized, with most of his notes and commentary written in journals, arranged chronologically. After a phone call from the Commander, however, Sandra instructed technicians to collect the sheets and blankets from the bed and the soiled contents of the laundry hamper.

Likewise, the kitchen and living room contained little information, though Sandra instructed technicians to collect the pillow cover cushion sleeves from the couch and chair and swabs from the surface of the television remote, magazines, the refrigerator and kitchen counters.

When the time came to search her room, Alberta reacted in anger, baring her teeth and screaming, her body language signaling aggression. At first, she blocked the door, threatening technicians until Roland interceded.

"Davis Franklin promise Alberta room is private!" she signed as Roland explained. "Davis Franklin say Alberta say who come in her room and who not come in."

"Can you explain to her that we have a warrant to search the entire house? Would she understand that? Can you tell her that the judge has more authority in this matter than her or Davis Franklin?"

Roland signed to the chimp, who seemed to object, wagging her head forcefully in response. Yet after a series of additional exchanges, Roland approached Sandra, whispering.

"Do you have a copy of the warrant?"

Five minutes later, Roland returned the document and Alberta sat on the couch, her arms crossed, pant-hooting, as Sandra and technicians entered her room. Roland remained close to her, consoling her, as she voiced intermittent protests in nonsensical syllables, full of nuanced emotion. The search went on for an hour before the room was cleared. Sandra was careful to instruct her crew to return all Alberta's things to their original places.

As she approached the table, Sandra held up a small vial, half-filled with what seemed to be a crystalline compound, with the appearance of salt or sugar.

"We found this tucked in the corner of a drawer in the bathroom. Do you have any idea what this is?"

"Alberta not know," she answered. "Mi think white is salt, but salt is for kitchen."

"Which is why it's peculiar that she would have a vial of a crystalline substance in her room," Sandra explained to Roland. "We'll check to see what it is. Other than that, this search is over. I apologize for the inconvenience."

She looked around Roland's body, waving to get the ape's attention.

"Alberta, thank you. It was really nice talking to you. You're a very smart... person!"

****

Johnnie Draco, Gordon Dunleavy, Luis Gutierrez, D'Artagnan Williams and Tom Holt arrived in Austin from different locations, but they booked rooms at the same hotel on East 11th Street, across from the state capitol. One by one, the law enforcement secret group members wandered down into the bar area, taking a table in the remote corner.

It had been an abnormally hot day in Austin, so the men seemed uneasy as they monitored the activity on and around the Capitol grounds, amid preparation for Saturday's rally. Something bad was going to happen.

The previous week had set the stage for the inevitable conflict, and though state and local law enforcement hoped for the best, it was obvious all were preparing for the worst. Two months earlier, "White America," a supremacist group, had won a petition to stage a protest rally at the state capital, ostensibly to exercise their First Amendment rights, but also for recruitment.

Local opposition to White America as well as groups from California, Illinois, New York and Ohio organized an anti-protest movement to converge on Austin with the goal of shutting down the protest and thereby hindering recruitment.

During the summer, there had been previous skirmishes between white supremacists and groups who protested their racist rhetoric. The earlier incidents involved name-calling, hate-speech, bottle-throwing, spitting and threats from both sides, and yet with each occasion for conflict, the degree of violence escalated.

In one instance in Florida, a group of anti-white supremacists caught an opponent and savagely beat him with a flagpole, sending him to the emergency room. At the same incident, there were scattered fistfights. Outnumbered, outflanked and overwhelmed, White America suffered wounds to members, beat-downs and intimidation so that many were forced to flee from their scheduled event. Undeterred, they planned another event in California, with the same result, though the casualties were more widespread and severe.

At the most recent event a month earlier, White America was ready for the anti-protesters. Armed with knives, blades and other close-range weapons, WA members even sought to instigate violence to exact revenge. Surprised by the weapons, the anti-protesters suffered many wounds at the hands of supremacists. WA leaders instructed members to "go after the niggers, since ya can't tell between whites who are with us and the nigger-lovers. Get the Mexicans too!"

Wounded and bruised, the anti-protesters vowed to come back with guns to the next rally, wherever it was, and responding, WA members vowed to arm themselves. The result was a potential menacing conflict in Austin, which many leaders across the country called on state officials to cancel or postpone. The rally was in independent Texas, where the governor insisted that "individual rights and First Amendment rights were supreme." The rally would proceed and the state of Texas would see to it that civility was maintained.

Johnnie Draco and his colleagues did not trust the Texas government and other state officials to quell the inevitable conflict. In fact, they suspected that more than a few prominent Texans were working directly with the instigators of the anticipated race war, so they were counting on a mixed-race cadre of colleagues from all branches of Texas law enforcement to work with them to minimize damage and the escalation of violence and hate.

"Of the 520 law enforcement agents on the ground tomorrow," NY police commander Tom Holt asked, "how many will be working with us?"

"According to the latest information available to me," Dallas lieutenant Dunleavy answered, "we're just shy of 200, which includes people we've got with the state police. It's gonna be a tough call out there tomorrow."

"I don't know why the attorney general won't just shut this thing down or postpone it!" LA detective Gutierrez complained. "Obviously, there are people living today who won't be living tomorrow if they allow this protest to go on. We're gonna lose some of our people."

"People'll die tomorrow for sure," Philadelphia chief D'Artagnan Williams insisted, "it's just a matter of how many, who they are, and how those deaths will influence this war. We have to realize our brothers-in-arms out there will also be affected. Whoever's behind this wants law enforcement to be a principal army in the war."

"We already know who's behind it," Draco interjected, wagging his head. "We can't prove who the shot-caller is, but we know who he is and who's backing im. As long as poor people are fighting and killing each other, they're happy to help."

"People are so stupid! I mean just look at them," Dunleavy sighed, referring to protesters with picket signs outside the window. "They all think they're so patriotic or progressive. Idiots! The rich play em, both sides. But a race war is a much better thing than a class war, right?"

"If we get the guy at the top," Draco continued, "it changes nothing in the big picture—they'll always play one groups against another. If we can get him, maybe we can open some eyes, start a real movement."

"Or get aboard an existing movement and help shape change," Williams nodded. "That's why we chose Our Lives Matter... except I don't trust that Demetrius Berry character, not as far as I can spit. If he's their spokesman, then I don't necessarily trust their leadership—especially since we've been fighting for so long and have so much at stake. Every last one of us are risking careers here, let alone our lives."

"I trust Natsumi Mitchell," Draco countered, "and Padmi Ravi. Demetrius is a racist who doesn't belong there. Natsumi understands what we're trying to do."

"But Natsumi Mitchell's going to be away for a while on that Vesey trial," Holt said. "And I don't know if Ravi's got the balls to deal with Berry and the rest of the people there who aren't not on-board."

"She's got the balls for the job," Draco answered. "I was out there when she was seven months pregnant, and she wasn't backing down from anyone. She lost her baby, and she never gave up. She's down for that cause, so I can only feel sorry for Demetrius if he tries to diminish it."

"Let's pivot to tomorrow," Williams began. "How are we going to know which cops are working with us, so we can coordinate?"

"Shoelaces," Holt answered. "Their shoelace on the left will be missing the nibs, you know, the plastic tips, and the shoelace will be a shade lighter from a mild bleach application. It's subtle, but you'll notice it with those without helmets—they'll have our faded red sign on the forehead, lipstick—a smudged kiss. Maybe we can work together, and maybe we can't, but we'll better know who's on our side. So far, this is our biggest challenge ever."

"He's right," Draco concluded. "This is where the rubber meets the road. Tomorrow morning, we officially begin the 'war against the war.'"

****

Detective Dana Murphy sat at her desk at Central Station, located on Vallejo Street, between Powell and Stockton, which was the busiest division in the San Francisco Police Department. The district comprised the Financial Quarter, Chinatown, North Beach, Fisherman's Wharf, and three famous hills: Telegraph, Nob and Russian. Elbow on the desk, she propped her face in her left palm, squinting at the medical examiner's report on her laptop computer screen. Over the last three days, she had gone over the report a dozen times. Something wasn't making sense.

In the Jennifer Alvarez homicide, the victim had died from cyanide poisoning, which was both chronic and acute. The chronic damage meant that the exposure had occurred over a sustained period of time, "likely for 30-45 days, meaning there was evidence of sustained daily exposure, though at non-lethal limits." According to the medical examiner, there were traces of cyanide on her skin and in her blood, liver and kidneys.

Traces of cyanide were also found on the clothes, bedding, furniture and smooth surfaces at her apartment, at Kendrick's apartment and at the house in the Oakland Hills, where the couple occasionally stayed when Kendrick was working with Alberta.

Absent the notion that Jennifer was being poisoned in all three places, Dana was forced to consider a scenario where the source of the poisoning may have been outside the perimeters of initial suspicion. Later that afternoon, a forensic team would go to Jennifer's former office to test for cyanide contamination.

The acute cyanide poisoning, however, was another matter. Dr. Singh indicated that the fatal dose was critical, meaning it had been sudden and was presumably lethal, though the level of cyanide toxicity already present in her body may have lowered the threshold for acute poisoning. Post-mortem analysis of lung tissue indicated "inhalation at a concentrated level in some aerosol form."

Few of the facts from the medical examiner's report fit the narrative that investigators Nick Jantzen and Tramaine Lee advanced from early on—that Jennifer Alvarez's death had resulted from Kendrick Vesey either trying to silence her about the Stockholm incident in order to save his career, or to collect one million dollars in insurance money. The time frame for the slow chronic poisoning pre-dated the consideration and issuance of the insurance policy.

Dana hoped she could get Kendrick to trust her rather than lump her with Jantzen and Lee, but not because she was certain of his innocence. She was convinced that he was involved in the poisoning somehow, but she did not think his intention was to kill his fiancée. If he was willing to share how he was involved, she knew she could get the district attorney to pursue a manslaughter charge as opposed to some charge relating to murder.

Checking her watch, she remembered a scheduled meeting with Jantzen and Lee, so after finishing her notes closing down her computer, she hurried down the hall to the conference room.

"What are ya sayin, Murphy?" Lee asked. "You wanna just cancel out the ME report and let this guy go? He did something. He's responsible."

"I'm not saying 'let him go,'" she responded. "This case is obviously not as simple as any of us thought. It wasn't a typical poisoning. I say we get him to trust us and tell him we'll get him a good deal from the DA to get him to talk."

"That Mitchell chick is never gonna let him talk," Jantzen sighed, "not for with that Davis Franklin payin her."

"She will if we've got Vesey dead-to-rights," Murphy explained. "We just need to get the evidence and find a way to connect the dots—even if it's something we can't absolutely prove. Franklin is tactical if nothing else. I have a feeling he'd prefer a deal to a certain conviction, and he's clearly nervous, trying to protect his image as a do-good philanthropist. He doesn't want this to become a bigger story."

"Did anything turn up in any of the searches?" Jantzen asked.

"They're searching Jennifer Alvarez's workspace this afternoon," Murphy answered, "but nothing incriminating so far, though all the chemical tests aren't in yet."

"From what I read," Lee commented, "there were traces of cyanide everywhere—in his apartment, in her apartment, at the Oakland house, on his clothes, her clothes, everywhere."

"One of the doctors said Vesey was suffering from some kind of cyanide poisoning as well, but not nearly to the degree Alavarez was," Jantzen added. "He was exposed when he was poisoning her, I figure."

"So what happens if they find traces of cyanide all over her office?" Lee asked. "His lawyer'll argue it all came from there and make it harder to prove anything."

"We don't have to worry about that," Jantzen shrugged. "Whatever they find today won't be a part of the original report. If they find cyanide there, we just won't share any of that information… for now."

Chapter 15

Natsumi's eyes glanced up occasionally as she scanned the pages of the
police report. He was staring again, albeit furtively. *For God's sake—Trevor
Reed's kids were almost her age, and he was married besides!* He wasn't bad-looking,
but he definitely was not her type. He had the annoying habit of sucking and
picking his teeth in public, and his fingernails were always filthy. *Creepy!*

The report was enigmatic, especially the passages about the distribution
of cyanide on surfaces at Kendrick's apartment, at the Oakland Hills home
and in Jennifer's apartment. Cyanide was on the bed sheets and her skin. It
was in the shower, on her clothes and on some of her dishes—and in the
same places at Kendrick's apartment. Jennifer was dead, but Kendrick, who
was obviously subject to similar exposure, appeared to be fine.

The district attorney put a motion before the court, requesting an order
for a doctor to perform a full physical examination on Kendrick to determine
the degree of his exposure. The subsequent report yielded that 1) chronic
cyanide poisoning was evident in subject's (Kendrick's) skin, though in
significantly lower levels than Jennifer's; 2) subject's blood lactate levels were
elevated, indicating slight cyanide toxicity; and 3) tests determined that
damage to subject's liver, kidneys and lungs was mild. At the conclusion of
the examination, doctors gave Kendrick an intra-muscular (IM) injection of
Sulfanegen to detoxify his body. Alberta also received a Sulfanegen shot for
good measure.

While it seemed that both Jennifer and Kendrick were slowly being
poisoned, the physical source of the contamination was a mystery. Detectives
seemed to believe the point source was somewhere in Jennifer's apartment,
where traces of cyanide compounds were found in higher concentrations. If
her apartment was ground zero for the contamination, the investigation was
not able to identify a nexus.

Trevor Reed was working on a request by the court to expedite the
return of Kendrick's physical and electronic materials, asserting that
depriving the professor of his active files and ability to work would cause
significant harm to years of revolutionary research work. He glanced over
again, only to meet Natsumi's annoyed glare.

"What?" she asked.

"Nothing," he answered, embarrassed. "I was just wondering if you
talked to Kendrick about the DA's plans?"

"Not specifically, but he knows it's coming. He'll be ready."

Trevor closed the laptop.

"Were you able to divine anything else from that police report? It would take some real contorted logic to go from what's there to come up with a murder charge."

"You know what they say," she answered, "'you can indict a ham sandwich.' A woman is dead and people are screaming for justice. DA's got to do something."

"True," Trevor nodded, "but I'm thinking it was something environmental, something she was exposed to at work or somewhere else. Whatever it was, she was bringing it back to her apartment, contaminating that and wherever else she went."

"That makes sense," Natsumi said, "and it would explain why her level of exposure was so much higher than his, but it doesn't explain the acute exposure in her lungs… after being home with Kendrick in his apartment for three days. The press had them hemmed in. She never went anywhere after they got there."

"Okay, and what did Kendrick have to say about all that? What did she do during that time?"

"He said she slept mostly," she answered. "He said she had been sick to her stomach and was taking medication—Tagamet, while insisting on drinking alcohol, so he just let her sleep. Dr. Singh says the fatal exposure was a cyanide compound in aerosol form, something she breathed into her lungs. So how is that possible?"

"Maybe someone from the crowd sprayed her with it at the airport or on the way back to the apartment. Did she have any enemies? Anyone who may have wanted her dead?"

"There was an ex-boyfriend under a restraining order," she said, scanning the police report, "but the detective who questioned him confirmed he was working down in Bakersfield during that week. Then there's her brother, Armando, who was very controlling and had some kind of obsessive animus against Kendrick. Jennifer once filed a protective order against her brother for stalking, and his best friend, Carlos, who Armando wanted for her, was warned by her job security for the same thing."

"There's something no one's seeing here," Trevor offered after sucking his teeth. "All this cyanide in all these places… If she didn't die when she did, the continued exposure would have probably killed both of them. If it was a murder attempt, then Kendrick was also a victim."

Trevor clicked the remote to turn on the television, flipping through news channels until he settled on CNN, where a reporter was summarizing the events leading up to "Confrontation in Austin." Selecting "DVR (Digital Video Recording)," Trevor played an earlier NBC broadcast titled "Jennifer Alvarez: A Life Nipped in the Bud," an obvious reference to her Mission Flowers project for Latino girls, "where hybrid seeds from Central and South America grew lush in fertile American soil."

"As tragedy often begets tragedy," the reporter said off-screen, "many wonder about the plight of little Alberta, the remarkable college-educated chimpanzee who reads, writes and is fluent in American Sign Language. Still more incredible, the ape is a mathematics phenomenon who has completed advanced calculus and logic courses at two Ivy League schools, regularly amazing professors."

Trevor turned up the television volume as coverage cut to Dr. Jacobs, who publicly lamented being separated from his precious little *Kipekee*—who had been unfairly ripped from his life in her infancy.

"The resultant trauma and feelings of abandonment have produced anger and resentment, which she has repressed because Dr. Vesey, in his short-sightedness, did not allow for expression. It's only a matter of time before her powder keg of repressed emotion erupts, and heaven forbid, I pity the soul who will be there to witness it."

"What do you think of that?" Trevor asked, nodding toward the television as he turned it off. "Is she's really that smart?"

"I don't know," she answered. "I watched her on TV, and then I met her in… I met her in person. She is smart—disturbingly smart, but when I listened to her answers to reporters, I sensed there was some anger and resentment going on. She was fuming at the press for talking down to her. Every one of her answers was passive aggressive, angry."

"Well, you gotta figure," Trevor sighed, "the smartest ape that ever lived has got to be smarter than a lot of humans, as weird as it is to admit. People naturally feel threatened."

"I heard that in Stockholm she beat a panel of math professors at finishing an abstract math problem. I won't be trying to match wits with her," Natsumi laughed. "My ego could not take losing to an ape."

"Have you interviewed her yet?" he asked.

"You know, Trevor, I was going to talk to you about that," she stammered.

"About what?"

"About the fact that I'm terrified of her, of Alberta. I don't know why. I realize she was raised with and by humans, but there's just something about her. I can't explain it. Please, can you interview her? Can you do that for me?"

"Uh, hell ta the no on that, Natsumi! Do I look crazy to you?" he laughed. "That's your job. They don't pay me enough to do something like that. Tell Davis Franklin I'll do it for a million dollars. Otherwise, no way!"

"Come on, Trevor. Please. I'll be forever in your debt. Why not?"

"Why not? I watched a video last night on YouTube where this little chimp literally went ape wild and tore a lady's face right off. Are you kidding me? Why do you think I wouldn't do an interview with a chimp for you?"

****

The city mayor did his best to persuade the governor to cancel or postpone the protest, citing his concern that the local police and state police were not adequately prepared to handle the thousands of protesters and anti-protesters swelling into Austin. A traditional peaceful protest would have been fine, but the two principal groups involved knew each other—with each side counting casualties after bloody clashes in California, Ohio and Illinois, each side seeking revenge. More than opponents with profound philosophical differences, these groups hated each other and wanted to exact maximum carnage.

"The First and Second Amendments are alive and well in the great state of Texas!" came the governor's strident reply.

On that morning, the American experiment regarding "the absolute right to free speech and the absolute right to bear arms" would be tested for practicality before the people of the United States and the citizens of the world.

Stationed in strategic positions along the police perimeter outside the State Capitol in Austin, Draco and the members of his core group, who they had named "The Loverboys" (for the lipstick "kiss" on their foreheads), directed hundreds of clandestine off-duty law enforcement officers from departments across the country who had volunteered to be "present" as "concerned citizens, dedicated to protecting cops and peaceful protesters."

On one side, the white supremacists and supporters were in Austin "to assert their right to exist and to protect the rights of White People in the United States of America," while a rejuvenated Black Power movement and its supporters sought to equal their voices with a counter message and to discourage recruitment opportunities at the event. With hostile individuals availing themselves to "open carry" weapon protections in Texas, both sides arrived heavily-armed.

The third army on the field was more covert, for fear of revealing its existence and goals, or exposing its membership. The Loverboy Elites and cohorts were 200 officers strong at the event, armed and ready to intervene in acts involving lone wolf assassins, conflicts with opposing groups and cops-versus-community confrontations.

Our Lives Matter, led by Queen Shabaz, was there to signal a peaceful protest to "white supremacy," which leaders and followers believed was the direct source of the racial divide in America. There was also a mixed-race coalition of Christian ministers and churchgoers present to call for a peaceful resolution to the escalation of tensions by appealing to God, who was a common denominator on all sides of the issue.

The sheer number of guns and rifles brandished was unnerving for peaceful protesters and local and state officers, who seemed outgunned at the event. A formation of specially-trained men and women, wearing riot gear behind shields, did their best to keep opposing factions separated so that, while opponents could shout slogans and angry insults across the divide, the erected barriers and police provided for no physical confrontation. Hostile rhetoric escalated over the first thirty minutes. A greater conflict seemed inevitable.

The initial skirmish began with a brick. Someone on the white supremacist side hurled a brick across the divide, which struck a Mexican protester in the head, drawing blood. Retaliation was immediate, with rocks, ball bearings and other small objects flying across from the other side. In no time, the air was filled with projectiles flying in both directions. Following predetermined protocol, the riot police, shields locked, began pushing each group back to widen the divide. The groups offered initial resistance, but both sides yielded ground.

Then there was an unmistakable gunshot, which ironically had been fired into the air by a protester, and yet a woman on the anti-protest side began screaming, claiming that she had been shot, when in fact she had been hit by a chunk of jagged glass. She held out her bloody hands as seeming proof. The man next to her needed no other pretense. Reaching up with his Glock 9-millimeter, he fired across into the crowd on the other side, inflicting palpable injury and the beginning of the small war. Shots rang out on both sides, along with screams and wailing from those who were wounded.

Police reinforcements quickly arrived, flanking both armies, closing. They fired tear gas canisters as they approached with rifles leveled at armed combatants, and they shot individuals who refused commands to lower their weapons. The smell of gunpowder filled the air, along with thick smoke and the overwhelming CS gas trailing from the canisters. In the haze, the sound of an automatic weapon rang out, simultaneous with the sound of bullets ricocheting off the shields of riot police.

In the chaos, other shots rang out, distant shots, from atop a nearby building. Two officers fell. Three more shots, and another officer down. Immediately identifying the man discharging the automatic weapon, a police sniper positioned atop a vehicle quickly put him down with a shot at mid-forehead, and yet there was another sniper on another building who was apparently targeting the police.

****

"How is she, Mia?"

"Not good," Mia answered standing. "Hey! Can we get some help over her?" she shouted toward a paramedic crouched behind the open back door of an ambulance. "This woman's been shot! She needs immediate medical care! Get your ass over here now, you coward!"

"What happened?" Phi asked. "Was she targeted?"

"I don't know!" Mia snapped, gesturing toward two paramedics who cautiously approached. "Goddammit! If you don't hurry your sorry asses up, she's going to die!"

Mia Melendez and Phi Truong had accompanied Queen Shabaz to Austin to lead the OLM protest, and they had participated in the protesters training session with her on the previous afternoon. On that morning, they had breakfast with protesters, emphasizing the mission: to call attention to the disparity in the value attributed to black and brown lives in America.

Queen was awkward at leadership because she was the new chairperson for Our Lives Matter, so the Austin event was her first foray in the challenge she faced in her elevated position. Embracing her role, she worked enthusiastically with local leaders, protesters and volunteers. She was standing in front of a chanting crowd when the shot rang out and she fell to the ground.

The bullet pierced her chest, bursting out her back before striking another protester in the leg. Witnesses insisted that the bullet, based on its trajectory, had not come from antagonists on the other side. Rather, the person who shot her was someone on the anti-protest side, either from a misdirected bullet or intentional assassination.

Queen labored to breathe, her words coming between the painful sounds of groaning and weeping.

"My kids!" she pleaded, her eyes desperate, blood trailing from her mouth. "Oh, my babies! I'm not gonna make it! My poor babies! Pray for me, Mia! I can't die here! Don't let me die! Please!"

The paramedics worked frantically, applying pressure to the wound and starting an IV while prepping for an emergency blood transfusion.

"Save me, God!" she called as paramedics carried her to the ambulance. "*Allah Akbar!* It ain't my time!"

****

Loverboy Elite D'Artagnan Williams was certain the shots had come from the roof, two stories above him. The hostile was firing a sniper rifle, and it seemed his targets were law enforcement personnel on the ground. From the window, Williams watched as a riot police officer was struck by an armor-piercing round and fell to the ground. He hurried up the stairwell, pistol in hand, and paused at the door, listening, waiting. When the next shot rang out, he slammed the door open, convinced the shooter was turned toward the street.

Startled by the sound of the door, the sniper whipped his head and shoulders around, and yet before he could follow with the rifle, his fate was sealed. Williams shot before aiming, hitting the man directly in the throat.

The shooter stiffened as the rifle tumbled to the floor. Clutching at his throat, the man fell backward to the floor on the other side of a counter, his army boots twitching in William's view.

Williams kicked at one of the boots, came around the counter and kicked the sniper rifle out of the shooter's reach. The man was barely alive, reaching out and still struggling to breathe. Down on one knee, Williams placed his glove-covered palm over the man's nose and mouth, holding firm until struggle ceased and the body relaxed. Withdrawing a small tube from his pocket, Williams turned the base to expose the bright red lipstick, and he drew a two-inch line across the dead man's forehead.

He stood and took a picture of the scene before retrieving the spent shell from the floor and hurrying from the room and out the building. Only after he was two blocks away did he approach a nervous officer along the perimeter that was purposed to contain the shooter.

"I'm very sure those shots were coming from that building right there," he said, indicating the place he had just left. "They were coming the building there, on Third."

****

"Roland, is it?" Natsumi asked. "Roland, thanks for doing this for me. You must think I'm silly, but I'm just not comfortable sitting so close to her. I hope she's not offended. Maybe you can tell her it's required by law that we can't be in the same room?"

"You want me to lie to her?" Roland asked.

"I don't know if you would really call that lying…"

"There is no law that says you have to be in another room, so that would be a lie," he answered. "You need to understand the rules, Ms. Mitchell. We don't lie to Alberta—not me, not Kendrick, not Davis. Never. Lying to her would only teach her how to lie, and we don't want that. Lying is a human habit, a nasty human habit, but you're a lawyer, so you wouldn't know anything about that, would you?"

"I'm sorry," Natsumi effused. "I just never really thought about it that way."

"It's also a matter of trust. Most people underestimate her intelligence. Her brain is so rational that she would see through a lie if there was the least bit of inconsistency. Trust me, there is nothing for you to fear by being in a room with her. She's not dangerous at all."

"There's something about her," Natsumi sighed, unconvinced. "I just have this spooky feeling about her. Maybe if we were at opposite sides of the room, with you in the middle?"

"Since I'm translating for you, Ms. Mitchell, that arrangement probably makes the best sense."

"She wants to know if you are the judge, Ms. Mitchell," Roland translated.

"Tell her 'no,' I'm not. Tell her that I am a lawyer who is helping Kendrick in this matter."

Natsumi waited for Roland to translate, so her face registered confusion when he didn't.

"Aren't you going to tell her?"

"You just did. Look, she understands everything you're saying. You're the handicapped person in the room. You're illiterate at American Sign Language. She asked if the judge is your ma… she means your 'boss.'"

"I am a defense attorney. The judge is the arbitrator of facts. During the trial, if there is one, the judge will make both findings of fact and rulings of law," Natsumi answered, turning toward Roland. "Do you think she understood all that?"

"Alberta wants to know the purpose of this interview."

"Tell her…" Natsumi stopped, redirecting to the chimp. "I am here to help Kendrick, Alberta, and you can help me do that. Will you answer a few questions for me?"

Alberta held her right arm up at face level, and making a fist, displayed a knocking motion while nodding.

"I'll take it that means 'yes.' Okay, first question: did you spend time with Kendrick and Jennifer together?"

Alberta indicated 'yes.'

"Okay. During the interaction between them that you observed, did you ever notice any disagreements, any fighting?"

Alberta indicated 'yes' and signed toward Roland.

"She says that because humans can talk, they have the ability to argue and fight with words. Apes never argue," Roland translated.

"What did they fight about?"

"They fight about flowers for the wedding, and colors. They fight about friend of Armando, Jennifer brother, and they fight about Alberta."

"Why would they fight about Alberta?" Natsumi asked. "For what reason?"

"Jennifer not like Alberta because Kendrick love Alberta. Jennifer not want Kendrick to see Alberta after them marry."

"Did Alberta ever fight with Jennifer? Did you two ever have a confrontation?"

Holding up her hand, Alberta extended the index and middle fingers together, tapping them with her thumb.

"That's a 'no?' Okay…" Natsumi said while scribbling a note. "Wait, would it be all right with Alberta if I used my phone to tape the rest of this interview?"

"Ya."

"Thank you."

Alberta responded by touching the fingertips of her right hand to her chin and extending an open palm toward Natsumi.

"That means 'thank you?'" Natsumi confirmed while repeating the gesture. "Well then, thank you," she said as she turned on the phone camera and aimed it toward the chimp. "Was there ever any physical violence between Kendrick and Jennifer? Did you ever see Kendrick hit Jennifer or shove her?"

"Alberta is not in elevator, but mi see Kendrick shove Jennifer when them is in elevator. Mi see on YouTube. Shove not same as murder."

"No, it isn't," Natsumi confirmed. "Did you ever see him hit or shove Jennifer when she was visiting him here?"

"No."

"Did he ever scream at Jennifer or threaten her?"

"No."

"Do you understand what 'murder' means, Alberta?"

"Murder mean when one person plan to kill other person, except when human law tell prison or police to kill other person."

"Unlawful premeditation," Natsumi nodded. "That's right. You understand that! Okay, do you think it is possible that Kendrick could have murdered Jennifer?"

"No," she signed, followed by Roland's translation. "Kendrick, him have no motive for kill Jennifer—to kill Jennifer. Kendrick loved Jennifer. Kendrick wanted to marry Jennifer till die—for life."

"Alberta, do you know of anyone else who may have wanted Jennifer dead?"

"Mi not know, but Armando love Jennifer too much for him brother. Him be Tony Montana, love sister too much."

Natsumi couldn't help but turn toward Roland, scolding.

"You guys let her watch that violent movie?" she sighed. "Alberta, did you ever see Armando hit Jennifer or shove Jennifer?"

"Mi not see, but mi see Jennifer cry. Mi see black mark on Jennifer face. Armando whip bitch ass."

"What was that? Nevermind, please don't repeat it," Natsumi said, glaring again at Roland. "The black marks on Jennifer's face, Alberta. How do you know that Armando is the person who hit her?"

"Jennifer say Armando hit her face. Pow-pow!"

"Did she tell Kendrick about it? Did Kendrick see the injury to her face?"

"Ya mon."

"Okay," Natsumi continued as she turned the notebook page. "Do you remember a week or so ago, when officer Ballesteros came by to search Kendrick's room and your room?"

"Ya."

The ring-tone on Natsumi's phone interrupted the interview.

"Hello? What! No! When did this happen? How is she? No!... I'm just finishing an interview. I'll call you when I leave. Make sure you answer. Bye."

Obviously stunned by the news, Natsumi bowed her head, tears in her eyes as she struggled to continue.

"Alberta, do you remember when Officer Ballesteros found something in the corner of the bottom drawer in your bathroom?"

"Ya mon. Her show Alberta jar of salt."

"Salt? Tell me, do you know how the 'jar of salt' got in your drawer?"

"Mi not know. Salt is for kitchen."

"One more question," Natsumi intreated, looking toward Roland and back to Alberta. "How did Alberta know it was salt in that jar?"

"Alberta taste," the chimp answered. "Alberta taste nasty salt in jar."

"Thank you," Natsumi signed, "that will be all. We'll talk again.

Once outside the door, Natsumi burst into tears, weeping, her heart sunken to the pit of her stomach and her vision blurry by the time she reached the car. Padmi had shared awful news: Queen Shabaz was shot at the protest in Austin and had died in the ambulance on her way to the hospital.

Chapter 16

"So now we hafta somehow come to a new understanding, Mr. Luck," Colin announced as he sat across from the smug billionaire.

"No. Now *you* have to come to a new understanding, son," the older man answered. "Me—I understand things just fine."

"Things have changed. Stakes are higher. Now were dealin with a paid hit, an assassination."

"Is someone dead?" Luck asked.

"Please! You already know someone's dead—a second OLM leader. You ordered the hit!"

Luck paused, puffing on the cigar.

"I don't think I ordered any hit. Why would I do that? I know nothing about the woman who died. I didn't know she even existed. I wouldn't be involved with that in any way?"

"You said you wanted the leader of Our Lives Matter out of the picture, to send a message to group leaders and the rest across the country. That's what happened, and I understand you paid $50,000 for it."

"Look, Cyanide," Luck insisted, leaning across the table to whisper. "The record will show that I have never paid that amount of money to anyone outside my business! If you were somehow involved in that assassination in Austin, I wouldn't be surprised. One of your ghosts? You are Cyanide, aren't you? You can lie about it, but I could probably prove you are. So if I were you, Cyanide, I wouldn't say another word about it. I have an obligation to support law and order and the rule of law, and you know how law enforcement feels about people like you, with you being a bad-ass criminal rap producer and all..."

They sat on the rooftop patio of an upscale bistro on Page Street in Hayes Valley in the Western Addition of San Francisco. They usually had breakfast, but Colin was agitated and was sipping his third Hennessey XO in forty minutes.

"I'm sure there'll be a federal investigation..."

"But you're too smart for those amateur investigators, Colin. You made sure nothing would link back to you, Mr. Brown University, *Summa cum Laude*."

"You're right about that, Mr. Luck. Bottom line, though—I'm complicit, and so are you."

"Don't say that. I don't like the sound of that."

"Me either," Colin nodded, sipping, "but over the years, I've learned a lot from you. I know how you think. I know how you operate."

"Really? And how do I operate, boy genius?"

"If something goes wrong and federal investigators start looking your way, you've already found a way to put this whole thing off on me. You're solid mostly, but if it came down to it, you'd put this shit off on me."

"Never."

"You want this race war because it's good for business, but I want my revolution because I need black and white folks to finally start takin this shit seriously. We gotta cover our own asses. That's why if it ever comes down to me and you and they start comin after me, I've got the evidence to take you with me. If my hands are bloody, then so are yours. We're in this together—to the end."

"Is that what you think you learned from me, Colin?" Luck asked, "You learned to blackmail a nice old gentleman who only tried to teach a confused black boy who wanted to destroy the country?"

Colin brushed his long dreadlocks back, ignoring the question.

"So what really was the point? Do you really think smokin that bitch'll change anything?"

"That's it! You're wearing some kind of recording device," Luck returned. "And you want me to talk about it? Come on…"

Colin stood, ripping his shirt open to expose his muscular chest and defined stomach. He patted his pockets and turned off his cell phone, placing it face-down on the table.

"Do I look like an amateur? I don't play games, but I always buy insurance. I think you're gettin old, Luck, and maybe a little senile. You insisted on this risk for both of us, but all it did was hurt us."

"You've been reading the news, huh?" Luck said, tossing a newspaper in front of his protégé. "Things are already changing. When Our Lives Matter staged an event in Austin last night to protest that woman's death, hardly anyone showed. They're scared. I counted only two white people in a photo from the event. White people are afraid to be out there now."

"I was in Austin that night."

"You saw the cops die?" Luck asked.

"Six."

"Six! And eight injured! That oughta get some traction. Fuel to the fire."

"So now you're cheerin the deaths of cops? How does this work, Luck? How do you profit from this?"

"I've told you all along—chaos and anarchy aren't bad things, especially if you know how to make disorder work for you. Hate and division are excellent devices to make the people give you what you want."

"And what do you want?" Colin asked.

"I'm a business man. I want to win—nothing else motivates me."

"And love of country?" Colin asked.

"You said it yourself earlier, Cyanide. We've gotta cover our own asses. But of course *you* would understand that—you're a black *and* a Jew."

Five minutes later, the tension between Justin Luck and Colin Stein-Whitaker had diminished. The discussion moved to various other subjects, from Justin's kids and grandchildren to Colin's parents to the future of rap music. Luck had already paid for lunch, so as Colin stood, ready to leave, Luck bade him sit for a final conversation.

"Did I ever tell you I actually admire ISIS, in an odd way?"

"Why's that?"

"They're very effective. They know how to win. If you really analyze how they operate, you'll know why. First, they have no compassion. Winning is everything, and second—their order is chaos, so they're unpredictable, which makes them unstoppable. I hate em, but I gotta admire em."

"And the point of you telling me that?"

"Well, if you read the news like I do—six newspapers every morning, plus network and cable television news—you'd realize that same model could be imitated right here in America with profound benefits to those who understand the potential. The government and country's gone to Hell. It can't be fixed. This war's going to be a good thing. It's about damn time!"

Colin squinted as he discerned Luck's implication.

"You're talking about actual sedition?"

"Not at all. I'd like to call it 'the exploitation of a resource that is a product of American injustice.' It's a good rap music message."

"I shouldn't be listening to this," Colin said, "but go on."

"Okay," Luck began while lowering the volume of his voice. "You see it a lot on the news now. You get these black guys—usually ex-military—and they get back to this country after their tours of duty and the country hates em. And their families are torn apart. Their kids hate em, their wives have moved on. And they've got PTSD or whatever, with no help from the government. At least 10,000 of em homeless, and no one wants to hire em, cuz they're killers, after all. And they can't have decent relationships, because they're not well in the head. They're stuck nowhere, and they're all really pissed off. A lot of anger there to exploit…"

"And that's where you come in?" Colin asked.

"Correction. That's where you, me and this race war come in, Colin. These poor ex-military blacks out there, millions of them, not to mention the Mexicans—they're an un-tapped army. They're all lone wolves, but we've seen the damage and destruction just one of them can do with an automatic weapon and anger we can exploit. So now imagine if there were a leader for them out there, a leader who could speak to these angry blacks, feel their pain, provide purpose and give their pitiful lives some worth and relevance. They need someone with an idea to empower them and someone else to give em guns. It's Helter Skelter, at long last."

****

Although the family of Queen Shabaz conducted a private funeral service and quick burial in coordination with their temple on 31st Street in Oakland, the OLM movement, supporters and the media staged a memorial for her downtown at Oscar Grant Plaza, two days later. Pastor Calvin King, a close personal friend, presided over a program that celebrated Queen's strength, warmth, intelligence, perseverance, goodwill, fairness, optimism and her ability to forgive.

"While the investigation is still ongoing," Calvin lamented, "I know that, to her very last breath, Queen never bore hatred for anyone—not even the person who took her life, and I am sure she asked the Lord to forgive that hateful person before she died. She was just that way."

After fifteen minutes of remarks and a short prayer, Reverend King invited a nervous fifteen-year-old soloist onto the stage, where she stood trembling before the choir and audience. After a tense silence, she sang *a capella*, soulfully, sorrowfully.

> *I've been buked [rebuked], and I've been scorned, yes.*
> *I've been buked, and I've been scorned.*
> *Children...*
> *I've been buked, and I've been scorned.*
> *I've been talked about, [sure as] you're born.*

It was seven o'clock as the summer sun trailed toward the horizon. Hot and unrelenting, its edges crept behind the buildings in the west so that a welcome shade encroached over the gathering. There were roughly seven hundred attendees, representing diverse cultures, ages, lifestyle choices, income levels and every skin shade, ranging from blue-black to transparent. The timbre of the song and the occasion evoked visceral emotion, as people stood holding hands, swaying, weeping and seeking to comfort each other in the wake of the tragedy.

Television and smart phone cameras captured images and video, immediately broadcast out to the world, containing bittersweet scenes of harmony and hope. Surely beyond all the protests, all the contention, the scapegoating, the blaming and the hate, there were occasions like this, however ephemeral, to embrace humanity and love, based on the principle of a shared dream... of unity.

The clear, haunting and prescient quality of the youthful singer's voice belied her age, transcending the five generations assembled that evening and causing many among the huddled masses to reflect on the words printed on the back of the memorial program.

It really boils down to this: that all life is interrelated. We are
all caught in an inescapable network of mutuality, tied into a
single garment of destiny. Whatever affects one directly,
affects all indirectly. – Dr. Martin Luther King, Jr.

"And now," Calvin continued, "let us all put our profound grief aside
so that we may listen to a few inspirin words from Ms. Natsumi Mitchell, the
persistent, steadying voice of the Our Lives Matter movement."

Seated next to the choir, Natsumi stood, wiping her eyes with a small
purple handkerchief, and took her place before the microphone.

"To all my brothers and sisters of all races in this movement, let me start
today by saying that Queen Shabaz died for *you* on last Thursday. She died
for all of us.

"Queen was shot as she stood, as she so fearlessly stood, objecting to
division in this country, objecting to inequality, objecting to the injustice in
the lives of people of color. No one knows who shot her. Maybe it was some
hateful bigot from across the police divide, or maybe it was some rotten apple
on the police force, or maybe it was someone who represents a faction that
does not want peace in America, ever—someone who sees some measure of
benefit in dividing us.

"Let's just take it down to the basic words. You've heard our chant: *No
Justice, No Peace.* Some of you are tired of it, but let me tell you today, it is a
slogan that should not and does not belong to our movement. It's bigger than
us. It should be America's slogan.

"Our country's founders were the first Americans to embody *No Justice,
No Peace*, and there absolutely was no peace until the Articles of
Confederation were incorporated as the founding principles for our new
nation. It's to our benefit that those brave individuals didn't shut up, just
shut-up already. Throughout history, silence and apathy have never been
solutions for righting wrongs or making societies and governments work
better. Direct action involves confrontation.

"But how is peace possible, when on a weekly basis, we turn on our
televisions and we're forced to confront another situation where an unarmed
black or brown man or woman has been killed in the street by armed police
officers? There's always explanation, and it's always the victim's fault. In the
end, the cops cover for each other, while the prosecutorial system falls in line.
As a result, there is no justice for us—no trials, no convictions and no
punishment.

"How is peace possible when we're stung by injustice so often, seeing
the undeniable lack of justice with our own eyes in the murders of Michael
Brown, Trayvon Martin, Eric Gardner, Dontre Hamilton, John Crawford,
Ezell Ford, Dante Parker, Tanisha Anderson, Akai Gurley, Tamir Rice—
twelve years old, Rumain Brisbon, Jerame Reid, Tony Robinson, Phillip

White, Eric Harris, Walter Scott, Freddie Gray, Sandra Bland, LaQuan McDonald, Bettie Jones, Alton Sterling, Philando Castile and Ibrahim Ravi, and that doesn't begin to scratch the surface in terms of the sheer number of those killed each year. Justice for all? Where is 'Justice for Us?'

"There can be no peace when we watch our family members and neighbors die unjustly, when we wait for justice, only to see the murderers acquitted, when police and the prosecutorial system assume we are 'expendable until proven innocent,' when cops lie and destroy evidence to legitimize the criminality of other cops. "Blue Lives Matter too, but it's redundant, because when blue lives are lost, there is always accountability.

"Queen Shabaz was my friend. We marched side-by-side for two years—not because we had nothing better to do. We both had careers, so we sacrificed to hold our country to a higher standard. She had a family—kids and a husband, so on Thursday, she made the ultimate sacrifice. A soldier for justice, Queen gave her life for us, for America."

****

There he was again, when after the memorial meal, she got back to her car—only this time he was seated on the hood, smoking a blunt.

"Ms. Mitchell, I must say it's good to see you again," he smiled, blowing out a puff of skunk-scented smoke. "I was pleasantly surprised. Good thing you had to take time off. Otherwise, maybe Queen Shabaz woulda been speakin at *your* memorial service."

"Who are you? I've seen your face somewhere, before the last time."

"It don't matter who I am," Colin answered. "I warned you, and now someone's dead. Your friend is dead because you wouldn't listen."

"It was you!" Natsumi demanded. "You killed her!"

"I'm disappointed that you think so little of me. Do I look like a killer? I'm just a ghost."

"Bullshit!" she objected, angry, pepper spray gripped in her left hand. "You just admitted that someone targeted the Our Lives Matter leader, that it would have been me if I was still there. You were going to kill me!"

She raised her smart phone instead of the pepper spray and activated the video camera, but Colin turned and flipped up his hoodie and turned his back.

"If you get the feds or anyone else involved, then you'll be dead for certain. Turn the camera off. Turn it off and we'll talk."

She clicked two still-frame shots of him before returning the phone to her pocket—still in video mode in order to record the conversation.

"Do you know who killed Queen Shabaz?"

"You did, Ms. Mitchell. I warned you about the consequences, but you wouldn't listen. I'm sorry about your friend, but this thing that's going on is bigger than you and your movement. You can't win."

"Like you said, it's a movement," she insisted. "It's bigger than me. So you know I can't shut it down."

"Then choose a new leader, and that person will die too, and the next leader after that—until you stop all the instigating and tell your followers to go home."

"Only results or disillusionment can end a movement. How do you think I can provide either of those?"

"That's why I came today," he answered. "I can get you results, but they won't be all the results you're asking for. I can get money for your group. I can get cover—legitimacy for you if you're willing to compromise. Just be reasonable for a change."

"I told you before. I'm not going to sell out my cause. If I did that, Queen's death will have been for nothing."

"What about all the other people who are going to die," he asked, "in and outside your cause? You already have Queen's blood on your hands. Who's gonna be your next leader?"

Always quick with a retort, she was lost for words.

"Ms. Mitchell, it doesn't have to be like this. You've won a few battles, but you can't win em all. No one can. At some point, you hafta understand that you've taken your movement as far as it will go. Celebrate your successes and cut your losses. Take a settlement and retreat. Believe me, you'll do more for your cause by quietly coming to terms."

"On some days," she sighed, "I wish I could, but I don't have many of those days lately, and today isn't one of them."

"The revolution's been overdue for years. America needs to confront its race problem, and revolution is the only way. People'll die for the greater good—black, white—everybody. From the spilled blood of the oppressors, change will finally come."

"No one else should have to die," she insisted.

"But they will. Your movement will never change anything. Dr. King, for all his lofty talk and big speeches, didn't really change anything. That will only come through revolution, when blood flows in the streets."

"Now I'm convinced," Natsumi said. "At first I thought you were full of yourself. Now I know you're full of shit."

"You wanna know my settlement proposal?"

"No, I want to know who you really are. You dress like a gangbanger, and you try to be hard, but you're not street. My guess is you grew up middle-class and went to college. I just have to wonder why you've succumbed to the slave mentality of white supremacy."

"The revolution is the only way to end white supremacy..."

"Let me finish," she interrupted. "You've gone this far with whoever owns you. They've used your extremism to enslave you. You've already betrayed your people, but it's not too late for you. You need to think long and hard before you accept those thirty pieces of silver, because you already know the outcome. You'll gain the whole world and forfeit your soul."

Chapter 17

While the police report became a part of the national television news cycle, facts contained within caused the story to explode on the Internet, with details going viral in four hours. Based on an anonymous tip, a street cop had gone to the roof of an office building in downtown Austin, where he found a sniper, dead from a gunshot wound to his throat. Ballistic testing and fingerprints from spent cartridges confirmed that the decedent was the rooftop cop-killer. According to the report, he was dispatched at close range—meaning there was someone else on the roof.

Speculation ran amok. Some suggested there was a second sniper, and that perhaps the sniper was the victim of an accidental shooting. Yet all the shots fired to the street came from a single rifle. Others guessed that the assailant was perhaps killed in a dispute with the supposed colleague who was secretly an undercover FBI agent.

Investigators found two handguns and two modified automatic AR-15s with five high-capacity 100-round magazines and three 60-round magazines. They also recovered 12 M67 fragmentation grenades—each with a wounding radius of 50 feet, an improvised explosive device and materials purposed for booby-trapping the entrance to the roof. The report called the man a "suicide-sniper," as he obviously did not plan on surviving the ordeal.

His targets were cops on the ground, and his plan was to take out as many as possible before detonating the device on the rooftop when the door was breached. Whoever put the bullet in his throat had saved perhaps two dozen law enforcement lives.

The shooter was later identified as former army soldier Warren Drayton, a destitute African American male in his early thirties with a history of mental problems, including PTSD and acute schizophrenia. Warren was impoverished, so there was speculation about how he had acquired four expensive firearms, over two thousand rounds of ammunition, the grenades and the materials used for the IED.

One reporter suggested it was inheritance money, since his mother had passed away a month earlier—until records revealed that she died a penniless invalid in a care home.

Where would a mentally and emotionally-compromised indigent get over $5,000 to stage a mini war-platform on that roof? That was the $10,000 question, and yet a greater quandary had to do with the other person on the rooftop—the person who shot him before he achieved his end. Either that person was a persistent danger because he was involved in the planning, or he was an undercover hero.

The police did not reveal the presence of a lipstick smear on the sniper's forehead. It was a deliberate marking, corresponding to the marking on another man found dead near a protest in Chicago two weeks earlier. Roger

Brown's body was discovered in a vacant office space downtown off Michigan Avenue, dispatched by a single gunshot to the head. Brown was also an African American veteran and he too, had a cache of new weapons and excess ammunition. When detectives rolled him onto his back, his forehead was conspicuously marked with red lipstick, a horizontal smear.

Circumstances surrounding the two murders were of concern to the FBI, who determined that the firearms and ammunition discovered at both crime scenes were untraceable or registered to dead persons. Glock 9-millimeters were used in both instances, leading investigators to conclude the cases perhaps had an assailant in common. Based on the absence of forensic evidence in both places, an FBI profiler suggested the killer was "probably a cop," a vigilante.

The FBI heard rumors about a nationwide secret brotherhood of law enforcement officers who called themselves "The Loverboys," with its "Loverboy Elite" leaders. According to stories, these badass cops went after the real horrible guys, whether they wore gang colors or cop colors—to save cops' lives and protect communities. Local police unions bristled at the mention of the group, insisting that any admiration would encourage them.

Draco sat with the rest of the group in the private room of a small Italian restaurant on State Street on the North Side of Chicago. Born and raised in the North Beach area of San Francisco, he knew good Italian food, and the *Brodetto Ai Frutti Di Mare* was delicious, though he preferred the rockfish they used at home to the whitefish in Chicagoland.

Seated directly across from him was Philadelphia inspector Williams, and counterclockwise around the table there was McCarthy from Boston, Snow from Chicago, Dunleavy from Dallas, Collins from Cleveland, Gutierrez from LA and Holt from NYC. Once the dinner plates were cleared and coffee was served, Snow told the server to get lost for an hour. Bottle of Bushmills Irish Whiskey at the center of the table and shot glasses all around, the men spoke in quiet tones.

"So far, we've dodged two bullets," Holt nodded, squinting as he threw back a shot, "but we took a hit on the third. Fourteen shot—six dead. It coulda been worse."

"We were focusing on black," Dunleavy explained, "but this perp was Mexican, or Honduran or whatever. All three were American citizens."

"And all three ex-military," Gutierrez agreed. "No question about it—someone's recruitin these guys and supplyin the guns and ammo—and not just these guys. They've been dumpin guns in minority neighborhoods for months."

"We need to apprehend the next one," Snow asserted, "but that's like belling the cat. These guys are dangerous, and they're crazy. No telling what someone's done to their heads. Suicide snipers! What do you think, D'Artagnan? You got the last one."

"I didn't have time to do anything but shoot," he answered, "and he had grenades, which I didn't know about at the time, but I wanted to make sure he was toast."

"What about you, McCarthy?" Draco asked. "You got the guy in downtown Chicago. You had to take the kill shot?"

"I wasn't takin any chances," McCarthy answered. "Instinct tells ya that. These guys got nothing to lose."

"The best thing would be to identify the next one and then follow im and get to im before he starts settin up," Draco offered. "We could probably get our eyes on the ground to help us out there."

"Someone with a bigger plan is helping these guys," Williams countered. "The sniper's perch is probably already set up before those guys are sent up. Who knows? Maybe we'll catch a break next time…"

"My concern is we're sitting on a powder keg," Dunleavy sighed. "So far, we've been lucky, but it's only a matter of time before we're gonna be at ground zero for America's next civil war."

"Call it for what it is," Gutierrez corrected, "a race war."

"Okay, I just got a text," Draco interrupted. "Demetrius is outside in the parking lot. I'm telling him to come on in."

Ten minutes later, Demetrius Berry sat before the group, a lowball glass in his unsteady hand. He was wearing jeans, a sweatshirt with a hood, tennis shoes and an Oakland A's baseball cap. He declined a drink from the whisky bottle on the table, requesting "gin and juice" instead.

"How was the funeral?" Williams asked.

"It was a funeral," Demetrius answered, "bunch of speeches, cryin, prayin, and then prayin some more."

"So what's next for Our Lives Matter?" Dunleavy asked. "Queen Shabaz—wasn't she the new leader and spokesperson for the group after Natsumi Mitchell left?"

"She was," Draco confirmed, "and now she's dead."

"Who'll be the new leader?" Collins asked.

Demetrius' eyes scanned the solemn faces in the room, seeking openness and acknowledgement. Only Snow nodded.

"I don't know," Demetrius answered. "We'll have a vote at our next meeting, which is on Wednesday night. They know I'm meetin with you guys, so they'll probably want to know what you know."

"What we know about what?" Holt asked.

"About who killed Queen Shabaz. You musta heard somethin."

Draco and the others remained silent, unresponsive.

"I mean you guys were right there, and you had other cops working with you. Someone had to see somethin. It happened in plain daylight."

"It wasn't a random shot, a stray bullet," Holt answered, "if that's what you're asking."

"Then what was it? Do you know?"

"Well, it wasn't the rooftop shooter that you saw on the news," Holt replied. "This shot came from the complete opposite direction—a sniper in one of the buildings on the other side."

"A sniper?" Demetrius asked. "So it was intentional. Queen was a target?"

"Yes," Williams answered, "and not because her name was Queen Shabaz. She was targeted as the leader of the Our Lives Matter movement."

"A couple of our observers reported seeing a suspicious man with a case heading into an office building two hours before she was shot," Draco continued. "They never saw him come out, but when they searched the location, they found the case, along with a Barrett M90 sniper rifle and spent cartridges. The bullet was a match."

"Description of the man," Holt added, "six-four, athletic, dark clothes, dark glasses, a beanie and African American."

"African American? He was black?" Demetrius asked.

"Are you surprised?" Draco responded. "Doesn't that prove our point? It was an assassination meant to up the ante in the race war that someone wants."

"But I saw on the news where the guy was white…"

"And what was the source of that story?" Holt asked. "A convenient black witness who provided no other detail other than saying he saw a white man with a swastika on his shirt running from the building?"

"One of our guys interviewed that witness two days after the story broke," Dunleavy added. "The witness admitted that he lied for money. Someone gave him that story to help shape the news narrative. He got two hundred fifty dollars for that performance."

Demetrius cocked his head, skeptical, before shaking it in disbelief.

"We have a picture of the man we believe was the shooter," Dunleavy insisted, "but it was taken at a tough angle and from a distance." He stood, handing the picture over to Demetrius. "There he is. That man killed your friend."

"You're the head of security for your movement," Draco stated. "You ever seen that man before? Maybe at one of your protests?"

"No!" Demetrius groaned. "Besides, it's not a clear picture. I can't really see his face."

"And if you didn't notice," Holt countered, "that large case you see in his hand in that picture—that's the exact same case they found upstairs next to the sniper rifle. That man's the assassin, no doubt about it."

"Make sure you let Our Lives Matter know that," Dunleavy said, nodding. "We're need you guys to help us de-escalate this situation, and others coming up. This war is just getting started."

"We have to find a way to counter an overwhelming false narrative," Draco concluded.

"This all don't make no sense to me," Demetrius argued. "My concerns are white privilege and white superiority. That's why I got involved in the movement in the first place. I don't know if I believe in this race war theory. I don't know if this arrangement between us is workin."

"Are you speaking for Our Lives Matter," Draco asked, "or are you speaking as Demetrius Berry, because you're an idiot, Demetrius. We don't give a crap about you and what you think. I'm calling Natsumi Mitchell tonight to tell her that maybe you're the wrong person for the job."

"Screw you, white boy!"

"I'm black, Demetrius," D'Artagnan Williams intoned, nostrils flared, "and I know bullshit when I hear it! Being a cop and black, I see it from both sides, and I'm tired of people who are in the way. The stakes are too high, so get up and take your black ass out of here. Either Our Lives Matter will send us someone else, or we'll get it done on our own!"

****

"Are you ready for this?" Natsumi asked.

"Ready as I'll ever be," Kendrick shrugged. "I mean, who's ever ready for it?"

He had gone to the barbershop in the morning, followed by a trip to the spa for a facial, manicure and pedicure. He had met with the Vice Chancellor for Primate Research at the University of California at Berkeley, followed by a tactical meeting with Davis Franklin and Roland Hughes. Finally, he went to the office of his attorney, Natsumi Mitchell, who explained the nature of the criminal charges against him, giving him an idea of what he could expect over the next few days. Miriam Wilke, Reed and Wilke's PR specialist, was also present.

"Those who are ready, they control the messaging," Miriam stated, "and those who aren't ready are the victims of messaging. If fortune favors the bold, then history is unkind to the meek. Today, Kendrick, you'll be insisting for them to arrest you, if in doing so you will help determine the cause and circumstances of Jennifer's untimely death. Make everybody know you're still grieving for Jennifer, your fiancée—the woman you loved. Remember, you are the protagonist in this story, as well as a victim."

"Just be careful about what you say, Kendrick," Natsumi added, "because the press is just waiting to pounce on anything that might seem salacious. Stick to your prepared statement, and we'll take it moment to moment from there. It's a symbolic arrest at best."

"Tell that to the Vice Chancellor," he countered. "She told me there's significant pressure out there from groups who want to have me removed, and some of them are donors. This arrest couldn't come at any worse a time, especially for Alberta. There's no way I'll let her fall under the control of David Jacobs!"

"I've watched Dr. Jacobs in interviews," Miriam nodded, confused. "He seems on the level. Wasn't he the one who discovered Alberta? He seems to really care about her."

"No, no! That's all an act. He's an asshole who wants to make money on her. Alberta knows that. She hates him. If he comes anywhere near her, she'll kill him!"

"Kill him? Are you serious?" Natsumi asked. "Roland Hughes told me she wasn't dangerous in any way. Are you saying she is, that Alberta is capable of killing a person?"

"I don't know," he answered, "but this is a different circumstance. Over the last three years, David Jacobs has been baiting her, intentionally provoking her, trying to scare or frustrate her to the point that she'll have an episode and lose her temper. He wants the world to see her is a potentially dangerous animal who should be in a cage or a lab."

"He certainly manages to frustrate you, Kendrick" Miriam observed. "Be sure to avoid all questions related to him in public. Just resort to 'no comment.' You understand?"

"I hate that man!" he answered while nodding.

"Hate is a provocative word," Miriam scolded. "You'll want to stay away from extreme words."

"I don't understand," Natsumi interrupted. "Why do you have such strong feelings about the man? What has he done to you, and what has he done to Alberta?"

"It's nothing he's done," Kendrick answered. "It's what he wants to do. He wants to exploit her. He wants to play with her brain, and he wants to clone her, or breed her."

"And you're obviously against that?" Miriam asked. "Against breeding her? Why not breed her?"

"Because she's a person, and you don't breed persons," he answered, pausing. "Would either of you want to be bred?"

The seconds of silence that followed interpreted the non-answer.

"Depends on who's breeding me," Miriam answered. "It seems you're taking the matter a little personal. Look, I understand she's a person, but many persons make small sacrifices in the interest of science. Wouldn't that be social responsibility?"

"Those people make voluntary sacrifices," he sneered. "They choose to become test subjects, and the experiments are explained. If Jacobs ruins Alberta's chance at gaining legal status, she remains an animal, a glorified pet, and she forfeits protective rights."

"I understand," Miriam countered, "but have you asked Alberta about it? How old is she now? Sixteen? Maybe she wants to breed, to get laid. It would be perfectly natural. Do chimps have sexual desires like humans? I understand they're quite promiscuous."

"You understand wrong, Ms. Wilke," Kendrick replied. "Like most other animals, sexual intercourse in chimps is purely for reproduction and the advancement of the species. There's no desire. With all the work she's doing, she doesn't need the distraction."

"You sound like a protective father," Natsumi joked.

"Or a protective boyfriend," Miriam added.

"There is nothing wrong with me wanting what's best for her," he responded. "I don't think either of you understand how truly amazing she is. Researchers say she's taken the Schrödinger's cat thought experiment to a new level."

"For whatever that means," Natsumi said, shrugging. "I can only imagine Jennifer felt a little threatened—not just because Alberta could literally tear off her arms, but because you dote on that chimp. You really do."

"If you take any questions today," Mariam advised, "don't answer any about Alberta. This is about you and Jennifer. It needs to be totally scripted. We don't want any new narratives springing up about what some people might consider as 'your unnatural relationship with a monkey.'"

****

Jacobs seemed nervous as he sat in the private doctor's office, twirling the vial between his fingers, gripping it in his palm to keep the contents warm. The lab, located on Russell Street three blocks away from Berkeley's only hospital, was unique because in addition to hundreds of human patients that came in on a weekly basis, the lab had established protocols to provide check-ups and preventive medical care for one nonhuman subject.

Dr. Lawrence Little began seeing Alberta at the clinic when she was three years old, performing an annual physical exam, which involved measuring weight and height, drawing blood for analysis, tapping points on her body to test motor control, checking her eyes, ears and mouth, and listening to her heart and lungs. She entered the clinic through a private access, unseen by patients in the waiting room, so that her presence would not spark alarm and bigotry. A sizable donation from Davis Franklin allowed the clinic to set aside an examination room just for Alberta, with separate equipment and instruments that would not be used on humans.

Dr. Little had never failed to be available to welcome Alberta to the clinic and perform the physical examination before, but an unexpected family emergency in Iowa meant that he would be gone for most of the week. Some of his appointments had been rescheduled, while others were covered by other doctors. As he watched Kendrick in custody on the television news, he concluded that the upcoming appointment would be postponed indefinitely.

Nonetheless, he received a phone call on that morning from Dr. Linden at the clinic, telling him that Roland Hughes had called in place of Kendrick, insisting he wanted to bring Alberta in for her annual physical examination. Dr. Little balked initially, because he was concerned that Alberta would be uncomfortable with a different doctor, but Dr. Linden persisted and convinced his mentor to relinquish, allowing the physical examination to proceed as scheduled.

Dr. Jeremy Linden was a University of California at Davis graduate, after having studied under legendary primatologist Dr. David Jacobs. While he was a medical doctor, a general practitioner, he had taken several undergrad classes in the anthropology department at Davis, where he fell under the tutelage of Jacobs. Jacobs had in fact written an effective and effusive recommendation letter to the University of Wisconsin-Madison Medical School, where Linden completed medical school.

For Jacobs, having a doctor on staff where Alberta got her physical exams was a plus, meaning that with a little convincing, he would have access to her medical records and other personal information. However, when he got news that Dr. Little, Alberta's regular doctor, would be out of town on the day of her physical examination, Jacobs realized there was a window for opportunity, however slight.

Obtaining the sample was a challenge, but Jacobs had a friend at the Houston Zoo, and so after locating the smartest male chimp in the country, the zoo primatologist restrained Erevu, a healthy male, and inserted a rectal probe. A slight electro-stimulation resulted in an adequate seminal sample. The electroejaculation was incubated at 37 degrees C for about 20 minutes for liquefaction and placed in the vial that was flown to San Francisco and later twirled between Jacobs' fingers.

Jacobs' proposal to Dr. Linden was bold and it required absolute loyalty from his former student, but Jacobs recognized a perfect storm of circumstances had suddenly materialized and acted quickly.

If Vesey had brought Alberta to the appointment, the scheme would have had no chance for success. If Roland had mentioned the appointment to Vesey, it would have been postponed and the plan was impossible. If Dr. Little had been performing the examination, the thought of tampering would have been unfeasible. If Jacobs didn't have "a man on the inside," he would have lacked a partner, a trusted collaborator. And finally, if Alberta had not been in estrus, or ovulating, any efforts to impregnate her were moot, though cloning would have remained a possibility. There were still major risks involved, but after fifteen years, Jacobs at last had a plan that could work!

"Roland Hughes and Alberta. We're here to see Dr. Little," Roland announced to the attendant at the back door.

"Right this way," the attendant answered. "Follow me to her examination room."

Roland assumed that the doctor who arrived was Lawrence Little, but Alberta seemed alarmed.

"She doesn't know you. She wants to see Dr. Little."

"Dr. Little is unavailable at the moment—family emergency out of town," Dr. Linden answered. "Dr. Little is like a father to me, Alberta. If you can trust him, you can trust me. Now, if you'll just have a seat on the table, we can begin."

Alberta glanced over at Roland, hesitant, until Roland nodded approval.

"She's a creature of habit," he said to the doctor. "She doesn't trust things that are unexpected."

Alberta remained suspicious, but she grew more comfortable as the examination progressed. Dr. Linden did and said all the things that Dr. Little did. He checked her eyes, ears and mouth. He listened to her heart in the front and her lungs in the back.

"Can you remove the smock, please?"

Roland translated Alberta's loud and animated objections.

"She's in estrus, Doctor, and she's always been a little self-conscious about it. She covers it up."

Beneath the smock, the pink sex skin in Alberta's genital area was swollen to a sizable protuberance, which for chimpanzee females indicated a readiness for mating. Estrus, or the tumescent phase, occurs every 35 days for chimpanzees and lasts between six to ten days. In Alberta's case, the genital area was swollen to the size of a large orange.

"How old are you, Alberta? Seventeen?" Dr. Linden asked. "You're an adult now, and that means your examinations going forward will include a check on your reproductive health. You don't have to be embarrassed. I do this all the time. We just want to make sure you remain healthy. Come on."

Reluctantly, Alberta removed the smock.

"Very good, Alberta. Now I need you to lie on your back and spread your legs. If you can, place your feet in the stirrups there. That's okay. You're doing fine."

Awkward about the procedure, Roland turned to face the back wall, listening closely as the doctor continued.

"Okay, what I'm doing now is inserting a device called a speculum so that I'll be able to gently scrape a small sample of cells for testing. It might make you feel a little uncomfortable, but it won't take long. And there—we're done. That wasn't so bad, was it?"

Alberta sat up, seeming embarrassed, humiliated, and she felt the distinct urge to urinate. Snatching the smock from the chair, she pulled it over her head.

"You're young and healthy, Alberta. I'm giving you a clean bill of health until next year. When the blood tests and other tests come back, Dr. Little will give you a call to explain them. Otherwise, you're free to go."

Ten minutes later, Dr. Linden sat with Jacobs in Linden's private office. "How'd it go?"

"Easy-Peasy," Linden laughed. "Under the pretense of a pelvic exam, I filled a syringe with the semen and attached it to a 30-centimeter polyethylene tube, and then I transferred a super sample of the semen to her cervix, which I made sure was raised in a prone position. Not the best of circumstances for results, but I gave her a sedative to make her sleep, and it was a concentrated semen sample. It should do the job."

"Very good, Dave," Jacobs smiled. "I could not be prouder of you!"

"What's going to happen when she's pregnant after never being mated? I'm sure Vesey and Franklin will be livid."

"They'll never discover the connection. Just think—it will be the first Immaculate Conception for a chimp, and when it's done, there's nothing anyone can do about it. I've waited fifteen years for this. The semen came from her half-brother. I've finally have a game-changer!"

Chapter 18

"Rot in Hell, bastard!" one woman in the crowd yelled. "I hope they throw away the key!"

"*¡Vas a morir, Pendejo! ¡Bestia negro!*" another jeered.

Kendrick bowed his head, thinking of Jennifer. What would she be thinking if she were standing next to him? Absent any other exculpating facts, would she believe he had something to do with present circumstances? Would she blame him for her death?

"*¿Quién le importa lo que piensen los demá?* she always said. "Who cares what anyone thinks?"

The more he thought about it, the angrier he felt. The autopsy and investigation concluded that Jennifer had been murdered. But who would have done that? Who would want her dead? She had no enemies, though Armando, in his tortured need to dominate her, didn't exactly act in her best interests. He even said, "I would sooner see you dead, *cariño*, than to marry that loser—Kendrick Vesey!"

If someone killed Jennifer, it would have been a murder based on motive. In Armando's case, the motive would have been retribution for disobedience. Armando found his Columbian father dead of a gunshot wound to the head when was only twelve. Jennifer, three years old at time, did not remember her papa at all. Stunned by the tragedy, Armando stopped attending school at the mission when he was fourteen to support his Mexican mother and siblings.

Armando's sacrifice sent the younger children to school, put clothes on their backs and helped move the family across the border from Mexicali to Calexico and later over to the Imperial Valley in southeastern California. The family labored on farms as migrant workers around El Centro, harvesting lettuce, tomatoes, artichokes and various other crops in season. The younger children learned the beekeeping trade, so even as the Alvarezes traveled from farm to farm, from apiary to apiary, they were able to trade their time and skills for pure, organic golden honey to sell.

While all the younger children went to school in California, Jennifer was the academic stand-out. She learned to read at four years old, and because she was fluent at English at such an early age, she could bounce back and forth between the two languages at will, speaking English without an accent. She was also conversant in Punjabi and Vietnamese, languages she learned from the migrant labor families of several of her young classmates.

Jennifer and her two older siblings had no idea that they were poor, disadvantaged and impoverished. Their childhood was rich in tradition, happiness, music, close relationships and memories. Jennifer was already in seventh grade when she discovered that some Californians resented Mexicans for living and working in the state. Racism was an unfathomable concept as she thought dark pigment in skin was rich and beautiful. When she saw a black person up close for the first time at fifteen years old, she was stunned by the young woman's grace and splendor.

While Jennifer received a full scholarship to UCLA during her senior year in high school, Armando continued to labor to support the family. Armando saw Jennifer's expected success in college and the corporate world she entered as the culmination of his own achievement, hoping she would recognize how much he had sacrificed. Her success honored his efforts, so he resented the independence she showed early on—something uniquely American in girls.

When he told Jennifer that he had chosen a good husband for her, she only laughed, and when she told him that she was in a serious relationship with a man, a doctor, who was African American, he lost his temper, resorting to bigotry and name-calling. When he realized that she did not share his Mexican nationalism, he tried to reason with her, reminding her of family tradition and the awkwardness of being affianced to a black person who did not speak Spanish and did not understand Mexican culture.

While he scolded his younger sister for her stubbornness, she felt proud, thinking herself tenacious and independent. Their relationship had been fractious over the last three months—since the wedding announcement—so for Kendrick, Jennifer's obsessive, controlling brother Armando could not be ruled out as a suspect.

Kendrick stopped and turned to face reporters in front of the door.
"A few words, if you please…"
The crowd fell silent, awaiting his expected statement.
"I loved Jennifer Alvarez. She meant everything to me. We had something special that very few of you would ever understand, but I am sure some do. I'm here today because the police are saying Jennifer was murdered. They say there's proof. Now I don't care what people think of me, but if my fiancée was murdered, then her murder has hurt me more than everyone else. How dare anyone accuse me! I'm volunteering for arrest because I want justice for Jennifer, and I will do whatever it takes to see that whoever took her away from me pays the price—blood for blood, life for a life—damn the consequences!"

****

Davis Franklin was seated at the desk in his large Sausalito business office, eyes narrowed and lips tightened, as he and a guest sat watching Kendrick Vesey's live public statement prior to his arrest. Both men were fixated on the flat screen television in the center of an adjacent wall. After the defendant's brief remarks, the mainstream news station immediately segued to a story about Kendrick's immigrant roots, tying it to a story about Jennifer's legal status. While Kendrick had become a U.S. citizen during high school fifteen years earlier, sponsored by an American uncle, Jennifer was still technically an undocumented alien, who would become legal after her marriage to Kendrick.

The next story involved a background on Jennifer and the lead-up to her murder, including the elevator incident in Stockholm and assertions by Armando, other family and neighbors about the obvious "inappropriateness" of the relationship, the inherent risks involved in crossing cultural lines and the unsurprising conclusion to the matter. Despite being a doctor and a professor at Berkeley, Vesey was "an animal who did not deserve Jennifer."

"While I probably wouldn't express my disappointment in those exact terms," Justin Luck shrugged, "I can understand where that Mexican family is coming from. I mean, why didn't Vesey just go out and find some Jamaican girl or some American black to marry him? This Jennifer girl and her success were all that poor Latin family had, and he stole that from them. I don't blame the family for how they feel."

"Except the facts will prove that Kendrick Vesey had nothing to do with Jennifer's murder," Davis countered. "I know Kendrick, and I knew Jennifer, and while far from being the perfect couple, they loved each other deeply. Kendrick would have never murdered her."

"And how many times have we both been surprised after trusting the wrong people?" Luck answered. "Come on, Davis, you know things are seldom what they seem. Besides, race relations are terrible in this country. They're at an all-time low right now. It's the same old story—the Mexicans don't trust the blacks, the blacks hate Hispanics and Asians because they're successful, and they all hate white people. Before it's all over, I think were gonna see black against black, brown against brown, white against white, everybody against everybody else—and won't that be somethin glorious to see!"

"Thousands of people are going to die for hate," Davis responded, barely looking over. "How is that America?"

"What were those two thinkin—different races, tryin to marry each other? A Jamaican and a Mexican? The *immigrants* are ruinin the country!"

Luck paused, smirked and smiled at Davis.

"But I've heard rumors from unnamed sources you're sympathetic to some of them. Wasn't that Vesey doctor working for you?"

Davis Franklin and Justin Luck had met twenty years earlier when billionaire Franklin moved his software empire, Tomorrow Systems, from San Jose to San Francisco. Barely thirty years old at the time, Davis knew little about real estate, let alone about negotiating a ten-year, multi-million-dollar, 200,000 plus square-foot lease for a building at the heart of the Golden Gate city.

It just so happened that 50-year-old Luck was involved in several commercial redevelopment deals in San Francisco at the time, so when the two met at a San Francisco Downtown Chamber of Commerce mixer on one Christmas Eve afternoon, Franklin found his new headquarters, Luck secured a lease for a quarter of his San Francisco office space inventory and a friendship began. Over the years, the billionaires ran into each other at political fundraisers, soirées and galas, sporting events, formal dinners and conferences, and while they were not close friends, they considered themselves "friendly."

Luck always joked that "we billionaires live in a small, small world—tiny actually! Because our investments are all over the place, we always end up talking to the same people, listening to the same pitches, staying at the same resorts, eating in the same restaurants—and in hot water with the same government agencies, mostly the IRS."

"It's bordering incestuous," he laughed. "We have to support our friends, we really do, because we all end up in bed with each other at some time or another. I like to make sure I'm always on top—I don't know."

At lunch in the building's swanky mezzanine level restaurant, Franklin and Luck discussed their respective families, the golf game, death and taxes, and at last Luck came to the purpose of the visit.

"You've probably heard that I'm being considered for a political appointment."

"Justin, you of all people!" Davis laughed. "Aren't you the one who's always said that 'politician' was just another word for 'a well-dressed, educated whore, acceptable to society?' You swear you have no respect for them, and now you want to be one? What's gotten into you?"

"I want to work as an outsider, you know, someone who's different, someone who can change things up, shake things up a little."

"What do you want to shake up? A martini?" Davis asked. "What exactly is your agenda?"

"Patriotism, you know," Luck answered, "I mean, what ever happened to the good old days? Don't you miss em? When Americans loved America and other countries respected us? The way things are now, it's impossible for anyone to even know what a real American looks like. Something's happened to us, to who we are, and it ain't good. You know it."

"That's no agenda," Davis said, wagging his head, "and I can be honest because I've known you so long. You're better off sticking to what you know—building things."

"That's just it, Davis," Luck responded. "Now, I want to help build a better America, and I want to do that as an outsider, and that's why I'm putting it out there to my special friends. I need money pledges, and I'm not talking about individual donations. I'm asking you—if I accept a political office, can I count on you, my old friend, to make a donation worthy of the level of success you've achieved in America? I'm talkin a Super PAC."

Luck watched his friend's face as a carefree smile became a stoic mask.

"I actually have a person, an ex-staffer from the House Ways and Means Committee, who handles those types of requests for me," Franklin answered. "Politics are tricky, and we've been careful to make sure we don't get caught on the wrong side of a major issue, or of history. The other thing—we can't afford to be partisan, except in rare, industry-related circumstances. I honestly cannot make any type of pledge until my team has vetted you. I'm sorry, Justin."

"That's all right," Luck interrupted, angry, his face turning red. "You're already on the wrong side of history, among other things. Politics makes strange bedfellows, Davis. I understand. So I may be forced to ask one of your competitors for help. I may have to."

"If that's what you feel you need to do," Davis nodded.

"Out of the blue," Luck interrupted, "you ever hear of a company called Cyanide Inc.?"

"No," Davis said after a pause, "No, I haven't."

"Of course you haven't," Luck sighed, unconvinced. "It's a small world, you know that. It's all right, I get it. True friends stab you in the *front*, right?"

Davis felt a tinge of regret after he returned to his office, but not because he had declined to support Luck. He rued being asked to take a political position, which he considered the equivalent of hubris—the idea that he knew better than anyone else, the notion that his ideas were superior. Luck, by all accounts, was a blowhard.

Davis considered himself a fiscal conservative, but he admitted a sense of progressiveness on social issues. He was aware of Justin Luck's political proclivities, which put the two men on the opposite sides of most struggles and movements—especially involving two issues that were most important to Davis—social justice and legal rights and protections for nonhuman persons.

Dr. David Jacobs was Davis' final scheduled appointment for the day, and he was on the record only after pleading for a fifteen-minute meeting "of major significance to Alberta and her future welfare." Davis was reluctant to meet, but he was curious about what the doctor would have to say, so he had set aside a few minutes at the end of the afternoon.

"Dr. Jacobs, good to see you again. Come on in. Sit down, please. Something to drink?"

"No thank you," Jacobs answered. "I just want you to know I really appreciate this opportunity. Thank you for being willing to hear me out in person."

"Make no assumptions about the fact that we're meeting today, doctor," Davis insisted. "You're here as a professional courtesy. You were the first, after all, to understand how uniquely special Alberta is, so I would like to believe that you have her best interests in mind."

"I do, I assure you," the doctor answered, "and you're right. I recognized her distinctive evolutionary advantages in her from the first day she was born. I'm sure you've heard me say it before, but her head was noticeably larger, so as a primate neuroscientist, I was naturally curious about performing a few cognitive tests. We analyzed an fMRI scan of her larger brain, comparing it to other chimp brains, and alternately with human brains."

Davis smiled, nodding. He had heard the description before, but he was still fascinated, still hungry for greater detail, some facet he may have missed in an earlier version.

"It turns out that her brain weighed more than twice that of other young chimps," the doctor continued, "while neuroimaging indicated the potential for near-human intelligence. When *Kipekee* was twenty-six months old, we encouraged her to perform a series of motor, memory, and intelligence tests, including pattern completion tests, or Raven's Matrices, that measured abstract reasoning—her fluid intelligence…"

The doctor's story always contained a degree of rancor beyond the mention of those tests.

"We were in effect able to create a map of her brain, purposed to determine how areas of her brain communicated with each other, and we found a strong connection between the frontal and parietal lobes. Both are involved in high-level mental function, which confirmed our other predictions about her intelligence…"

The doctor paused, clearly emotional about the subject.

"And just as we had begun publishing our findings to the greater intelligence research community, that damn Southwest Foundation board sold her out from under us!"

"Yes, I know," Davis stated, unemotionally, "because I bought her. And since that time, I have used my resources to assure she's had the care, nurturing and opportunity for growth and living up to her full potential. We've had our differences about the matter in the past, doctor, but she has had a much better life outside, experiencing freedom and free will as Alberta, opposed to living caged in a lab as *Kipekee*."

"Yes, we've had our differences," the doctor answered, assuming an air of humility. "And perhaps you were right. Your resources, individual concern and money influence have made a difference, but if you really care about her, then you have to start facing reality."

"Reality about what?"

"Well, there's never been another subject like her before—not that we've ever known of. Who knows what she'll go through as she transitions from the young chimp novelty to a mature, thinking and rationalizing adult with the intelligence to understand humans and human society, with all its double-standards, lies and contradictions? You've already opened Pandora's Box. Vesey gave her access to the Internet. It's only a matter of time. The clock's ticking."

"The clock's ticking?" Davis asked, "To what end?"

"It's only a matter of time before the profound cognitive dissonance she is no doubt now experiencing will cause a major mental breakdown... or worse. She was better off in a lab. She will never be a human, Mr. Franklin. It was a mistake to try to make her a person, but that is not why I'm here."

"So why are you here, doctor?"

"I am here to offer my services. I'm here to help you. The fact that Dr. Vesey is otherwise occupied, accused of murder, must be devastating to Alberta. Who of us could imagine or understand what she's going through? And Roland Hughes—his credentials say 'primate neuroscience research,' but he's nothing more than a babysitter who sees himself as her friend."

"Dr. Vesey would never agree to any involvement on your part."

"Dr. Vesey was just arrested on murder charges. Who knows how long he'll be gone? All that matters to any of us right now is Alberta's welfare."

"Alberta hates you, specifically," Davis sighed, wagging his head. "I'm sure you mean well, and she has never been violent, but I'm afraid she would injure you on sight."

"Because of the misinformation and outright lies Vesey's been feeding her for years. She has to know that I mean her no harm," Jacobs insisted. "I'm not trying to put her in a lab, I swear. Vesey hates me, and he's put it in her mind that I'm somehow the enemy!"

Jacobs stopped and took a breath to calm himself.

"And that's where you could help Alberta, Mr. Franklin. You can talk to her. You can explain things to her. She trusts you. Please tell her that I am not the bad guy Vesey says I am, that all I've ever wanted is to help her from the day she was born. Only you can change her mind about me."

Davis thought for a moment before answering.

"To be honest, I'm not certain that I trust you, Dr. Jacobs, but I do realize Alberta is at a crucial or critical point, with very few doctors available who could begin to understand the complexities of being the world's first legal nonhuman person and fighting the fight. I'm not even sure you do. So I'm not saying I will talk to her on your behalf, but if I did, what could you promise me?"

"I can promise to adhere to any and all protocols that you set up for me. I recognize and respect you as her conservator and protector. I can promise I'll put her welfare above all else, to sacrifice my own scientific curiosity to ensure her personhood. Vesey's lost touch with Alberta. I am deeply worried about her, Mr. Franklin. I believe that without my help she's going to snap eventually. She's going to do something horrible, wicked, something very ugly. I'm the only one who can save her from the vortex of intellectual conflict and cognitive dissonance that will definitely destroy her and your hopes for nonhuman person protective rights. All I need is your help so I can save her."

****

"As acting chair for tonight, I apologize for cancelling last week's meeting, but with the funeral and members' schedules, I wasn't sure if we would even have a quorum to enact proposals," Padmi said. "This week it seems everyone's here, including Natsumi, and Demetrius, who was away in Chicago."

"If I might interrupt," Calvin King cut in while raising his hand, "to propose a moment of silence in the memory of Queen Shabaz. On the last time we met, she was our chairperson."

The motion quickly seconded and approved, the group fell silent with heads bowed for over a minute.

"As I understand," Lyndsey commented after the pause, "the police in Austin have opened an investigation surrounding her death, which they are calling a murder. She was clearly assassinated."

"But why?" Phi asked. "Do they think someone specifically targeted her, or were they aiming at our movement in general? Outside this room, who would have even known she had taken over as chair?"

"No one would have known," Natsumi answered. "When she became chair, we specifically decided that we would no longer disclose our leadership structure to the public. It's odd."

"Well, I don't know," Mia began. "Maybe they were aiming at the person who was the biggest target. I don't say nothin bad about the dead, but Queen was a big woman, ya know. She probably stood out from everybody."

"Had to be 300 at least, maybe three and a quarter," Demetrius seconded.

"For whatever reason, it is devastating to all of us, "Padmi concluded. "You met with Draco and his cop friends last week, Demetrius. What are they saying about it?"

"The same thing you're all sayin," he answered. "It was definitely a hit on us, maybe to make a statement or scare us or start up this race war they been preachin about. First, they said the shooter was white, and then they said he was black. If you want my opinion, I think those cops might be the ones tryin to start up this race war."

"Did you have any problem with Draco or any of his friends when you were there?" Natsumi asked.

"Other than the fact they believe in white supremacy and I don't, no. I ain't had no problem," he answered, "other than that black cop is worse than them white cops on that issue—he's an Uncle Tom with something to prove to the massa. Other than that—no, I ain't had no problem."

"As I understand," Natsumi replied, "they would rather you didn't come back to their meetings. They want us to send someone else. I recommend Padmi."

"Oh, I get it, Natsumi," Demetrius responded. "I can tell you been talkin to white boy Sergeant Draco behind our backs again, and now that you got better things to do with your law firm and your big case, you just stopped caring about the reason Our Lives Matter came together in the first place. Since when did we let cops tell us what to do?"

"I call foul," Lyndsey interjected. "That is so over the top, Demetrius. Everyone here knows meeting with them was not about cops telling us what to do. We have to work with cops, white and black. That's a given. Your problem is you don't play well with others."

"With all due respect, Lyndsey, you weren't there," he argued. "You weren't there to see how they all talked down to me, especially that rude black bastard, D'Artagnan."

"I believe we're getting ahead of ourselves," Padmi called out, retaking control of the meeting. "Let's return to order. Queen was our chair, and now she's gone. I was her co-chair, which presently makes me our temporary chair. To preserve order, we need to re-establish our chair and co-chair positions."

"Agreed," Natsumi nodded after being recognized. "So in the spirit of preserving order, I nominate Demetrius Berry to be our next chairperson. He rightly stated at an earlier meeting that he has the experience and seniority, and it's true that women have dominated in that position. Demetrius deserves equal opportunity."

Padmi's face registered a sense of betrayal—other faces in the room followed. Certain that she would automatically become the next chair, Padmi believed she had opened discussion for the consideration of a new co-chair. Even if her best friend was going to nominate a person ahead of her, why would it be Demetrius Berry, a man poorly-disposed for leadership and lacking good judgment?

"I, I don't believe that nomination is in order."

"Sure it is," Natsumi insisted, winking at her friend. "Draco and his friends specifically requested you to take Demetrius' place at their meetings. It's an important assignment."

"Okay," Padmi sighed, hesitant. "Are there any other nominations for chairperson for this committee?" and after a silence, "Is there a second?"

"I second the nomination," Calvin King nodded. "It's about time a man got into leadership."

"If there's no further discussion," Padmi affirmed, "we'll move for a vote."

"Wait!" Demetrius interrupted. "You guys can't just nominate me as the new chair. No one's even asked me if I wanted to do it."

"We all remember how hard you lobbied for the position a few weeks ago, Demetrius," Heather answered. "You accused us of being sexist. Why would we need to ask you now?"

"Because I don't want to be the chair now. You had your chance, but no—I decline. It's too late."

"Why are you declining now, Demetrius," Natsumi asked. "What's changed in three weeks' time?"

"I'm still handling security," he answered, "and there's no one who could do it if I wasn't there."

"Security is not rocket science, Demetrius," Mia scorned, piling on. "There's no reason Padmi couldn't handle it the way you have for the last two months. It's just a switch. She can do security, and you can become chairman like you wanted a few weeks ago—when you were still handling security."

"Get it through your heads!" he snarled. "I don't want to be the chairman now. I nominate Mia Melendez."

"Padmi, members of the executive committee," Natsumi announced, "I think a different motion is in order, one that supersedes our current discussion—a membership motion."

"And what is your motion?" Padmi asked.

"I believe someone on this committee has another agenda, which is to ruin us. I believe that person leaked that Queen was the new chair, and that's why she was targeted and murdered. I believe that same person does not want to be the chair because he knows the new chair will be the next target. My motion is a membership motion that relates to the security of our movement, and so I move that Demetrius Berry should be removed from this committee and expelled from the Our Lives Matter movement, and without discussion, I move for an immediate vote by roll call."

The vote was unanimous to remove Demetrius from the committee. Demetrius scanned the faces in the room, angry, contemptuous.

"That's all right," he said. "Ya'll goin in a different direction than when we started this. Ya'll sellin out. You can blame me if you want, but you still don't have a chair, and if you believe Natsumi, who of you would wanna be chair?"

"I'll be the next chair," Natsumi snapped. "I might have to work some things out with my firm, but I'll take the job, and if that means I become the next target, so be it. Dr. King said every step toward the goal of justice requires sacrifice, suffering, and struggle, the passionate concern of dedicated individuals."

Demetrius sighed as she looked up from her notes.

"You serious, bitch?"

"Goodbye Demetrius. You can leave us now."

Heather Kaplan was stationed by the door as Demetrius made his slow exit. Pivoting as he passed, she surprised him by slapping him across the face.

"That one was for Queen. She's dead, and you're to blame, Demetrius! Now get out!"

Eyes popping with rage, he immediately drew back his arm to retaliate, fist clenched.

"Demetrius, no!" Calvin shouted across the room in his loudest "Pastor" voice. "No! That's a woman. Don't you dare. If it's true what Natsumi told us, then you had that comin. Now you go on outta here. If you wanna talk about things when hot heads cool down, you give me a call."

Demetrius dropped his arm, eyes narrowed in anger as he realized he failed to intimidate the outspoken, defiant white woman.

"I'm sorry about Queen," he called to the group. "If I said something that made someone target her, it wasn't intentional. Ya gatta believe me…" Sensing only anger from the committee members, he sighed, calling out a comment before he exited. "It shoulda been Heather."

Chapter 19

"What were you thinkin?" Colin demanded. "It was all I could have ever wanted, all we could have ever wanted! You could have been right there, my brotha, calling the shots, making the statements! In on both sides!"

"They didn't even mean it," Demetrius sighed. "It was a test. They woulda never made me chair. The minute she put my name up, I knew they were gonna try'n get rid of me."

They were meeting in the Compton, California recording studio of rap producer, 'Cyanide.' The space was a converted three-story office building on Long Beach Boulevard, equipped with eight recording rooms, a sound stage, a video production facility and the spacious executive office where the two men sat.

"At this point, I just don't care. Our Lives Matter can kiss my black ass!" Demetrius fumed. "They was all wrong anyway. What they call 'unity' was just another form of submittin to 'white supremacy.' Things won't ever be right in this country as long as white folks remain in positions of power. It's all about the revolution, ma brotha—shockin the nation, killin white people. So what now?"

"Well, first things first," Colin answered. "Who will be the next chair?"

"Natsumi Mitchell. She knows she'll be the next target, but she wants to do it anyway. Let me shoot her ass!"

"Wait!" Colin interrupted. "Natsumi Mitchell—I thought she was tied up on that Kendrick Vesey case? What are you saying?"

"I'm sayin after they voted me out, Natsumi wouldn't let anyone else be chair. She said she had to do it. She says that case is an easy case to win—it'll be over after the first hearing. No one'll know she's chair anyway—they're keepin it a secret."

"That changes everything," Colin sighed. "How many people know she did that? Just the people at the committee meeting?"

"They won't be makin a public announcement. Why?"

"Natsumi Mitchell shouldn't be a target. It'll send the wrong message. You have to tell your contact it's someone else."

"Why? You told me that if I became chair, you couldn't guarantee my safety. Now you're tryin to protect that bitch? If I didn't know any better, I'd say you're bein soft on her. You told me you didn't have a heart—that you ate it, but now you wanna protect that bitch?"

"That's not it," Colin sighed as he opened the top desk drawer.

"Then what is it, 'Cyanide? Cold-Blooded Killa, architect of the revolution—the man who sends the ghosts.' You said yesterday the new leader was gonna die no matter who it was, and now you wanna change the rules?"

Cyanide did not answer the question. Instead, he took out an oversized balisong knife. Twirling it without looking, he performed a Zen rollover and a cherry picker before he returned to casually flipping the butterfly blade. Stopping with a jerk, he slammed the knife point into a pitted cedar block on the desk surface

"I'm not changing the rules. I just don't want Natsumi Mitchell dead. She could be useful."

"I've known Natsumi for two years," Demetrius said, ignoring the threat of the knife. "If you're thinkin you might have a chance with her, just forget it. She's a stuck-up bitch. I'm gonna tell em Natsumi's the new leader."

"No, you won't," Colin said, taking up the knife and twirling it again. "When I talked to her, she was a spitfire, but underneath that feminist activist shield, there was passion and conviction, which is rare."

"I hope you don't think she'd ever be interested in you," Demetrius scoffed. "She's an educated, high-powered lawyer with connections, which means she probably likes white boys—maybe that cop, Draco. What makes you think she would ever fall for a hardcore, uneducated rap producer with a criminal record? You might be big time in the rap underground, but you're outta your league there, my brotha."

"Maybe I am, but I'm not gonna expose her to danger just yet. I think, with proper motivation, she could further our cause."

"Trust me, Cyanide. I know her. She'd never even take you seriously. She'd see you as a project, some disadvantaged demographic. She might even try'n help you, but you'll always be a 'dumb nigga' in her mind. She ain't far off from white privilege herself, bein she's only half-black in the first place, ya know."

"I don't have time to worry about that," Colin responded, closing the knife. "I need to think about what I'm gonna do with you. We had you embedded in two key places, and in one week you blew em both. You've lost all your utility to us."

"That ain't true. I still have knowledge. I know who those cops in that secret brotherhood are, the Loverboy Elite—and what they're tryin ta do, and I've still got someone inside Our Lives Matter who trusts me. Padmi Ravi is gonna take my place with those cops, but she'll be reportin back to the committee, and that someone on the committee will report back to me. Nothin's changed in terms of the information I can provide."

"Except you ain't as smart as you think you are, Demetrius. Apparently, for all your self-assessed smarts, Natsumi and the others figured you out, and those cops probably figured you out too. Who's to say your so-called friend on the committee won't be feeding you false information just to throw us off?"

"I trust him," Demetrius insisted.

"I trusted you. Plus I paid ya, nigga, and what did that get me?" Colin shouted, slamming his fist on the desk. "What did that get me?"

"I'm sorry."

"You're sorry? I thought you was Demetrius," he sighed. "Funny how when folks screw up, they always tryin ta change they name ta 'sorry.' Give me the name you're gonna tell em."

"A name?" Demetrius asked, seeming confused.

"A name of the new chair, and don't tell me it's Natsumi Mitchell. You have to give your contact somethin, someone. So give me the name of the new chair you're gonna leak to your upline. Who is the new leader of Our Lives Matter?"

It didn't take long for Demetrius to understand what Colin was intimating.

"Right, right. Okay, I got a name for em. The new leader of Our Lives Matter is a white bitch named Heather—Heather Kaplan."

****

The hearing was set for 2 p.m. at the San Francisco Superior Court's Hall of Justice at 850 Bryant Street, between 6th and 7th Streets. Natsumi had taken the occasion to first visit with Kendrick Vesey, who was housed in the jail on premises.

"I've never been locked up before," Kendrick complained, dressed in orange custody-only inmate clothing. "How long before I'm out of here?"

"I'm here today for a special hearing," she answered. "After reading police and medical reports from the investigation and consulting with my co-counsel, it seems your best witness is Alberta. Ordinarily, it would be unthinkable to have anyone but a human or direct evidence for witness testimony in the preliminary hearing, but Alberta is unique to the courts, a quasi-legal nonhuman person, and I have on-hand respected, prominent scientists and psychologists who are willing to go on record asserting that her testimony will be credible."

"What?" he asked, "you mean that's all we've got, with all Davis Franklin's money? Putting Alberta on the stand? She's all we got, if they'll even admit the testimony of a chimpanzee? I smell a fix. What about the fact that they found traces of cyanide at Jennifer's job, at her brother's house, in her apartment and at her ladies gym? Someone was trying to poison both of us! How is this happening to me?"

"Calm down, Kendrick. In their investigation, inspectors Nick Jantzen and Tramaine Lee seemed to ignore any exculpatory evidence, any character evidence and the reality that you loved your fiancée. Their minds were already made up. It's the system and how it works. They were focused on the DMSO solvent found at your house, which contained an element of a toxic substance that could be cyanide—and the fact there were so many trace samples of the poison found in your apartment and in the Oakland house."

"And you think the Court would be willing to have Alberta take the witness stand?"

"It would be remarkable, a first ever, but it's something I could argue for, with the backing of experts in the scientific and academic communities. She's a cognitively complex animal, capable of high-level, full duplex communication in the English language, in ASL. All we would need is an interpreter for the 'hearing audience,' meaning the judge and jury, if we go to trial."

"And how could she help me?" he asked.

"Well, she was there," Natsumi answered. "She knew both you and Jennifer, and she was present at the time when the alleged poisoning was going on. She could attest to the nature of the relationship, on your behavior and Jennifer's, on any other possible explanation for the poisoning, or about other people and motives. You've got nothing else. If the judge allows it, her testimony couldn't hurt."

"Except that this whole thing will become a spectacle. They're accusing me of murder, Ms. Mitchell. Putting Alberta on the stand would only make the hearing all about her—the world's smartest monkey. I know how people react to her, and most feel threatened. My innocence would become secondary—and that doesn't even begin to consider the harm that would come to her by exposing her to the worst in human exploitation."

"Let me put it this way, Kendrick," Natsumi insisted. "Do you have anyone *else* who could attest to the nature of your relationship with Jennifer? Is there someone else you know who could help exonerate you or corroborate your version of events that led up to her death? Do you any other witnesses? That's what you need to be thinking about now."

Kendrick shut his eyes, his face strained in frustration.

"No. If I had known Jennifer was going to die right then and there and it was going to be poison, I would have made sure I had someone around to help me prove my innocence, but it doesn't work like that. If someone poisoned her, I'm sure I was set up and they knew I'd be on my own."

"If someone set you up, then they didn't realize you actually did have someone around who could help exonerate you. Within the next thirty minutes, I plan to go before a conservative California superior court judge to make a case for Alberta taking the stand. If you're against it, please let me know now and save me the trouble."

"Really? Do you think it could work—her testifying?" he asked. "I mean, without the circus?"

"I can't make any promises about a circus environment, but my job is to kill this in the preliminary hearing so it never goes to trial. In my humble legal opinion, I think Alberta's our best bet. She's our best witness…"

Hesitant, Kendrick nodded, but Natsumi had a coda.

"As long as she doesn't do something crazy… like throwing her poo at the judge."

****

Irving Carroll, the deputy district attorney objected to the Alberta-as-a-witness argument immediately, though he could not help ending with a zinger.

"So, instead of a kangaroo court, Counsel is asking to set this matter in a chimpanzee court?"

California Superior Court Judge Tamara Weir, however, did not laugh or even break a smile. She was stern and serious as she listened to alternating arguments, suppositions, answers and rebuttals. It was a criminal trial worthy of careful deliberation, and the motion was one that carried potential landmark implications, especially in the area of nonhuman rights, which was an emerging area of law.

"This is not a difficult proposition, given the expert witness affidavits and testimony that you already stipulated to, Counselor. Again, what is the basic objection you are making?"

"Well, your Honor, I would begin with the issue of prejudice, and also the availability of this witness to the prosecution. This famous chimpanzee has been in the defendant's charge for almost fourteen years. Naturally, she would feel a degree of loyalty to him, especially if she is as intelligent as they say she is and she understands the complexities of the complaint against him. Besides that, we don't believe we could effectively interview or cross-examine this witness."

"What does that have to do with her answering basic questions in direct testimony and cross examination?" the judge asked.

"That would depend on the scope of questions asked," he answered, "and the prosecution would be at a loss about how to treat this witness. In our briefs, we included Tennessee v. Reyes and Michigan v. Johnson, where there is a precedent for the presence of animals 'in the courtroom as emotional support for children,' and we twice cited the Harvey and Harvey study on scent evidence having to do with bloodhounds, but there is no precedent for an animal or nonhuman person being used as a material direct witness in a criminal trial. The prosecution objects to the very notion of it."

"Ms. Mitchell?" the judge asked, looking over to the defense table.

"There's no precedent, because Alberta will be the first nonhuman person recognized in the U.S. Court system. Of course her presence would have nothing to do with the emotional support of the defendant. But there's no doubt Alberta is a remarkable person who's at least as intelligent as the average human who testifies before our courts on a daily basis. We've presented supporting scientific evidence, and the global scientific community backs that assertion: she's an intelligent person, capable of full-duplex communication and should be able to direct testimony in a court proceeding.

"I also submitted an opinion by noted primate neuroscience researcher Roland Hughes," she continued, "who asserts that Alberta does not understand the human concept and rationale for being untruthful—for lying in other words. Like any witness, she will answer direct questions truthfully, which is all the court could ask for under any circumstances, and better. We all watched the tapes of her minutes ago. I don't think facts involving her credibility and competence are in dispute, your Honor."

"But apes are powerful and dangerous animals," the prosecutor maintained. "Even if she is capable of 'full-duplex' communication, how would the court expect us to conduct an interview with Alberta without endangering the investigator conducting that interview? You have before you, your Honor, an opinion we presented by Dr. David Jacobs, the man who first discovered Alberta as an infant in a Texas facility. In that opinion, he warns the public that under Kendrick Vesey's lax care, Alberta was becoming increasingly unstable, and I quote, 'she could go into a Bezerker rage at any given time without notice.' So given the physical strength advantage that chimps have over humans and potential for mayhem, how would you reasonably expect us to send one of our investigators into such a precarious situation?"

"I interviewed Alberta," Natsumi answered, "without fear or incident under the direction of Dr. Roland Hughes. The prosecution could do the same, or they could simply conduct a Skype interview, which Alberta is accustomed to doing. Frankly, I don't understand the premise of the prosecution's objection. The crux of this matter is about the innocence of Dr. Kendrick Vesey, who is under indictment for the alleged murder of his fiancée. The issue is not Alberta, though she's a key witness for both sides. The overriding question in this hearing is, 'will her testimony be credible and true, and does it help the triers of fact arrive at a just conclusion?'

"We all understand that this is a landmark case, your Honor, involving the legal status and the testimony disposition of nonhuman persons, but let us not forget the victims in this case, Jennifer Alvarez, and her fiancé, Dr. Kendrick Vesey, who wants nothing more than justice for the murder of the woman he would have married last Saturday."

"I've read your briefs and listened to your arguments," Judge Weir announced in summary thirty minutes later while rendering her decision, "and I find in favor of the defense. The fact that direct witness testimony by a nonhuman person has never been admitted in the history of U.S. Courts notwithstanding—in this case, the testimony of the nonhuman person, Alberta, will be admitted as evidence in the preliminary hearing, which is set to begin the day after tomorrow."

****

"Are you telling me that Kendrick is going along with this?" Roland asked, perplexed. "Kendrick is okay with you bringing Dr. Jacobs in here, in this house?"

"At this point, I'm more concerned about Alberta's welfare," Davis answered. "Kendrick hasn't been around for three weeks, and while you've been helpful, you lack the enduring bond he had with her. With all due respect, Roland, you're no Kendrick Vesey, and for good reason. You were around in a limited capacity when she was younger, you've only been around consistently for the last six months. Dr. Jacobs, on the other hand, has a far-reaching history with Alberta, and he's a noted expert. He was the first authority figure in her life, which might be helpful under the present circumstances."

"And because of that, she hates him," Roland objected. "Do you know what would happen to him if he walked through that door today? It wouldn't be pretty, I assure you. She'd make him a choirboy—bite his nuts off! You're the boss, but trying to bring the doctor here is a horrible idea."

"What if I talked to her?" Davis asked. "What if I told her that to help Kendrick, she would have to be nice to Dr. Jacobs for a few weeks, but only until Kendrick comes back?"

"She wouldn't believe you. She sees Jacobs as the greatest threat to her legal status, and Jacobs has gone out of his way to exasperate and agitate her, threatening to make her a lab specimen."

"Jacobs insists that it was Kendrick who portrayed him in that way to her—that the opposite is true. He says he only wants to help her."

"If you believe that," Hughes answered, "then Alberta might be a better judge of human character than you are. Her hate has nothing to do with Kendrick. Jacobs is a wicked man. Kendrick knows it, Alberta knows it and I know it, but you're the boss. I'm listening."

"What if you were to talk to Alberta before I did, Roland?" Davis asked. "What if you were to tell her to give Dr. Jacobs a chance to help her and help Kendrick? What if you were to tell her she was wrong about Dr. Jacobs— that Dr. Jacobs is a good man?"

"That would be a lie," Roland answered. "From what I know of him, it would be untrue. Alberta has a problem understanding the concept of lying, Mr. Franklin. She has a cognitive dissonance dilemma that's become more profound since Kendrick was first accused, and forcing a contradiction of what she already knows is risky. I can't lie to her because she trusts me. Our relationship is built on trust and honesty."

"I'm not asking you to lie to her," Davis sighed, "but would you be willing to ask her to give Jacobs a second chance? You can tell her the truth—

that it's temporary, and I'll make sure you're always there to protect her. I'm asking this as a personal favor, because I'm worried about her."

"As am I," Roland nodded.

"You've already said she's having psychological problems with Kendrick's being gone," Davis continued. "It may be selfish on my part, but I have so much invested, not just in her, but in the future of nonhuman persons. I have other projects. If you do this for me, Roland, you will have a billionaire in your debt. Will you please at least talk to her for me?"

Later that evening as Roland and Alberta were seated on a couch and chair after dinner watching *Dateline*, Roland turned toward her and switched off the television.

"We've always been honest with each other, right?"

"Honest what for? Kendrick is dead?" she signed. "White police—them kill Kendrick in jail?"

"No, it's not that."

"Roland turn off *Dateline* when mi watching. Him say something important?"

"Yes, and I know it's something that might make you upset."

"Why white human hate black human?"

"White humans don't hate the black humans," Roland answered. "I'm a white human, and I like Kendrick, who is a black human."

"In logic," she signed, "some and most white human hate black human. Why? White human believe black human is not really human, is not person? Inferior? No protection under law? Illegal immigrant is not human? Mexican is not human?"

"I don't get it," Roland sighed. "Who is telling you this? Let me guess. You've been watching TV?"

"Mi watch news. Police is white human. Police kill black human. Police never get punish."

"It's complicated. Sometimes the news doesn't have the opportunity to tell the entire story."

"Natsumi Mitchell on news. Her say police kill black human, police not get punish. Her say police lie."

"That's not entirely true, Alberta. Many police are black humans, so the police don't hate black humans. The problem is that police must start listening to the black humans. They must learn to understand the black humans' concerns."

"Why Roland turn off TV?"

"I turned off the TV because I wanted to talk with you about Dr. Jacobs."

"Alberta hate Dr. Jacob!" She almost said that she wanted to kill Dr. Jacobs, but she stopped short, remembering Kendrick's earlier admonition. "Mi hurt Dr. Jacob."

"Does Alberta want to help Kendrick and help other nonhuman persons?"

"Yes," she signed. "Roland trick Alberta?"

"No, it's not a trick. I've always been honest with you, so I'll tell you outright. With Kendrick gone, Davis Franklin wants Dr. Jacobs to come in here and help us, help Alberta."

Roland expected a wild, angry, unintelligible outburst and Alberta did not disappoint. She went on for a minute before she finally stopped to catch her breath.

"Are you done?"

And then she went on for another minute. He sat, making a 'raspberry' sound with his lips as he sighed.

"Are you quite through, Alberta? We really must talk."

"Dr. Jacob come here? Stay here?" she signed, her expression anxious, incredulous. "Kendrick not come back?"

"No," Roland answered in a re-assuring voice. "Kendrick will be back. He's definitely coming back. Davis Franklin just wants the doctor to come in and help us out a little while Kendrick is gone. The work must continue, and it's been a month since you and Kendrick have worked together."

"Alberta work with Roland. Not work with Dr. Jacob."

"I'm not a doctor at biological anthropology like Kendrick or Dr. Jacobs. While I can only do so much with you, Mr. Franklin is insisting that the work he is paying for continues. He says that because Dr. Jacobs has known you all along, he's the most logical replacement for Kendrick, but only until Kendrick is free."

"Davis Franklin smoke ganja? Alberta not work with Dr. Jacob!" she signed before crossing her arms.

After a quiet phone call from Roland, Davis entered the room thirty minutes later. He was alone, since he did not require a translator.

"Congratulations, Alberta—I understand you're providing direct testimony in Kendrick's preliminary hearing. That's huge! It moves us one step closer to your legal status. Natsumi's done a great job."

He sat, reached across and stroked the back of her hand.

"You're your own person, Alberta, so I can't tell you what to do. If you don't want to work with Dr. Jacobs, that's your choice. But I'm asking you to trust me. Presently, I have a team of lawyers working on a national initiative relating to the legal status of nonhuman persons like you. The work Kendrick was doing was important in terms of the science we have to present—necessary work that came to a screeching halt one month ago."

"Mi not like Dr. Jacobs. Him bad man. Him Anansi!"

"I'm simply asking you to work with Dr. Jacobs, Alberta, for just a little while—as a favor to me. Please understand that I am aware of your concerns about him, and I can assure you you'll be safe. I'll make sure that Roland is also here at all times. I only want what's best for you, so I'm begging you to help me out here."

"Decision Alberta choice? Mi say 'yes or no?' Not Davis Franklin, not Roland, not Kendrick?"

"That's right. I will respect whatever you choose to do, but I hope you'll realize that the legal status of nonhumans persons is bigger than you or your problem with Dr. Jacobs. Think of all the lives that will be affected. We're changing the world."

Alberta contemplated Davis' request for a moment before signing her answer.

"Mi work with Dr. Jacob if mi read police report about Kendrick. Mi worry about Kendrick. Davis get police report for Alberta?"

Franklin seemed confused and uncomfortable.

"Well, I suppose I could arrange to get the police report to you, Alberta."

"Complaint too. On computer? Mi read on computer."

"Okay, if that's what it takes. But why do you want to see the police report?"

"Mi ask to know," she answered, baring her teeth, nodding in finality.

Chapter 20

Draco stood outside the perimeter of the protests in the Maricopa County city of Phoenix, Arizona, within its downtown section. He and his colleagues had been apprehensive all week. There was an undercurrent of mayhem pervading the region, from many of the schools and colleges along Highway 17 to the bars and taverns in the downtown area, extending all the way to Scottsdale. It was nothing tangible; it was just a spirit in the air, one of escalated tension and disquiet.

The Loverboy Elite were especially alert because an ancillary group that provided communications intelligence informed Draco about heightened chatter involving a clash, a martial confrontation between two of the most polarized voices in the escalating quarrel about race—the black and brown separatists versus the white separatists. While both sides shared similar hate philosophies, it seemed the leaders were spoiling for a mini-war to settle old scores.

It didn't help that two featured news stories for the week involved protests related to the killing of an unarmed black motorist in Indianapolis and the fatal shooting of two teens in a Chicago neighborhood that resulted from a panicked female officer who fired into a moving vehicle. Additionally, the news of the killings followed on the heels of a story from Charlotte, North Carolina, where a group of middle-aged, blue collar white workers beat three UNC students who were protesting for Our Lives Matter outside Hearst Tower in the downtown area.

"Copy that. If it's true, it worries me. This is no natural turn of events. Our man Justin Luck is behind it. Only problem is: at this point, there are so many potential flashpoints. There's just no way we're going to be able to be on top of all of them."

"Well, what about Our Lives Matter?" the voice on the phone replied. "You said their Padmi Ravi's organized a committee of watchers at various events who will report through text messages?"

"That's the general idea, D'Artagnan," Draco answered, "but this is all new real estate for us, and the ground here is constantly changing. They know we're here and we're trying to stop this first major skirmish, this war-trigger event. If it happens, we'll be fighting the battle from behind. The race war will be ahead of us and in full force, civil order be dammed."

"Lotta chatter comin in from friends, Draco, some of it pretty damn scary," D'Artagnan sighed, "but I get the feeling Luck knows we're out here and who we are, so while it's crazy, we have to seriously vet everything we hear and discover. We have one enemy. The rest of it's all collateral damage."

"This'll be the first skirmish in an all-out war," Draco added, "which moves it from wild conspiracy theory to headline news. The fuse is lit. At this point, we can't stop it. We can only focus on containing it."

"I have to realign our men and resources over the next hour," D'Artagnan commented, almost to himself. "What have you heard?"

"Well," Draco answered, "ground zero will be at 24th Street and Camelback Road—the stage of various previous protests. Looks like we're seein a subtle accumulation of opposing forces in that area—a lot of weapons, body armor, comm equipment. We've got the leaders of the United Aryan Coalition over there, and the Black/Brown Resistance—both anarchist groups who've been preaching and stoking this war for years."

D'Artagnan took one last look through the binoculars.

"I'll redirect and we'll migrate that way now. What should we be looking for?"

"I wouldn't know," Draco answered. "There's definitely a powder keg growing over there. It's looking like four or five separate hyped-up militias, locked, loaded and armed to the teeth. They've spent years getting ready for this. I guess we'll be looking for the fuse, the first shot—whatever it'll take to let slip the dogs of war."

****

"Where Dr. Jacob take Alberta? Mi no wanna go," Alberta signed, nervously scanning the blurred landscape through the glass pane at her left. "Where Roland?"

"Roland is at the university at a lecture. He'll be back at noon. We're just having a little field trip, that's all, you and me—an educational trip."

Comfortable at the steering wheel of his leased Lexus GS 350 F Sport Sedan, Jacobs took the John Daly exit off 280 South, continued onto Skyline Boulevard and drove north for ten minutes before turning right onto the Great Highway. Glancing out the window, Alberta saw a sandy beach and beyond that, the vast, majestic Pacific Ocean.

"Where we go?"

"It's a surprise. You'll see."

"Mi no like surprise."

"Come to think of it," the doctor laughed, "neither do I. But what about irony? Do you like irony, Alberta—if you even understand what the term means?"

"Irony mean Dr. Jacob discover Alberta when baby and Dr. Jacob think him be rich man. But Dr. Jacob be poor man—always be poor man with bad breath."

"You're very funny, Alberta," Jacobs sneered, "but you're wrong. One way or another, you're going to make me a rich man. I know it, and I deserve it."

Weaving through traffic, Jacobs moved into the far-right lane and made a turn, where immediately a large sign glared before both their eyes: *San*

Francisco Zoo. Alberta's first inclination was to panic, but Kendrick had taught her how to better manage her emotions. She thought of Kendrick just then as she turned and forced herself to smile at the doctor, all the while studying his body language and decorum.

"Field trip? Where is field? This is beach."

"Yes. I imagine you've never been to a zoo before. That being the case, I made special arrangements with the zoo board of directors to set up a private guided tour, just for you. I thought you might like to see how the other side lives, and maybe you could see some of your relatives."

Alberta was angry, but she pretended to be dismissive.

"Them more your relative, Jacob."

Inside the gates of the zoo, Dr. Jacobs, assisted by the facility's great ape veterinarian and nervous security guards, strapped and secured Alberta into a wheelchair, placing a sign around her neck that read, "Wild Animal – Extremely Strong and Dangerous – Do Not Approach within 30 Feet at Risk of Great Bodily Injury."

As the veterinarian wheeled Alberta toward the first exhibit, the African Region toward the left, the majority of nervous zoo goers gave the entourage a wide berth, though a few in the crowd recognized the chimp from television news show appearances and approached to ask occasional questions and take pictures… from a distance.

Alberta, Jacobs and the group first the viewed the ostriches and the savannah ungulates, which included the kudos, zebras and giraffes, and then they visited the African aviary, where they saw Marabou storks, crowned cranes, Waldrapp Ibises and Hamerkops. Then it was on to the Jones Family Gorilla Preserve.

While there was a wall of viewing windows that allowed the group to see the gorillas up-close as they rested, played, ate and interacted with each another, Alberta could hardly breathe as she read the graphics that attempted to tell the story of what someone had termed "these gentle giants." Alberta realized that she could not imagine what gorillas behaved like in the wild, but she sensed the sadness, misery and humiliation these apes felt in a life that was merely a display for humans. The gorillas were miserable. Her anger grew.

Wasting no time, Jacobs directed the guides to head for the Primate Discovery Center, where the chimpanzees were housed. Nothing Alberta had ever conceived could have prepared her for the experience. There she saw with her own eyes what she never could have imagined—a terrible thing that humans obviously sanitized in its transferal to the computer or television screen—the humiliating display of chimpanzees for purposes of human enjoyment and "discovery." She seethed all the more inside.

There, across the moat before her, was an ugly exhibit, with drying weeds, an unappealing structure made of wooden poles and platforms, a silly hammock, rudimentary toys, play ropes, a water bowl, a food bowl and shacks for sleeping quarters. She saw a few chimps lying about, inactive, despondent. They seemed mentally-ill, like frontal lobotomy patients in a poorly-run institution, but once the gray-bearded alpha male noticed her outside the enclosure, he began a loud sustained protest that people heard from 200 meters away, eventually drawing a small crowd.

"Push her closer," Jacobs insisted.

The nearer the zoo veterinarian pushed her, the more violent the alpha male's angry protests became, and he was joined by the other jealous chimps in the enclosure as the spirit of a murderous frenzy ensued. Alberta could tell the chimps hated her, that they would tear her limb from limb if given an opportunity. For the first time she could remember, she feared for her life, though she tried not to show it.

"Push her even closer."

Alberta cringed noticeably as the pupils of her wide eyes dilated, her back pressed hard against the back of the wheelchair. She wanted to kill Jacobs. Barring her teeth, she growled and vocalized all the aggression she was feeling toward the alpha male, startling him initially. Straining against the straps holding her, she seemed poised to viciously attack him, her eyes intense and sharp canines on display. Rolling her eyes back, she howled.

Confused, the startled alpha male froze before beginning another half-hearted charge and quickly turned away, disappearing into the shelter. The other stunned chimps followed.

"How would you like to live here, Alberta, with them as your roommates?"

"Mi kill you! Take Alberta home now, Anansi!"

Amused, Jacobs laughed.

"How about the zoo? How about that for irony? I'll take you home. Roland doesn't know we're gone, but we've got one more stop to make, if you don't mind."

She thought to attack him as he drove south along the Great Highway, the beach to her right, but she realized he was her only ride home. If she hurt him, there would be no way for her to get home to wait for Kendrick. If she hurt him, then human law would come after her. She determined that if she was going to hurt him, she would have to bide her time.

Instead, she reached over and ripped the upholstery off the passenger door panel, squeezing the plastic, wood and leather material in her hand.

"Stupid ape! I'll have to pay for that! Now you better make me money."

He stopped along a remote stretch of the beach, pulling the car off the highway before parking.

"It's time you and I came to a precise understanding." With those words, he withdrew the Springfield Armory 9-millimeter pistol from under his seat. "Do you know what this is? Have you ever seen a gun like this up-close? Or better yet, have you ever seen what a firearm like this can do?"

He reveled in her discomfort, which was transformed to abject fear when he pointed the barrel toward her, aiming at her forehead. She vocalized panic and alarm in chimp terms.

"Ironic, huh?" he said, waiving the gun. "You wait here."

Alberta sat frozen in terror as Jacobs exited the car, opened the trunk and began setting up something like an easel on the remote, secluded beach. He reappeared five minutes later, approaching her window with a honeydew melon in his hand, seeming to match up the globe with her head.

"That's about right, isn't it? This melon is your head," he announced, confirming her fear. "Now get out of the car and come with me."

Attaching a leash to the collar he earlier put on Alberta's neck, Jacobs led her to the place where he had set up the display, ten yards away from the loud, incoming waves.

"Get over here!" he demanded, motioning with the gun. When she arrived, he placed the melon on the small stand that he erected at Alberta's eye level. "Again, the melon is your head."

As he and Alberta stood ten feet away, Jacobs aimed the pistol and suddenly fired. *Kapowww!* The explosion from the gun was so loud and violent that Alberta dropped to the ground, traumatized, cringing, shaking, urinating on herself. Her ears, unprepared for the loud shock of the blast, could no longer hear. There was only a low, persistent ringing.

The fragmented melon, ripped open and ravished, lay on the ground in pieces, seeds scattered along a wide area on the sand. Next, Jacobs aimed the gun toward Alberta's face.

"I know what you're thinking: *if he doesn't kill me now, I'll kill him the first chance I get.* We both know you're stronger than I am, Alberta, but this is my equalizer here," Jacobs said, opening his jacket to show a leather holster, "and I keep it on me at all times. Don't think I would ever hesitate to use it if I feel threatened by you in any way. And if you tell anyone I've threatened you, I'll deny it, and then I'll kill you. I'll shoot you dead in the head, you understand?

"Vesey's made you think you're something special, but I was first to discover you. You're a little smarter than most, but you're still an ape, a beast, a wild animal. If I have to shoot you, I'll tell everyone it was self-defense, that you attacked me, and I'll walk away from your dead body. In the end, no one'll mourn the death of one dead chimp—person or no person. Your death might be in the news cycle for a day, but then life will go on. You won't matter. Believe me, no one will care."

****

At near sunset in Phoenix, the Valley of the Sun, the temperature only seemed to be rising as numbers on both sides along 24th Street and Camelback Road rose to the hundreds, a perceptible roiling boil of agitated separatists, activists and hate-filled anarchists. Shadows were creeping westward from the eastern horizon, draping strategic repositioning of militias and the stockpiling of weapons in shaded enclaves beside and between structures all along the divide. There were more than 3,000 fighters on each side. Apprised of the situation, the President had called in the National Guard, but it would be hours before their numbers would justify safe intervention.

"Are you sure you're all right, Billy? You don't look so good," Tamara McCracken noted in her Alabama accent as she rubbed the temples of Billy Joe Martin, the leader of the United Aryan Coalition. "It's really going down tonight. I know ya got a lot on your mind."

"Look up ta the sky," he said. "See that?"

"What?" Tamara asked.

"Chemtrails! That's a sign. The government wants this war just like we do, but not for the same reasons. They're druggin us with chemtrails ta make sure this war happens tanite."

As Tamara looked toward the sky, she wondered about the numerous white vapor lines that seemed to hang overhead. If they contained chemicals, then the entire area was affected.

"Taday is your big day, Billy. Here, this might make you feel better."

The cream she rubbed at his temples contained a trivalent chromium ion, which used a matrix of zinc and gallogermanate to host the ions, the chemical structure of which created a labyrinth of "traps" that captured excited infrared energy and stored it for an extended period. In short, the infrared energy in that cream produced a glow that was visible only through nighttime goggles.

Billy Joe, persisting in the notion that he stood at the brink of history and the reshaping of America, leaned back, enjoying this final indulgence from a very attractive woman, her gentle fingers massaging his temples and forehead, though he discerned annoyance from his peers. He thought of Jesus in Bethany at the house of Simon the Leper, when the woman, Mary, came with an alabaster jar and anointed his head with valued perfume, "an expensive nard."

When the murmuring became too pronounced, Billy invoked the memory of his lord, speaking in prophetic words.

"Ya'll let her be. Ya'll leave her alone. He she's tryin ta do a beautiful thang fer me. The weak and disloyal will always be with you, and you can help them whenever you want, but I won't always be here—not if the niggers and other savages get their way. For all we know, she might be anointin me for ma grave."

At the same time, across the divide, the leaders of the Black/Brown Resistance were being similarly pampered and prepared by a good-looking brown-skinned woman. She had, over the last several months, become the confidant and lover of Javier Brown, a thirty-something charismatic leader of mixed black and Puerto Rican heritage. Javier cared little, neither for his own life nor the lives of his followers. A true nihilist, his solutions involved the complete destruction of both sides, along with American society.

Hadassah Gonzalez Blackburn remained at his side, encouraging his ambitions for the upcoming battle, but she also had the trivalent chromium ion ointment, infused with fragrant perfume, which she applied to his face and head. Under a freestanding canopy that served as a makeshift command center, Javier and lieutenants sat, heads bowed, game faces on, as Hadassah attended to each, applying the ointment to three of the four leaders, careful not to touch the fourth, Jerome Martin, who was Javier's hotheaded and fiercely loyal protégée.

"What do you think's gonna happen tonight?" Hadassah asked Brown.

"Somethin that's never happened before in this country," he answered. "This revolution will be televised. America will finally have to answer for white supremacy—inherent racism and its history of persecution of non-whites. Finally, tonight, white blood will flow in a river so wide the world'll never forget the cost of America's racial sins. I don't care if I die. I just wanna kill me some white people—by the hundreds—by the thousands if possible."

"Well, I hope you don't hold it against me if I don't stick around," Hadassah apologized. "I'm not a soldier, cuz I have two kids at home who need me to stay alive. I'm all they've got."

"You go on," he nodded, "but you watch, and if you're close enough, you'll record history in the making. It will be the second and final revolutionary war in the history of this unjust, crooked country."

"I'll be watching," she answered, careful to return the large jar of ointment to her bag. "I'll say goodbye now since I know I will probably never see you again. *Revolution is the only way, baby!*"

"Revolution is the only way!" he yelled, returning the maxim, followed by calls of the refrain from his loyal lieutenants. "Tonight, we put the fear of God in white people. Tonight, white America bleeds!"

****

In a building two blocks away, one sniper awaited instructions, while a counterpart, a block beyond the divide, glanced through a night-vision scope, scanning for his own marks. He followed with the rifle as several targets' faces glowed infrared in the area around the canopy. He knew he would have to dispatch the first three targets quickly—within seconds—before the resulting panic began, and he knew his counterpart would do the same. It would be a coordinated effort, taking out actors on both sides—that based on a visual cue—a random flare that would burst ten degrees west of north in the twilight sky.

None of the targets realized their immediate peril or the betrayal by the trusted women who had infiltrated their ranks. Consumed by the rhetoric and passion of their separate causes, none realized their radicalization had made them the unwitting tools of less extreme, more calculated players in world affairs. The next few minutes would make America's race war a forgone conclusion.

****

"Natsumi, I'm glad you answered. I just received a report from a source that there's at least one sniper stationed in in a building within your proximity," Draco warned, "and since we know you're a target, I strongly suggest that you and your people retreat to a secure position. You can't lead if you're dead."

"Thank you. Point taken. We'll retreat," she answered, nervous, glancing up at building windows. "Things look really bad down here. If this situation gets out of hand, it's guaranteed thousands of people are going to die. What are you guys doing? When's the National Guard coming?"

"They're here. They're just mobilizing. They can't go in until they can fully assess the threat and know they can overwhelm it. They won't go in just to get massacred. They have to maintain their advantage."

"That won't be easy, believe me. I'm on the ground," Natsumi warned. "I don't like what I'm seeing—so many automatic, military-style weapons, so many fighters, and body armor. It's a war zone. Aleppo in America!"

"You just get your people outta there. No telling what's going to set this thing off."

Draco's next call was to Williams, who was coordinating the efforts of the Loverboys on the ground.

"Talk to me, D'Artagnan."

"With Padmi's help, we think we've located and isolated one of the snipers in a building. I just don't know I can get there in time, because it seems he's booby-trapped the main entrance, which will take me some time. I'm going in through a third-floor window. It's a long shot, but it's all we got right now. Chances are they have a redundant sniper or snipers out there somewhere. Uphill battle!"

"It's our worst fears, come to pass."

"Have you tried prayin, Johnnie? Sometimes, that's all you've got, and it works."

"Bad timing," Draco laughed sarcastically. "If God was a player in any of this, we'd have never been here in the first place. God might not be dead, but he sure sleeps a lot—too much for me to be a solid believer."

****

A flare at ten degrees west of north lit the darkening western sky! Instantly, the spiked, staccato shooting from both positions began. The first to fall was Javier Brown, a bullet through his forehead, and then his lieutenants, one by one, in quick succession, leaving only Jerome Martin, who hunkered, trembling, behind the com array. On the other side of the divide, Billy Joe Martin lied on his face, the back of his head missing, cerebral neural gore oozing onto the pavement. His top-ranking, hand-picked replacements were also dead, two of their faces gone.

All around, Javier Brown's forces were in a panic, with most, lacking immediate leadership, inclined to flee. Yet one of the survivors of the initial onslaught—Jerome Martin, was more angry than afraid. Calling orders to the leaders of the ground forces, he was intent on gaining the advantage of the first offensive.

"Kill them all! Shoot now, before they know anything! Fire away! This revolution is on!"

The opening salvo was deafening, accented by blasts from shoulder-launched munitions and loud explosions. For a moment, all seemed eerily silent, except for the sounds of wounded men and women screaming in agony, and then the sustained exchange began in earnest, with frenzied forces charging both ways across the divide.

Pandemonium ensued as panicked fighters fired weapons without restraint, often into the backs and heads of co-patriots. The bodies fell, though many were trampled. Within the first ten minutes, 500 were dead, and casualties mounted with each loud exchange from automatic weapons. Far from the romantic idea of war and the thought of killing enemies on the other side, the carnage resulting from the increased efficiency of domestic American war craft was gruesome to behold. Dismembered arms, legs, hands, fingers and skull fragments littered the area as the ground, in the surreal light of grenade explosions, flowed red with blood.

The Antifa division was better prepared for battle than most. Its leadership intact, its infantry group advanced, shields erect, while artillery mounted on nearby buildings targeted and shelled enemy weapons and positions, exacting heavy casualties and breaking through the line.

At the divide, some combatants swung chains, heavy pipes and bats, while others wielded knives and swords, hacking wildly, inflicting horrific wounds, some mortal—some worse than mortal. There was confusion at the center, as the race war was not merely a conflict of black against white, or brown against white—but white against white—leaving white supremacists confused.

Roughly forty percent of the fighters on the protesters side where white, or they seemed like white persons. Since combatants could not be identified by their uniforms, many of the white separatist fighters were suspicious, turning on each other. At the same time, when casualties among the whites who were fighting alongside the blacks and browns began to mount, Jerome Martin ordered them to pull back to support and security positions for their own protection.

The sheer number of bloodied inert bodies on the ground was a sight unseen in generations on American soil. News cameras, albeit positioned on drones or a good distance from the conflict, captured the bloodbath for the world to see. While family and friends across the globe cringed in horror, the enemies of America and terrorist groups reveled at the sight of a slaughter they could only imagine after years of failed efforts—the sight of Americans massacred by the thousands, at their own hands. It was an American racial/civil war, the judgment of Almighty God!

****

"I'm in the building! I followed the sound of the shots. I've got the hostile trapped on the other side of the door here," D'Artagnan advised in a whisper. "There's no way I'm going in there alone, and somehow I don't think he's gonna wait in there for the SWAT team to arrive. I need team back-up now! Right now, goddammit!"

"Just get outta there, D'Artagnan!" Draco screamed into the phone. "You won't have support for at least five minutes. Let him go. Fall back! Film him! Take a picture, but get outta there!"

"Pulling back. I'm not stupid," the Williams answered. "I'm headed back toward the stairs. You shoulda told me that two minutes ago before he knew I was out here. Wait! He's comin out. This is gonna end bad!"

Ten seconds later, Johnnie Draco heard the exchange of gunfire and a man groaning in agony.

"D'Artagnan! D'Artagnan! What's happening? D'Artagnan, are you there?"

For the next minute, all Draco could hear was labored breathing, and then another shot.

"D'Artagnan!"

"I'm hit, Draco. When are they comin? I think I got im!"

Chapter 21

For San Francisco Superior Court Judge Tamara Weir, it had already been a trying day. She was up at three a.m. to prep for an interview on the *Good Morning America* show at four o'clock (over two hours before sunrise), followed by a *Today* show interview at five. While she knew Alberta's direct testimony before a U.S. court was landmark relative to the nation's disposition on nonhuman person recognition and protective rights, she felt pressure from the presiding judge of the San Francisco Superior Court to publicly discuss her ruling and its implications before a national and international television audience.

The first interview, however, had been pre-empted by coverage of the conflict, or race war, that had spilled over from the previous night. According to a National Guard spokesperson in Arizona, over 2,300 persons had died during the night, in addition to scores of injured persons who over-filled local hospitals and clinics. Of the 1,500 and more at medical facilities, nearly one-third had sustained "critical to near-mortal injuries."

The President declared the entirety of Phoenix and Maricopa County under martial law, showing force by placing a contingent of 10,000 Guard forces at the divide and at the perimeters of the city. Early resistance by groups on both sides was met with overwhelming retaliation, employing formidable weapons and tactics, resulting in roughly 200 more deaths before militias on both sides retreated to positions outside the city to prepare for the next fierce and angry conflict.

It was a huge news morning, with networks and news affiliates reporting on similar though smaller flare-ups in Los Angeles, Oakland, Denver, Dallas, Chicago, Milwaukee, Detroit, Miami, Philadelphia, New York and Washington DC. Congressional leaders called a special session at 3 a.m. to consider whether to invoke the National Defense Authorization Act (NDAA), mandated under Article I, Section 8 of the U.S. Constitution.

This provision "would allow Armed Forces of the United States to detain covered persons pursuant to the Authorization of Use of Military Force," thus allowing the United States military, under the direction of the President, to act as a police force and arrest or use force against any person (including American citizens) suspected of terrorism. Further, the act allowed the federal government to hold these persons without trial indefinitely.

Many conservatives blamed recent underground rap music lyrics for the fighting, and several named rap producer Cyanide as an instigator. Highlighted, many of his lyrics called for a "revolution" that would make America's streets flow with blood. "Red Streets," Cyanide's personal anthem to the revolution, had been downloaded for free over 38 million times. On social media sites, he compared his recent rap songs to speeches by revolutionary leader Malcolm X. Cyanide's message was a call-to-action, coinciding with Justin Luck's dumping of more than 100,000 illegal weapons in inner-city neighborhoods.

Over the course of the morning, broadcast and cable news networks interviewed panels of judges, lawyers and legal experts about the advisability of taking such an unprecedented step—the NDAA. Some called it "a blatant, unabashed abandonment of the Constitution and our founding principles," while others saw it as "dangerous federal overreach" by the President.

A *GMA* producer called Judge Weir at the local San Francisco television news studio on Front Street, telling her there would be no room in the news block to air her discussion about the preliminary hearing, though the hosts would pre-record the interview, "to cycle it in at a future time." The *Today* show postponed its interview indefinitely, much to Judge Weir's relief, as she planned to hear preliminary motions for the hearing at nine.

During the interview, the judge weighed in on the constitutionality of the National Defense Authorization Act before pivoting to explain her rationale for allowing testimony from Alberta as a "legal nonhuman person," marking the first time a U.S. court had ever recognized a nonhuman person witness for direct testimony in a criminal trial. As expected, most of the host's questions focused on Alberta, her intelligence and the implications the ruling would have on the growing issue of nonhuman rights.

"I consider every case on its individual circumstances and merits," the judge remarked, "but beyond the more lurid and press-worthy issue that you in the media are intent on discussing is a man—incarcerated and accused of murder. My job as a judge is to determine whether there is enough evidence to hold him over for trial. The NHPRP issue, meaning the Nonhuman Persons Rights and Protections controversy, though valid and indeed interesting to consider, is not at issue during the hearing, as I have already ruled on that matter."

At the courthouse on Bryant Street, a bailiff opened the court session at exactly nine o'clock. Deputy District Attorney Irving Carroll and co-counsel were seated at the table on the left, while defense attorney Natsumi Mitchell was joined by co-counsel Trevor Reed at right. Roland Hughes sat in the front row of the gallery, gripping a leash, attached to a leather harness that was strapped over Alberta's shoulders and around her waist.

Seeming a bit uneasy, deputy district attorney Carroll stood, glancing back toward Roland and Alberta.

"Your Honor, with all due respect, having a powerful wild animal loose in the courtroom makes me and my co-counsel a little nervous—especially since it's an adversarial setting and we're men. What if she gets mad at us for our questions? I've heard chimps go for the nuts to bite em off. We're respectfully requesting an order from your Honor that the monkey should be caged. She's a wild animal."

"She's a legal nonhuman person at this hearing, Counsel," the judge answered, "and she is attached to a leash that's attached to a sturdy behaviorist—Dr. Roland Hughes, who ironically meets Michigan People v. Johnson and seems to be no less than two hundred pounds. I think the leash will suffice."

"I continue my objection to her being on a leash," Natsumi called out while standing. "Not only is Alberta a peaceful person, but she's a thinking, feeling, rational person. Having her on a leash is humiliating to her, as it would be to any other rational person."

"Ms. Mitchell," the judge responded, "you must remember that your own co-counsel agreed with the district attorney on this point—maybe because he's a man, but he's also admitted he isn't all too comfortable with her being so close, having nothing more than a leash to restrain her. You want no restraint, they want a cage. I believe the leash is an adequate compromise."

"And what about when the public comes in for the hearing?" Carroll asked. "They don't get to weigh in on this?"

"Counsel, we've posted an advisory in good detail at the courtroom entrance," the judge countered. "The notice clearly informs that Alberta will be a witness at this hearing, and that she is on a leash. Those who want to attend this and any other hearing will attend at their own risk. It's telling that there's not an empty seat in the gallery."

"So how is this going to work, your Honor?" Carroll asked. "I'm not seeing any discovery on her expected testimony. I understand she's a defense witness. So how are we going to do this?"

"The same way we do it at any other preliminary hearing, Mr. Carroll. You'll present your case and witnesses, and then the defense will present theirs. And since the attorneys present are not fluent at American Sign Language, a translator will facilitate the exchange of testimony between questioners and Alberta as a witness. Don't make this any more difficult than it has to be."

With the courtroom filled and the defendant present, the judge returned, calling the court to order. Moments earlier, the courtroom stirred as all witnessed the reunion between Alberta and the defendant. Upon seeing Kendrick, Alberta rose and leapt into his arms, hugging him, weeping. She stroked his face and kissed him on the forehead, and Roland allowed her to cling to her conservator for a couple minutes before prying her fingers away and guiding her to the "reserved" front row of seats in the gallery.

Sitting next to Trevor, Dr. Kendrick Vesey seemed depressed and demoralized as he stared forward, hands folded in front of him on the table. He had a full beard the last time Natsumi saw him, so his appearance had improved since they spoke last. She smiled over at him, thinking to herself that he was very handsome after the shave and haircut… *a little hot even, but no way!*

After an opening statement, prosecutor Carroll brought on three witnesses in an effort to establish a timeline and sequence of events. The first witness was Matheo Larsen, a security guard employee that the DA had flown in from the hotel on Hornsgatan in downtown Stockholm. The man did not speak much English, so Carroll had arranged for a translator.

Under oath, Matheo testified that he discovered Jennifer's inert body on the floor next to Kendrick, outside the elevator, barely conscious and groaning in pain—with a huge knot and bruise on her forehead. Matheo said he was initially suspicious of Kendrick's story that she had passed out, bumping her head as she fell. When he checked the elevator video the next day and saw the altercation, he alerted the hotel manager.

The prosecution's next witness was the paramedic who first encountered Jennifer, unconscious, in the bedroom at Kendrick's apartment after the couple returned to San Francisco. He said her breathing was shallow and she was unresponsive. There was no indication of trauma. Jennifer seemed to be in a deep sleep. When Carroll asked if she could have been saved if Kendrick had called the ambulance earlier, the paramedic was uncertain. He suspected poisoning initially and had indicated that assessment to Kendrick.

Under cross-examination, however, the paramedic admitted that Kendrick, who thought Jennifer was stressed out about the wedding and that her medication had made her lethargic, might not have known the degree of her medical dilemma. The paramedic said it was impossible to determine how long Jennifer had been unresponsive, and perhaps Kendrick did not have the medical training to understand that she had slipped into a coma.

The final timeline/sequence witness was the medical examiner, Dr. Medha Singh, who described the nature of cyanide poisoning, providing her insight and opinion about how and why Jennifer died. Based on levels of toxicity in Jennifer's blood, skin, tissue and organs, the poisoning had been slow and sustained, with exposure occurring over weeks, if not months.

Dr. Singh pointed out, however, that the over-the-threshold lethal dose was separate from the slow exposure poisoning. In the doctor's opinion, Jennifer had inhaled cyanide "in some aerosol form," as there was ground-glass attenuation apparent in both lung fields, along with inflammation indicative of exposure to cyanide. The doctor believed the exposure to Jennifer's lungs had occurred eight to ten hours before paramedics arrived.

"Dr. Singh, can you provide any medical explanation for the slow poisoning?" Natsumi asked in cross-examination. "Could it have been environmental?"

"That's possible," the doctor answered, nodding, "but probably not environmental."

"I'm no scientist, doctor, but I've read that cyanide is produced naturally in the human body, and it's exhaled in extremely low concentrations with each breath. Is that true?"

"It is indeed."

"Is it also true that cyanide is produced by over 1,000 plant species, including sorghum, bamboo and cassava? It's in smoke, and it's in water? It's fairly abundant in our everyday environment, is it not?"

"It is," the doctor answered, "but not at lethal levels, nothing close to the levels found in the decedent's body."

"But doesn't the toxicity threshold vary from human to human?" Natsumi asked. "I mean, isn't it possible that exposure at a level that might kill one person—that same level of exposure might not kill another person?"

"That's true," the doctor answered. "There is no question the decedent suffered long-term exposure, but her body contained levels of toxicity that would not have resulted from casual environmental exposure. There was direct exposure, evidence of slow poisoning, either through the skin or consumption, and the inhalation exposure that resulted in her death."

"Just one more thing," Natsumi said while scanning the examiner's report. "I noticed that the toxicity level in her lungs was relatively low, perhaps under the lethal threshold. Is that true?"

"It wasn't an extremely large amount," the doctor answered, "but since she already had high levels of cyanide present throughout her system, it probably didn't take much to get her to that lethal level."

"So whatever amount she inhaled and you found in her lungs, doctor, may not have been enough to kill the average person? The exposure that put her over the threshold could have come from an environmental source?"

"Objection, your Honor," Carroll shouted. "Question calls for speculation?"

"Sustained," Judge Weir nodded. "And if there are no further questions, this court will recess until 1p.m."

****

"He was here in Phoenix!" Padmi answered. "None of us knew why, you know—after we kicked him out. Calvin saw him. He was just standing there, somewhere behind us, and then *boom*! Someone shot him in the head. There were all kinds of other leaders around, so we're thinking he had to be targeted. No one knows what to think. Do you think Draco's group did it to make sure he wouldn't talk to anyone?"

"No way. They're focused on the race war, so Demetrius was nothing to them. I need to know—did anyone leak anything? Could anyone know we kicked him out?"

"The only person I told was Draco," Padmi responded. "As far as anyone else knew, he was still in charge of security detail for OLM."

"So once again we were targeted for assassination. Where are you now?"

"I'm still on Camelback Road. The National Guard is pushing us back."

"Sorry about Demetrius, but you need to get out of there, Padmi. Whoever's targeting us—they know who we are. They'll go after our leadership before they go after anyone else. I know this! Get out of there now! They know who you are. They're targeting our leadership!"

In the light of day, hostilities between amassing militias had abated, though the National Guard across the country, governors and local law enforcement expected flare-ups to resume after sundown. The media finally began to focus on the unusual omnipresence of "contrails," which the conspiracy theory proponents called "chemtrails"—the source of the unrest. As a precautionary measure, the President ordered a 6 p.m. to 6 a.m. curfew in most major cities and scheduled a speech to the nation for 8 p.m., EST.

There were a few instances of racial conflicts in San Francisco, but local groups calling for tolerance and peace had organized to bring the city together. However, there were many reports of fighting coming in from Oakland, San Jose and Sacramento. National and cable broadcast news presented a picture of America in turmoil, with scenes of battle and conflict coming in from states along the coasts, in the south and along the northeast.

"This is the realization of the White Nationalist Movement!" a Wyoming man missing his front teeth shouted toward the camera. "We said it! We're finally takin our country back! We're makin it great again!"

Across the country, casualties continued to mount, with an estimated 11,000 persons killed by noon. Sad stories and gruesome, bloody scenes dominated the news until editors made the extraordinary decision not to broadcast scenes of violence and devastation in hope of quelling the anger and hysteria.

When coverage of conflicts moved to the Internet, the government began to selectively shut down gruesome and inflammatory video segments and comments, beginning with social media sites and moving to websites and email servers of known hate groups.

When organized militias began marching from rural areas toward populated cities, the government scrambled fighters and sent troops to establish "no-go" zones. For the paramilitary group in Missouri that shot down an U.S. Army helicopter with a shoulder-launched surface-to-air missile, reprisal was swift and severe. Three F-18s circled, literally scorching the Earth beneath the feet of the militants, burning 1,800 men, women and children to death to set an imperative precedent.

Hate groups in a few European cities sought to imitate America's violence as a show of solidarity—mostly targeting minority communities, but relative governments were prepared. There were a few flare-ups that were violently answered by ready military forces. Yet the world's attention and cameras had turned toward the race/civil war in the U.S., with Russia's leader suggesting that the fighting had sounded the death knell to capitalism and American arrogance.

****

Judge Weir gaveled the court to order at exactly one o'clock before delivering the court-mandated remark.

"In light of the civil unrest presently occurring across the country—beginning tomorrow morning, this court will stand in recess until further notice by order of the governor of California and the president of the United States."

She looked toward Kendrick.

"The good news for you, Mr. Vesey, is that we'll hear the remainder of the prosecution's case this afternoon—and the defense case, if we're lucky. If I've heard enough to render a decision, we'll either hold you over for trial or you'll be going home today. The bad news is that if we *don't* resolve this matter today, there's no telling how long we'll be waiting to resume. Let's get this matter concluded today, Counsels."

Deputy district attorney Carroll nodded, calling the first of his crime scene/motive witnesses, beginning with San Francisco Police Inspector Dana Murphy. During direct testimony, the inspector described the crime scene and the results of the investigation, indicating that detectives discovered traces of cyanide all over Kendrick's apartment, including countertops, dishes and flatware, in every room, on linen, bed sheets, pillows, furniture, toothbrushes, and in the shower and drains. The investigation showed similar cyanide contamination at Davis Franklin's Berkeley residence and at Jennifer's apartment.

The prosecution's next witness was investigator Nick Jantzen, one of three detectives who inspected what he called "two of the three crime scenes." Jantzen said "traces of cyanide were everywhere! Once we knew the extent of the contamination, we feared for our own health."

Though the questioning was brief, Carroll, seeking to establish his overall theory, posed a final question.

"According to the report, Inspector, did you find any irregular substance in the defendant's bathroom, under his sink?"

"Yes, we did. We found dimethyl sulfoxide, which is abbreviated DMSO. It's a solvent."

"Thank you, Inspector. No more questions."

The third prosecution witness was Inspector Sandra Ballesteros, the detective who investigated the Berkeley residence where Kendrick had a room and where Alberta lived. Interviews established that Jennifer was a regular visitor. Ballesteros confirmed that her team found traces of cyanide all over the house—in high enough levels for her to call in an environmental engineering specialist team to clean up the house.

The firm, which was well known in northern California for cleaning residences that had previously been used as meth labs, issued a report indicating the contamination was "pervasive, in every room of the house." Finally, Ballesteros testified that the team had found a vial of a white crystalline substance, similar in appearance to salt or sugar, which the lab later determined contained potassium cyanide.

The final prosecution witness was Armando Alvarez to establish motive. Armando helped introduce a letter that Jennifer had written to him, complaining about problems in the relationship. Two lines of the letter referenced an angry argument, bordering on violence, related to "Alberta, that wicked monkey!" In another letter, Jennifer described Alberta as a two-faced, manipulative monster who "had Kendrick wrapped around her finger."

Armando described the relationship between Kendrick and Alberta as "sick and perverted. I dunno what disgusting thing was goin on between him and that monkey, but it was definitely unnatural, weird!"

Armando also helped introduce the insurance policy in his possession that Jennifer and Kendrick purchased on her life, which was purposed to provide Kendrick as beneficiary one million dollars in the event of her death.

"Kendrick was horrible to my sister. He never loved her. He was in it for the money. That monkey was always first with him. He murdered Jennifer. Kendrick Vesey murdered my little sister."

Armando's comment drew an objection from Natsumi, which the judge sustained. With its final witness questioned, the prosecution rested its case.

The judge glanced toward the other bench.

"Call your first witness, Ms. Mitchell."

"Very well. The defense calls Alberta, America's first legal nonhuman person."

Alberta sat in the seat in front of the court, across from the judge. The swearing-in was awkward for the judge, since she did not know if Alberta understood the concept of God. She instructed the clerk to replace the words, "I swear" with "I affirm," and the words "so help me God" with the words, "under pains and penalties of perjury."

"Where is the Bible for the oath?" Alberta asked the clerk through the translator.

"We don't use a Bible any longer, Alberta. Do you understand the Bible?" the judge asked.

"Alberta reads Bible every day," the translator answered. "Mi—I know God. God is Jah-Jah. Mi—I won't lie—so help mi Jah-Jah."

"Very well," the judge answered, impressed and surprised. "You may begin, Ms. Mitchell."

"Alberta," Natsumi asked as she stood. "Did you know Jennifer Alvarez?"

The witness answered through the translator.

"She says 'no,'" the translator answered, "she did not know Jennifer Alvarez, but she saw her two or three times a week for over two years. She says she only saw Jennifer when she was at the house, so she did not know her well."

"Okay, I can accept that," Natsumi answered. "You saw her a couple times a week for over two years? Can you tell me why she visited the house so regularly?"

"Because she told Kendrick she loved him and she wanted to marry him," was the answer. "She loved herself more."

"In fact, Kendrick and Jennifer were going to get married, is that correct?"

"Yes," the translator pronounced carefully, "but Jennifer is dead. Dead people cannot marry."

"That's true. Alberta, I understand you watch television and you are frequently on the Internet. Have you watched or have you read about Kendrick being arrested by the police and charged by the district attorney and the people of California for the murder of Jennifer Alvarez?"

"Kendrick did not murder Jennifer Alvarez," was Alberta's answer through the translator.

"Did you read details about his arrest and this case on the Internet?"

"Yes."

"Do you understand the definition of murder, Alberta?"

"Murder is when one person kills other person, and there is a motive for money, hate or revenge. Kendrick did not kill Jennifer."

"Do you understand what motive means, Alberta?"

"When someone murders," she answered, "human law says a murder must have motive, means and opportunity. Motive is reason *why* someone murders. Kendrick had no motive."

"Did you ever see them fight? Did you ever witness any arguments between Kendrick and Jennifer?"

"Jennifer went to his room at night," Alberta answered, "and they closed door. Then Jennifer made loud noises for long time, but they weren't fighting—no words. Then she made more noises, not angry noises. They were breeding, never fighting. He had no motive."

"Was Kendrick nice to Jennifer?"

Alberta glanced toward Kendrick, sympathetic, before turning back to the lawyer.

"Kendrick loved Jennifer with his heart, all the time. He would never kill Jennifer."

Natsumi returned to the defense table to get another report before beginning a new line of questioning.

"Do you recall an occasion with Sandra Ballesteros, an inspector with the San Francisco Police Department, along with two other investigators, came in to inspect the house where you live?"

"Yes. They made my house chaka chaka."

"Do you remember that they found a vial somewhere in your room, and they brought it out?"

"Yes."

"Do you know what that was?"

Alberta seemed confused.

"It was a jar."

"Do you know what was in it?"

"I knew after I smelled it. It was salt."

"It was potassium cyanide salt. Do you know what that is?" Natsumi asked.

"Cyanide is poison."

"And how do you know that?"

"Science class. Chemistry class."

"Did you know you were inhaling something poisonous, something that could have killed you?"

"No," Alberta answered, her face and pouted lips displaying incredulity. "I'm not crazy!"

"Do you know how that vial got in your room, Alberta?"

"No. I found vial under the sink."

"Had you ever seen that vial before, anyplace else? Had you ever seen it anywhere else before the day you found it?"

"No."

"Okay, and after finding it and tasting it, then what did you do with it?"

"I put vial back where I found vial. It wasn't mine."

Natsumi neared the witness to ask the last questions.

"Alberta, when you were interviewed by Inspector Ballesteros, did you say, 'salt is for the kitchen'?"

"Yes," the chimp nodded.

"Did you, at any time, take that vial to the kitchen?"

"No. I put vial back."

"Did you, at any time, take that vial into Kendrick's room or anywhere else in the house?"

"No."

"Thank you, Alberta. I have nothing else."

Carroll chose to remain seated during his cross-examination.

"Okay, Alberta… hi. You said you never saw Kendrick and Jennifer argue or fight? They were a couple for two years? You're saying they never had a fight? Do you know what we mean by 'fight'?"

"I know fight. A comb fight your hair this morning and him lose—not fair fight. Hair choke comb to death. Carrol old shoes and wrinkled pants—them still fighting now."

As the courtroom erupted in laughter, the judge had to bow her head briefly to hide her amusement.

"A fight is an argument. Fight is hitting and biting. Kendrick and Jennifer did not fight."

Feeling the heat glow in his cheeks, Carroll tried not to react to the barb, but he realized he would have to choose his words more carefully.

"Well, did they ever disagree about anything?"

"Ya mon. They're only human," the translator stated awkwardly.

More laughing.

"Do you remember what they may have disagreed about?"

"Something little."

Carroll glanced down at his notes.

"Did they ever disagree about you, Alberta?"

"Maybe, but I never saw them disagree."

"Let me ask you this, Alberta. Did you get along with Jennifer? Did you ever fight with her?"

"Fight? Jennifer was a little human. She would be crazy to fight me. You're bigger, but you're hiding behind the table."

"Did you get into any arguments with her?"

"She could argue with Alberta. She did not understand American Sign Language."

Frustrated, Carroll raised his voice.

"Did you like her? I've read enough to know you don't know how to lie to the court. Did you like Jennifer Alvarez?"

"No. I did not like Jennifer."

"Did you hate her?"

"No. I did not hate her, but I did not like her."

Carroll stood, still remaining behind the table.

"Why didn't you like her, Alberta?"

"I did not like Jennifer, because she did not like me."

The final witness for the defense was Kendrick's financial adviser, CW Webb, who testified that Kendrick's net worth was a little less than six million dollars, and that his annual income, which was a combination of his UC Berkeley salary, his work for Davis Franklin, speaking fees and royalties, was over $350,000. He also indicated that Kendrick had donated the monies from his Nobel Prize award—an amount totaling $1.4 million—to a charity organization that was dedicated to advancing the rights and interests of nonhuman person protection rights across the globe.

"This man just gave away over a million dollars," Natsumi concluded. "Why would he expose himself and Alberta to slow cyanide poisoning to murder Jennifer Alvarez for a one-million-dollar insurance claim?"

It was already 6 p.m. by the time the final witness direct examination and cross-examination ended. Judge Weir, tired and concerned about a disturbing text message from her daughter in New York, sighed before her summation.

"I'm very sorry, Mr. Vesey, but it is already too late to hear closing arguments, let alone for me to deliberate and render a decision today. Sadly, this court will stand in recess until such time our governor deems appropriate, but with events unfolding the way they've been today, who knows? As a result, you will continue at the jail until I have an opportunity to finish hearing this matter and render a decision.

"Alberta, it has been my honor to hear the testimony of the first legal nonhuman person in a U.S. courtroom. This court appreciates your effort to come and testify today. Counsels—the events in this court today are truly historic. I anticipate closing arguments appropriate for the level of discourse.

"For everyone, this is a trying time for our country. I pray that we will all come through it wiser and more determined to put forth that last full measure of devotion so that we will experience a rebirth of freedom. May God bless the United States of America. This court stands in recess until further notice."

Chapter 22

"Is he conscious yet?" Draco asked, "or better yet, is he gonna make it?"

"It was a serious wound," the doctor answered, "but I think he'll survive. He's still under sedation, which means you won't be able to make any sense of what he might tell you, and frankly, he probably won't understand any question you might ask."

"What about your other patient?" Draco insisted. "What about D'Artagnan Williams, my brother-in-law?"

"Mr. William's wounds are a bit more serious. One bullet tore through his abdomen, while the other nicked his femoral artery. He's lucky he didn't bleed out on the spot. We've stabilized him, but right now, he could go either way. He's headed to the nearest hospital."

The Loverboys' local base of operations was inside a warehouse outside Phoenix. They had set up a temporary command center with a computer bay and a half-dozen workstations, a secure phone system, a war room, a lab, a weapons locker and an area with two beds, which served the purpose for triage and medical treatment, if required.

Six hours earlier, the facility received two patients, victims involved in a shootout against each other. The sniper/instigator caught D'Artagnan Williams off-guard by kicking open the door while firing his semi-automatic weapon. Unable to find cover, D'Artagnan stood his ground, firing back. In the sequel, both the shooter and D'Artagnan went down, with D'Artagnan suffering the more serious injuries. Within minutes, however, Draco and Loverboy support arrived, accompanied by a paramedic team.

Both injured parties were treated on the spot and immediately transferred to the warehouse, where doctors went to work to save both lives. Once stabilized, D'Artagnan was transferred to a hospital, while the shooter—instead of being turned over to local authorities, was held for future interrogation and the intelligence he could provide.

To Draco's surprise, the shooter was not an American—not a disadvantaged, disaffected ex-military minority male. Initially, intelligence experts thought the injured shooter was Ukrainian, until they brought in a Loverboy who was a specialist in Slavic languages. Based on documents retrieved from his person and data extracted from his mobile device, the shooter was "Crimean, of Russian extraction."

"We just finished our investigation of the room where he was hulled up and the motel room he rented. He's not KGB, but he's associated in some way."

The revelation came as a shock to Draco and the others, as they were certain they were dealing with a domestic attempt at sedition in America's large cities, motivated by financial gain. Instead, they were forced to consider the involvement of a foreign actor, and the implications were troubling. If a foreign power was involved, then its underlying motivation would be much more sinister—the destruction of the United States of America and its ideals.

"We're in over our heads," Draco explained. "I think we need to call a Loverboy Elite Committee meeting. We came into existence because we didn't think our bosses would react to the threat we saw and no one believed. Now it's bigger than us. It's no accident the hostile we have in that room is Russian, and we can only assume the other shooter was also Russian."

"You're right, Draco," McCarthy from Boston chimed in. "I don't know if our target is tacitly working with the Russians or if the Russians saw an opportunity. I'm guessing they've inserted themselves America's growing civil unrest to exact maximum damage on this country and what we stand for. We're gonna have to figure out what we're gonna do, and soon. Fourteen thousand Americans dead in 48 hours. It's the worst day in history for American casualties!"

"So who do we trust?" detective Gutierrez asked.

"I know someone who's got a relative with a CIA connection," Draco answered, "and she can be trusted. We need to bring the executive committee together so we can come up with a course of action. D'Artagnan might not make it—we're praying for him. A lot of us will lose our lives before this is over, but here's the future of our country at stake."

"I'm ready to die. It's ironic we're fighting for the same ideals our founding fathers risked their lives for in 1775," McCarthy added, "except we face longer odds—all sides hate us, and we're up against billionaires, our departments and our fellow officers—and now the Russians."

****

"I didn't come to meet you, Luck," Colin explained, "because I can't trust you anymore."

"That's ridiculous!" Luck responded. "What's wrong with you, Colin? What's changed?"

"Who killed Demetrius? I can't help thinkin it could've been me, partner. Was someone shootin at me? Maybe the sniper missed. I was standin three feet away from him. I had his blood all over me. You never tell me someone was gonna take him out. Why? Because they were aimin for me?"

"Calm down!" Luck insisted. "I have no idea what you're talking about. Maybe it was one of your 'ghosts.' I know nothing about your friend, Demetrius, except that he failed us, or whoever he was dealing with. Now you're telling me he's dead?"

"He was taken out—just as sure as I coulda been taken out if someone knew who I was or what I look like. I was standing right there. You know it, or you should know it. Did you order that? Who are these damn people, these foreigners you're workin with? And what's this business about chemtrails?"

"I can't tell you that," Luck answered, "but I had nothing to do with that loser Demetrius getting killed—had to be a stray bullet. The people I work with charge for what they do, and that thug racist sack of shit wasn't worth the bullet, believe me."

"All the same," Colin countered, "I know how you operate. You'd just as soon kill me than pay me. You don't even like black people. It's all business for you. After I saw what happened to Demetrius, I've decided to assume a lower profile with you until this little war is over. If you wanna find me, you're gonna hafta learn how to navigate the LA underground and deal with my ghosts. Otherwise, we do everything by phone."

"A lotta gratitude you're showing me, Colin, after all the time I've spent trying to teach you, trying to help you. And to think I've known your parents since you were a little black Jewish boy—long before you changed your name to Cyanide."

"You wanna think I'm Cyanide, but you don't know," Colin scoffed. "It really doesn't matter now. The country's gone to hell—just the way you predicted. Didn't you say after all this shit went down—your race war and all—the true winners would just 'divvy up all the spoils? The more ruthless, the better. Screw the weak, screw the masses!' Ain't that what you say?"

"Get off your soapbox, Colin. You wanted your revolution, and now you got it. You'll have a big following by the time the smoke clears. Who knows? Maybe they'll make you the King of the Blacks, and maybe the Jews too, and Mexicans. They'll need a leader. You'll be their leader."

"I don't trust you, Luck. You'd take me out first chance you get. We'll take care of business by phone from here on. No one'll be listenin in. The government's got its hands full these days."

"I'm really insulted, Colin, but okay. I need you to help me out with something."

"With what?"

"Well, you've talked to Natsumi Mitchell—the black broad you have a hard-on for over at Our Lives Matter? Demetrius told handlers about that."

"Now he's credible?"

"Anyway, she knows an Oakland cop named Johnnie Draco. She's working with im."

"So?"

"Draco's in big with the Loverboys—that rogue cop group, mostly in the cities—that's been fighting against the war. They've been after me."

"I know who Draco is? What about him?"

"Well, there were two pro shooters out there last night. It was their job to make sure the war got started. They took out a few key people to ignite the fire, and it worked perfectly, as we saw on the news this morning."

"Alotta people died," Colin agreed, "and by all accounts, tonight'll be worse."

"It will once the sun goes down. Anyway, I understand one of the Loverboys downed one of the shooters in a bloody gunfight. The shooter's hurt, but he's not dead. The Loverboys have him."

"And why should I care?"

"Because I need to know who this shooter is. I don't deal directly with contractors when it comes to anything that might get my hands bloody. There are brokers for that. I'm always two or three steps removed, but with the war escalating, the government's going to be very interested in this shooter if they talk to him, and I don't want it to come back to me… and you."

"Me? That's yo shit, yo deal. Leave me out of it."

"You're involved in it all right. You can't play dumb. You knew what you were getting with me. Fifteen thousand people are already dead. You think they'll cut you any slack?"

"What do you want me to do, Mr. Luck?"

"I need to know where the shooter's from. I have a sneaking suspicion he's Russian, and if he is, then we're screwed. I need you to talk to Natsumi Mitchell and set up a meeting with Draco."

"Shit!" Colin stammered. "Are you tellin me you invited the Russians in on your American race war? They're here! Are you crazy? Russia ain't no joke—especially in this!"

"No, Colin. I didn't invite the Russians in. It turns out one of my business associates may have done so without my knowledge. I can't say for sure. I'm trying to fix this—believe me, but I need your help."

"They still hang people for treason, Luck. You're on your own."

"Listen Colin, you're in this until I say you're out! Your revolution is already sedition. You don't think that's treason? You're as responsible for this war as I am. If I hang, you'll hang right beside me, so cut the crap. We need to find out who that shooter is and where he's from. You get a hold of Natsumi Mitchell and set up that meeting with Draco, you hear? You talk to him and get back to me—sooner rather than later. Who knows what they'll find out about him… and us."

"I think your problem is bigger than that, Mr. Luck," Colin answered. "If the Russians are involved, they'll want to make sure there is no arrow pointing back to them. They won't risk a war with America. They'll take out the shooter and anyone else who could implicate them. They know you're involved, but they don't know anything about my black ass, and I aim to keep it that way. This is Cyanide's revolution—not mine. I'll set up the meeting as a final favor, and then I really am out. I won't hang next to you because you'll already be dead. The Russians are gonna merk your ass!"

****

"Okay research subject 104—we're back at Thomas Young's 1803 famous double-slit experiment. What was he trying to prove?"

Dr. David Jacobs was at Davis Franklin's Oakland Hills home with Alberta in the space that doubled as a classroom and lab. The specialist and his subject were not alone. An hour earlier, a film crew from the science department at UC Berkeley had come over to document the ape's exploration and grasp of quantum mechanics. The same group that had recorded her work in theoretic inorganic chemistry. Accustomed to the routine of taping, both the doctor and subject had fallen into practiced roles and patterns, displaying no evidence of the tension between them.

"Wave theory of light," she answered through the translator. "Young use diffraction experiment. Him project light through two slit in plate to show light on back screen. Young—him think light want to show on screen like two bright band. That mean light is particle. But light show as like dark and bright bands—both. Surprise. This mean interference is like wave in water—that mean light act like wave too. Bright band mean particle and dark band mean wave. That mean light is particle *and* wave at same time."

"A good attempt, research subject 104," Jacobs said, smiling toward the camera. "I think you understand the experiment, but you didn't do a good job at explaining it. In my opinion, you were trying to get it all out too fast. It came across as gobbledygook. You knew what you were saying, but I don't think anyone hearing you would."

Alberta pouted her lips, disappointed and embarrassed by the critique on camera.

"I think you can do better," Jacobs explained, shaking his head. "We'll try again tomorrow, and then we'll begin on the work of Max Planck."

The doctor glanced toward the crew.

"Any questions?"

The director was quick to respond.

"I have a question for Alberta," he said, cameras still rolling. "We've been doing this, this documentation, for what, three years? Obviously, Kendrick, who started this with us, isn't here. What's it been like to work with another doctor?"

"Kendrick is good doctor," she answered. "Kendrick is brilliant. Him is genius. Him not murder Jennifer. Him have no motive. Kendrick belong in house with Alberta."

"We hope Dr. Vesey returns soon, but what is it like working with Dr. Jacobs, the researcher who discovered you?"

"I, I think this would be an appropriate point to stop taping," Jacobs interrupted. "I've determined that this research subject has a few residual issues relating to some of Dr. Vesey's unconventional ideas and practices. I'm working to recondition…"

"Jacob lie!" Alberta interrupted emphatically. "Dr. Jacob—him chupid! Him fassyhole. Mi no like Dr. Jacob," she finished before crossing her arms.

Embarrassed, the doctor asked a favor of the director.

"We're still in an adjustment period. I would appreciate if you would edit that last comment out."

Fifteen minutes after the crew departed, Jacobs decided to clean and reload his 9-millimeter pistol in Alberta's presence.

"You think you're so smart, you stupid little monkey! Don't think I won't kill you, because I'd love to watch you die. I might get in a little trouble, but it'll pass. In the end, you're just an animal, an overrated pet. It won't matter. No one'll care."

"Alberta not scared. If Jacob kill Alberta, Jacob always be poor man, eating with bad teeth, talking with bad breath."

"What is 'chupid' anyway? Some jungle Jamaican way of saying stupid? Not very clever."

"Fassyhole!"

"And what does that mean? Are you trying to call me an 'asshole'?"

After Alberta signed to better explain the expression's true meaning in nuance, Jacobs was instantly insulted, remembering she signed that particular insult on tape.

"If I kill you," Jacob's sneered, "I'll get a sample of your DNA so I can clone you. It's no big deal. It's been done before…"

As the doctor neared, Alberta noticed the empty leather holster under his coat. He took a seat on the desk, staring directly into her eyes, tapping the pistol on his thigh.

"You know that's what you are, don't you? You're just a clone from a government experiment. You think it was just random that some stupid chimp was born with the brain of Einstein? I could show you the study. You were no accident and you're not special. You're just a clone from a failed project that was created in a petri dish. I was in on it. Stop thinking you're special. I can make a hundred of you—a thousand! That's why it wouldn't matter if I killed you."

"Jacob lie. Mi read record. Mi read report. Human cannot clone primate now. Impossible seventeen years before now. Spindle protein."

"I doctored the records when you were born. I doctored that report because the trials we performed weren't sanctioned in the U.S. The first legal nonhuman person my ass! You're just a lab experiment and nothing more."

Alberta studied his face, analyzing his expression for an outlier to betray his assertion.

"You talk about Jah Jah," he continued. "What a joke! You don't even have parents. The chimp you thought was your mother—she was just a troubled lab animal that needed something to cling to. You're a cooked-up experiment with no parents, which means you can't have a soul, which means your Jah Jah doesn't even recognize you. You're a lab freak, a genetic experiment!"

He pointed the pistol at her face.

"You pull a stunt like that again and I really will kill you. You got me?"

Alberta was focused on his coffee cup. In the time that he'd been in the house, the doctor averaged no less than four of five cups per day.

Him so arrogant, him never see it coming. She wanted to believe he was lying, but doubt and fear began to invade her thoughts and memories. *Jacob is a evil bastard!*

"Did you hear me, Alberta" Jacobs repeated. "I said, 'you got me'?"

"Mi get you, yes" she answered, her eyes intense, focused on the stained cup. "Mi get you good!"

****

Most of the entire country dreaded sunset on the second night, and most in the great melting pot experiment were surprised at the degree of unspoken resentment and hate that had bubbled to surface during what could only be called the country's first major race war. In keeping with America's ideals, the thought of a race war was inconceivable until the previous night. America had always been the land of liberty, freedom, opportunity, diversity, inclusion and higher aspirations, and yet it seemed that the very principles of that democracy were on trial before the world.

During the day, the President called the National Guard to arms, directing forces to shut down and secure the country's major cities. New York City was on lock-down, with subway trains and all public transportation parked at 5 p.m.—under the direction of the Secretary of Transportation. Businesses were shuttered as most nervous residents watched national news updates behind locked doors, while military forces rounded up the homeless, forcing them into overnight shelters around the city, provided by New York City Emergency Management. Other metropolitan areas adopted similar management strategies.

As darkness crept westward across the country, nearly every major city literally went dark, as the Secretary of Energy shut off streetlights and business lighting during nighttime hours. Military jeeps and armored vehicles patrolled business districts, major streets, parks and neighborhoods, enforcing the "6-to-6 curfew." From within their homes, Americans watched the President's 9 p.m. Oval Office "Appeal to America," during which he condemned the violence in harsh terms, invoking "America's better angels."

"We are up against perhaps the single most consequential challenge we have ever faced as a nation. Ironically, the greatest existential threat to America has come from within our borders, with Americans turning on

Americans. Yet our challenge is more profound than that. Our utmost threat does not come from within our borders even, but from within our own hearts as Americans. Never before has America's character been put to a greater test. This is not us. Over the next few days, we as Americans will reveal to the world and to history just who we are.

"When I look within my own heart, I see an opportunity for Americans to come together now as we never have before. I see an opportunity for America to live out the words of her creed, to reveal the great vision and aspirations of our Founding Fathers. More than a geographical territory on a map with borders, America is a vision rooted in our hearts and ideals, defying borders, and that vision is the light of the world."

The President's address was followed by news that the U.S. Senate and House of Representatives had convened emergency sessions to take up issues dealing with the National Defense Authorization Act (NDAA). In separate sessions, national legislators hotly debated the propriety and extent of the President's reach, with disputes about executive power and control on state and city levels. Those powers had rested with respective governors and mayors until the military leaders, under direction of the President, took over.

In the interest of "national security," state and local law enforcement agencies answered to military leaders, who followed executive orders and directives of the President and his Secretaries: the Secretary of Transportation had power over all forms of civilian transportation; the Secretary of Defense over all water resources; the Secretary of Agriculture over food resources and facilities, livestock, plant, health resources, and the domestic distribution of farm equipment; the Secretary of Energy over all forms of energy; and the Secretary of Commerce over material services and facilities, including construction materials.

Many state governors were appropriately concerned that while the major cities and related assets were locked down and secure, the conflicts and the battlegrounds on the second night of America's race war would be localized in smaller cities, towns and communities. Throughout the day, the mostly white militias from rural areas of Pennsylvania, Michigan, Montana, Idaho, Missouri, Texas, Mississippi, Alabama and other states readied themselves, strategically positioning troops at the outskirts of cities with minority populations that were vulnerable to domination and occupation.

Domestic terrorist organizations of all racial and political affiliations, operating in unprotected cities, took to the Internet to call members for assembly in preparation for battle. In the large cities, the National Guard's presence was formidable, intimidating and effective, but in American's small towns and communities, the Guard knew they were outnumbered and outgunned. It would take at least five days to assess the risks of engaging the various groups spread out across the country.

In the smaller cities, government drones were scrambled into the sky in numbers that would have been inconceivable two days earlier. In some places, residents glanced up at surreal skies, filled with swarms of unmanned aircraft in various sizes and shapes, buzzing about this way and that way, though never colliding. It was like the scene of an alien invasion in a sci-fi movie. At times, the skies seemed dark with them. They just kept coming! The media documented nine separate drone body and capability types features called "The Drone Wars." *Who knew the government possessed such awesome capabilities!*

The bold and foolish sharpshooters who took potshots at smaller drones were faced with larger, more powerful drones that descended from the heavens and that, from great distances, obliterated militia positions, taking out entire buildings in some cases, while killing and wounding dozens of people with every missile fired.

As the sun set across the United States, Americans knew that soon would begin the second night of reckoning for America's original and erstwhile unatoned-for sin: historical and institutional racism. Even as reality set in, the personalities in American media recognized the complicity of the press in the bloody race war that they, corporate America and establishment Republicans had wrought.

In an America where ratings trumped fairness, where profits trumped compassion, where the pursuit of "a lurid story" trumped the truth—in an America that feigned deafness to dog-whistles, race-baiting and cries of the oppressed—in the reality of that America, a few in the media sought redemption in a "collective conscience," and these few hoped to reestablish their rightful role in government as a watchdog rather than a lapdog.

But that night proved to be the bloodiest night in the history of America. While the National Guard had effectively protected the great cities, they were helpless to prevent small town carnage in the darkness. In states across the country, enemies engaged with automatic weapons, RPGs, mortars, with chemical and biological warfare and crude arms, right down to knives, bats and brass knuckles.

Most had no idea what they were fighting for, and yet they fought on anyway, to the death. They fought for what they believed, though not because they believed in anything but their burning anger. They fought for a distant, vague, ephemeral America that never truly existed—a false image of America held out to them by an elite class that pitied the fools in their minds, but felt no compassion for them in their hearts. *Poor slobs!*

The sun's rising across the country revealed thousands of slaughtered and butchered bodies, in fields, along the streets of towns, and clogging rivers and streams. Initial drone data estimated 40,000 Americans were dead, with skirmishes still being engaged in the western States. Two networks published graphic photos online and during their broadcasts to illustrate the horror and tragedy of so many lives lost.

That morning, the federal government deployed the Army and Special Forces to liberate small cities and towns in the South and Midwest, potentially pitting soldiers against family members and friends, creating wounds and scars that would never heal. As hundreds of millions across the world watched, a single conclusion emerged: Even if America survived, the country would never be the same.

Chapter 23

It was the winter of despair, it was the spring of hope, it was the season of darkness, it was the season of light, it was the epoch of incredulity, it was the epoch of belief, it was the age of foolishness, it was the age of wisdom, it was the worst of times, it was the best of times, yet all was and was not lost in a night of blood and gloom, in a day of growth and optimism. Not mice to bell the beast of battle, naïve children dared to speak, and childlike carried conscience forward—thus a turning point.

The populist, hate-mongering legions in the continental United States as well as their opponents, however, had lost all semblance of sanity and decency. As a visible sunline trailed eastward north-south across the country, the line illuminated the reality of America's first race war, though not its first war about race. The face of the sun shone on hatred and division, on intolerance and intransigence, on illogical anger and irrational fear. "*E pluribus unum*," or "Out of many, One," had transformed to "*Odium de multis*," or "Hatred of the multitude."

As the sun crept higher to expose the forced civility the larger cities, there was a sense of normalcy, except for the presence of the National Guard and U.S. Army troops throughout. As morning progressed, trains, buses and traffic went from non-existent to bustling, airports resumed flights, people returned to work, and stores reopened as populations cautiously edged forward, testing the fluctuating temperature of democracy. Despite Martial Law, there was a report of a bloody battle at Westlake Park, a plaza in downtown Seattle, just after sunrise.

Early on, individual states reported casualties coming in from the smaller cities: in Tempe, Arizona—798 dead, in Idyllwild, California—273 dead, in Newport, Rhode Island—1,073 dead, in Ketchum, Idaho—101 dead, in Gatlinburg, Tennessee—73 dead bodies, in Beaufort and Greenville, South Carolina—803 dead or missing, in Williamsburg, Virginia—1,500 casualties, and in Langley, Washington—500 persons, or half the city's population lost after a battle against an approaching militia. By noon, an estimated 18,000 had died in conflicts ranging from race wars to anti-government militias settling scores with local political leaders.

The idea of peaceful protest, set forth in the First Amendment of the United States Constitution, had yielded to chaos. Local government takeovers by defiant para-military leaders controlled over one hundred small towns across the country. By noon, a loose confederacy formed through various Internet social media sites, and a national leader was chosen: Everett Mann, a naturalized American entrepreneur and scientist who had made a fortune in genetic engineering.

For fifteen years, Mann was a popular voice in the re-emerging white populist movement, which played on fears of a "browner America," where white males and their families would be marginalized and excluded by the very powerful and wealthy nation that whites themselves had created. Mann warned that America was being taken over by liberal women, blacks, homosexuals and other minorities who were under the subtle control of wicked, rich, manipulative Jews.

Mann's idea for the confederacy of para-military-run small American cities was to first establish complete control, and that would mean herding up the blacks, Mexicans, Asians, Arabs, Muslims, homosexuals and Jews and placing them in "detainment facilities," where they could "do no harm." He insisted his proposal was for the minorities' own protection—from suspicion and acts of mayhem, warning that "the actions of a few bad apples might lead to justifiable punitive actions against their entire groups… to keep white Americans and their families safe."

In towns and cities where the militias held the overwhelming advantage in numbers and weapons, the round-up progressed quickly and orderly, though in many towns, the militias persecuted and injured minorities to instill fear and establish whites as the indisputable dominant group. It was a well-organized, coordinated effort, conceived long before the first shot in America's race war was fired.

In the cities and towns where the numbers of minorities and arms were more substantial, however, battle lines were drawn and skirmishes were fought flesh to bone, with over 80,000 civilians nationwide fleeing cities, displaced from their homes and businesses, helpless to confront either side in the escalating clashes. In some towns, the police department opposed the militias, fighting to protect their communities, while in other locales, law enforcement joined the confederacy, with elected or appointed officials sometimes acting as leaders.

The news personalities of mainstream media were aghast, interviewing U.S. Senators and Representatives, Supreme Court Justices, governors, state officials, political commentators, religious leaders and activists who were completely stunned, who were at a loss about how "something like this could have happened in America so unexpectedly." While most admitted that the possibility always existed, no one believed it would actually happen.

Most of the nation sat numb, staring blankly at television and cell phone screens in collective shock and denial about the redefinition of America occurring before their eyes. They watched footage of fellow Americans— black, white and varying shades of brown being forced at gunpoint into barbed-wire-topped confinement facilities. They watched scenes of mob violence and senseless shootings of unarmed men and women who seemed non-compliant, successful or ambitious. They watched frightened, weeping children being placed in separate pens, away from their parents, families divided. *It could not happen in America – not the America most Americans knew or respected!*

There were stories of war atrocities in Jasper, Indiana and Bloomington, Illinois, with heated, protracted conflicts in the suburbs of Detroit, where militias were met with equal force from black and Hispanic nationalist groups, resulting in tragic numbers of dead or wounded Americans. Although the largest cities in Ohio were locked down for the curfew, there were hotbeds of gunfire exchanges in enclaves across the state.

The federal government tried to disperse troops into some of the more contested cities, but government troops were confronting too many skirmishes, with too few troops deployed in conflict areas and too little time for an adequate response.

In a few "ideal areas," the military tested the efficacy of a new, "anti-collision" experimental AR-15 rifle drone, armed with .556 NATO bullets. A little more than forty-five inches across, the drone was capable of perimeter protection and long-distance sniping. This gas-operated drone rifle fired from a 10.5-inch barrel and carried a one hundred round drum and was operated from a tablet in a remote trailer with fifty operator bays.

It was fascinating for those watching on live television to see the scores of new military weapons on display that day, though horrific to realize they were being tested on Americans. Despite the advanced weaponry, the fighting was ubiquitous, so the thousands of drones had little overall effect. If there was a SNAFU in the declaration of Martial Law, it was evidenced by the collapse and capitulation of America's most valued small towns and cities. The central government had too little time to react.

Nations great and small watched in disbelief and horror the devolution of America, watched the detention of some of its citizens based on race, religion and political disposition as hate, guns and military-training trumped love, brotherhood. Instead, America's greatest sins—racism, injustice and inequality were forced onto the world stage for history to judge and condemn—especially in the conspicuous hesitation of America's most respected political leaders to condemn the actions of the militias. The great American experiment teetered on failure.

"How did we, as a nation, get to this place?" one prominent clergyman mused aloud on air. "How did no one see this coming, and if so, why didn't someone do something about it? Sweet Jesus! Lord have mercy on our punished souls!"

Notwithstanding, there were some instances of injustice and atrocities from minority-controlled small towns and cities where whites were rounded up and locked in fenced-off pens, "for their own protection." One black activist, when speaking on a cable news network, provided a notable distinction.

"What no one is understanding here," she opined, "is that this is America's second 'revolutionary' war, and not its first 'race' war, as many have mislabeled it. And yes, I will call it a 'war.' But I beg you to understand—this war is not about black versus white, or minorities versus white, or somehow Jews versus white. There is not a war against white people or minorities. That's a false narrative! I say those who oppose this so-called war today and going forward are the true firekeepers of America's soul. They are our last and only hope."

"But most Americans don't see it that way, Natsumi," the television news host differed. "In the minds of white nationalists, and black nationalists for that matter, it's all about race and hate and years of suppressed anger and resentment that has now boiled to the surface. In times of war, laws fall silent. Ideals fall silent."

"In the words of Dr. King," she answered, "we can no longer afford to worship the God of hate or bow before the altar of retaliation. Love among ordinary Americans is the only solution for the problems in this country."

****

Roland Hughes was surprised by the sudden announcement of the curfew, so when the street lights shut down at 5 p.m. on the first full night of fighting, and when major roads began closing, and when military vehicles with loudspeakers began rolling down the major thoroughfares issuing restriction warnings, Roland was stuck in the apartment of his domestic partner. Events of the day had moved so fast that he was caught unaware as the city of San Francisco began its shut-down.

Panicked, he called Alberta to make sure that she was safe, and then he called Jacobs, who was already headed to the Oakland Hills home. Roland asked the doctor if he could stay with Alberta until the morning. Jacobs complained, though he agreed to stay until 7 a.m. Careful not to breach protocol, Roland then called Davis Franklin, apprising him of the situation.

"I'm a bit disappointed in you, Roland," Franklin commented, seeming irritated. "We both promised Alberta that you would always be there when Jacobs was there. I'm worried something might happen. Alberta's set to provide official testimony in a legal proceeding. That's huge! Do you realize how far we'll be set back on our project if something happens to Alberta... or Jacobs for that matter? It's a recipe for disaster: he goads her and she hates him—no loss of love between them. Don't be surprised if get there to find one or both of them dead."

Roland Hughes was born 37 years earlier in the port city of Liverpool, England. His father was the assistant to the British High Commissioner to Tanzania, who was often gone for long stretches of time, so Roland grew up under the influence of his mother and six aunts—he, along with his five sisters. Thaddeus Hughes, Roland's father, usually returned to England in August during the summer, and he stayed for three months, returning to Africa in November, at the start of the annual wildebeest migration that began in Serengeti National Park.

When Roland was fourteen years old, he accompanied his father to Tanzania to witness the migration, and yet he found little fascination in the unthinking, primal beasts on the plains. The scene reminded him of some high schooler's CGI project. Next to his father's suite, however, the sixteen-year-old daughter of the High Commissioner had a chimpanzee as a pet, and Roland could not get enough of Aladdin, her remarkably intelligent simian companion. By the time Roland returned to England six months later, he was determined to spend his life working with chimps in behavioral studies, and interfacing humans with their closest nonhuman relatives.

While in college at the University of Edinburgh, Roland volunteered on projects with the Jane Goodall Institute, purposed to protect habitat for apes and other primates at Gombe Stream National Park, located in western Kigoma Region, Tanzania, ten miles north of Kigoma. Passionate about chimp conservation, he worked with the institution, which eventually took him to Durham, North Carolina, at Duke University.

When he heard about Alberta and her potential, Roland immediately submitted a curriculum vitae to Davis Franklin, offering himself as a volunteer assistant in "experimental primate research studies." Kendrick eventually became closer to Alberta due to their working relationship, but Roland had known her longer—from the first day that Franklin acquired as a baby. Roland did not brag about it, but he and another Franklin research assistant comprised the first family unit that Alberta experienced outside a lab facility, and they helped shape her world view.

Roland had been in a romantic relationship for eight years, but his partner never wanted to get married and later cheated. On the rebound for six months, Roland had finally found someone who understood him and his grueling work schedule. They had gone out to a sidewalk café on Market for lunch and back to the apartment when they realized the city was closing due to the fighting. They had ignored the initial warnings, assuming the commotion was just another demonstration or protest… until the military vehicles began to roll down the streets.

"Oh shit! I need to get back home!"

It was too late. The Bay Bridge was already closed and all freeway traffic was in the process of being cleared, beginning at the tolling station at

Interstate 80 in the East, to the 101 at Golden Gate Bridge in the North, and down to Redwood City on the 101 in the South.

It was surreal to see all activity in the city come to a halt at 6:30. The city of San Francisco took on the appearance of a deserted movie set, while in the East, Oakland was silent and still. The final flight to land for the day at San Jose International Airport, a Boeing 767, had arrived at 6:37 to find all but one terminal dark.

On the road at 6 a.m., Roland sped across the Bay Bridge toward Oakland in his silver Peugeot 307, all the while cursing drivers who were slow to respond and others who cut in front of him. Swerving in and out of lanes, he finally caught a little daylight in traffic just before merging onto the 580 in Albany near the Hoffman Split. The rest was easy. Fit and athletic in his youth, Roland had begun putting on five or so pounds a year since his early thirties. At five-feet-ten-inches tall, he weighed 248 pounds, though he maintained a new, sugar-free, paleo diet regiment since the week he began dating again.

He sighed as he saw that Dr. Jacobs' car was in the driveway and the house was still standing—without the presence of police, an ambulance or "crime scene" tape! Rushing to the door, he slipped his key into the lock and shoved the door open, calling as he entered.

"Dr. Jacobs? Dr. Jacobs, are you there?"

Hearing no response, he panicked, fearing the worst. He rushed toward the library.

"Dr. Jacobs! I need you to respond. Are you okay?"

He immediately went to Alberta's room and tried to enter, but the door was locked.

"Are you in there, Alberta? Where is Dr. Jacobs?" No answer. *Davis Franklin is going to be absolutely livid!* he thought. "Alberta! Please tell me where Dr. Jacobs is!" Still no answer.

Were they both dead? Numb from panic, he rushed through the large home, slamming doors open, checking closets and other places were Alberta might have hidden the body.

"Alberta! Oh no you didn't! Please tell me you didn't kill him!"

Then Roland saw a shoe—seemingly attached to an inert body, just on the other side of the couch. He played the *Look! – Don't Look!* game for a few seconds, but he realized he had to know—for better or for worse… for Alberta, and all her potential.

Rounding the couch, he saw the body sprawled on the floor, on its side—in something that resembled a fetal position. After the initial shock passed, Roland began to notice several irregularities. First, there were no signs of a struggle. The half-filled coffee cup and saucer rested undisturbed on a nearby table. If Alberta had attacked the doctor, there would have been a lamp or table knocked over, and there would have been… blood, since chimps are notorious biters. No blood, no sign of a struggle… and the doctor was still breathing!

But there was something else. As Roland crept closer, he cringed, embarrassed. The doctor's trousers and boxer briefs were down around his ankles so that his hairy legs were bare. Inside the doctor's jacket, Roland noticed the gun holster, but it was empty. As he grabbed Jacob's wrist to take a pulse, Roland glanced at the man's genitals, fully-exposed, again noticing something odd: they were still attached and they seemed to be sprinkled with salt and pepper.

If the salt and pepper was the work of Alberta, she was obviously making a statement—that she could have bitten off the doctor's balls if she had wanted… *and relieved him of his shriveled penis at the same time.* Yet there was something else odd. There was what seemed to be a short stick protruding from the back—from the doctor's anus.

"For the love of God, Alberta! What did you do? Why?" he called toward her room.

Jacobs still lay unconscious, so after considering two unpleasant options, Roland thought it best to remove the stick while Jacobs was asleep to spare the doctor the pain and embarrassment. Kneeling beside the doctor, he reached down, tugging at the stick, but it would not budge. Next, Roland found a pair of pliers in the garage and returned, hoping Jacobs would remain asleep throughout the procedure.

The stick was firmly lodged and would not move with the first few tugs—probably because it was buried so deep that only one-half inch was exposed. The other problem involved Jacob's rectal response. On one occasion, Roland thought the stick was coming out until Jacob's sphincter involuntarily contracted to reclaim it. Yet something relented as Roland thought to give up and call 9-1-1. There was slight movement, and past a certain point, the sphincter did the rest of the ejection work.

"For the love of God, Alberta!"

Much to Roland's surprise, it wasn't a stick at all—and then he realized why he had such difficulty removing it. Rather than lodging a stick in there, Alberta had apparently shoved a still-green plantain up the doctor's rectum— *a still-green plantain that measured at least ten inches.*

****

Draco returned to Phoenix to monitor the condition of fellow Loverboy and brother-in-law D'Artagnan Williams. His sister, Elizabeth Williams, had come with her children from Philadelphia. Aramis, Draco's 23-year-old favorite nephew, was still dressed in the black slacks and blue button-up shirt as part of the Philadelphia police department uniform.

Although D'Artagnan's condition had stabilized over the last 24 hours, his condition was still critical. The family visited him briefly in the recovery room after the second of two surgeries required to address the gunshot injuries. One of his kidneys, wounded beyond repair, had to be removed, while his right lung had partially collapsed due to the trauma from one of the gunshot wounds. Two of his ribs had fractured on impact, allowing air to leak into the pleural space, creating crushing pressure on the lung. By doctor's orders, the visit was brief.

"I have to go back tomorrow, Uncle Johnnie," Aramis said, "because they're telling me things are going to get worse in Philly. I don't see how. When I left the department yesterday, the Army was there, and we had some arrogant colonel from California calling all the shots."

"It's worse than your dad and I ever imagined," Draco answered, "It's hard to imagine the sheer number of people already dead. It's so bad they stopped showin the bodies on the news."

"But you can still see them on the Internet," Aramis explained. "Before I came to the hospital, I watched a news story that said we're on pace to have the bloodiest three days in any modern country's history. Who could ever imagine it? Americans killing Americans… in a war!"

Johnnie and Aramis looked up at the television screen in the cafeteria at alternating shots of angry leaders from both sides, vowing retaliation at sundown.

"We're fightin for the soul of America here, and we don't care about dyin. We'll fight tooth and nail, blood and bone—right down to our last man. We ain't givin up! Let's make America right again by makin America white again!"

"Let em bring it," the opposing leader sneered. "We ain't scurred. We been fighin this war for over four hundred years, so we ready. We been dyin everday since we got here, so we know about dyin. But now is a time ta kill, and today, we gonna let the other side get a long taste of dyin. As they say in Narleans—*Bon Appetit!*"

The morgues and funeral homes in small America were overwhelmed by the number of bodies showing up at hospitals, sparking fears of local disease epidemics as the corpses began to decompose. Some cities decided to burn the bodies, while others, concerned about last rites and respect for the dead, commandeered refrigeration food storage facilities, first freezing and then stacking the bodies to best utilize space. The federal government sent refrigerated storage trucks to communities that requested them.

Yet there was a constant supply of dead bodies coming in from all quarters. The existing hospitals, despite setting up triage stations prior to accepting patients, were poorly-equipped to handle the sudden influx of critical patients.

The Federal Emergency Management Agency, or FEMA, commandeered large retail stores to be used as shelters and set up tent hospitals next to overwhelmed medical facilities and in other crucial locations to lessen the demand. After an Internet video from a shelter went viral, rumors spread quickly across the country, suggesting policies at the FEMA facilities encouraged "restrictive intervention," which favored "letting nature take its course," rather than saving lives.

"What's happened to this country?" Aramis asked. "This is all straight out of a nightmare. How did we allow this? Where did we go wrong?"

"The people out there dyin don't have a clue, Nephew," Draco answered. "The American people got played. They're just pawns, shills—too ignorant to know any better—dumbshits with Second Amendment rights! Just hear me: whenever you've got something erupting on a scale like this, you'd better believe there's some powerful person or people in the background, pulling the strings. This situation didn't just happen. It was engineered, scripted—right down to the news stories we're watching."

"That's what the Loverboy Elites are trying to do?" Aramis interrupted. "You're trying to get to the person or group behind it?"

"That's what we're trying to do."

"Then I want to be an Elite, Uncle," Aramis insisted, "I don't care what happens to me. I'm ready to die to save this country, because if this continues, there won't be a country left."

"D'Artagnan was… or is, an Elite," Draco countered. "But being an Elite is more than being a soldier, ready to die. It's understanding the history of this un-American crusade and the dangerous people behind it. Besides, your mother is my sister. I don't know if she'll ever forgive me for getting your father involved. It's out of the question with you. Just be a shoelace/lipstick Loverboy for now. We're going to need you out there, ready to go, for when the final battle begins."

The news broadcast ended on an unexpected note, one that seemed to gain resonance and inspire hope in many across the country. The story played out in Quitman County, Mississippi, when a para-military force from Oxford, 5,000 strong, began to march the fifty-mile distance to claim the communities of Crenshaw, Sledge, Clarksdale and neighboring towns.

Notably, the town of Crenshaw, numbering 868 persons, was 71% black. The town of Sledge, numbering 529 persons, was 75% black, and the town of Clarksdale, numbering 17,900, was 68% black. Oxford, on the other hand, numbered 18,000, and was 72% white. Yet the militia pulled not only from Oxford, but from surrounding, mostly-white areas.

When news began to spread that the militia was marching on Quitman County with the intention to subjugate blacks and other minorities and to establish territorial detention facilities, city leaders and townspersons quickly came together to decide a response. They would organize a resistance: the "Mili-Minute Men and Women of Quitman County," comprised mostly of blacks and whites, with two dozen or so others, including Native Americans, Asians and Latinos.

As the 5,000-men-strong Oxford militia along Mississippi 315 approached Sledge, the nearest and least populated of the three towns, they were surprised by the number in the makeshift territorial army assembled two miles outside the municipality—7,000 strong, armed and ready for battle, with reinforcements arriving from the towns of Falcon, Marks, Lambert and Crowder. The television cameras arrived as the two groups set their positions, roughly one mile apart from each other.

The Oxford contingent had planned to rout Sledge, Crenshaw and the smaller towns, picking up new white recruits while instilling fear in the countryside. Leaders expected Clarksdale to capitulate in the face of fear and overwhelming numbers. In Clarksdale, there were at least 12,000 blacks, so it would take the entire militia, the momentum of the smaller victories and "the good white people" of Clarksdale to corral the minorities in that town and put them behind fences.

Faced with insurmountable numbers against them, the Oxford group mounted a half-hearted offensive and were repelled soundly, suffering heavy casualties. Then the Mili-Minute Men and Women launched a fierce attack, driving the invaders to retreat so that many were caught fleeing in fear on national television coverage, a humiliating defeat.

Johnnie Draco and Aramis Williams watched with a hopeful nation the spectacle of a community of ordinary Americans triumphing over hate. The Mili-Minute Men and Women of Quitman County were nearly evenly split, black and white, with women making up a quarter of the volunteers. Yet they provided an early blueprint and insight for success in the disquieting conflict: Unity Trumps Hate.

In interviews, jubilant leaders of the group were quick to advocate their strategy and recommend it to other small communities around the country, and yet the transfixed world who watched remembered best the words two children spoke.

"Some people are trying to call what's happening a race war, but that's a lie," a ten-year-old girl told a reporter, "a lie that some bad people wanna spread. My parents came from Clarksdale ta fight because they believe in America. We're Skittles. Look at us—all the different colors making America beautiful and great."

"My daddy's white and ma mamma's black," a twelve-year-old boy from Crenshaw explained. "I got black cousins and white cousins, I got black grandparents and white grandparents, I got white friends and black friends.

How is it we let anyone can tell us we have to hate each other and fight each other and lock each other up... and kill each other?"

"I say this to all the grown-ups who are tryin ta make up this war," the ten-year-old continued, "if we kids was doin the same thing—hatin and fightin and callin names—we'd get a beatin with a hickory switch. If we know betta, how come so many grown-ups don't get it?"

Chapter 24

"What was the last thing you remember?" Roland asked. "Do you remember anything at all?"

Jacobs was slouched on the couch, his pants pulled back up and glasses returned to his face. He seemed disoriented and uncomfortable.

"I don't know. I can't remember anything. I was sitting here, I think, going over my notes on my iPad—waitaminute, where's my iPad?"

"I didn't see an iPad when I came in," Roland answered. "What happened?"

"I told you I don't remember," Jacobs responded, irritated. "I think I was here going over my notes, and the next thing I remember, you were waking me up. I must have passed out."

"I don't know how to tell you this," Roland said, "but when I came in and found you, you weren't sitting in the spot where you are now. You were on the floor."

"On the floor?"

"Yes… and your pants were down, around your ankles."

"Oh my God!" the doctor exclaimed. "What happened?"

"I have no idea. That's why I'm asking you. Now either you pulled your pants down or someone else pulled them down."

"All I remember is I was sitting here…"

"Uh, there's more in case you don't already know," Roland continued.

"What?"

"Well, it's not an easy thing to say, so I'll just say it: when I found you, you had this plantain inserted in your rectum."

The doctor's eyes bulged at the sheer size of the fruit that Roland displayed.

"Again, I'm figuring either you did it, or some other person did it."

"I didn't do that!" Jacobs protested, cringing from newly-realized pain. "I would never do that!"

"I see you're feeling it now. It'll definitely feel worse the next time you go to the crapper, believe me."

"I don't know what happened…" the doctor mumbled.

"I would say most likely you were drugged, maybe something in your coffee?"

"Alberta!" the doctor snapped. His hand went to the holster for his weapon. "My gun! It's gone! She took it!"

"What are you doing with a gun?" Roland asked. "That's a hard, fast rule with Davis Franklin. Absolutely no guns in the house. You knew that!"

"Well, with all the race wars and fighting going on out there," Jacobs stammered, "I thought I might need protection. I don't usually carry it. I thought I left it in the car, actually."

"Then maybe that's what you did. I can't imagine why Alberta would ever want to take a gun from you. You probably left it in the car."

"Yeah, I think I did," Jacobs said, cringing as he tried to stand. His buttocks tightened, sensing the soreness deep within his rectum. "But my iPad. It was here. I'm sure Alberta took my iPad… and my phone. I need those back."

"Let me go get her," Roland sighed.

With Roland gone, Jacobs eyes scanned the periphery, stopping at the half-full coffee cup. Thinking, he remembered making the coffee. It was his third cup, so after placing it on the table, he went to the bathroom to "drain the vein." Only then he remembered that third cup of coffee having a somewhat "salty taste." At the time, he imagined his gums were bleeding, since he did not spend the night at home and had not brushed his teeth earlier.

He picked up the coffee cup, sniffing it, daring not to drink again. *It had to be the coffee! Alberta put something in the coffee!* She must have drugged him when he was in the bathroom. He adjusted his pants around his waist, wondering about the salt and pepper containers next to the coffee cup. And then he re-examined the large, still-green plantain. *Oh, my God!*

"Alberta's on her way," Roland called out as he entered the room. "We'll figure this out."

After about two minutes, Alberta ambled into the room, defiant to the doctor, even smiling and pouting her lips. Seated at a dining room chair, she crossed her arms and blew him a kiss.

"Save it, Alberta," Jacobs seethed. "What did you do with my iPad?"

"Mi download all him data," she signed. "Email, message, document on mi cloud. Same for phone. Mi use Jacob fingerprint for him phone. When mi done, mi put iPad, phone in Jacob car."

Jacobs appealed to Roland.

"That's illegal! It's an invasion of my privacy and that of the university. Some of that information is protected by intellectual property rights. Do you have the codes to her cloud? I need all that information erased."

"What are you so worried about?" Roland smirked. "She's just an animal. What could she possibly do with downloaded data?"

"She knows what she's doing!" Jacobs sneered, his eyes squinting. "I need access to her computer now!"

"Sorry," Roland shrugged. "She has her own username and password. It's her cloud. We could ask her to erase your information."

"I'll get a court order if I have to," Jacobs warned. "I want it erased immediately!" He glared at Alberta. "You'll be very sorry if you don't."

Alberta made a face and barked before reaching for the plantain, sniffing it and pretending to pass out, falling off the chair.

"I don't think you'll be able to get a judge to issue an order with all this craziness going on," Roland sighed, "let alone get someone to enforce it. Alberta, why did you take Dr. Jacobs' devices?"

"Dr. Jacob lie. Him come in this house before him work for Davis Franklin. Him know what is in drawer and cabinet in kitchen. Him know what is in drawer in mi room. Him come before, but him lie."

"Have you ever been in this house before that first day I brought you here?" Roland asked.

"Of course not!" Jacobs answered. "This is ridiculous! Call Davis Franklin. I'm sure he can order her to do it."

"This is odd. Why would she say you've been here before?"

"I have no idea why she'd say that. She's losing it!"

"Him have picture of mi room. Date on picture before him come," she signed.

"That's not true," Jacobs protested. "She probably looked at something I downloaded and had on my device that and mixed up the date, but no, I was never here before."

"Alberta does not lie because she cannot conceive of the concept," Roland remarked. "For example, Alberta, why did you sprinkle salt and pepper on Dr. Jacobs genitals?"

"Mi want him to know mi could eat him ball if mi want, but him ball is too small, small like peanut. Jacob think him is smart boss, but him chupid fassyhole."

"Why did you stick that plantain in Dr. Jacobs' arsehole, Alberta?" Roland asked. "Why did you do that?"

"Why mi rape Jacob?"

"Yes, I guess you could call it that. Why did you rape Dr. Jacobs?"

"Mi rape him because him rape mi. Mi pregnant because him rape mi."

"I've had about enough of you, you damn ape!" Jacob screamed, lunging and kicking at Alberta, who leaned to one side, slapping his foot away.

"Doctor have test to prove."

"If that weren't so disgusting, it would be laughable," Jacobs sneered. "I can't even respond to something so absurd."

"What do you mean he raped you, Alberta?" Roland asked, confused. "How is it possible you could be pregnant? What test?"

"On-line. Mi buy nonhuman primate pregnancy test kit on-line. Mi pregnant."

"That's impossible!" Roland exclaimed. "How could you possibly be pregnant? You haven't been mated. What, are you going to have a baby Jesus chimp? Or are you saying you're going to have Dr. Jacobs' baby?"

"Disgusting!" Jacobs groaned.

"Mi remember. Something not right in Dr. Little office last time we go. Dr. Little not there for check-up. Other doctor, Dr. Linden—him is there.

Mi remember, Dr. Linden do test on mi pum-pum. Him put something in mi pum-pum. Dr. Linden put man-juice in mi pum-pum and now mi pregnant. Man-juice from chimp. Mi find Jacob letter to Dr. Linden in Jacob email."

"Is that true?" Roland asked, glaring at Jacobs in disbelief. "If she's pregnant, are you responsible? I'll have to tell Davis Franklin about this."

"No, she's just making that stuff up," Jacobs replied. "I'll admit, I underestimated her EQ, but based on today, I'm certain she's capable of incredible manipulation and mischief. I think she's a danger to people, and she should never have access to a computer and Internet and credit cards after today. I'll tell Franklin!"

"But she doesn't lie. If she says she's pregnant, then she's pregnant."

"If she's even capable of reading a pregnancy test! She obviously read it wrong. It happens, even with humans. She's unfamiliar! She's guessing! Don't bother Franklin with something that isn't true. We'll order another test."

"Oh come on, David," Roland sighed, "we both know there won't be any UPS or any other deliveries for at least the next few weeks with this civil war going on out there, and when deliveries start up again, they'll be so backlogged. It'll take months."

"Maybe I can find one at UCD. Let me at least try to do that. Don't go to Franklin with this. Let me prove myself right. If that doctor did something to make her pregnant, I had nothing to do with it."

"Well okay," Roland nodded, "if you can find a nonhuman primate pregnancy test over at UCD, we'll retest her within the next few days. If not, I have to go to Franklin."

Jacobs spoke directly to Alberta.

"For my own health concerns, you little bitch, what did you use to knock me out?"

"GHB—date rape drug. Mi got on-line. Too easy, for thirty-five-dollar. If you mash ants, you fine him guts."

"Roland said you can't lie. Did you see my gun?"

"Yes, mi see gun. Mi see gun in car and on beach. Jacob shoot gun at melon, call it Alberta head. Him point gun at mi head. That is gun? Yes, Alberta see gun."

****

"Sergeant Draco?"
Draco stood, expecting the worst.
"Yes?"
"He's stabilized and capable of answering a few questions now."
"Thank you."
"Are you going to call in the feds?" the doctor asked.
"That depends on what he tells us."

Door closed, Draco and McCarthy approached the patient, who was handcuffed to a post. Taras, a Crimean translator, stood next to the bed, gripping the patient's hand.

"Hello Sergei," Draco began. "We are not with the American government. If you help us, we will see that you get back to the Ukraine and your family."

Taras took great care to share the content and sentiment of Draco's statement. Sergei answered through the translator.

"I shot police and people. Why will you help me?" Taras translated.

"Because you're an agent, not an actor. We're more interested in the American you're working with."

"My father is dead. My family is poor. I work for man in Ukraine, not an American."

"Then the many you work for works for American. If we give you to the American FBI, you will never go back to Crimea, and whoever you work for—the American CIA will kill him right after they kill you. If you wanna die and you want your family to die—fine. But if you wanna live and see your family, you'll need to call your friend. We have a secured, untraceable line. I need an answer now."

The patient and translator exchanged words that seemed to be an argument, and then Taras answered.

"He says he knows the laws of America. He wants to talk to a lawyer."

"Tell him that's not an option. It's either us or federal government agents. They're in on it, so they'll just kill you and your family to cover their asses. Your government will help your family, because they're in on it too. Talk to us, help us catch one bad American, and you go home, to whatever pay they promised you. You can tell them you were injured and had to lay low for a while. I just need a confirmed name."

"I don't have a name," Sergei answered.

"Chances are this is an inside deal. We're sure there aren't many players involved. They sent only two of you, right—two pros who'd get things started and get out? I don't think there's direct KGB involvement and whoever's behind this had tacit Kremlin authorization. I don't care about that. I just want the name of the American involved. We can leave Crimea and Russia out of it. We need the American."

After a lengthy exchange between Sergei and the translator, Taras turned back to Draco and McCarthy.

"He says he has a boss who might know the name of the American. Maybe his boss will tell him, maybe he won't. He says his boss will not answer on an American secure line. He says he needs his phone."

****

"I'm glad you changed your mind and came to meet me, Colin," Justin Luck said with a smile. "Some of our investments have gone well, and some have not gone well, and though you say you don't care about it—you'll be richer than you ever imagined. This race war will pay our families dividends for the next two decades—much longer than I'll live."

Colin stared at his collaborator through dark glasses.

"I'm concerned about what hasn't gone well. Our goals were different in this business. Success for you isn't necessarily success for me."

"What's not gone well? The Loverboys have one of the Russians. It's a long shot, but if he talks, we'll have no protection—not from the Ukrainians, the Russians or my friends in the government."

"What does that mean?"

"It means we'll be exposed. We'll have targets on our backs. That means either prosecution or assassination—most likely assassination."

"Why me?" Colin asked. "I had nothing to do with the Russians. Russians don't even do business with niggas."

"I used your name—Colin Stein-Whitaker, as the actor on our side."

"You did what?"

"Couldn't afford to have too many people involved," Luck answered. "Your name doesn't sound black, and my name is too well-known. Everyone's heard of Cyanide, but no one knew who Colin Stein-Whitaker was, at least until now. I figured it would fly under the radar."

"Are you outa your mind? I don't believe this!"

"Believe it. The guy they got is some Sergei Rahimkulov. I know because now I've got someone inside the Loverboys."

"I'm done with you. I didn't agree to any of it. I'm a rap producer and an American revolutionary. I didn't sign on for any of this James Bond spy shit!"

"Like it or not, you're in it up to your eyeballs," Luck said, nodding his head. "The good news is those Loverboy Elites don't want to turn this shooter over to the FBI, because they know I have friends over there. The Loverboys don't know who the rest of my friends are, but they know me, and they'll soon know you. They want to use Sergei to connect us to a few treasonous events that have happened across the country over the last eighteen months."

"Us? Eighteen months? We've been workin together only six!"

"You've known me your whole life, Colin. Stop trying to worm your way out of it. It's you and me. You know—get richer, or die tryin."

"Your shit is pollutin my shit! What has this shooter told em?"

"Nothing yet. That's where you come in. I already told you the good news. Now I'm going to tell you the bad news."

"What?"

"I'm going to get you in there, but you're going to have to cut off your dreads and cover your tattoos. You're going to have to look like a cop. It's risky, but it's our only hope."

"Oh, hell no!"

"We don't have a choice."

"You better find another choice. I go in there and get killed—and you blame all this shit on me. That ain't happenin. Send one of your people. You said you had someone in the Loverboys."

"We can't afford to have anyone else directly involved. Increases our liability. Maybe we could send one of the ghosts."

"We? No. Figure something else out, Luck. I ain't gonna die to save your ass, and my ghosts are my ghosts."

"We're out of options."

"Send your son in there—send Luck Jr. He's white. He'll arouse less suspicion than me."

"My son knows nothing about this," Luck grumbled, his voice quivering. "He's my future. I can't afford to have him involved in any of this."

"Oh come on, man! I ain't stupid. He knows everything you do. He's running your businesses. He stands to lose in this just like you and me."

"Besides, my son's too recognizable."

"Luck Jr.? If I said he wasn't the most generic-lookin white boy I ever seen in my life, I'd be lyin. He's a clone of every preppy white boy on every college campus in America. I've seen him plenty times, but if someone stuck him in a line-up with a bunch of other typical-lookin college white boys, I swear I wouldn't be able to pick him out."

"My son isn't a killer."

"Oh come on! He's all over the Internet, shootin lions, rhino, leopards and even elephants in Africa. I don't know when I ever killed any of those. He's a killer all right. He just needs to add 'Russian' to his list."

"My son is not going to be involved. You are."

"Oh yeah?" Colin responded, smirking. "It's like you said earlier, Luck—you're out of options."

Luck's face became beet-red.

"You know by now, Colin, of course, that there were two Russian pros who came over here for the job. Two—you understand? The Loverboys got one of them, but the second guy hasn't left the country yet"

"Oh, so you're tellin me that if I don't go in there and get myself killed for you, you're gonna send this other Russian pro after me? I'll take my chances on that one. I'll go to my underground kingdom, hang in places where a Russian'll stand out like a sore thumb."

"The other pro is in Connecticut, Colin," Luck said, his voice trailing off. "Now I know you and your old man have never gotten along, but your mother is another story…"

"Are you threatenin my mother?" Colin responded, anger breaking in his voice, murder in his eyes. "Come again with that if you're bold."

"You heard me, Colin. You have a choice to make."

"You don't know me," Colin said, standing. "Just like the arrogant, patronizing asshole you are, Luck—you underestimated me. You thought I was gonna go on a suicide mission for you? Well how about this? If I had my gun right now, I'd shoot you in your withered old face, right between your beady eyes, and take a shit on your mouth. You wanna know my choice? I'm comin after your precious son. First, I'm gonna kill that bitch punk-nigga, and then I'm comin after your sorry ass!"

****

Event coordination between over 30 major U.S. cities would have been daunting even without restrictions imposed by the Army, to which organizers complied. The permit process stalled early on, yet owing to the stalwart efforts by the OLM Steering Committee and volunteers, all but three permits were approved. Corporate sponsors of the organization rented auditorium facilities, PA systems and large television screens, and covered security costs. Correspondingly, the major networks and cable affiliates patched in markets so that the event was scheduled to go out to over 100 million viewers.

Our Lives Matter's "Communities Across America" project was a direct affront to alt-right groups across America who sought to consolidate territories in small America, an effort to find common ground between the country's coastal or aqua-based large cites, which were largely liberal and Democrat, contrasted with the rural, agri-based townships and communities on wells and government-apportioned water, which were conservative and Republican.

Communities Across America focused on the reality that the differences in America had less to do with race and more to do with community, geography and economics. Front and center were the simple folks in the community of Quitman County, Mississippi, who stood up to a numerous, well-armed, organized militia from Oxford. Their story highlighted blacks, whites and others, standing together against forces that were un-American in their means and ends.

In Quitman County, community trumped hate, unity trumped fear and cynicism and faith in fellowman trumped racial division and animosity. On that afternoon, the nation came together in large cities and small towns, in rural areas and neglected enclaves—a nation reflecting the diversity of "the huddled masses" and the resilience of their roots, reflecting "the wretched refuse" and the strength of common bonds, reflecting "the homeless and tempest-tossed," and the sheer power of human will.

From the early morning, people streamed into the cities and towns, holding hands, embracing, chanting words of hope and unity. The images of black, white, Latino, Asian, Native, Jew, Muslim, wealthy and impoverished—singing together, beaming, smiling in the wake of the bloodiest, most horrifying night in America's history, was a stark contrast to the thousands of bodies sprawled on smoldering fields in the morning and the dirty, gore-smeared, weeping faces of old men, women and children, suffering behind barbed-wire fences in a gray backdrop.

The auditoriums filled quickly, and the parking lots and lawns around them bustled with activity beneath huge screens that mirrored similar gatherings in other large cities—a media link that united tens of millions on the ground and over a hundred million across the globe. For all the despair and disillusionment resulting from America's second race war, Communities Across America represented a ray of hope, a glimpse of the lamp beside the golden door.

Beginning in Atlanta, a procession of speakers, some eloquent, some plain, shared compassionate and inspirational words on screens across the country in synchrony. A speaker from Seattle followed, telling a touching story about a group of local high schoolers in rural Washington who refused to allow the grown-ups, in many cases their own parents, to lock up their minority friends and families. A speaker from Denver described one community's blood-drive that saved over one hundred lives.

In some areas, local alt-right militias considered firebombing or otherwise interrupting the OLM protest to the civil war, but in most places, the numbers were overwhelming, while security measures in others provided little opportunity for an offensive.

A speaker from Jackson, Mississippi, described how the last two days had re-opened festered-over, long-forgotten wounds and memories of slavery, while Elena Ginsburg, the daughter of a Holocaust survivor read from the diary of her mother, whose family was incarcerated at Buchenwald. She wept, expressing a final sentiment.

"Never again we all said, but here we are!"

Every speech and reading presented that afternoon contained an appeal toward hope and our better angels. In San Francisco, Natsumi Mitchell introduced the final speaker, a person she had admired for as long as she could remember, who embodied the best qualities of a modern progressive, a champion of disadvantaged women and a leader in the fight for gender equality in all aspects of life. Perceiving the history of the moment, she felt humbled as she introduced her famous aunt.

"It is my privilege and honor to introduce a woman who has been more than a leader, but one of the foundations of the San Francisco community, a deputy district attorney, the leader of a women's empowerment movement and a presidential appointee, but to me, she's my aunt and mentor. Please welcome Destiny Mitchell, U.S. Senator from the great and glorious state of California."

"Where do we go from here?" Destiny said in oratory. "What will we do, knowing that tonight, as the sun sets on America, there will be more bloodshed. Thousands of Americans will die, sacrificed upon the blood-stained altar of hate and division. Many thousands more will suffer the loss of liberty. They will be herded like cattle, confined in the equivalent of concentration camps. They will be deprived of their possessions, their children and, in many cases, their very lives."

The dais was situated at the center of Yerba Buena Gardens, at the cultural center of San Francisco, where an estimated two million persons had traveled or assembled to share in the peaceful nationwide protest. Aerial footage showed a landscape covered with people and large screens for fifteen blocks beyond the park. Senator Destiny Mitchell, a city favorite daughter, paused to consider the potential impact of the day.

"For so many of us, it was inconceivable that America could ever again succumb to a war based on race, but it's happened. What can we as ordinary citizens do? Do we wait for the President to solve this? Do we wait for Congress to do it? Is it up to the Army to get it done? No. It's no one else's problem to solve. The greatest military force on earth is feeble compared to power and strength of the American people. The character of America is embodied by citizens, not politicians. It is now up to the American people to do what no one else can.

"All we have to say is 'no. No More!' It seems too easy, but you have the power to act today. If individuals are being illegally detained in your communities, you must stand up against it, tonight and tomorrow and from now on. You must oppose injustice, even if it means sacrificing your personal comfort and safety. You must make perpetrators accountable. If individuals are being injured or killed in your communities and no else has the courage or numbers to oppose those actions, you must document it, on your phones or whatever devices you might have. Record faces, words, actions, license plate numbers. Document these crimes!"

Destiny held up her smart phone.

"I've got my camera. I'll be out there tonight. OLM has created YouTube channels for every state where videos can be anonymously uploaded. The enemies of America must know that they will have to answer for their actions, that there will be a record for later. If you don't have a cell phone with a camera, go out and get one before the curfew begins. Tonight, we prove that our Great American Experiment is the best model for all the worlds societies and governments—the best for humanity!"

Chapter 25

"Sergei," the doctor pronounced carefully, "this is Sergeant Draco. He is not with the American FBI or CIA, but he wants to talk to you again."

Sergei glanced up at Draco as Taras the translator refreshed his memory about details from their previous discussion. Straining from the pain of the gunshot wound to his abdomen, Sergei mumbled a reply in Crimean.

"He says he does not know about any American. He does not believe you are not the American government."

"Tell him I'm just a cop who loves my country and I am after an American traitor. Tell him I don't care what he's done. If he helps me identify this traitor, he can go home to his family."

"He says how does he know this isn't set-up," Taras offered.

"I can't prove it to him. He is going to have to trust me. All I want is the American. If I were with the U.S. government, I'd be trying to blame the Russians."

"He doesn't know the American," Taras insisted. "He was following orders from his boss."

"I'm sure his boss knows who the American is. Tell him we don't want his boss either. We want any documentation that can prove the American's involvement. We'll leave his boss out of it."

After a lengthy exchange lasting over two minutes, the translator turned back to Draco.

"He says if you can really help him go home, he will help you. He has heard of an American, but the American does not talk to his boss. The American has talked to his boss's boss. He says he has a favorite nephew who works for some Fancy Bear group. He says maybe this nephew can find something out about the American for you. His boss won't talk to you."

"Then can we talk to the nephew?" Draco asked.

"His nephew won't take a phone call," the translator answered, "but Sergei can send him an urgent message. He asks, if he can get this information for you, you will let him go?"

"Tell him he can stay until he's healthy enough, and then he can slip quietly out the country. If he needs money for travel, we'll take care of it."

Minutes later, Sergei and the translator send off a message to the nephew, who asked his uncle to "stand-by."

Fatigued and in agony after the stress involved in the exchange, Sergei self-administered another dose of morphine and drifted off to sleep.

"Do you think there really is a nephew?" Draco asked.

"Oh yes," Taras answered. "I've heard about this group he works for. If anyone can find something, the nephew can."

"I thought for sure Sergei wouldn't talk to me. I didn't seem he would at first. What made him change his mind and decide to trust me?"

"He didn't change his mind, and he doesn't trust you," Taras answered. "He trusts me. My grandparents and his grandparents grew up in the same village near Staryi Krym in Crimea. We share some of the same family. We're distant cousins."

****

Natsumi had already reached her car when she recognized the figure of the man, and then his face.

"I've figured out who you are," she said as she approached her car in the parking garage. "I just listened to Red Streets. I recognize your voice. You're Cyanide—the rapper/producer and business entrepreneur from LA. No one's seen your face, but that's your shtick."

"Is that what you think?" he answered. "Cyanide comes in many forms. Maybe there's more to me than what you see."

"I'm sure there is," she challenged him. "It seems you're also a thug and someone involved in conspiracy to commit murder, at least in the murder of Queen Shabaz."

"I tried to warn you, but you wouldn't listen. You're as much to blame as I am."

"Neither Queen nor I was willing to abandon our cause. As you can see from the sequel, there was just too much at stake for the country. We weren't going to betray black people and all the blood sacrifices invested in our history. You're just a lowlife sell-out, exploiting and misrepresenting black culture."

"If I'm so bad and you know so much, Miss Thang, why haven't you already told your new friend, Johnnie Draco, who you think I am?"

"Have you turned on the news, you idiot?" she asked incredulously, "Do you realize how many Americans have died in the past few nights? Do you realize how many more are locked up in outdoor pens at this very moment? No, I have more important things to think about than the ego of a narcissistic rap producer. When this is all over, you'll pay for what you've done."

"Aren't you gonna ask me why I'm back?"

"Why are you back?"

"To do you and your cause some good," he said. "I'm speaking to you through my avatar because I wanna help you. You need to listen to me and trust me, unless you wanna lose another friend."

"No! There's been enough blood. What are you saying?"

"I can save a life. What's her name? Heather?"

"Heather Kaplan! No, you don't! You better not—"

"After the protest this afternoon, they're gonna kill her. She's the new leader of OLM, isn't she? It's best you call her back ta the base and put her on ice for a few days."

"Heather's not the new leader," Natsumi protested, "I'm the new leader. Who said Heather was the new leader?"

"It don't matter. If ya'll don't get her hidden away somewhere right now, she'll be dead tonight."

Natsumi was already dialing the number.

"No answer." She called another number. "Padmi! Heather's the next target. You've got to find her and get her hidden somewhere. Find her now!"

She turned back toward Colin.

"Why are you telling me this?"

"Because I need you, and I need OLM. You won't actually make a difference, but I need you to win, if even for a moral victory."

"Moral victory?"

"He had it all figured out... except you... and me. He underestimated us. It's so much bigger than he is and he can't even conceive it."

"What are you talking about?" Natsumi asked. "Who is this person?"

"The man behind the race war? Who else? Your friend Queen—Demetrius gave her name to that man's assassins. His es-FBI goons killed Queen, just like they gonna kill this Heather chick."

"Who is this person? Who killed Queen?"

"He wanted a race war, I wanted a revolution. He's the one who's been sabotaging your rallies and who's spent millions of dollars puttin guns in the inner cities. He set this whole thing up. It took years for them to create the race bomb, but he lit the fuse."

"What's his name?"

"It don't matter. You wouldn't believe it if I told you, but you will—you will when you see what happens tomorrow."

****

It was the third night in America's race war, which had transformed to become its second civil war. It was the bloodiest by far. Fighters on all sides had been battle-tested, lost friends and family, and become entrenched in their thinking. They no longer fought for white pride or equality or the soul of America. They fought to kill their enemies—the demon forces set against them. During the day, would-be soldiers streamed out from the Army-controlled cities with weapons, ammunition, reinforcements and animosity. Fathers in all America's great cities sent their sons off in sacrifice to Thanatos, the god of war and death.

The U.S. Army tried to anticipate potential areas of conflict, but command struggled with misdirection and misinformation by leaders on both sides who wanted to press the war forward. The OLM protest rally, however, had an unanticipated effect. In California, work teams from the power company PG&E came together to liberate detainees in the regions they served across the state, and in rural areas, the fight was intense, with significant casualties to employees.

In many of the detainee camps, the prisoners were prepared for liberation and were ready to fight to the death for their freedom. Across the country, prisoners were freed, while occupying militias began to suffer significant losses.

The alt-right militias simply could not contain the huge numbers of blacks, Latinos and Asians in their facilities and were forced to surrender prisoners and territory. Desperate, leaders reasoned that if they lost the war, they would make a statement that would resound in throughout American history. The order went out: fight to the death, deplete your ammo, kill the enemies of America—all the minorities. Kill the Jews and the Muslims!

In a community near Modesto, California, Senator Destiny Mitchell joined an OLM effort to liberate what militants had called "Jew Camp," where seventy-eight members of that community had been detained at the edge of a vineyard. A convoy of vehicles had approached in a bold effort to overwhelm the guards to free the prisoners.

The order had already gone out, so soldiers had been selected to carry out methodical execution orders, beginning with the suspected Muslims, and then moving to the Jews. Unarmed OLM recorders, unable to resist and unable to look away, watched as Muslim prisoners, men, women and children, were systematically executed without compassion. Within two hours, an estimated 19,000 perished across the country.

Then to the Jews. In the community outside Modesto, John Deitch, the regional leader, surveyed the enclosure where the suspected Jews were being held. He walked among the detainees, condemning them, reminding them of their sins and predicting their destruction. Then he recognized one particular face.

"Hey! Don't I know you?"

"I have never seen you before," the man responded.

"No, I *know* you," the leader insisted. "I know you. You work at the bank. You're the manager. You denied the loan on my house. Thanks—I lost my house, and then my family."

"I don't remember. I meant no harm to you."

"But you ruined my life, damn Jew! When did you ever care about anybody? Much less Americans!"

In a fit of fury, Deitch beat the man across the head with a nightstick, terrifying the other prisoners in the background.

"You had the power then, Jew banker, but I have the power now!"

"Yes, yes I remember you now," the banker said. "You wanted a loan and you had the 479 FICO score. A Protestant wouldn't have given you a loan!"

He earned another blow to the back, but he laughed to himself, hoping he would be able to share his heroic retort with friends when that night of persecution was over. At the same time, OLM leaders arrived with 200 volunteer soldiers and a State Police contingent in an effort to liberate the camp. Initially, there was an exchange of gunfire before many in the occupying militia faded back into the darkness, surrendering ground. Heather Kaplan was among the OLM leaders, accompanied by Senator Destiny Mitchell. Both were disgusted by the signage over the enclosure.

"Jew Camp? Are they serious?" Heather scoffed.

"It's disgusting. Let's just get them out of there," Destiny agreed.

One of the men knocked the lock off the gate with a sledge hammer, and Heather and other OLM members began guiding the prisoners out. Several older members had succumbed to the cold and had to be revived. As the last of the detainees exited the enclosure, a thin, bespectacled, twenty-something man approached.

"Are you Heather Kaplan?"

"Yes… who are you?"

"It's your turn to die, Jew bitch!"

He fired a single shot into her abdomen at point-blank range. Her eyes widened in surprise as she gripped her stomach. Then he turned toward Destiny.

"And you too, nigger bit—"

He did not finish the word. Destiny had already drawn her weapon, a delicate-looking Glock that flashed pink before she shot three times, center mass. The man dropped his gun and fell to the ground, clutching at Heather's feet. Quivering on the ground, he fired a final shot.

"I'm hit!" the banker yelled. "Hurts like Hell! Someone help me!"

"We need an ambulance and paramedics over here now!" Destiny screamed, training her gun on other possible would-be assassins. "Who is this guy? We need these people outta here before someone else gets hurt!"

The assassin turned out to be a man named Michael Finkelstein, who had changed his name to Mike Finch. The son of a Hasidic Jewish family, he became radicalized at a Wyoming college, returning to California to join the alt-right movement. Through the chaos, it appeared he was the only shooter, purposed specifically to go after Heather.

Senator Mitchell's bodyguards were quick to respond, hurrying her into a black SUV and clearing a way for the paramedics. Destiny seemed stunned, eyes fixed as two tortured faces seemed to follow her—the sense of shock on Heather's face at the moment she was shot, and the brief flash of terror in the assassin's eyes when he realized he had been outdrawn. He was already dead, but there was hope for Heather.

"Look up, Senator," one of the bodyguards said. "I'm sure someone got that on tape. You'll be famous. How many other senators in this century have been in a gunfight and won?"

"You'll have a new nickname," the other bodyguard laughed. "Destiny Mitchell, the gun-slinging Senator from the Wild, Wild West, state of California!"

****

Draco was awakened by the sound of gunfire. Someone had shot at the front door. The next shot came through one of the two windows at the front of the warehouse.

"Everybody down! What the—?"

Another shot through another window. There were seven men in the building: Draco, Dunleavy, captured shooter Sergei, translator Taras, a doctor and two police officers. acting as indoor Loverboy guards.

"You guys see anything?" Dunleavy called to the sentries outside.

"Nothing!" one of the armed men crouched behind an armored car answered. "I'm thinking it's long-range. Someone with a scope."

"Anyone hit?" Draco asked.

"I don't think so," another voice called in. "If he wanted to hit us, someone would already be dead. I think he's shooting at the building!"

Another shot slammed against the metal door.

"See what I mean!"

"Why would someone be shooting at the building?" Dunleavy asked.

Suddenly, a shot rang out from within the building, from the room with the prisoner. Draco and Dunleavy rushed toward the room with guns drawn.

"What happened?"

Sergei began gagging and then he began to cough up blood. One of the guards stood there with a gun in his shaking hand.

"It was an accident. I heard all the shooting out there, so I drew my weapon. I was startled by that last shot and my gun just sorta went off. It was an accident. I'm sorry."

"An accident?" Draco screamed. "There are no accidents. Who is this guy?" he asked Dunleavy, glaring at the nervous guard. "Let the doctor get in there!"

The doctor rushed in to examine the gunshot wound to Sergei's chest. The patient was gasping, struggling to breathe, obviously in the throes of death.

"Accident?" Dunleavy said to the shooter. "Cuff im," he told the other guard, "unless you're in on it with him."

"No sir!" the guard answered as he snapped one of the cuffs on. "I just met him yesterday. I had my suspicions about him this morning. He was acting funny after he got a phone call. I shoulda said something."

"*Moja, moja obitelj!*" Sergei groaned, "*Obećao si mi!*" His back arched a final time, his face contorted with pain, and then he exhaled, lifeless, sinking back to the mattress.

"You better hope everything checks out with you," Dunleavy warned the shooter. "If you come up dirty, we'll execute you on the spot. We're in a war here, and it looks like you chose the wrong side." He nodded toward the other guard. "Get his wallet, his phone, his background, his Internet codes. I wanna know everything he's done and everyone he's talked to. If he refuses to cooperate, your orders are to execute him, clean, back of the head. That was no accident."

"So now we're screwed!" Draco grumbled as the guard took his prisoner away. "Back to square one. He was going to give us a name."

"We were close," Dunleavy agreed, "but nothing is guaranteed. At least we know there's an American involved."

"But we don't have a name?"

"Draco, Dunleavy—" Taras nodded as he entered the room. "Sergei's dead, but I think we've caught a lucky break. As you remember, we emailed his favorite nephew this afternoon, asking about the American, and this computer genius nephew did the work. He doesn't know his uncle Sergei is dead yet, but he sent back what he found, and yes, the American has a name."

"Thank God!" Draco sighed. "We've waited so long to nail this asshole! I can't believe it. Is it him? Is it Luck?"

"Surprise," Taras countered, "it isn't him. We all thought for sure it would be, but no. Turns out to be a name none of us have ever seen before. Basically, a nobody."

"Who is he?" Dunleavy asked.

"His name is Colin Stein-Whitaker, a pretty ordinary guy who graduated from Brown University. Black father is a doctor and Jewish mother is old money."

"So we're looking for a black Jew... who is not Lenny Kravitz or Drake?" Dunleavy asked.

"Then that's who we're looking for," Draco affirmed. "Colin Stein-Whitaker—shouldn't be too hard to find. A black Jew? Maybe he's in the music business too?"

****

"Colin? Colin! I'm so glad you took my call!" Luck effused. "I've got great news! You remember that problem we were talking about, right? Well, it turns out that I was able to take care of it on my own. You don't have to do anything. The threat to us has been neutralized."

"Good for you, Luck," Cyanide said coolly, his focus trained on a table across the restaurant, his eyes fixed on one face. "You took care of your business. Now I have to take care of mine."

"What does that mean, Colin? You had to know I wasn't seriously threatening your mother. I was just trying to get your attention. You do know I wasn't threatening your mother, don't you? She's been a great friend for a long time. The other guy's already gone home. You know me. I was just talkin out my ass. I didn't mean any of that."

"Right…"

"Where are you right now?" Luck asked. "Are you in California?"

"New York… City. Manhattan."

Immediately nervous, Luck looked up his son's number and typed a text.

Justin – where are you now?

"What are you doing in New York, Colin? Music business stuff?"

"No, this business is of a more personal nature."

Manhattan restaurant on East 77th for a meeting, Dad. Why?

"Where exactly are you then, Colin?"

"Manhattan restaurant for a little meeting," Cyanide answered.

"Are you at that spot on West 51st? I know that's your favorite?"

You need to leave right now. Your life is in danger! Get out now!

"No, I've grown tired of that place. Thought I'd try that old time-tested spot on East 77th."

"Colin, we're partners. Tell me you're not going after my son. Our business is between you and me, right?"

"Right," Cyanide sighed. "You, me and someone's mom."

"I took you under my wing, Colin," Luck complained. "Will you give me the benefit of the doubt? I was never going to hurt your mother."

Leave now!

"Speaking of the woman whose life you threatened," Cyanide sighed. "I spoke with her this afternoon. Two of the Loverboy Elites went by to talk to her. They said they *someone* gave them Colin Stein-Whitaker's name, insisting Whitaker hired some Russian assassins to come to America to start this race war."

"Oh no! I had nothing to do with that. That Russian couldn't have told them anything. He's dead. He died this morning."

"You're good, Luck," Cyanide said. "And because I know you so good, it only stands to reason that you've sent someone after me to, ya know, to clean up any loose ends."

"I would never double-cross you, Colin! We're partners! You're like a son to me."

"I'm flattered. But then, you'll still have a son."

"Colin, please don't kill my son! He's my legacy. He's Justin Luck, Jr. He isn't involved in any of this. I kept him out of it purposely. He's a good kid, a good son."

"I see him texting. You must've warned him, but like you, I'm a careful planner. I'm here, and you're there, so let me give you the play-by-play."

"Please, Colin. I'll give you anything. You want money?"

"Colin's mother is an heiress, Luck. He was never in it for the money. It was the thrill, the game. Okay—Luck Jr. is getting up, but I have this sneaky suspicion he isn't feeling so well. Hand to the stomach—I was right."

Justin Luck Jr. cringed after he stood, nearly doubling over from an abdominal contraction.

"I'm acquainted with server in this place, and she told me Luck Jr. always has tea and milk after lunch, a habit he adopted from his European mother. Unlike me, the server was hard-up for money, so just today, she made up a special tea for him…"

"You bastard! You poisoned my son? I've already warned him, and I've called 9-1-1."

"I figured you would, but because of your little war, Luck, emergency services aren't exactly what they used to be in this town. And poison? When did I say I poisoned him? Poison's not my style. Yes, there he goes, and it looks like he left his phone on the table."

"He's leaving?"

"When the server made up the special tea, she added a tasteless powdered ingredient, Miralax—it's a hellava laxative. If your son was constipated, it would have taken a whole day, but Justin Jr. is healthy, eating all that wholesome, organic food. His bowel's already clean as a whistle. The first cup of tea should've done it, but he just finished his second. No, your son isn't poisoned, but he's gotta go. It's either that or shit his pants in the middle of this fancy restaurant."

You have to leave the restaurant, Justin! Leave the building now. Someone there is trying to kill you! No shit!

"No poison, but there a couple of niggas in that bathroom that'll make him wish he had a cyanide pill ta chew on. That restroom has three stalls. The two on the outside will be occupied. A third nigga is gonna man the door. It'll be quick, but they'll make sure ta tell im before he dies that it's because of you and your lyin ass, and because his ass was complicit. He should've known better. Ignorance and a silver spoon are no excuse."

"No! No, Colin, please. Spare my son! Call your ghosts off. I'll be a wasted man. He's my legacy!"

"All the more reason. He just went in. God can't save him now."

"Oh God! No, please!"

Two minutes later, three men exited the restroom. One minute after that, Luck's summoned police arrived. After rushing into the bathroom, they found Justin Luck Jr., strangled to death, his head stuffed in his own unflushed toilet.

"And now I'm coming for you—just for the thrill of it, just for the game."

Chapter 26

"In other words, I'm just stuck in here?" Kendrick complained.

"With all the fighting that's still going on out there," Natsumi answered, "there's not much we can do besides wait. At least it will give our detectives some time to dig up something in the way of exculpating evidence. It's a circumstantial case, but cyanide was everywhere."

"I was poisoned too!" Kendrick insisted. "Why would I poison myself?"

"You're a professor, Kendrick," Natsumi continued, "but when you've dealt with the criminal court system as long as I have and as long as the judge has, you've seen some very strange things. Why would you poison yourself? We've had cases here where perps have shot or stabbed themselves in the legs or stomachs to throw the blame in some other direction. We need something more than the fact that you were poisoned too, and so far, we don't have much to go on."

Natsumi sat with Kendrick in a legal visiting room at the jail on Bryant Street in the city of San Francisco. Three days of Martial Law and nighttime curfew, along with the indefinite court recess, had slowed activity at the jail. The sheriff, fearing the racial fighting and strife might carry-over at the jail between inmates and inmates, between inmates and guards and between guards and guards, put the facility on a 24-hour lockdown. The lockdown had been especially difficult for Kendrick, who had never been incarcerated before.

"I'm not saying I'd take it, but did they offer us a deal?"

"'Guilty to a lesser charge of manslaughter,' based on the fact that you could have poisoned her outright, but you didn't. Intent would be hard for them to prove. Based on the less-than-lethal amount of cyanide in Jennifer's system, we could argue that there was an intent to poison, but not to kill."

"But a manslaughter is a homicide too, isn't it?" Kendrick asked.

"It is," she answered, "though it's a lesser crime."

"With a homicide, I'd lose my teaching credential, and I'd probably lose my position in Oakland with Davis Franklin, so I'd lose Alberta."

"Yes, those are probable consequences, we know that."

"Then we have to fight this, and I have to win. Alberta's personhood is too important. You've accomplished something we couldn't for years! The California legal system is recognizing Alberta's legal testimony in a Superior Court. That's one step closer!"

"I'm a lawyer, but nonhuman protective rights aren't my specialty. What does that mean to you, legally?" Natsumi asked. "I should know, but do you apparently do? What are you and Davis Franklin actually fighting to accomplish?"

"Let's not leave Alberta out of it. It's really her personal fight. We're just assisting in ways we can. Davis Franklin has the money, and I'm creating the scientific and empirical documentation. In the past, the fight for personhood related to rights of the unborn, but in order to be a person, an entity has to meet two criteria: he or she has to possess continuous consciousness over time, and she would have to be capable of framing representations about the world, formulating plans and acting on them. Finally, there's social responsibility, a sense of duty to others. That's what I've been documenting with Alberta, which is why I have to get out. Dr. Jacobs is trying to destroy everything we've worked for."

"You believe Alberta is a person," Natsumi asked, "in the same way that you and I and the guard out there are persons, with God-given legal rights?"

"You don't?" Kendrick replied. "If you ever take the time to really talk to her, you'll realize she's more a person than most of the people you know."

"But if she's a person," Natsumi continued, "what would the status be with all the other chimps? Do we ban them from zoos and research? And what about the Africans who kill and eat chimps as bushmeat. Do we make that a crime tantamount to murder? And what about other primates, and elephants, and dolphins?"

"We're talking rule of law in the United States for now. In 2015, an American court granted a writ of *habeas corpus* to two chimps at Stony Brook University, making them legal persons and challenging the college to provide a legally-sufficient reason for their imprisonment. We lost that case. We lost another in 2017, but we're just getting started in this country."

"You're right, this country will someday have to deal with that," Natsumi sighed, "but look around. There're bigger problems in the world than personhood for animals, even cognitively complex animals. You see what's happening out there? My good friend Heather was shot last night, and my aunt was almost killed. I'm needed out there. I don't know how much I can do for you, Kendrick. No offense, but my bosses made me take this case as a favor to Davis Franklin."

"Are you saying you don't want to help me, or Alberta?" Kendrick asked.

"It's not that, Kendrick," she sighed. "I was in the middle of my own movement when they pulled me out of it to defend you. Again, no offense, but this is an ordinary murder case—circumstantial, though not overwhelming on either side. I would just rather be out there, where I could make a difference."

"And you don't think you'll be making a difference by helping me?" he asked.

"It's a routine murder case."

"Do you think I'm guilty?"

"I don't know. Obviously, Davis Franklin and Alberta don't believe you are."

"Do you think I'm responsible for Jennifer's death? Have you put any real effort into researching this case, or are you too busy feeling sorry for yourself because you don't get to play activist on TV?"

"Excuse me," Natsumi responded, offended. "I've put research and effort into this case—like have done with every case I've worked over the last five years."

"Then tell me, have you ever considered that maybe someone else might have killed Jennifer in order to frame me, especially after that elevator incident in Stockholm? Have you done anything besides offering a chimp as my best witness? Davis Franklin should fire you for legal malpractice."

"Look Kendrick, I know you're tired of being locked up, but it isn't helping when you take your frustrations out on me. I'm doing the best I can for you."

"Are you really?" he challenged. "What have you done for me that any rookie public defender wouldn't have done? Stop going through the motions! Do your job, dammit!"

"I suppose you know that better than I do," she retorted. "Do you know what things are like out there? What do you expect me to do?"

"Realize that Alberta's fight is your fight, and there are persons out there who don't play fair, who would find a way to lock me up in the same way they would kill your movement. Why can't you fight your fight here?"

"Because the fight's out there."

"It's here too," he argued. "It's the same fight. Alberta is fighting for the same rights and protections that American slaves and women fought for in the late eighteen and early nineteen-hundreds—the same that your movement fights for."

"But they were humans. You can't equate a chimp to humans."

"And why not?" he shouted. "Alberta is a sensitive, sentient being who understands this world we're living in. She's as much a person as anyone you know! Don't you think white men felt the same way about women and blacks the way you feel about Alberta—that to grant them legitimacy would somehow take something away from them? Why do you resent her?"

"Please!" Natsumi interrupted. "I don't resent her."

"Then talk to her. She can help you. I know you don't believe it, but she can. She can help you help me. I'm sure she's frustrated with your reluctance. She'll challenge you intellectually and physically, but that should only prove her point. Stop being such a bigot and realize that personhood is not determined by DNA. It's determined by the individual, that person's deliberate actions and thoughts—reality and the real world, language and verbal behavior. Do your job, Natsumi! Or do you think it was a coincidence why Davis Franklin chose you?"

****

"Roland," Jacobs fumed, "I'm insisting that you remove her devices from her, and tell her you won't return them until she provides the login and password for where she has my data stored."

"You have your devices back, Jacobs," Roland answered, "and you've already told me you checked that your data is intact. Nothing is missing. No foul as far as I'm concerned."

"But she's copied my files, notes and emails. They contain sensitive and protected information. I want those back! I need those back. If I were in charge, I'd confiscate all her technology. She doesn't need it!"

"And for that reason, you are not in charge," Roland sighed. "Why are you so threatened by her? What is going on between you two?"

"She drugged me and shoved a banana up my ass! And she did it because I'm onto her. I can see what you and Vesey never could, what Davis Franklin is blind to. Alberta's not a person. She's a freak of nature and she's ramping up to hurting someone, maybe killing someone!"

"Did you bring the primate pregnancy test?" Roland asked.

"They didn't have one at UCD."

"That's okay. Alberta ordered one online. It'll be here tomorrow. Of course, you know if she is indeed pregnant, you'll have to answer to Davis Franklin."

"Yeah, I know that, but I need to talk to her… alone."

Roland hesitated, recalling the gun holster he saw under the doctor's jacket a day earlier.

"Do you have your gun?"

"Do you see a gun?" Jacobs answered, opening his jacket.

"Well, I'll have to ask Alberta if she's willing to speak with you alone. Give me a minute."

Jacobs remained calm until Roland had gone inside Alberta's room and closed the door. Then he went to the kitchen and retrieved a 9-millimeter from the top of the cabinet over the refrigerator. He tucked the gun in his back waistband, where it was concealed by his blazer.

A few minutes later, Alberta exited the room and took a seat at the kitchen table before crossing her arms, making a face at the doctor and offering him a plantain from the fruit basket.

"Can you give us a moment, Roland?" the doctor asked, glaring.

"I'll be in my room. I trust both of you will behave," Roland answered. "Text me if you need me," he signed to Alberta before leaving.

"I want all my data returned today," the doctor demanded.

"Clone? Jacobs say him clone mi. If him can clone mi, why him make mi pregnant?" she returned. Why him not take tissue sample? Why him not take Alberta egg?"

"Give me back my intellectual property, you damned ape!"

"Mi read you note, mi read you email, mi read you text," she said, tapping the temple of her head. "Already up here. Already know."

"You know nothing."

"Mi know Jacob pay Dr. Linden to make mi pregnant. Mi know Jacob cannot clone mi. Mi know Jacob hate Kendrick, and him come to Kendrick apartment when no one home. July 31."

"That's ridiculous!"

"Mi saw picture on phone. Jacob is at house before Jennifer die."

Jacobs reached back to the waistband under his jacket and drew the gun.

"Text Roland and I'll put a bullet in your head right now!" he warned. "I'll take my chances that the U.S. courts aren't yet ready to charge me for murder for shooting a threatening, conflicted chimpanzee."

Alberta crossed her arms and turned her head, defiant.

"Look at me, Alberta. I want all the data you downloaded off my devices. Give Roland your login and password so he and I can go in and delete what you've stolen from me."

Uncrossing her arms, she held up her right hand and extended her middle finger.

"Don't test me, Alberta. I will shoot you!"

"Jacob shoot mi back?" she signed. "And mi pregnant, and mi Davis Franklin money? Jacob go to jail for something. Jacob be pretty girl for bad man who want sex in jail."

"I don't want to shoot you, but I will," he threatened. "I'm asking you, person to person, Alberta. Give Roland the codes so we can go in and delete my data, or give me the storage devices you've put them on. I'm only trying to protect privileged information belonging to my clients."

"Maybe it is not murder to kill Alberta," she signed, turning fully toward the doctor. "Jacob spit in sky, it fall in him eye. Alberta die, email is evidence. Mi text Roland now."

Jacobs quickly slipped the gun back into his waistband.

"This isn't over, Alberta," he said. "I will kill you and cut your baby out of you and have what I want, the embryonic stem cells. Chimps have not yet evolved to even conceive of how savage and efficient humans can be—not even close. That's why you're bushmeat and stuck in zoos."

****

San Francisco Police Department Inspector Dana Murphy was tired of taking orders from the Army, and she was tired of the curfew. She wanted to do some real work, beginning with a re-examination of the Jennifer Alvarez murder case. She did not believe from the beginning that Kendrick Vesey murdered his fiancée. The facts didn't support the charge, but more than that,

Dana had a gut suspicion that there was something more complex going on, and her intuition was seldom wrong.

She began by examining the reports detailing evidence collected during the search of Kendrick's apartment, Jennifer's apartment, Jennifer's workplace, her gym locker and Davis Franklin's Oakland Hills home. All those places contained traces of cyanide, but Jennifer worked out at a women's only gym, which meant she was contaminated somewhere else, and she carried traces of cyanide wherever she went. The exposure could have occurred in one location, a point-zero of sorts, and she could have contaminated other places by carrying it there on her skin and clothes.

She lived in her apartment alone, so it was doubtful that the exposure occurred there. Her brother, Armando, visited on occasion, but interviews yielded that he lacked the intellectual sophistication to indulge in the poison arts. If it hadn't occurred at her apartment, that left Kendrick's apartment and Franklin's Oakland Hills home, since cyanide levels in her office and at the gym indicated secondary contamination in significantly lower levels.

Still, Dana did not believe Kendrick was guilty. She interviewed him twice and she believed him, regardless of the evidence… and that left only one other possibility. Curious, she re-read inspector interviews from the investigation, eventually realizing something she had not considered earlier.

After a phone call to the district attorney, Irving Carroll, Dana received courier-delivered transcripts from the arraignment and the preliminary hearing. With every page that she read, she became more convinced of her suspicion until she finally called the deputy district attorney back and asked for a meeting.

"I know it sounds crazy," she insisted, "but if Kendrick Vesey didn't poison Jennifer Alvarez, it's the only other viable possibility to consider."

"You're right, it does sound crazy!" Carroll nodded, his eyes widened. "Now if Jennifer's neck was snapped or her face was ripped off, you might be able to make people believe the ape was responsible, but slow poisoning, with cyanide? That just don't sound ape to me."

"You were there in the courtroom, I wasn't," Dana argued, "but you heard her testimony. She's got an Einstein brain. Under direct examination and under oath, mind you, she proved that she understood the definition of murder. In her words, she said murder was 'when one person kills another person, and there is a motive—for money, for hate or revenge,' and then she went on to define motive. You don't think it's possible?"

"That the ape was trying to poison Vesey and Alvarez? Hell no! Why? Where's the motive?"

"Love!" Dana insisted, passion in her voice. "She's in love with Kendrick Vesey. You couldn't see that? And she was poisoning Jennifer to get her out of the picture. Jealously—it's the oldest motive in the book."

"That is… kinda… way out there. You know that, Dana, don't you?" Carroll asked. "You're a talented inspector, and I've come to respect your judgment over the many years we've worked together, but if I went to my boss with a theory like that, he'd laugh me out of his office and tell me to clear out mine."

"It's sounds a little crazy, yes, but it makes perfect sense. It brings all the puzzle pieces together—the vial of cyanide salts found in Alberta's bedroom, the incident in Stockholm, her lack of feeling or regret about Jennifer's death. Everything!"

"Look," Carroll sighed. "I'll admit I was impressed with how smart she was. At first, I thought it had to be a gimmick. But if she's that smart, then she'd have to know Vesey would never fall in love with an ape. That's sick. She'd have to know that."

"You're a man, so you wouldn't understand," Dana countered. "Sometimes it's just enough to have a man's exclusive attention, his heart. Sometimes a woman doesn't need anything else."

"But Alberta's not a woman! She just an ape, a chimpanzee. She's an animal, not a human."

Dana's phone rang just then, and so holding her palm out in a gesture of apology, she took the call, nodding emphatically as he listened.

"Yes! Yes, thank you for getting back to me so fast. Yes, it's exactly that 'something else' I was looking for. Please send it to my cell phone right away."

"What was that?" Carroll asked.

"A call from a friend of mine in records, and it seems just yesterday morning, a man, a Dr. David Jacobs, filed a confidential police report in Oakland complaining that a chimp had drugged him, stuck a banana in his ass and downloaded or otherwise stole his intellectual property, along with a 9-mm handgun."

"And you think that was Alberta?"

"She's not a human, but in the Oakland police report and in the murder of Jennifer Alvarez, she's definitely become a person-of-interest."

****

It was a close call. Because no one knew what he looked like, he was able to easily fool the cops stationed at LAX airport. There was another group in the terminal, however, that seemed to be onto him. They had anticipated his every move. In the end, Colin was forced to slip out a private utility door, leap down 15 feet, spraining his ankle, bribe a couple baggage handlers, and ride with the luggage until he was next to a field.

Hopping from the cart, he crawled across the grass and scaled the chain-link fence, spending most of the night jumping at every sound as he made his way to an airport access road. Using the phone that he bought from one of the baggage handlers, he called his crew to pick him up, and then he descended into the LA underground.

Strange, he thought, but the second group searching at the airport knew him as Colin Stein-Whitaker. That was the name one of the questioners used. Justin Luck must have sent them, since few besides his mother and Luck knew the convoluted mystery involving Cyanide and his ghosts and avatars. The man who had approached obviously did not make the connection and did not recognize him as Cyanide. He only said the team meant "Colin Stein-Whitaker" no harm if he could help them get Luck. The man was a cop or cop-related, so Colin didn't trust him and gave him the slip.

Get swazey, go underground and see how it all plays out, he figured. He still couldn't believe Cyanide had gone through with his plan to kill Luck's son. He knew the old man had to be pissed, but Luck would be loath to publicly risk exposing Colin as Cyanide, since he couldn't be sure and since in doing so, he would expose his own involvement in sedition against the United States government. For the moment, it would remain a private battle, with Luck in his New York castle and Colin in the LA underground moat.

Before the murder in New York, Colin explained his situation to his mother and urged her to take a sudden, unplanned trip for a few weeks to an undisclosed location as a precaution, and he made sure the "go" order on Luck Jr. wasn't issued until he knew she had left the country. About his father, Colin told Luck, "Go ahead, do me a favor." Luck had called Colin several times since Luck Jr.'s murder, but the avatar did not take the call. Using a phone from his stash of untraceable, disposable cell phones, he dialed the private number.

"Until now, Luck, I don't think you ever took me serious. To you, I was just another nigga you could control, but as I told you earlier, you miscalculated. I tried to trust you, I tried to believe you, but you screwed me at every turn. You might hate me now, but I've forced you to respect me."

"You killed my son, you bastard! Of course I hate you," Luck responded, feigning calmness. "Where are you now, Colin? Are you still in New York?"

"You already know where I am. You sent your people after me."

"I've spent the last twelve hours grieving for my son and comforting his family," Luck explained. "If someone was after you, they weren't my people. My people will be coming though."

"You might want to keep them close, because I'm still coming for you. You underestimated me before. Folks like you can't afford to make the same mistake twice."

"And niggers like you can't afford to crawl out of the gutter you live in. I didn't underestimate you at all. With all that black persona you put out there, it just slipped my mind that you were half-Jew. Only a Jew could do something so wicked."

"Oh yeah," Colin half-laughed, "like sedition, like using your money and influence to instigate and initiate a for profit race war in America—like inviting the Russian government in to help? All those guns you bought and distributed in the inner-cities and the money channeled to alt-right groups and militias—you think I didn't find proof that someone linked to the government in Russia provided the financing?"

"You're lying. You can't bluff a bluffer, and I'm the best at bluffing. The only name that comes up in any of the Russian transactions is yours—Colin Stein-Whitaker. It wasn't me who was after you. It's the CIA and FBI."

"I have the proof—documents, recordings, video—proof you started this war," Colin insisted. "Do you know how many Americans have died in the last three nights? Over 90,000. That's a lot of American blood on your hands, Luck, and when people find out you were behind it, I won't have to do anything else—but that would be too easy. I need to make sure you recognize that I'm smarter than you are, that I'm better than you. All you have to do is say it to me. That'll be enough. I'll destroy my evidence."

"What will be enough?"

"Tell me I'm smarter than you, that I beat you."

"You're not smarter and you haven't beat me," Luck answered, his temper flaring. "You'll be just another dead nigga before the week's over. And do whatever you want to do. Who are people going to believe? Me or you?"

"I got the hard goods on you. That's all that'll matter."

"I'm the big dog here, Colin, and you're just a flea on my ass."

"Good analogy, Luck," Colin laughed, "but sometimes you're better off being a flea on a dog's ass, especially when there's a car coming. Alotta times, I've seen a big dog get his ass run clean over, kilt dead on the spot—blood all over—and even then, there wasn't one bit of harm come to that flea."

Chapter 27

"Mi watch Natsumi on TV yesterday. Her fighting why?"

"I'm fighting injustice," Natsumi answered. "Do you know what that is? Injustice?"

"Injustice is when something is not right. Good have punishment, bad have reward. Poor die, money people live. Lie is success, truth is shame. Hard worker have nothing, rich, lazy son have everything. Mi know injustice."

"Yep, you're right. That pretty much sums it up," Natsumi smiled, nodding toward Roland, who was acting as translator and was a stocky body between the two females at the kitchen table of the Oakland Hills home.

"Our Life Matter," Alberta signed, "what injustice them fight for?"

"We fight for equality under the rule of law. Black and brown people are being profiled and punished disproportionately under the law, and black and brown men and women are being killed by law enforcement agencies, with no effective accountability. It's very frustrating for those in our communities, especially for those who work in and trust our justice system."

"Why black and brown?" she signed. "What is wrong with black and brown?"

"Nothing. It's just racism. Unfortunately, there are some people who think they're better and more deserving just because they're white. In fact, in some places in America, it's the prevailing opinion."

"Because them white?" Alberta signed, frowning. "How can white make someone smart? That is racism?"

"Yes, that's what it is—bias or animus based on race."

"Race? Explain race."

"Race has to do with differences between people, like color and hair texture and facial features—things that cause people to regard and treat each other differently."

"Black is race?"

"Yes. Black is a race."

"Brown is race?"

"Brown is not exactly a race, but brown gets combined with black because it's not white—which is a race, according to American society."

"Muslim is race? Jew is race."

"No, people who are Muslims are followers of the religion Islam, in the same way that Catholics follow Christianity and Jews follow their sacred customs and traditions. People who discriminate on the basis of religion are bigots, but they're not necessarily racists, since most religions contain various racial and ethnic groups. Why are you asking me all this, Alberta?"

"Mi ask to know. Tall is race? Fat is race? Deaf is race?"

"No, being tall is not a race. It's just a human characteristic—like being fat or deaf."

"Not logical," Alberta signed, frustrated. "Natsumi contradict Natsumi! Color is human characteristic! Pretty is human characteristic!"

"Yes, but humans don't usually discriminate to such an extreme degree because of height or weight or looks. For instance, tall people as a group have never been enslaved or subjected to genocide on the basis of their height, or weight people for that matter."

"Stupid is race, ugly is race, homosexual is race? Human is Homo."

"No," Natsumi sighed. "For all intents and purposes, race has more to do with color and where people originate in the world—specifically black, white and Asian."

"Mi want to join Our Life Matter. Mi want to be member. Alberta life matter."

"Of course it does," Natsumi answered, "and that's why you have Roland here, and Davis Franklin, and Kendrick. They are all proof that your life matters."

"All good, but mi want world to know Alberta life matter. Alberta life matter, and life of other chimp matter. Life of all person matter. Person life matter."

"You're right, Alberta, but that's not what our movement is about. The fight for nonhuman rights must be fought at some time, but it's not my fight."

"Natsumi is black. Alberta is black. Same fight."

"Not exactly. You and I aren't black in the same way. Our Lives Matter is fighting to save lives unjustly taken, institutional racism and white supremacy."

"Mi too!" Alberta signed frantically. "Mi fight same things! Alberta is black."

"You're not black, Alberta," Natsumi sighed, wagging her head. "You don't understand black—it's more than a color. It's a culture. This is not your fight."

"Alberta is black like Natsumi is black. Alberta is more black! Mi female like Natsumi is female. Same fight!"

"You're an ape, Alberta," Natsumi said, "I'm a human. Regardless of what color you are, it's not the same thing."

"Alberta is person and Natsumi is person—same fight. Both black, both female, both mad. Both fight injustice. Ape is race? All human is race? Ape is different race?"

"Apes are a separate species. Races are divisions among humans. It's hard to explain, Alberta, but we're not the same."

"Who invent race? When human say ape is not person, that is racism? All human is person?"

"Yes."

"All human is smarter than all ape? This why human is person?"

"I wouldn't exactly word it like that."

"Autistic human is not smart human, but always is person, always more person than Alberta," she said, invading Natsumi's personal space. "Human do not want Alberta to be person. Why human is afraid?"

"You got me there." Natsumi said, backing, nervous. "Waitaminute! Kendrick warned me you would do this! You're testing me. You caught me off-guard. I'm sure I failed on both counts!"

Alberta crossed her arms, shaking her head, indicating failure.

"Took you a minute there," Roland chuckled.

"Well, I stand corrected, Alberta. I guess you're more human than I ever imagined, but I think you have a hidden mean streak."

Pleased that she had made her point, Alberta wanted to spar a while longer, but she was more interested in sharing what she had discovered. She opened her laptop and invited Natsumi to examine the pictures, from a distance.

"Look at date. July 31. Picture taken on Jacob camera," Alberta indicated. "That is three month before Jennifer die."

Natsumi seemed surprised as she looked from the computer screen to Roland's face.

"Where did these pictures come from?"

"Dr. David Jacobs' camera apparently," Roland answered. It's the first time I'm seeing them. Wow!"

"But how?" Natsumi persisted.

"Mi download from Jacob phone when him sleeping."

"Then you have to understand we can't use any of this as evidence. It wouldn't be admissible in court."

"That mean him not come to here on July 31?" Alberta asked.

"No. Apparently he was here," Natsumi answered, "but because you didn't follow the rules for obtaining evidence when you downloaded his phone, I won't be able to use it."

"Ya mon. Mi no care. Mi prove Kendrick never kill Jennifer. Jacob kill Jennifer. Jacob use poison to kill Jennifer. Him make Kendrick go in jail."

"Do you have proof of that on your computer?" Natsumi asked.

"No. Mi have proof Jacob come to here July 31. Have proof Jacob come to Kendrick apartment July 28. Why him come? Him hide cyanide salt here, inside mi room. Why?"

"I don't know," Natsumi answered, shaking her head. "Even if he did break in here and hide the potassium cyanide in your room, that doesn't prove anything. Jennifer died at Kendrick's apartment, and the fatal dosage was found in her lungs. You've been resourceful, Alberta, but it's not nearly enough."

"Police report, them say them find something in Kendrick apartment," she said as she prepared to finger-spell for Roland. "Police, them find

DMSO, mean dimethyl sulfoxide. It is solvent. Jacob hide DMSO in Kendrick apartment."

"Okay, maybe you're going somewhere with this. Why would Dr. Jacobs hide DMSO at Kendrick's apartment?"

"Relationship. Chemistry. Cyanide salt and DMSO is like perfect marry. Complete dissolve. Potassium cyanide and DMSO together, name is 'Liquid Death.'"

"Okay, so combined together, those two things are lethal," Natsumi began, intrigued. "Is there anything you downloaded that suggests Jacobs had some way of combining them to poison Jennifer Alvarez?"

"No mon, not on mi computer. Mi know Jacob poison Jennifer. Kendrick never poison Jennifer."

"But that's not enough, Alberta," Natsumi sighed. "You really don't know. What you're saying is what you believe, but you don't have any proof. Even if Jacobs was in both places, and even if he did plant those two compounds as you believe he did, it doesn't prove anything."

Frustrated, Alberta began an unintelligible rant that initially scared Natsumi. Cringing behind Roland, she peeked at the ape, who bowed her head, ashamed for losing her temper.

"How to prove? How to prove Jacob kill Jennifer? What mi need for evidence?"

"Look Alberta," Natsumi consoled. "It's complicated. Something like you're suggesting would be next to impossible to prove—even for an expert detective, and believe me, we've had trained investigators working on this case for weeks. I know you care about Kendrick. I'll tell him how hard you tried."

"Not try. Mi prove. Mi prove Jacob poison Jennifer."

"How are you going to do that?" Natsumi asked. "There's nothing in the police report to go on, and there's nothing in the information you downloaded to your laptop. How are you going to prove it?"

"Mi brain is working, is thinking, is figuring thing out. Mi prove."

"You are a very determined… chimpanzee," Natsumi sighed. "I'll say that much, and if you somehow find a way to prove this theory you're suggesting, I'll be a believer, and I might be one of the loudest voices beside you in your fight for nonhuman rights."

****

The fourth day of America's race war was the most significant, because it was the day the nation found its soul. Pictures of Americans in "protection camps" with barbed-wire fences on American soil flooded the Internet. Images of bloodied, weeping American children and the elderly haunted thoughts throughout the day. In small communities, once-quiet townsfolk began to speak out against the sieges and confinement camps, demanding the release of detainees. Once hesitant religious and conservative leaders appealed to the fundamental principles of justice and democracy—equality, justice compassion, goodwill and love.

"Ma daddy fought in the Second War," one elderly woman from Missouri said to a reporter. "He come back wounded cuz he was fightin the Germans against this very same thing. What they're doin here in Camden Point just ain't right. We all gotta come together and make that militia let those people go."

As midday was transformed to late afternoon, America tested its commitment to equality and justice—the idea that all Americans were equal under the rule of law and whether Americans would go to battle for the concepts of fairness, moral rightness and sanctions for human rights violations. Yet the underlying values put to trial were those of tolerance, cooperation and compromise, which had been undermined during the short-sighted nationwide campaign to reject political correctness.

In a movement that leaders called the "March on Detainment," community members of all races, cultures, ethnicities and religions began a march on the organized "detainment camps" in an effort to free American prisoners and immigrants who were illegally detained. Many in these groups coordinated with the American military in instances where larger and more organized militias refused to release prisoners.

Americans across the country praised the movement's effort with each report of a detainment camp being shut down. By 4:00 p.m. EST, it was clear that the tide had turned and the ambitions of America's second race war had fallen short of expectations. Again, the instigators had underestimated the decency and goodwill of the white majority in the nation, the determination of the oppressed, the resilience of the American spirit and the strength of American ideals. Notwithstanding, the country readied itself for another bloody, horrific night.

At 2 p.m. in San Francisco, four hours before the curfew, Our Lives Matter staged a protest at Oscar Grant Plaza to support the National March on Detainment in what many hoped would be a death blow to the effort to sustain a race war in America. Many other speakers, liberal and conservative, had flown out to support the protest, including a former governor of Indian heritage. The various speeches encouraged patriotic involvement, which would make a statement in history and to the world. On that day, America's lofty rhetoric came to terms with reality.

Natsumi, at the offices of the *Aegis Foundation* on Montgomery and Washington with her Aunt Destiny, chose not to attend or speak. Padmi Ravi led the Our Lives Matter contingent, introducing guests and moderating the event. Though unplanned, her concluding remarks were aired on television news networks and broadcast across the globe.

"America is a nation of immigrants," Padmi shouted. "I come from a family that immigrated here from India when I was five years old. In my experience, I never saw myself as anything other than an American, loyal and patriotic. In my American youth, I was taught I lived in a country that was unlike any other—a place where words like 'democracy,' 'freedom' and 'justice' had real meaning and resonated from coastline to coastline, from American to American.

"I speak uniquely as a child of immigrants and a lawyer, but over the past few days, that vision of America has been called to witness before the world. The evidence has been presented over the last three nights, over the last election, over many court cases where racial minorities, mainly African American males, have been killed by law enforcement, and by police and citizens who claim to 'stand their ground' with zero accountability. The world is watching. How will America answer?

"Fascism, we thought, was an outdated concept, and the very idea of the military citizenship that we have witnessed in small America, in 'fly-over America' these past three nights, the idea of authoritarian nationalism that we've experienced! Just how will America answer to the last three nights of chaos and injustice requiring Martial Law? We might feel embarrassed now, but then again, we have an opportunity to reaffirm our democratic roots. We have the opportunity to redefine who and what we are as America and Americans in the 21st Century.

"Tonight, I am an American only—not an immigrant, not a woman, not an Indian, not a Hindi and not a member of Our Lives Matter. I'm just an ordinary American who is committed to saving our country, which is still great, though yet imperfect. Some of us will die tonight in the fight, yes, but in honor of those who have suffered and died in our history so that I could stand before this nation to make my plea, I am willing to pay the debt forward. We can do this only if all Americans come together in an unabating commitment to save America. America will survive this trial."

****

Once the 6 p.m. curfew began, Colin sat at the corner table in an empty soul food restaurant he privately owned on Long Beach Boulevard in Compton. He was alone and becoming increasingly paranoid. His "Secretary of State," Eddie-Roc, and the Ragna-Roc ghost were ever-present. He trusted no one else—not at least in the days that loomed ahead. Colin was deep underground, but he knew something or someone was coming. Ragna-Roc, the most severe member of the crew, had strangled Justin Luck Jr. and stuffed his face in the soiled toilet. Agitated energized, he was eager to go directly after Luck Sr.

Eddie-Roc, on the other hand, operated on a more public level, so his focus over the last few days was to "draw the fire." A UCLA Business School graduate and astute entrepreneur, he handled Cyanide's vast network of businesses and associates and was the chief operating officer of Diabolical Records, a division of Cyanide Inc. Earlier in the day, Eddie-Roc met with two undercover cops who were inquiring about Cyanide Avatar. They seemed to be offering a deal.

"They said they know who you are, that you're actually some kind of spoiled rich kid, and you're half-Jewish. They're talking treason and some connection with the Russians they can prove, but they say they know you were set up. They want the real boss on that deal. They want you to give them Justin Luck."

"Okay, I give them Justin Luck and then what? And how do they expect me to give them Justin Luck?"

"You have to go on record with the FBI."

"Oh hell no! That ain't happenin! I'm not the real Cyanide."

"They want to talk to you," Eddie-Roc said as he lit up and inhaled.

"Who?" Colin asked. "Me, or someone they think I am?"

"Well, one of the cops was from here. Gutierrez—he grew up in the 36th Street barrio in South Central, and he was with some white boy from Boston. They say they've been after Luck for years, and they know he's behind all this shit that's happening now."

"Tell me somethin I don't know."

"Whatever Luck did, he's got all the evidence pointing back to some spoiled rich kid from Connecticut, a 'Kaepernick,' Luck calls im—playin the 'black' card to make a name for himself. They're sayin you're Colin Stein-Whitaker and you started up this revolution because you hate white people, and you brought the Russians in it because you hate America. The perfect set-up."

"You don't think I knew what Luck was doing?" Colin asked after hitting the blunt. "And once Luck leaks that Cyanide is an Ivy League brat who first pimped and then sold out blacks in America for profit, he figures he'll turn everyone against that rich kid, right?"

"You knew all that?" Eddie-Roc asked.

"Ain't happenin. I don't know if you wanna believe I'm Cyanide or that rich kid, or we're one in the same," Colin said, "but never underestimate the value of an Ivy League education. Illustrious men like Justin Luck have illustrious enemies. When I realized Luck was tryin to play me, settin me up, I went out and found someone more powerful than he was and cut a deal over there. Where Luck loses, someone else wins."

"Who's more powerful than Luck, and why would he help you?" Eddie continued.

"A guy I know," Colin answered. "I met him through Luck, but they ain't friends. They're more like frenemies."

"A guy you know?" Eddie asked. "Don't tell me it's Davis Franklin."

"Davis Frankin?" Ragna chimed in. "The baller billionaire with that smart chimpanzee? He's tryin ta make her a human. Alberta, *that's* her."

"Davis Frankin?" Ragna chimed in. "The baller billionaire with that dope-ass chimpanzee? I like that little bitch! Alberta, *that's* her."

"It could be," Colin answered, "but Franklin can't be bought. When I give him all the shit I got on Luck—how Luck and his friends have worked for years to start this race war that's killed almost 100,000 people, how he dumped guns in black and brown neighborhoods and how he involved the Russians in a treasonous plot against America, this guy has the juice and connections to take him down."

"As powerful as your new friend is, it would still be a big risk on his part to go after Luck," Eddie advised. "I mean, on that level, all those guys've got their businesses tangled up with each other, all guilty of somethin. Take down Luck, and he'd be hurtin himself. He'd be hurtin other billionaires and big corporations. Why would any billionaire do that?"

"Because while Luck's got his cause, which is creating division, keeping the so-called lower-class people in this country from ever puttin their heads together or getting anything, this other guy has his own pet projects."

"But didn't you just say they were friends?" Eddie asked.

"They've come down on different sides of this race war. Luck is the instigator, but Franklin—he's helping out the Our Lives Matter movement. In fact, an attorney on his payroll is the main leader in the movement. Luck wanted to take her out, but I couldn't let that happen."

"Who's is she?" Ragna asked.

"You've seen her on TV. Her name's Natsumi Mitchell, and she's the niece of Destiny Mitchell, U.S. Senator from the State of California."

****

Scenes of opposition to the militias and detainment camps flooded all aspects of media across America and the world. There were stories of liberation and tears of regret, the beginning of widespread healing. Local, state and beltway politicians made patriotic speeches, invoking the Founding Fathers and calling on ordinary Americans to show the world that tolerance, compassion and unity are stronger than hateful rhetoric and bigotry. America's race war lasted four nights and claimed over 100,000 lives, but the nation proved itself resilient in the face of its greatest trial.

In many large cities, people defied curfews, peacefully coming together in great crowds, celebrating the end of the fighting, mourning those lost and reclaiming the lofty ideals central to Americanism. In smaller towns, communities walked along the roads, singing spirituals, opposing hate and freeing prisoners. Never had Americans loved the ideas of liberty, inclusion and goodwill more than on that night when the people reclaimed the nation's soul.

Notwithstanding, there were some unpatriotic confederates who resisted the spirit of unity and goodwill that flooded the country, who hoped to continue and escalate the war, but the opposition to Americans fighting or imprisoning other Americans was overwhelming. Even the most dogged militia leaders realized the war had been roundly rejected and sent their soldiers home, where they initially melted back into the population. America had learned its lesson—that conditions should never exist again to pit American against American in a war about race.

"Not exactly the result we wanted," Luck said, "but it was a good thing. War is always a good thing, and this one was smart. America was so worried about an attack coming from abroad that they let it happen. They'll learn to be more careful next time. Anyway, we'll make money on it."

"Money's good, but it isn't everything," advisor Bartholomew Morton countered, patting Luck's left shoulder before sitting across from him at his office desk. "You lost your son in the war. I'm sure there's no amount of money that could make up for that loss."

"I guess you're right. It was the war. I lost him because of the war. He was a great son. I know who's responsible, and I'm going to make him pay."

"I thought it was a random attack," Everett Mann asked, "some jealous black nationalists wanting to kill a successful establishment white male. That's what the paper said."

"That's exactly right, but it wasn't a random attack," Luck answered. "The successful establishment white male they were trying to punish was me, and they did it. They knew he was my son. It was personal."

"And you know who was behind it?"

"Colin Stein-Whitaker, a Black Judas," Luck answered, tossing a file across the desk. "He put the blacks up to it. That's the name and there's the proof. You still have a special relationship with the FBI?"

"Absolutely. What do you need me to do?"

"It's all in that file: sedition, treason, conspiracy to commit murder, with times, dates and names. Tell them Whitaker should be considered armed and dangerous. Tell them if one of their agents gets a little nervous and accidently shoots him—kills him and his friends, I won't be too sad about it. I'd probably be glad. Really glad."

Chapter 28

Inspired by the events of the previous night, the reality of 100,000 dead Americans, the speeches and the calls for unity, the American people demanded action and accountability, especially after an unknown source leaked a story to the press about 100,000 illegal guns being dumped in inner-city neighborhoods and funding to alt-right groups to fuel an American race war. The suggestion that the Russians and American traitors were involved, despite denials by the CIA, incited anger against the current administration and Congress, who patriots and media analysts cast as weak in the face of foreign aggression and interference in American affairs.

Hard-pressed by constituents, congressional members and state executives introduced legislation to address criminal justice reform, including the powers and accountability of police agencies, the responsibilities of district attorneys and grand juries in investigations and indictments, independent, community-based law enforcement oversight and overall transparency. The leadership of Our Lives Matter, Mothers Who Care and other protest groups were included in discussions for immediate and sensible reform.

Concerned about the 100,000 illegal guns—over half of those described as military-style weapons—dumped in inner-city neighborhoods, Congress for the first time introduced legislation purposed to significantly reduce the number of firearms on city streets. Twenty percent of the weapons had been distributed in Chicago and Philadelphia alone. Despite pushback from the NRA, the Congressional House Speaker and Senate Majority Leader were able to push two-of-five gun-reform packages through committees during the first day.

The urgency for reform was echoed on state and local levels, with California taking the lead by offering cash for illegal guns turned in to state-administered weapons recovery stations. The City of Miami offered temporary immunity from prosecution for wanted felons surrendering unlawful firearms. Long-stalled government-sponsored job-creating infrastructure programs were immediately approved. Under public pressure, the corporate community introduced plans for enhanced job creation and announced widespread support for a higher minimum wage.

In San Francisco, Natsumi trailed Roland's silver Peugeot 307. Roland suggested they could all ride together, but Natsumi was not comfortable at such close quarters in an enclosed area. More than that, Alberta was accustomed to riding in the passenger seat next to Roland and had already strapped herself in. *Backseat to an ape?* She was disturbed by the thought.

With the court's permission, they were headed to Jennifer Alvarez's apartment in the Mission district. Alberta had insisted to Natsumi that she wanted to investigate the crime scene to "solve the murder." Natsumi laughed initially, but when she realized Alberta was serious, she reflected on Kendrick's advice and called police detectives to arrange the visit. She didn't dare tell anyone why she had brought the chimpanzee to the apartment.

Jennifer's clean, modernly-decorated apartment had remained untouched since the initial investigation. A warm, fuzzy picture of her and Kendrick was the centerpiece for the coffee table in the living room, while two colorful paintings, gifted from a student artist—one of her Colombian "Flowers," hung on the walls. Jennifer hated clutter, so most surfaces in the apartment were orderly and clean. There were no magnets, notes or pictures on the refrigerator, and unused kitchen appliances and utensils were stored out of sight.

"Have you ever been here before?" Natsumi asked.

"No," Alberta signaled, and then she signed. "Jennifer, her have rule: no monkey in house."

"So, what do you think you're going to find here? The detectives were already here twice."

"Mi is thinking about slow poison—how Jacob use slow poison to kill Jennifer. Him come to Jennifer apartment July 28. Him take picture. Where him put poison? Poison here, but detective come two time and them not find poison. Them find poison in mi room. Jennifer never come in mi room. Poison is here. Mi look."

"You're going to find it?" Natsumi asked as she crossed her arms, standing next to the kitchen table. "And two sets of trained police detectives somehow missed it?"

"The more them look, the less them see."

"Knock yourself out then," Natsumi sighed, almost laughing before looking over at Roland. "I know she's smart for an ape, but this is bordering on ridiculous."

"For whatever it's worth," Roland smiled, "thanks for indulging her. She's got her mind made up that she's going to save Kendrick."

"Well, I guess it can't hurt," Natsumi shrugged.

"At least you allowed her to try. I figure if she gives it her best shot and she can't prove Ken is innocent, it might help her accept the possibility that she won't be seeing him for a very long time, if ever again in her life."

"She seems very attached to him," Natsumi commented, crossing her arms. "She's very protective of him. Is that normal?"

"Chimps are our nearest relatives, Ms. Mitchell," Roland answered. "You have to understand that we aren't so different. Their lifespan is 60 years—pretty close to ours, and during their lives, they develop many deep bonds, just like we do."

"You told me you've known her longer than Kendrick. Why isn't she as attached to you?"

"Persons like and bond to who they like," he laughed. "It's very personal. Who knows? I met her earlier, but I didn't see her as much. Maybe it's because Kendrick's better-looking than I am. Who would you rather bond to, Kendrick or me?"

"You're both good-looking, but why should it matter?"

"Ms. Mitchell, I think you've got to get over this erroneous notion that you're somehow better and smarter than Alberta is. Admitted, not all chimps are so intelligent, but I imagine, on many levels, Alberta's not very different than you are."

"I have a hard time believing that," Natsumi huffed, wagging her head.

"I've been watching your speeches on television over these past few weeks, and I'm a little surprised, because it's hard for me to believe that you of all people would base your judgement on a person's appearance—that you're unwilling to consider an individual on her singular merit."

The sound of the front door hinges interrupted the discussion as Dana Murphy burst into the room.

"I heard you guys were over here, and I heard you brought Alberta. Is she still here?"

"Why are you here, Inspector?" Natsumi asked. "I cleared this with the commander."

"No official reason," Dana gushed, out of breath. "I'm just curious, that's all. Why is Alberta here?"

"She's re-investigating the crime scene," Roland offered with a smirk, "she's trying to solve the murder."

"You can't be serious? Really?" Dana asked Natsumi.

"Look," Natsumi answered. "Dr. Hughes says Alberta's been profoundly affected by the sudden and sustained absence of Kendrick Vesey. As a doctor who understands her, he thought it would be helpful to indulge her in this. I figured, what could it hurt?"

"Nothing, I suppose, but it's just weird," Dana said before turning to Roland. "Dr. Hughes, I understand you've worked with Alberta and other chimps for at least two decades. Can I ask you a question?"

"You can, and I'll even answer," he said.

"Okay, do you think it's possible for a chimp like Alberta to fall in love with a human? Do you think it's possible that she might be in love with Kendrick Vesey?"

"Oh, I think they've formed a bond, a close attachment through knowing each other and working with each other—much the same as you form bonds with your co-workers, but I'd hardly call it love, and certainly I don't think she could ever be 'in love' with him."

"But she's different, isn't she, doctor?" Dana continued. "Isn't she a person—like a human? A human person can fall in love, and love is a strong motivator. Isn't that why she's here trying to help Kendrick?"

"She can't be in love. Her brain isn't wired to work that way," he sighed, dismissive.

"Sorry to cut in here, doctor," Natsumi interrupted, "but didn't you just tell me she's not very different than I am? You don't think it's possible?"

"I don't."

The discussion stopped abruptly when Alberta came into the room with a small, square body powder box in her hand. Unfamiliar with Dana, she cupped her hand against her body to hide the black and white box, trimmed in gold. She did not need to sign to Roland, because he read her expression.

"Alberta, this is Inspector Dana Murphy with the San Francisco police. She's okay. I trust her. She can help us. What's that in your hand?"

"Mi find Jennifer powder, powder her put on her skin. Mi think Jacob—him put cyanide in Jennifer powder. Slow poison."

"How would you know if there's cyanide in that powder box?" Dana asked slowly.

"Mi smell cyanide," Alberta answered. "Mi smell cyanide in Jennifer powder."

"Is that possible, doctor?" Natsumi asked.

"Physiologically speaking, yes," he answered. "For humans, over half of our approximately 1,000 olfactory genes that detect smells don't work. For chimps, it's about a quarter. Short answer—she can smell things we can't, so it's possible she can detect the smell of cyanide if she remembers it. We know she's already familiar with the smell from the vial in her room."

Unafraid to approach the chimp, Dana stooped.

"Alberta, I'm a police inspector," she said as if talking to a child. "If you give that powder box to me, I can take it to the lab and have it tested."

Alberta snatched the box away from Dana and finger-signed something toward Roland.

"What's wrong?" Dana asked.

"It's the way you're speaking to her. She thinks you're mentally-challenged. Retarded. She thinks you might hurt yourself if she gives it to you."

"Well, tell her I'm not."

"You can tell her," he laughed. "Just speak to her like you would to anyone else."

"Alberta, I'm clearly not mentally-challenged. I need you to give me the box so I can have it tested."

Alberta looked toward Roland, handing over the small box only after he nodded.

"How did you know to check the powder case for the cyanide?" Dana asked. "How did you know cyanide would be in there?"

"Mi read police report and medical examiner report twenty time, and me think: where Jacob hide cyanide? Cyanide on Jennifer skin. Powder go on skin—same color as cyanide. Poison so easy to hide."

"Why didn't your detectives think of that?" Natsumi asked Dana.

"I don't know. Maybe because they're men. Who would have thought to test a body powder box for cyanide? Uncanny how she knew."

"I think your detectives ought to feel embarrassed," Roland jibed.

"I read the medical examiner's report too," Dana said, confused. "If the cyanide was in the powder box, and powder was applied on her skin, that wouldn't have been enough to kill her. How did it get in her bloodstream and in her lungs?"

"Are you asking Alberta, or is that a rhetorical question?" Roland joked.

"Something's not making sense to me. It just seems oddly convenient that she would want to come over here, and then she miraculously finds this powder box and smells cyanide. Do we even know for sure it's Jennifer's powder box?"

"If you're asking if Alberta brought it with her, that's a 'no,'" Natsumi answered, "This is her first time ever being in this apartment, and we all came empty-handed."

"It's still not making sense," Dana mumbled. "There's something we're missing. I'll take this box to the lab and have it analyzed and dusted for prints. If the powder is mixed with crushed cyanide salts, we'll know the method, or at least part of it. But maybe there won't be any cyanide in the powder at all. I'm not sure if I'm ready to put my full trust in the nose of a love-struck chimp."

****

Draco and Gutierrez were in Los Angeles watching the conclusion of the OLM rally in Venice on Ocean Front Avenue. The rally was incident-free, with attendance by whites reaching over fifty percent. The California state governor introduced Senator Destiny Mitchell, who was the keynote speaker. After the rally, the Loverboy Elites sat at a bar in Long Beach.

"Colin Stein-Whitaker's still a ghost?" Draco asked.

"Most people in the underground believe he's Cyanide," Gutierrez answered, "but there're some who don't and say Cyanide was here well before Whitaker came along. Some of em are sayin he's dead and others insist he isn't a real person."

"What do you think? Is Whitaker Cyanide?"

"The underground sees Whitaker as a great entrepreneur and rap producer—like Kanye with an Ivy League education, but no one really even knows what he looks like. He's either Cyanide or Cyanide's main avatar. Those in the 'know' call im Cyanide Avatar."

"I heard the FBI's got a team down here looking for Whitaker at Luck's request, but the Bureau's pretty much got their hands full these days with all the killing and chaos of the war. They'll have a hard time finding him in the aftermath."

"I talked to one of Whitaker's associates this morning, a guy named Eddie-Roc. He contacted me," Gutierrez said. "He says Whitaker's got the smoking gun that started the war, says Whitaker's gonna keep it unless we can prove to him what we're gonna do with it, says the only way out for Whitaker is if we take down Luck."

"Did you tell him that's what we're trying to do?" Draco asked.

"He says Whitaker knows all about us and what we're doing. He doesn't think we're capable of taking Luck down by ourselves, and he doesn't trust us. He says one of the Loverboy Elite is dirty, says we're amateurs if we don't realize one of our Elite is working for Luck.'"

"No way! Did he say who?"

"No," Gutierrez answered, "but he says Luck's friends got someone in there to kill our Russian shooter because a Loverboy Elite set it up."

"It was just me and Dunleavy," Draco said, almost to himself. "Did this Eddie-Roc say what we'll have to do to prove what we're gonna do with his evidence—this smoking gun?"

"He said we gotta clean house first. Get ridda of our spy, get ridda the traitor to our cause."

****

"I'm glad you took the time to meet privately with me, Ms. Mitchell. I know how valuable all our time is with everything going on out there."

Dana Murphy and Natsumi Mitchell sat at a quiet table in a small restaurant in Chinatown on Grant Avenue. Both had bowls of wonton soup.

"I'm actually surprised at how quickly things are going back to normal in the city," Natsumi said, after sipping from the white ceramic spoon. "I understand they're still having problems in some of the rural areas in the valley."

"It's worse in other states. I hear Missouri's still a mess, with a small war still raging."

"Well," Natsumi said, "Like Lincoln said after the last civil war, 'these dead shall not have died in vain.'"

"Your cause?"

"Our Lives Matter. The lives of ordinary, underrepresented, disenfranchised Americans matter. That's the only way we can go forward. I hope now we all can unite to advance that cause."

Dana took a deep breath, pausing for an appropriate period.

"I asked you to meet me because something's been bothering me about the Vesey case."

"And what's that?"

"You didn't believe me earlier," Dana began, "but I was never convinced that Vesey had anything to do with poisoning Jennifer Alvarez, and after yesterday, I'm even less convinced."

"I believe the same," Natsumi said. "Vesey loved that woman. They'd planned a life together. There is no reason he would've killed her."

"But you believe that someone else killed her? Maybe some other person murdered her?"

"Waitaminute," Natsumi interrupted. "Are you trying to suggest that maybe Alberta murdered Jennifer Alvarez?"

"You mean you haven't considered it? I did, and I was unconvinced until she somehow discovered the body powder box this afternoon. What are the odds? The detectives completely missed it, twice. I know she's supposed to be smart, but those were seasoned detectives."

"I'm sure it's embarrassing, but maybe they honestly missed it. I can vouch for her—she didn't bring anything with her. She's basically naked all the time."

"There are other bodily crevices, you know. How long was she out of your sight?"

"I believe she's clever," Natsumi smiled, "but not that clever. She didn't bring anything in. Besides—a powder box?"

"Well maybe she discovered it when Jennifer was visiting Vesey in Oakland. That would explain it. Detectives found that vial of potassium cyanide in her room. She could have crushed some of the salts and mixed them with the powder during one of Jennifer's visits. That's why she wanted to go to the apartment to look—because she knew the box would be there."

"But we have no idea if Jennifer ever even took the powder box to the Oakland house. You're giving Alberta a lot of credit, Inspector. But why would she go through such elaborate means to poison Jennifer Alvarez?"

"Because she's in love with Vesey," Dana answered. "It's the only thing that makes sense. She was jealous of Jennifer and was worried she would lose Vesey once the two of them were married. She murdered Jennifer so she wouldn't lose Kendrick."

"Murder?" Natsumi remarked, confused. "She's a chimpanzee. Do you really think a chimpanzee could be capable of murder, of malice aforethought, premeditated intent?"

"Vesey, Franklin Davis and Dr. Hughes have been saying it the whole time. She's a person—not so different from you and me. We're women. She could be jealous. Don't you think it's at least possible?"

"I don't know," Natsumi sighed, thinking. "Off the record, Alberta's implicated another person, a Dr. David Jacobs, who she believes poisoned Jennifer. She's got records and emails from his laptop and phone."

"Really? And how did she get those?"

"She drugged him, borrowed his devices and downloaded them."

"Seriously? But see what I'm talking about?"

"She found pictures from his phone of break-ins to Kendrick's apartment, Jennifer's apartment and the Oakland home. She's trying to prove Jacobs is the murderer."

"All she's proven so far is that it's either him or her," Dana asserted. "It has to be one of the two. What would the doctor's motive be?"

"Jacobs is the doctor who discovered Alberta," Natsumi answered, "and he thought the discovery would make him rich, but Franklin bought Alberta from the research facility where Jacobs had her before he could exploit her. Roland says Jacobs is currently broke and in debt—that Jacobs believes Franklin and Vesey stole Alberta and turned her against him. When Kendrick was arrested, Jacobs became his replacement at the Oakland Hills house, so it's to his benefit that Kendrick is conveniently out of the way."

"I've saw Jacobs on TV a couple times. He was never on our radar, because he came along after the fact."

"Alberta has proof, albeit inadmissible," Natsumi explained, "that Jacobs was around prior to Jennifer's death—at all three crime scenes in fact."

"You think they might be in it together?"

"Alberta hates him, and if you've watched him on TV, he's not a proponent of nonhuman rights. They weren't working together."

Natsumi's ring-tone interrupted the discussion. She would have ignored it, but she recognized the jail prefix and decided to take Kendrick's call. In a calm voice, she re-assured him that court would reconvene within days and she would visit him at six o'clock that evening.

"In a way, I feel sorry for Kendrick," Dana said after the call. "He lost his fiancée, after all, and then to be accused and jailed for murdering her! If he's innocent, what a cruel twist of fate!"

"He's innocent."

"With Alberta and her vaunted Einstein brain," Dana continued, "I'm inclined to think it was her, that she murdered Jennifer Alvarez. Alberta's in love with Kendrick. He's an attractive man in many respects. In addition to testing the powder in the box, I've had the lab dust it for fingerprints. If Jacobs' fingerprints are there, we'll be able to consider him as a suspect, but if only Alberta's prints are there, I think we'll have our answer."

****

"Are you okay in there?" Roland asked, "Did you do it?"

One knock meant "yes."

"Well, come on out. We can wait on the result together."

After another minute, Alberta exited the bathroom with the tube from the test for "hemagglutination inhibition for urinary chorionic gonadotropin" in hand.

"Embarrassing!"

"Yes, but necessary," Roland groaned. "Do you see anything yet?"

"Ring be in tube," she signed, showing the ring in the tube.

"So you're pregnant? That Jacobs! What a bastard! He lied to me. He did this."

"Jacob make me pregnant."

"This is mind-numbing. That snake! I don't know exactly how he pulled it off, but he obviously did. What to do? We have to tell Davis Franklin."

"Jacob," she interrupted, "him want mi baby."

"We'll have to ask Mr. Franklin what to do."

"Why we ask Franklin? This is mi baby."

"But this is his project. We'll have to ask him what he wants to do about the baby. For all intents and purposes, he might decide that we have to abort it."

"No!" she signed. "Mi not project! This is mi baby, mi choice. Alberta is person."

"You're right, but this pregnancy changes everything. Now, there will be another one of you… maybe."

"Alberta is person, yes or no? What Franklin say? What law say?"

"Yes, you're a person, Alberta, but Davis Franklin has a lot at stake here. We have to tell him."

"No, Roland do not tell him. This is mi choice. Mi share this with Roland, not Franklin."

"Why not?" Roland asked. "Hasn't Franklin been good to you?"

"This is not about him be good to mi. This is about mi as person. Person have choice. Alberta not choose to share baby with Franklin."

"Well then, that puts me in a precarious position," Roland responded. "Davis Franklin is my boss. He pays my salary. I don't think he would be very pleased if he found out I was keeping secrets from him."

"Franklin want Alberta to be person. Mi choice. Him understand. Real person can choose. Legal person can choose. Franklin, him understand."

"You want to *have* this baby?" Roland asked.

"Yes."

"Alberta, you have to understand. This baby might not be born with an Einstein brain like you. Einstein's children were not born with his same brain. Jacobs did this trying to make money on the baby. I'm still wondering where he was going with it. The baby would be Davis Franklin's property."

"No! Baby is person! No one property."

"I'm sorry. You're right. The baby would be a person because it was born to a person. I think that would be the case, legally—unless the baby is an ordinary chimp. Why would Jacobs do this?"

"Him tell me him shoot mi and cut baby out. Him take chance with court to see if mi is real person."

"Then we must tell Davis Franklin this!" Roland exclaimed. "We have to make sure that Jacobs can never come here again."

"No, Jacob think him smart, but him not smart. Franklin not need to know. Jacob kill Jennifer. Mi prove. Jacob cannot escape."

"Just so you know," Roland added, "someone made a police report saying they heard gunshots this afternoon coming from somewhere on the property. Nearest house is a half-mile away, but do you know anything about that? Did you hear anything?"

"Race war happen. Many gunshot," she responded.

"I'm just about sure I smelled gunpowder when I came back."

"Race war. Gunpowder everywhere," she answered. "Let Jacob come. Alberta is ready."

"What are you going to do? What is your plan, Alberta?"

Eyes guarded, she smiled.

"Play fool for catch the wise."

Chapter 29

"What ever happened to that guard?"

"What guard?" Dunleavy asked.

Draco and Dunleavy had met at Dealey Plaza in Dallas, on the west edge of downtown at the convergence of Main, Elm and Commerce Streets—a place the locals called the "triple underpass." Draco had dropped into town without notice, pressing for a face-to-face meeting with his Loverboy Elite colleague.

"What are you getting at, Draco?"

"You know—the guard who accidentally shot Sergei Rahimkulov, our Crimean assassin and witness. You were going to have the guard checked out, remember? You didn't think the shooting was an accident. You were going to check out that guard…"

"Well, I did," Dunleavy answered. "Snow and I checked his record of service, possible ties to Luck, his personal life and bank records. I'm still not convinced he wasn't involved, but he came up clean."

"Really?" Draco asked, "And we're all supposed to believe Sergei's shooting was an accident? Sergei Rahimkulov—the best last chance we ever had to get Luck?"

"I was more pissed about it than anyone," Dunleavy sighed. "You saw that. You were there."

"So where is this clumsy guard now?"

"Well, once we put him through the grinder—which was intense and took over 48 hours, he was cleared and he went back to work for Phoenix PD. He's still a Loverboy, but he's on probation."

"What would happen if I reopened the investigation?" Draco asked.

"Why would you do that?" Dunleavy responded. "Are you saying I'm not capable of conducting a basic investigation? I told you—I checked him out, and he came back clean."

"But what if McCarthy and I went to Phoenix and we asked him a few questions about the shooting? What if we told him he was involved in a treasonous act that resulted in 100,000 dead Americans? What if we told him we would ignore his involvement in the plot if he gave us the name of the person who paid him to 'accidentally" shoot and kill Sergei?"

"It sounds like you've already talked to him," Dunleavy scoffed. "What did he tell you?"

"We haven't talked to him yet, but we're planning on questioning him in the next two days. We thought we'd come to you and give you a chance to explain what you found out about the accident before we confronted him. Is there anything you want to tell me?"

"You know, Johnnie—you and I have been friends for over ten years. It sounds to me like you're accusing me. What is it? Come out with it. Do you think I'm working for Luck?"

"I know you've been having money problems, Gordon," Draco said quietly. "You've got three kids in college. I know hard that is. I had to short-sell my house in North Beach this spring to pay my debt. We all got it bad, but country comes first."

"Are you seriously accusing me, Johnnie? I'm so insulted I don't know what to say. I'm a Loverboy Elite. I recruited you, remember? I trusted you, and now to hear this from you—that you're somehow accusing me of selling out my friends and my country? What could be worse than that? You've obviously shared your suspicions with McCarthy. Who else?"

"We want to know if what happened to Sergei Rahimkulov was really an accident. No one's accusing you. We just want to talk to the guard who shot him for ourselves. Over 100,000 Americans are dead. We want to punish whoever was responsible, and those who helped him."

"Do whatever you want to do," Dunleavy snapped. "You're looking for a scapegoat. I had nothing to do with the race war. I don't have a racist bone in my body. My record will show that—no matter what the guard might tell you."

"Then you have nothing to worry about," Draco answered. "I've always respected you—like a brother. I'm prayin this has nothing to do with you."

"How do we know it wasn't you, Johnnie? Maybe you put the guard up to it? Maybe you're working for Luck?"

"Maybe..." Draco answered. "Let's just ask the guard."

****

"Inspector Dana Murphy seems to be stuck on the notion that Alberta murdered Jennifer," Natsumi said to Kendrick. "You know Alberta better than anyone. Is that even possible?"

She had arrived fifteen minutes earlier at the jail within the San Francisco Superior Court's Hall of Justice at 850 Bryant Street. Smiling, she told Kendrick she had just spoken with Superior Court Judge Weir, who indicated the preliminary hearing would resume in four days. Yet the extended imprisonment had taken a toll on Kendrick's spirit. His sad eyes signaled despair.

"Do you think it's possible? For Alberta to commit murder?"

"That's what Davis Franklin and I are fighting for. We *want* for it to be possible. You know the law better than I do, Natsumi. In order for Alberta to commit a murder, she would have to be capable of malice aforethought, premeditation—and if she is capable of premeditation, then she would have to be a person, and the state would be forced to recognize that."

"This isn't making sense to me," Natsumi argued. "Are you telling me you believe Alberta could have murdered Jennifer?"

"No, not at all," Kendrick replied. "She didn't do it, although you need to understand that she was capable of doing it. She may have even considered it, but she chose not to, proving again she's capable of framing representations about the world, formulating plans and acting on them—or in this case, *not* acting on them."

"You don't believe Alberta is responsible for Jennifer's murder?"

"I know she isn't," Kendrick answered. "Alberta knows how much I loved Jennifer. She would have known how miserable losing Jen would make me feel. She wouldn't do that to me under any circumstances."

"Do you think Alberta's in love with you?"

"That's an odd question. Why would you ask me that?"

"It's what Inspector Murphy believes," Natsumi insisted with a shrug. "She thinks Alberta may have murdered Jennifer because she didn't want to lose you once you two were married."

"Alberta is not wired to have those feelings."

"That's the same thing Roland told me, but if Alberta is capable of framing representations about the world, if she's capable of malice aforethought, then why wouldn't she be capable of feeling love, of being in love?"

"That's you two women and your silly sense of romanticism," he commented.

"Maybe that's you two men and your lack of sense about the female heart. Why are men so obtuse about feelings other than their own?"

"Have you seen Alberta lately?" Kendrick asked. "How is she?"

"Roland and I took her on a visit to the crime scene at Jennifer's apartment this morning."

"Crime scene?" he asked. "Why's that?"

"It seems Alberta's determined to prove your innocence. She believes it was Jacobs who poisoned Jennifer—that he poisoned all of you. She found a body powder box at Jennifer's place that she insists contains crushed potassium cyanide powder."

"Is that true?"

"Inspector Murphy's having it checked at the lab. Murphy's suggesting that if Alberta's right, maybe she's the person who put the poison in the powder box."

"Jen never brought her make-up to the Oakland house. She was bare-faced after work when she came to see me, and she always got ready for dates and events at her apartment or mine. It's impossible for Alberta to have put the poison in there."

"Do you think Jacobs could have done it?" Natsumi asked.

"I don't know how he would have had access either. He's never been to Jen's apartment, or mine for that matter."

"But he has," Natsumi countered. "Alberta has the proof, although I can't use it in court."

"Jacobs was at Jen's apartment? What proof?"

"Photographic evidence from his phone and computer, with time and date stamps. Jacobs was in both apartments and at the Oakland home."

"That's a mind-boggling idea, even for her. You mean Alberta went over to Jen's, a place she'd never been, and she found something the detectives overlooked?"

"Depending on what Murphy comes back with, yes."

"Does that change anything having to do with my case?"

"Unfortunately, no," Natsumi answered. "Even if there's cyanide in the powder box, that doesn't make you innocent. For all investigators know, you're the one who put the poison there."

"Do you think the district attorney has made a good enough case to prosecute me?"

"That'll be up to the judge. I honestly have no idea on this one," Natsumi answered. "Again, do you think Jacobs is the one who poisoned Jennifer?"

"If she was poisoned and he was there, then yes. He's desperate for money and he's devious. He's been on this bent for fifteen years. He did it. I'm sure of it."

"I don't have the evidence to prove that or even to introduce the theory at the preliminary hearing during closing arguments. We have four days to come up with something."

"What's Alberta saying?"

"She thinks she's going to save you. She says she's thinking."

"Is she playing her Mozart music? Smoking cigarettes?"

"Are you serious? I've heard classical music, but I had no idea she smokes cigarettes. Unhealthy habit."

"Only when she's stressed and thinking," Kendrick said. "Tell her we only have four days."

"Why? Do you think she can really solve a case the police detectives and Davis Franklin's detectives couldn't? Gotta give her credit, but no one's that smart."

"I've never underestimated her. Does you think she can solve it?"

"No, I don't, but if that powder box comes back and there's cyanide mixed in with the powder, I'm one step closer to believing."

****

"We can't afford to keep waiting here," McCarthy complained as they sat outside the Phoenix police station, "Time is a limited resource these days. They need me back in Boston. Chief Brady revoked my leave. No one gets any leave. It's crazy in Beantown."

"We'll just follow him for half the day," Draco said in a re-assuring voice. "If nothing happens, we'll approach him and question him. You'll be back at work tomorrow."

"Well, there's his car. He's headed out," McCarthy called as he started the rental SUV. "We'll follow him for half the day and see what happens."

Draco and McCarthy had converged on Phoenix during the previous evening and met at a hotel, three miles away from Sky Harbor International Airport. They talked about Colin Stein-Whitaker's intimation that the Loverboy Elite had been compromised.

It was hard to believe, since the Loverboys' existence came about when a network of honest cops met to complain about the culture of corruption, fraud and outside inducement occurring in their respective police departments at the highest levels.

The Loverboys' mandate was to quietly expose or embarrass the worst offenders within their respective departments and crooked players on the outside. Throughout their three years of existence, they had managed to force five police chiefs into an early retirement, including one who chose "retirement by gun in mouth." Prominent in that mandate, they went after district attorneys, private lawyers and businesses who colluded to make a mockery of justice and to profit on corruption.

The chief tenet of their mission was an oath that every Loverboy had to speak aloud before he was sworn in, solemnly pledging "to uphold the goals, mission and objectives of the Loverboy brotherhood" and "to perform my duties to the best of my ability in the service of the Loverboy brotherhood." New members pledged "to support the membership and its endeavors," and most importantly, to work toward the Loverboys' principal requirement of "clean hands," or remaining ethical in all activities, but especially those related to the Loverboy brotherhood.

While on missions, the Loverboys identifying feature was the kiss or lipstick mark somewhere on their faces, or when in stealth operations, the missing nibs, or plastic tips, from the left shoelaces. Missions, orders and directives came from the Loverboy Elite, a group of nine leaders who received alerts and information from a renegade faction composed of members from two quasi-government intelligence agencies.

The idea that one of the Loverboy Elite had been corrupted by Luck was hard to fathom, let alone Dunleavy, who had written the mission statement himself. Draco asked intelligence sources for a work-up on Dunleavy two days earlier and was concerned about what came back. There was a record of considerable debt, relieved by questionable bank transfers that did not coincide with the Dallas Police pay schedule or his retirement accounts.

"You think Dunleavy's dirty?" McCarthy asked as they watched officer Reynolds and his partner responding to a domestic dispute.

"I hope not," Draco answered. "It would shake the brotherhood to its foundation. Imagine the cynicism that would create. 'Dirty hands' at the top? I don't even want to think about the consequences."

"Isn't he the godfather to one of your kids?"

"Yeah, he is—to Stephen, the youngest," Draco answered as he read a message on his phone. "There's some good news!"

"What's that?"

"Dunleavey's still in Dallas. He went to work today, which means he isn't worried about what Reynolds might tell us. Maybe he's clean."

McCarthy started the black SUV and began following the patrol car again, this time headed north along the I-17 corridor to exit on Indian School road.

"Maybe we'll talk to Reynolds after this stop?"

"Yep," Draco nodded. "We'll have our answer and we can put the matter to rest."

The patrol car made a wide right turn on North 24th, drove for a half mile and turned again into the parking lot of a large apartment complex. McCarthy followed, but only to the parking lot entrance. From the SUV, McCarthy and Draco watched Reynolds exit the patrol car, approach a building and disappear up a staircase.

"Rough neighborhood," Draco said, sighing.

"Better him than us," McCarthy laughed. "I did my time in shit neighborhoods. Meth heads—look at em."

Three minutes later, they heard the distinct sound of discharge from weapons—five or six gunshots in rapid succession. Reynold's partner, still seated in the car, spoke into the radio and exited, cautiously approaching the building. McCarthy gunned the engine, sped toward the building and screeched into a parking space before the he and Draco exited, guns drawn, calling out to the startled officer.

"We're cops! We heard the gunshots. Did you call it in?"

"Yeah, but I don't expect back-up anytime soon," the officer answered, noting the lipstick smear on Draco's face. "It's the race war. The city's still in chaos. You're Loverboys, aren't you?"

"Might be," McCarthy answered, glancing over at the crowd that began to gather. "We're going up. Keep all these people away from the stairs, and watch your back."

At the top of the stairs, Draco noticed that one of the doors along the corridor was ajar, and so moving toward the door with his back to the building he shouted in.

"Police officers! Drop your weapons! We're coming in!"

When Draco peeked around the corner, he saw the first body, face down, a pool of blood surrounding the face. It was Reynolds—the dark blue uniform shirt and insignia made him easy to identify. The room was still, but Draco thought he heard or sensed heavy breathing in the distance. Leading with his gun, he stepped into the doorway, immediately recognizing a flash that he assumed was a weapon. Relying on instinct and years of experience, he fired four shots in quick succession and watched the body slump over.

McCarthy, gun drawn, followed Draco into the room, edging past the fallen officer to the body of the shooter. After kicking the gun out of reach, Draco used his boot to roll the dying man onto his back. He and McCarthy immediately gasped in shock, because they knew the face.

"Snow? Chris? What are you doing here?"

Christopher Snow was a police detective from Chicago and one of the Loverboy Elite. He was mortally-injured, bleeding from a neck wound, struggling to speak.

"What the hell are you doing here, Snow?" McCarthy asked.

"The, the kid was dirty," Snow strained to answer, gagging, blood trailing over his lip, "he was workin for Luck. I came to question him. He, he fired on me."

McCarthy glanced over at Draco.

"Let's get im outta here before we get too much attention."

"Yeah, we're gonna get you to a doctor, Chris. We need to wrap that wound."

Snow's inert body between them, the Loverboys walked him past the curious crowd and put him into the SUV's backseat. McCarthy then drove alongside to Reynold's partner who was standing on the sidewalk.

"I thought you called this in?"

"I did, but I knew they wouldn't rush over here. These are meth apartments."

"Wouldn't have made a difference. Your partner was dead when we got here." McCarthy eyed the lipstick smear on the officer's cheek. "It's safe. You can go up. Are your hands clean? Your partner's sure weren't."

The officer held up his hands.

"Clean hands! Loverboy for life. I'll take care of everything here."

Detective Christopher Snow died an hour later as the SUV sped up I-57 North. McCarthy stopped the van shortly afterward so that he and Draco could reposition the body before the onset of rigor mortis.

"Another thirteen hours and we'll be in Chicago," McCarthy sighed, resigned.

"Just look at it this way," Draco groaned in sarcasm. "When we get there, you'll have just enough time to fly back to Boston in time for work."

****

"Have you ever been in this apartment before?" Inspector Murphy asked.

"No," Alberta indicated. "Never see Kendrick apartment. Him never show mi."

"Then why did you want to come here?" she continued. What do you expect to find here?"

"Evidence," Roland translated to Dana and Natsumi, "every mickle make a muckle. Everything count. Mi look."

Earlier in the day, Dana called Natsumi to inform her that the body powder box that Alberta discovered at Jennifer's apartment did indeed contain powder that was mixed with crushed potassium cyanide—in lethal concentration. Researchers had also lifted an unknown fingerprint from the case, which Dana believed belonged to either Alberta or Jacobs. Neither had prints on record.

Natsumi then drove over to the Oakland Hills home to tell Alberta news of the discovery and to relay Kendrick's message from the previous day: *we only had four days, but now only three.* Alberta was insistent about searching Kendrick's apartment, so Natsumi made appropriate arrangements with the court for access. Then she called Dana and the DA to make certain all parties involved knew what was going on.

"Where do you want to start?" Natsumi asked.

"Kendrick room," she answered as she travelled down the hallway and disappeared.

Alberta was thorough in her search, checking gaps between the mattress and the bed frame, under the carpet in the room's corners and behind light switches and electrical outlets. She checked his clothes in the chest of drawers and in the crevices of all the furniture. Then she went to the bathroom and began to check there. The detectives had removed most of the contents from the drawers and cabinets, so there was not much to be examined. Still, Alberta lingered in the bathroom.

"It was either luck the first time, or Alberta's got to be the killer," Dana insisted.

"But how?" Roland asked. "She's never visited either place. I can vouch for that."

"Maybe she has and we just don't know about it."

"She's a chimp," Roland countered. "She can't drive, and chimps don't generally have a stealth mode while moving through a human city. What— you think she hailed a cab? Called a Lyft?"

"San Francisco is full of a lot of strange characters," Natsumi agreed, "but I think people would notice a chimp going in and out of this building."

"What does that leave us with?" Dana asked. "What is she—eighteen? How could she be so smart? Do either of you really believe she could succeed where four of our best-trained detectives were stumped?"

"She is just that intelligent," Roland assured the women, "and yes, she's still a teenager. Her brain isn't yet fully developed."

"Then maybe we all should be scared," Dana said, incredulous, "and maybe humans should think twice about extending personhood and legal rights to other species. Roland, you said she was born in a lab. Is it possible that scientists altered her brain or gave her drugs to heighten her intelligence—like in the movie?"

"That didn't happen. I've read all her medical history and records, and Davis Franklin's had her since she was two years old. It's natural intelligence—from an Einstein brain, which is perhaps one in a billion for chimps, and even rarer if you include humans. Her intelligence comes from that brain, not some miracle drug."

"Well, she isn't human," Natsumi commented, "but there's no doubt she's a person. I don't think even you would disagree about that, Dana. As a person, maybe she should be entitled to some legal rights and protections—no matter what the implications are or how much it scares people."

"That'll be all fine and good," Dana retorted, "until Alberta becomes the leader of a 'Chimp Lives Matter' movement. No equivocation intended, Natsumi, but you know what I mean."

"And what would be so wrong with that?" Roland disagreed. "Chimps share 99% of our DNA. That's only a 1% difference, and despite that, they have the legal status of pets, the same legal right to protection and justice as a goldfish—the same as a guppy, or a pet cockroach."

"But where does it all end?" Dana asked. "We have to be able to draw the line somewhere. That 1% apparently makes a huge difference. Maybe saying so makes me a species elitist, but we're better than apes, much better! I'm convinced of that."

"We are, Dana?" Roland sighed, rolling his eyes. "Have you been watching the news? The hate and the fighting? We sure are proving that!"

"What about poor humans in third-world countries?" Natsumi asked. "How do they they fit your or America's definition of 'persons'? They have no human rights or protections? And what about felons who've been stripped of their rights?"

"They're still humans," Dana insisted, "as opposed to wild, savage animals."

"What if an alien race came from outer space, and they were a little smarter than humans, maybe 1% smarter?" Roland asked. "Would they be entitled to a superior status on Earth just because, by their subjective or technological standards, they're smarter and 'less savage' than we are? Should they have more of a right to justice and protection under the law? Should humans then be stripped of their rights and be forced to submit to an inferior status?"

"No, it's our planet."

"Why? Because we're a little smarter than the second smartest species here? On another planet or next to another species we haven't met, perhaps we'd be the goldfish."

Alberta's re-emergence from the hallway abruptly ended the debate. She held an iPad in her hands because she had taken some pictures.

"Let me guess. You solved the murder?" Dana asked, sarcasm flavoring her voice.

"Mi not find DMSO, mi not find cyanide. Everything is gone. Detective take everything."

"The detectives were thorough. They did their job. They checked everything," Dana confirmed. "Other than traces of cyanide on surface areas, on the bed linen and in the carpet, there was nothing else."

"Where Jennifer sleep when her was sick? Her in Kendrick room?"

"Apparently on the bed," Dana answered. "Our detectives suggested he sprayed her with cyanide in aerosol form while she was sleeping."

"But the amount of cyanide in her lungs alone would not have been enough to kill the average healthy person," Natsumi argued. "Jennifer already had near lethal levels in her blood. Your detectives' aerosol theory doesn't account for that."

"It's the only theory out there," Dana countered, "and we all know Jennifer Alvarez didn't commit suicide. The deputy DA has a circumstantial case, but he thinks he can win it. No one else had the means, motive and opportunity—no one but Kendrick."

Alberta finger-spelled a word to Roland.

"Smudge?" he asked. "Where?"

After a sign language exchange that went for twenty seconds without translation, Natsumi interrupted the discussion.

"What are you two talking about?"

"Alberta said she noticed a slight smear of residue on the mirror. It wasn't powdery, so it wasn't the cyanide. She took a picture of it."

"If it's there, let's all go back and look at it," Dana countered. "What about it?"

"She wants to know if your doctors can test to see what it is—if there are chemicals in it. She says that might be important."

One at a time, Dana, Natsumi and Roland examined the smear, which seemed to have been wiped, leaving a slightly-oily residue three-quarters of an inch in length.

"Did the detectives test this smear, Inspector Murphy?" Natsumi asked. "Maybe she's onto something… again."

"How do we know Alberta didn't just put it there?"

"Small, small dot." Roland translated. "Dry."

"What exactly do you think this is, Alberta?" Dana asked, perturbed.

"DMSO," Roland answered for her, "she says there's DMSO in that smear."

"How would she know?" Dana sneered. "DMSO doesn't have an odor. Not even a chimp could smell it. A bloodhound couldn't smell it."

"Mi guess," Alberta answered. "Mi know smear. Mi see same smear at mi house. That is Jennifer-smear."

"Well Inspector," Natsumi began, "Alberta was right the last time. Can you get a team over here to test that smear for the presence of dimethyl sulfoxide?"

"Okay, I'll do it," Dana shrugged after a pause, "but this doesn't help Kendrick. Even if she's right again, even if we find DMSO there, what does it prove?"

"Smear prove murder," Alberta answered through Roland, "smear prove how Jacob murder Jennifer."

Chapter 30

"So why is Mr. Stein-Whitaker seeking an audience with Mr. Franklin?" the lawyer asked. "If the explosive information he's offering is truly valid, why doesn't he just go to the FBI?"

Edward Simmons, whom Colin called his "Secretary of State," did not seem at all related to Eddie-Roc, though they were one in the same. Mr. Simmons, unlike his underground rap music counterpart, wore a conservative, privately-tailored business suit and appeared clean-cut and professional.

"The FBI can't be trusted," Simmons answered. "Mr. Whitaker doesn't think the entire agency is corrupt, but there're enough people in key positions who Luck can control. If we give them what we have, the information will somehow get lost, classified or debunked, and no one will hear about it. I'm sure Mr. Franklin knows it that works. He's got friends over there too."

"There are other people with connections," the lawyer persisted. "I ask again, why Mr. Franklin?"

"Because Mr. Whitaker also has information, directly from Luck, that Mr. Franklin is secretly one of the biggest financial and legal backers of the Our Lives Matter movement. Luck considers Franklin an enemy, because there's also proof that Franklin has provided key support to the Loverboys—the police brotherhood working for years to take Luck and his friends down. Luck wants revenge, and he'll be able to exact it when he gets his government appointment."

"And what does Mr. Whitaker want for handling this evidence against Luck?"

"He wants the assurance that Franklin will use it to destroy Luck... completely, so he can go back to living a low-key life—without having to worry about Luck's friends showing up. That's all he wants."

"Excuse me for a minute," the lawyer said. "I have to make a call."

When the attorney returned fifteen minutes later, he was prepared to speak on behalf of his boss.

"First, Mr. Franklin cannot be directly involved. He wants plausible deniability if Luck ever publicly accuses him of leaking the information. Every billionaire has his own Achilles heel to protect."

"Mr. Whitaker figured as much," Simmons responded. "That's why he wants to leak the information through the Loverboys, who would be all too eager to take credit for finally sacking Luck."

"With all due respect, Mr. Simmons. The Loverboys come from law enforcement agencies all over the country, and you must know your boss is already on the FBI's radar, with rumors that he is hiding here in Los Angeles. It's no secret that Cyanide's been working with Luck the entire time and helped him instigate the race war. The Loverboys would arrest your boss on the spot."

"You're mistaken there. Mr. Whitaker is not Cyanide, though he's been Cyanide's avatar in this business. It's Mr. Whitaker who has the evidence that'll bring down Luck."

"And he's going to personally hand that evidence to the Loverboys?" Franklin's lawyer asked. "He wouldn't trust them and they wouldn't trust him."

"The information will come through a person who has nothing to do with Mr. Whitaker?" Simmons replied. "What if it came from a person who both my boss and the Loverboys trust? A person who even Mr. Franklin trusts?"

"Then I'm sure Mr. Franklin would definitely want to know who that person is."

"You're no doubt familiar with the name," Simmons insisted. "It's Natsumi Mitchell, one of the founders of Our Lives Matter and someone who is working directly with the Loverboys. She's also working on a big case that's important to your boss. We'll pass the information through her to the Loverboys, and your boss can work through them."

"Mr. Whitaker knows Ms. Mitchell? And she knows who he is?"

"Let's just say they're informally acquainted."

"And Ms. Mitchell has agreed to this arrangement?" the lawyer asked.

"Not yet, but Mr. Whitaker is confident she will."

****

"What is your *real* name?"

"Ya know ma name," the young man answered. "It's the only name ya need ta know."

"Ragna-Roc is not your real name."

"Oh, my real name? It's Ghost IV, cuz no matter how hard you look, you won't find a trace of me nowhere. Not a single record nowhere, and I'm not the only one."

Ragna-Roc sat in a makeshift interrogation room with his four captors, a large, armed guard at the door. Earlier in the day, he realized someone was following him, so he took his pursuer through the motions to get a better look. The man was black, about six-foot-three, and he seemed awkward in the hood. He moved like a soldier.

First, Ragna "gutted" a local restaurant, meaning he went in the front door and quickly left through the back door. Either the man would follow him or he would wait outside. As Ragna exited and began travelling down the alley, he noticed another "government-type" on his tail, following less discreetly—another black man. *How many are there?* Glancing down the alley, he spotted a third man waiting at the end.

He wanted to head for the subway, where he could go underground, but all the escape routes were blocked. *How did they know he would gut that particular restaurant?* They must have been on his trail for days. Options— he was carrying two guns, his 9 and a .22 burner with four bodies on it, but he was light on ammo, especially going up against three or more soldiers. He couldn't run and he couldn't hide. He could have gone out "smokin," but he didn't want to die in an alley like a dog—not when he could still provide Cyanide with some tactical advantage.

The main interrogator, a white man seated across the table, tossed a folder filled with photos on the desk surface, opening it.

"A ghost? Not so much. Ghosts don't show up on cameras. You did. Take a look. Right here's a time-stamped picture of you and another black male in New York five days ago, standing outside the bathroom of a Manhattan restaurant on East 77th Street. And there's another one of you, going in. And here is one of Andrew Luck Jr., going in that same bathroom. Here's another one of you and your partners coming out of the bathroom. Pretty good likeness in that one. It's you."

"So ya'll got pictures of me going in the bathroom in a Manhattan restaurant. A black man cain't use the bathroom there? I sorry. I guess I didn't see the 'White Only' sign posted outside."

"The last two are of Justin Luck Jr., strangled to death, his head stuffed in the toiled that you and your partner didn't bother to flush first. Just the three of you in that bathroom—and Justin Luck Jr., upstanding citizen, husband and father of two, somehow came up dead."

"And who are you? FBI? Ya gonna arrest me?"

"We're not the FBI and we don't arrest people. We capture people."

"For what?" Ragna challenged.

"Revenge."

Luck arrived two hours later, sneering in disgust as he entered and looked on Ragna's face. He ordered the interrogators out of the room and had the armed guard brought in, gun drawn.

"Black piece of shit!" he hissed as he sat. "You murdered my son!"

"Ya murdered ma son!" Ragna spat back. "Ya murdered ma father, ya murdered ma brotha, ya murdered ma mother, ya murdered ma friends. It nevva stops."

"Where is Colin Stein-Whitaker? Where is that bastard? You tell me!"

"Why would I tell you?"

"You'll tell me if you want to live."

"Live?" Ragna laughed. "I just saw the proof they got of me merkin yo son. Ain't no way ya'll wanna let me live."

"You never met my son. I know you were only acting on Colin's orders," Luck said, trying to appear sympathetic. "I know how it works. I might even be able to use a guy like you someday in my business. Just tell me where I can find Colin, or Cyanide as you call him, and we can talk."

"Who's Colin? I work for Cyanide, but he don't let no one see his face," Ragna laughed. "And you think you've seen it, Mr. White Man? I know how it work," he continued, his face becoming serious. "You was workin with Cyanide through an avatar. You promised Cyanide a lotta big thangs, and ya then went back on every last one of them. Ya meant ta do him dirty from the start. Instead of threatenin me, you need ta watch yo back, cuz he's comin fa yo ass."

"He's small-time. I'm not worried about him," Luck sighed. "You see what kind of resources I got? They found you, a so-called ghost, didn't they?"

"Cyanide's comin after you. This shit is turnt up. He got nine ghosts he call his Supreme Court? Me—I'm the Minister of War."

"I know about his damn ghosts, and it's all bullshit."

"Twelve ghosts—all recruited cuz we got no records nowhere. I was born and left in a boarded-up ghetto apartment—no birth record. I nevva went ta school, got no family, nevva been to a hospital, nevva been arrested, and I got scar tissue for fingerprints. Same with the rest, and some of them is white too. All trained ta kill, and they're all after a bounty Cyanide put on ya balls."

"I'm not worried. I'm well-protected from the likes of you."

"I'm sorry—it must be some kinda racial language misunderstandin. When I said 'yo balls,' I wasn't talkin about you, personally. I was talkin about ya family—the otha kids, ya wife, ya close friends—all the people you care about. His ghosts are out there now. So with all ya money and power, you might just see Cyanide face-ta-face one day, but you won't have no one around ta tell about it."

****

"Christopher Snow is dead."

"Oh God! You're kidding me!" Dunleavy exclaimed. "What the hell happened?"

"Seems he was shot in Phoenix," Draco answered, intentionally vague.

"Phoenix? What was he doing in Phoenix?"

"I was hoping you could tell me."

Draco had knocked on Dunleavy's office door, unannounced. Earlier in the day, he and McCarthy left Snow's body with some Chicago Loverboys, who were tasked with creating a cover story and notifying the family.

Uncomfortable with the incursion, Dunleavey sat at his desk, feeling anxious, even a little confrontational.

"Don't play games with me, Johnnie. What's the deal?"

"I'm just trying to figure out why Snow would go to Phoenix to re-interview Reynolds. Did he somehow know that me and McCarthy were on our way there and were about to do the same thing? Did you tell him we were headed there?"

"Was it supposed to be a big secret?" Dunleavy snapped back. "I mighta mentioned it. So what?"

"Coupla strange things at the site of the shooting, Gordon."

"Like what?" Dunleavy asked.

"Snow was wearin body armor. I had to wonder. Why would he need to wear body armor to question a Loverboy cop?"

"Because the kid was dirty."

"But I thought you and Snow already questioned him and cleared him? Didn't you tell me that two days ago?"

"Well," Dunleavy answered, "after you mentioned it, we got to talkin, and Snow—he had a couple of follow-up questions."

"That goes against procedure, and you both knew that!" Draco objected. "There always have to be at least two interrogators at all times in a 'dirty hands' investigation."

"Well, then you just broke your own rule, Johnnie, because I'm only lookin at one interrogator in front of me, and don't tell me you came all the way to Texas to have a friendly conversation. That's not why you're here! You came to accuse me of dirty hands."

"I didn't come to accuse you, Gordon," Draco insisted. "I'm actually hoping you'll have a good explanation, and one that makes sense."

"Whatever happened in Phoenix, apparently Snow was there, and you and McCarthy were there. I was here in Dallas, as you already know because you checked. What more explanation do you expect?"

"I'll just ask outright then," Draco stated, frustrated. "Have you and Snow been compromised? Were you both working for Luck?"

"You insult me," Dunleavy huffed.

"Swear to me on your mother's grave. Swear to me you're not working for that evil bastard! That's all I'll accept. Swear on your life!"

"I'm not doing that. I've known you for twenty-five years. Believe me or don't believe me. That's up to you."

"Either one or both of you were working for Luck. My gut and the circumstances say both. Why, Gordon? Why would you throw away 30 years of good you did? For a bribe!"

"You have no faith in me, Johnnie."

"No, I don't at this point," Draco growled. "Your hands are dirty."

"And so are yours, if you really believe I'm dirty."

"My hands are clean," Draco answered, wagging his head in disgust.

"If you think I'm guilty, Johnnie, what are you gonna do? Turn me in to the FBI? Have me arrested and my career trashed? Is that what you're gonna do?"

"It's not personal, but I'll do it if you don't withdraw from the Loverboys immediately and retire from your job here at the Dallas Police Department."

"All that, but you won't expose me to the Loverboys as a Loverboy Elite with dirty hands?"

"If you withdrew and retired, I'd see no reason to do that—tarnish your reputation."

"But won't that make you dirty too," Dunleavey scoffed, "if you don't expose me?"

"I've known you for twenty-five years. I owe you that dignity."

"Bullshit! You have your own selfish reasons. You won't expose me because doing so would destroy the Loverboys. Imagine that! Dirty hands at the top! Dirty hands in the Loverboy Elite! Why then, the whole movement becomes a fraud! Your entire disillusioned membership would quit on you. Don't act like you're doing me any favors!"

"I'm not trying to hurt you."

"But you're tryin to preserve your precious Loverboy brotherhood, and in doing so, you're sellin out your cause. Remember that oath we all took? You would rather lie to the movement to keep it intact than tell them the truth and maintain your so-called principles. If I'm as guilty as you say I am, it would be your responsibility to expose me, but you won't, for self-serving reasons. That's why you're a sellout—just like every leader of every movement in history. I no longer have any respect for you and your useless movement. Get outta my office!"

****

The reception after the solemn memorial service for Heather Kaplan was a celebration of her life. Her body would not be buried for at least a week, as funeral homes were overwhelmed by the sheer number of dead people arriving. In some areas, bodies were being frozen prior to embalming, since the formaldehyde and phenol in the arterial solution resisted freezing. During the service, Heather's mother, Claire, assured friends and family that her "beautiful little girl" would be "interred in two weeks' time" and that four shomers had been appointed to remain with the body.

Four hundred people crowded into the synagogue to mourn the death of the fiery redhead pediatric doctor whose life had been so selfless. The only child of an older couple, Heather had followed in her father's footsteps and had taken over his children's medical practice after he died. Many undergrad friends from USC were in attendance, as were associates and colleagues from the University of California at San Francisco School of Medicine.

Rabbi Sara-Rachel Ben-David, Heather's best friend since second grade, performed the eulogy and led the reading of the psalms. Her husband, also a rabbi, led the recital of *El Maleh Rachamim*, the Memorial Prayer. Heather's favorite first cousin recited the Mourner's Kaddish. After the final prayer, over eight hundred gathered in a great room at the Moscone Center for an evening meal and remembrances of a life lived.

After the dinner, family and friends traded stories about Heather, from her time volunteering with the Peace Corps in Namibia to several "Doctors without Borders" stints in Guatemala and Panama. Heather, very pretty, had never married because she was always too busy, though there was never a shortage of longing, obsequious male attention. She did not resent men, but she found most of her suitors "pathetic."

"Heather was a heartbreaker because she was so honest," Sara-Rachel joked to Natsumi, seated at her left. "I always pitied the men who tried. It was a fool's errand. She loved her work too much."

"She was a warrior with the heart of a saint," Natsumi commented. "Never afraid to speak her mind."

"Along with my senior counterpart, I will be introducing a U.S. Senate resolution honoring the memory of Heather," Destiny Mitchell added. "She was liberating a detainment camp. She exemplified the best of American values."

Natsumi decided to use Uber rather than drive because she suspected he might show up at her car again. She was so angry about Heather's death that she feared what consequences would come after she pepper-sprayed him, tasered him and beat him bloody with her heavy flashlight. He was large and muscular, so she fretted to imagine the level of violence in retaliation if her weapons failed.

As the dark blue UberBLACK Lexus LS460 approached her condominium building, she remembered that Draco had texted during the reception dinner to let her know he was back in Oakland, while offering condolences for Heather. She thought to call him to ask what he found out about Cyanide. Doing her own research, she had discovered Cyanide's "thing" was invisibility. There were no photos of him discoverable anywhere, and then there were his "ghosts," who operated in his underworld, and his "avatars," who represented him to the public.

As she exited the car, she cringed, imagining someone was watching her. Scanning the periphery, she clutched the pepper spray in her shaking hand as the driver pulled away from the curb.

"Who's there?" she yelled, regretting she had not phoned Draco. "If you're there, come on out now. I'm dialing 9-1-1 in five, four, three…"

"You're gonna call the cops on a ghost?" a male voice spoke from a position behind her.

Turning suddenly, she squirted the pepper spray in the direction of the voice, but no one stood there.

"That wasn't nice," the voice said as a silhouette emerged, standing fifteen feet to her left. "You were really gonna pepper spray me?"

"You killed my friend!" Natsumi blurted. "You killed Heather."

"I didn't kill your friend," the calm voice said. "Remember? I tried to warn you. I tried to save Heather—like I saved your ass. She was good people."

"Your revolution killed my friend!"

"No more than your movement killed your friend. But you know and I know people've been out there dyin every day before all this. What's new? And where did it get you?"

"You obviously don't read the news," Natsumi scoffed. "We just got two bills passed in Congress that will be on the President's desk tomorrow morning—one on gun regulation that will significantly reduce the number of guns on the streets, and another that will compel DAs to prosecute cops who kill civilians in clear-cut cases, like the ones we protest."

"And you think you did that?" the voice asked. "You think Our Lives Matter did that?"

"Our Lives Matter testified before the committee that drafted those bills. We helped create those bills."

"Civil rights attorneys come a dime a dozen. Ain't it a little funny that during all the time you been protestin, Washington didn't wanna give ya'll the time of day? But now alla sudden, they've got you helpin em write they bills. I wonder why that is?"

Natsumi understood the insinuation as she reflected on the first time she spoke with him.

"It wasn't because of your so-called revolution. What we had was a race war. It was a terrible thing. One hundred thousand people died. Americans turned on Americans… over race."

"It was a revolution and people died, but more significantly, a lot of white people died," the voice answered. "It's like I told you—when white people start dyin, that's the only time things change in this country! Revolution made em take this race shit seriously."

"Your voice—it sounds different," Natsumi interrupted, squinting in an attempt to make out the man's shrouded face. "And you're shorter."

"Ma voice doesn't matter, and I take many forms."

"So are you the real Cyanide? Or are you one of his ghosts or avatars?"

"What does it matter? They're my words, no matter who does the talkin."

"What do you want from me?" she asked.

"I wanna help your movement. I come bearin a gift. You'll probably take the credit for that too."

"What kind of gift?"

"Do you have a cop friend, a white boy, by the name of Johnnie Draco?"

"I know Sergeant Draco, yes," she answered.

"Draco's a Loverboy."

"A lover boy? Excuse me. I know him, but it's never been like that."

"No, the Loverboys are a secret order of cops who were tryin ta stop the race war. Draco's one of the leaders."

"Okay," she answered, nodding. "He did tell me that. The idea sounded absurd until a week ago."

"Did he tell you the name of the person who was behind it the race war?"

"I think he said no one would believe it," she answered, still straining to see his face.

"It's Justin Luck," he announced.

"No way! Justin Luck? You mean those rumors—those conspiracy theories were true? Seriously? That's huge!"

"I brought proof. I never trusted him, so took out insurance. I've brought the emails, payoffs, recorded conversations, solicitation for murder and video evidence. All you gotta do is give it to your boyfriend. Luck can't pay or talk his way outta this shit."

Natsumi felt annoyed at the second reference to Draco as her boyfriend, but she was more overwhelmed with the revelation that Luck was responsible for the race war.

"I always wanted to believe he was a secret bigot, but I never imagined there'd be proof!"

'Luck ain't no bigot," the voice argued. "He's a businessman."

"Right, just like you don't hate white people."

"I don't hate white people," he countered. "I just understand how real change comes, and ain't no real change ever came in this country till white people started dyin. I just leveled the playin field. In this country, only White Lives Matter, and the rest can just keep on dreamin and hopin… while they're dyin in the streets every day."

The darkened figure reached over a placed a briefcase on the sidewalk.

"It's all in there. Tell Draco he can't do nothin with that all by himself, or with the Loverboys for that matter. Luck's got too many friends at the FBI and in government. Tell him he needs to go see your boss's friends. Your boss's friends'll be able to take that asshole down."

"My boss? The Reed and Wilke firm has been around for a while, but my bosses don't have that kind of juice."

"No, I meant your 'real' boss—Davis Franklin. You need a dog to eat a dog. Franklin's probably the only one in the country who can pull it off. You said it—100,000 Americans are dead. When people realize Luck was responsible, I'll be surprised if folks don't lynch him on the spot. He'll get his."

"What about you?" Natsumi asked. "You were involved in sedition against America along with him. They'll come after you too."

"Like you care about what happens ta me. But again, you don't know me?"

"You're Cyanide?"

"But who or what is Cyanide?" he proposed, "You've never seen Cyanide. You have never even met Cyanide. You've just been dealin with his ghosts—with his spirit… for the last time."

Chapter 31

"Thank you for taking the time to speak with me, Kendrick," Dana said as she sat, "off the record. Did you tell Ms. Mitchell I'd be coming?"

"No, you asked for a private meeting and I agreed," he answered, "for as private as a meeting can be in this place. You said you wanted to ask me a few questions?"

"Yes, about Alberta. Her testimony in court proves she understands the concept of premeditation and murder. I figure if you can think it, you can do it. Has Alberta ever talked to you about committing murder?"

"We've talked about murder, yes," he nodded.

"Has she ever talked about murdering a human?"

"She's been angry at times," he answered, reflecting, "like any other person, and during those frustrated times, she's said things, but no, she's never talked about murdering a human."

"She's said things. What kinds of things?"

"Basically, that she would protect herself if she felt threatened."

"Threatened by who? By Jennifer? She felt threatened by Jennifer because Jennifer was going to take you away from her."

"No, not at all."

"In the transcript from the court, she says 'she did not like Jennifer,' and since you and Ms. Mitchell insist that she doesn't know how to lie, we have to take that to be true."

"Okay," he sighed. "They didn't like each other very much."

"Kendrick, do you realize Alberta is in love with you?"

"Oh please! No, she likes me, and I like her. We've been working together for over seven years, so there's naturally an attachment. But love? You don't understand Alberta."

"Maybe you don't understand Alberta, Kendrick," Dana countered. "Maybe you're so caught up in your work that you don't realize how…" she sighed, suddenly sad, "how love works—especially when it's one-sided, and there's a heart is breaking, and she can never share how she feels."

"She has a rational brain…"

"Persons don't love with their brains," Dana interrupted. "They love with their hearts. You were engaged to Jennifer, for God's sake! You don't know that?"

"You're right," he nodded, closing his eyes, remembering. "I know that."

"If you really think Alberta should be a person, with protections, rights and respect like the rest of us, then you have to give her credit for being able to love. She's in love with you."

"I don't know," Kendrick sighed. "Even if she was, what difference would it make?"

"It would provide motive. It would explain why she did it."

"Even if that were true," he conceded, "it wouldn't explain how. She had no means or opportunity. She's never been to Jennifer's apartment, or mine for that matter."

"That's what I'm trying to figure out," Dana answered. "She's clever. She had never been to Jennifer's apartment, but somehow she found the body powder, laced with cyanide. And then in your apartment, she pointed out a residue on the mirror, which she said she knew was Jennifer's smear, and asked us to test it for the presence of DMSO. Turns out she was right again. Dimethyl sulfoxide was present. She knows something. She's involved somehow."

"I don't believe that," Kendrick countered. "She might be capable of murder, like all persons are, but she would never kill anyone."

"You said earlier she indicated she would protect herself if she felt threatened. If she didn't feel threatened by Jennifer, then who was she referring to?"

"Dr. David Jacobs. Alberta hates him, and he does everything he can to push her buttons. He's the doctor who discovered her."

"So she threatened to murder Dr. Jacobs?"

"Not literally."

"I have information about a strange incident between those two involving violence and a large plantain, but I can't share it now. Why does she hate him?"

"Because he does not believe in her right to personhood," Kendrick answered, "because he suggests that he wants to do laboratory experiments with her brain. He wants to make her a test subject again, so he can make his millions off her."

"Didn't he have her the first two years?" Dana asked. "Didn't he discover her to the world?"

"Because he thought she would make him rich. But after Davis Franklin acquired her and began the quest for her legal personhood, Jacobs became bitter and did his best to provoke her into a savage, violent animal act. He's betting that an animal act of violence from her will dash her personhood hopes for good."

"What are you suggesting, Kendrick?"

"If anyone had a motive to kill Jennifer, it was Jacobs. By killing her and somehow framing me, he's managed to get me out of the way. I'm here— he's got Alberta! And as one of the world's foremost expert primate researchers in the world, he offered himself to Davis Franklin, knowing Franklin is eager to submit research for upcoming trials. Jacobs is the only person in the equation whose destiny changed for the better after Jennifer was murdered."

****

They agreed to meet at a cool coffeehouse on Broadway in Oakland. Natsumi placed the briefcase on the bench seat, close to her, nervous thoughts putting her on edge. While driving, she fancied a car was following her off the exit the ramp to downtown. Three blocks away from the coffee shop—there it was again. Inside the shop, she caught one hulking man staring in her direction too often, always glancing away when her eyes confronted his. She was certain it was the same man in the car that was tailing her.

She hoped Draco wouldn't be late, because she really wanted him to take possession and responsibility for the highly-significant carrycase. She hadn't dared to open it to examine its contents because she believed that, as an officer of the court, exploring the documents within would have required disclosure or reporting—or sworn testimony if an investigation or hearings eventually ensued. And worse—after what she had learned about Luck, she imagined he was capable of sending someone to kill her if he knew about the damaging contents of the briefcase.

Natsumi trembled, terrified to the point of screaming when the creepy man approached her table grabbed her shoulder, lurking over her, his eyes fixed on the briefcase.

"I'm sorry if I scared you, Ms. Mitchell. I'm here as backup for Johnnie. Relax—you're surrounded by friends. He's on his way."

Relieved, she exhaled, recomposing herself. She had researched the Loverboys earlier in the day and had learned the group had been instrumental in tactical response, military support and community relations during the war and its aftermath. In an offhand way, the President credited early monitoring, intervention and "the selfless sacrifices of unsung heroes in Loverboy ranks' as a major factor in limiting the war's scope and the number of casualties. Draco had been telling her the truth all along.

She thought Johnnie was handsome for an older man—older, meaning he seemed to be in his forties. Steamed milk in front of her, she watched him steady his coffee cup on a saucer as he approached the booth and sat across from her.

"So that's the briefcase?" he asked.

"That's it."

"And you actually met with Cyanide?"

"Now that I don't know," she answered. "After all I've been through, I thought I was talking to him when we met three times before, but last night, he seemed like a totally different guy. Cyanide brags about avatars and ghosts, so who knows?"

"Yeah, the closer we think we're getting to him, the more layers we discover. I'm beginning to think Cyanide isn't an actual person. Maybe it's all a front for another billionaire. Maybe it's big business? Maybe it's the Russians?"

"As long as we're talking crazy theories, I was wondering if Davis Franklin could be Cyanide."

"Davis Franklin?" Johnnie asked. "Funny you should say that. Friend of mine in LA told me I had to go to Franklin to take down Luck."

"Isn't that bizarre?" she asked. "Did you know Justin Luck was behind the race war?"

"From the beginning. We tried to stop him. I understand he was working with this Cyanide person, who has some connection to a Colin Stein-Whitaker, who by the way, gave us the dirt on Luck."

"Colin Stein-Whitaker—who's that? Truth is we don't know who or what Cyanide is—just like most people didn't know anything about the Loverboys. You never told me."

"Okay," Johnnie confessed, "what have you heard about us?"

"You're the cops who tried to save America from the race war."

"Yeah," he sighed, wagging his head, "that's us, and the race war happened in spite of us. We failed our mission. We're done."

"What are you saying? You throwing in the towel, Johnnie? The Loverboys are done?"

"We failed. One hundred thousand Americans died. Hate won."

"So why would you quit?" Natsumi asked. "We're at the beginning of change. There's still so much more work to be done."

"Not for the Loverboys. We failed. We're history."

"But not the things you were fighting for," she countered. "Not your mission."

He bowed his head, reflecting on his last conversation with Dunleavy.

"Natsumi, you're involved in a movement. What happens when you realize your movement can't possibly bring the changes you promised your believers—the people who have trusted you?"

"That's a good question," she answered, "and it's one I deal with it every day. Queen is dead, Demetrius is dead, and now Heather. They believed in our movement. They died for our cause. The movement can't fail them now."

"But there's a time when a movement outlives its purpose," Johnnie said, "and a time when people realize it's all vanity. Things will never change. A movement can never really make a difference."

"We've already made a difference," she countered. "New laws are being written and enacted today. Things are changing."

"Laws can never change hearts, Natsumi. I was out there. I saw the hate, fear and resentment. It's everywhere. I watched Asian teenagers celebrating after killing every white person at a senior care home, and I had to shoot an old man my father's age after he killed a pregnant Mexican woman. There's so much hate in this country. It's naïve to think changing laws'll change anything."

"What about Justin Luck?" Natsumi asked. "You don't think taking him and his friends down will make a difference?"

"There'll just be other billionaires to replace them—people who thrive on hate and division. Nothing will change."

"That's a cynical way of seeing things."

"Luck was paying off some of the Loverboys," Johnnie sighed. "At least two of my friends at the top were taking his money to betray our cause."

"Every cause has its Judas," she nodded, "and some have two, but you're right—laws don't change hearts. Hope changes hearts. Selfless actions change hearts."

"Maybe," he replied, unconvinced. "So what's next for Our Lives Matter? If you think I'm cynical, go out on any street corner today and ask around. We just had a race war that impacted every family in the country. There's not a lot of hope going on out there."

"It only takes a drop to fill an ocean," she said with a soft smile. "You didn't stop the war, but you got the man you were after. You were successful. You're taking down Justin Luck."

"Did you look in there?" Johnnie asked, nodding toward the briefcase.

"Do I look cray-cray to you? I've got my hands full with the Vesey murder case. Luck's your next battle. I've done my part by delivering it."

"You're not even a little curious about what's in there?"

"I have to do the closing argument for a preliminary hearing in the morning where an ape is the star witness. Whatever's in that briefcase, however amazing, does not begin to compare with Alberta."

"Alberta's the chimp who's becoming a person, right?" he asked. "Is she really that smart? I've watched some of her interviews. She talks like a retarded kid."

"You're wrong. She's scary smart. That's just a private language she developed with Vesey, but don't let it fool you. I'm a little terrified of her, personally," Natsumi admitted, cringing, "but somehow she's convinced she can solve Jennifer Alvarez's murder."

"A chimp solve a high-profile murder? And you think she can't?"

"That's what scares me—the thought of what'll happen if she succeeds?"

****

"You're gonna tell us where we can find Cyanide, or you're gonna end up like your friend, Ragna-Roc. Today, he's a real ghost," Luck advisor Bartholomew Morton sneered. "Speak up, Eddie-Roc!"

"My name is Edward Simmons, and I called my lawyer minutes before you and your goons kidnapped me. I've got a GPS chip embedded in my head. We have FBI friends too. You can't do anything to me."

"You work for Cyanide. He ordered the murder of Justin Luck's son and several Our Lives Matter leaders. He's guilty of treason against the U.S. government and conspiring with the Russians. It's guilt by association."

"I work for Cyanide Incorporated, a legal U.S. corporation operating in full accordance with domestic business laws and practices. This 'Cyanide' you're after has nothing to do with my employer."

"They're one and the same," Morton barked, "so you can cut the shit, Eddie-Roc! And we know Colin Stein-Whitaker is Cyanide. It's only a matter of time before we find him."

"Really?" Simmons laughed. "You think Colin Stein-Whitaker is Cyanide? And you're really former FBI?"

"Whitaker is Cyanide," Morton retorted. "He told Luck that himself. Stein-Whitaker as Cyanide was working with Luck on the race war all along. Luck has a secret video of him revealing his identity. He admitted it."

"For a billionaire, your boss sure is gullible. You don't think Cyanide knew what Luck was up to? He put Stein-Whitaker up to that—Whitaker was pretending to be Cyanide. He has a history and records, so he could never be a ghost. He's just Cyanide Avatar. The other Cyanide, on the other hand, is a ghost—the realest ghost of em all. He was born in a shopping cart in South Central LA."

"I call bullshit. This is all a bluff," Morton countered. "Whitaker is Cyanide. We know that."

""No. Like me, Whitaker is just an avatar—Cyanide's best avatar. Cyanide Ghost ain't even Cyanide! Whitaker was not in New York when Luck's son was murdered. Check your facts. Whitaker was in LA. Cyanide Ghost was at that Manhattan restaurant, callin the shots—not Whitaker."

"Well, if Whitaker isn't Cyanide," Morton asked, "why's he hiding?"

"Because he's waiting for Luck to fall. It's only a matter of time before people realize your boss was responsible for the race war. In fact, it'll be on blast by tomorrow. Whitaker staged it all, set him up—but in the end, there'll be proof that he wasn't involved in any way. All the evidence will point to Luck and Cyanide Ghost, the true architects of the race war and revolution. Luck's out there—he's a public figure, but the real Cyanide is and will always be 'the God from the Machine.'"

"I don't believe you."

"Access your FBI database," Simmons insisted, tossing a document on the table. "Whitaker and Cyanide Ghost have never even been on the same coast at the same time. That was intentional and premeditated. They've never met in person. It was all a set-up, and your boss fell for it, like the dumb bitch he is. Heads-up, Morton—you're on a sinking ship. Get your ass off, or you go down with Luck and the rest of his bitch organization."

****

"It is the understanding of this court that the defense has rested. Shall we move forward on that understanding, Ms. Mitchell?"

"I'm sorry, Your Honor, but the defense has not rested. We would like to recall a witness."

"Okay, and which witness would that be?"

"Alberta, whom this court, the Superior Court of the state of California, has recognized as a legal nonhuman person for the purpose of direct testimony."

"My understanding," Judge Weir said, "was that the defense had rested at the close of our last session. Is there something new to be considered?"

"There is," Natsumi answered. "Alberta has asked to amend her testimony to the court on the investigation related to Jennifer Alvarez's murder. She believes she has pertinent information that will affect your judgment in this matter. Until this time, she has not revealed it to me, which is why I have not shared it with the prosecution team."

"New information?" the judge asked. "The court will hear it."

Returned to the witness stand, the translator in place, Alberta seemed intent and confident. Natsumi asked the questions.

"It is my understanding that you believe you know how Jennifer Alvarez was murdered. Is that true?"

"Yes, I know."

"You do realize that human detectives have been working on this case, and they have not reached a conclusive result for lack of evidence. Are you telling this court that you, as a nonhuman person, have discovered something that human detectives could not?"

"Some humans are smart, but some humans are not so smart."

"So you're saying you discovered something the human detectives missed?"

"The evidence was there, the humans were there—but they never saw it. Real eyes realize real lies."

There was laughter and murmuring in the courtroom from those who understood the reference.

"What did the detectives not see?"

"They did not discover the potassium cyanide in Jennifer's powder box. There was potassium cyanide, ground-up, in her powder box. When Jennifer put on her powder, she put on cyanide."

"But as the medical examiner testified," Natsumi questioned, "potassium cyanide in her body powder would not have killed her. It may have made her sick, as it apparently did, but it wouldn't have killed her."

"Dr. Jacob's put the cyanide in her body powder box. I have proof. He went into Jennifer's apartment when she wasn't home. That is when he put cyanide in the powder box."

"Objection!" the prosecutor called out. "Assumes facts not in evidence."

"Sustained."

"Your Honor," Natsumi interrupted, "there is photographic evidence from Dr. David Jacobs' cell phone that he was physically in Jennifer Alvarez's apartment prior to her murder and that he had the means to add ground-up potassium cyanide to her powder box. We're not ready to introduce it as evidence because of the way it was acquired, but I can introduce a report from the San Francisco Police laboratory that indicates a significant amount of potassium cyanide was present in the powder box."

"Very well. I'll take other matter under advisement. Please continue."

"So having potassium cyanide in her powder box does not explain how Jennifer Alvarez died, Alberta," Natsumi continued. "Are you saying there was something else involved?"

"I can prove that Jennifer die because she was exposed to 'liquid death.'"

"What is 'liquid death,' Alberta?"

The translator struggled to re-work the syntax and find the approximate words.

"Liquid death is a combination of potassium cyanide and DMSO, which is the solvent—dimethyl sulfoxide. When they're combined, humans die fast."

"You discovered the potassium cyanide in the powder box in Jennifer's apartment, but you would agree that all by itself, it wouldn't have killed Jennifer. Do you know how that potassium cyanide would have been combined with dimethyl sulfoxide?"

"I discovered a smear on the mirror, a Jennifer-smear."

"Jennifer-smear? You found residue on the mirror at Kendrick Vesey's apartment that you called a 'Jennifer-smear.' When you found it, you asked San Francisco Police Inspector Dana Murphy to have it tested for the presence of DMSO, or dimethyl sulfoxide. Is that true?'

"Yes, that is true."

"Why did you believe DMSO was present in the 'Jennifer-smear'?"

"Because DMSO is other element in liquid death."

"Your Honor," Natsumi said, "I would like to add a second lab report to the record, relating to a residue discovered on the bathroom mirror of Mr. Vesey's apartment. It's the residue Alberta identified as the 'Jennifer-smear.'"

She handed the document to the judge before turning back to her witness.

"You were right, Alberta. That smear did contain DMSO residue. You're not a detective. So how did you know dimethyl sulfoxide would be present in that residue?"

"Because it's Jennifer's smear."

"Can you tell us why you call that a Jennifer-smear?"

"Jennifer always wore perfume—too much. She was always spraying perfume, all over the place. It smelled bad."

"Objection," DA Carroll interjected. "Misleading, and calls for speculation by a person who is clearly not an expert."

"Overruled," the judge answered.

"Please continue," Natsumi urged. "The Jennifer-smear?"

"When she sprayed the perfume, she always sprayed too much, and the extra perfume always sprayed on mirror. That is why the Jennifer-smear."

"And what does that have to do with the murder of Jennifer Alvarez?"

"After Dr. Jacobs put potassium cyanide in her powder box, Jennifer put the powder on her skin…"

"Objection, your Honor!" Carroll complained, "Counsel is leading the witness."

"Overruled."

"Okay" Natsumi continued, "we get that. We understand the powder she put on her skin contained potassium cyanide. Please continue. Then what did Dr. Jacobs do?"

"Then Dr. Jacobs put DMSO in Jennifer's perfume bottles. When Jennifer sprayed the perfume that was mixed with DMSO on her skin that was covered with powder and potassium cyanide, the chemicals combined— sodium cyanide and DMSO. They became liquid death, and Jennifer died. That's how Dr. Jacobs murdered Jennifer. Check Jennifer's perfume bottles."

The chamber erupted in chaos as the import of Alberta's words resonated throughout the courtroom. Her words lingered in the air, with the realization that she had put a theory forth that finally described in detail how Jennifer Alvarez was murdered. Police investigators and FBI profilers in the room struggled with her explanation, seeking a logical flaw, but in the ensuing bedlam, no more a reasonable alternative emerged.

Frustrated and angered by Alberta's testimony, Armando Alvarez stood, yelling a profane-laced series of simian insults before launching a banana in her direction. He was in the act of launching a second banana when one of the sheriff officers tackled him to the floor.

Pounding the gavel, Judge Weir ordered Alvarez out of the courtroom and held for contempt. After the commotion, all eyes returned to Alberta, who had endured the threat and insult with a comportment that could only be described as "dignified."

It was an awkward moment as onlookers were forced to consider the reality that a chimpanzee had solved a murder where human detectives, with all their technology and training, could not. When investigators checked Jennifer's perfume bottles, they would find the presence of DMSO, a substance that should not normally be there. Dimethyl sulfoxide alone mixed with perfume was mostly innocuous, but when sprayed in aerosol form to combine with powder that had been laced with potassium cyanide, it was liquid death—extremely toxic and Jennifer's certain demise. Alberta had put it all together.

Next, Natsumi recalled medical examiner Medha Singh to testify about whether it was possible to poison a person in the way Alberta suggested, asking if Alberta's description of the poisoning was consistent with the facts of the case.

"Her theory would explain the light layer of cyanide found on the decedent's skin," Dr. Singh explicated. "It would also explain the chronic exposure, which was notable in the neck and upper chest area, where one might apply powder and spray perfume. Consistent? I would say 'yes.'"

"And would it also explain Mr. Vesey's exposure and the cyanide residue found on the bedding and in other places at Ms. Alvarez's and Mr. Vesey's apartments?" Natsumi asked.

"It would," the doctor answered, "as well as the contamination at the Oakland Hills residence. The record indicates that Alberta suffered a level of cyanide exposure, which would also be consistent in such a scenario."

"And what about, as you stated in your report, 'the ground-glass attenuation apparent in both lung fields, along with inflammation indicative of exposure to cyanide'?" Natsumi asked while glancing at her notes. "Would that be consistent with Alberta's theory of events causing Ms. Alvarez's death?"

"Objection, your Honor. Calls for speculation."

"Overruled."

"Well," the doctor answered cautiously, "it could be. I would imagine that if the decedent had recently applied the cyanide-laced powder, and powder particles remained suspended in the air at the time she sprayed the perfume, it would explain the ground-glass attenuation in the lungs—that is if she inadvertently breathed in the perfume in aerosol form. It would account unexplained fatal exposure. It's possible that's how it happened."

Natsumi's final witness was San Francisco Police Inspector Dana Murphy, who testified about the investigation work done by city detectives as well as the inspection by Alberta. Struggling to save face for the inspectors, she admitted that investigators had missed the powder box at Jennifer's apartment and the 'Jennifer-smear' at Kendrick's apartment. Alberta however, she insisted, had an advantage because had access to Dr. David Jacobs' smart phone and computer.

"And in your investigation, Inspector Murphy," Natsumi asked, "what did you learn about Dr. David Jacobs and his possible involvement in the murder of Jennifer Alvarez?"

"He is definitely a person-of-interest, but we've just gotten started in the new investigation. We—all with the district attorney's office, are aware that some of the evidence involved might be inadmissible in a courtroom proceeding, but we're investigating the same theory that uh... Alberta put forth."

"Finally, the Court would like to thank Alberta for her landmark testimony, which made all the difference in this hearing for me. Alberta, I personally wish you success in your quest for personhood. Never stop fighting. It's a little ironic that we, as humans, are full of such hypocrisy. Without debate, we have provided that ordinary corporations are persons, and we've granted them legal rights and protections without considering they have ta distinct advantage over us—their potential immortality. We did this long before you came on the scene, Alberta, but watch yourself—the world and indeed history are watching you."

Two hours after closing arguments, Judge Weir had reconvened the court for the purpose of stating her judgment. She rambled on about nonhuman persons' legal status and their potential involvement in national courtroom proceedings before coming to her ruling.

"In the matter of the people of the state of California verses Kendrick Vesey, I find that, based on the probable cause required to convince a reasonable jury that the defendant has committed the crime as charged, there is insufficient evidence to hold Dr. Vesey over for trial. I hereby order his immediate release. This hearing is closed."

Chapter 32

"I'm pleased that Kendrick was exonerated," Davis Franklin responded, beaming, "but the fact is Alberta solved a murder case where the detectives could not. Do you realize how much coverage that'll get us? Think of the implications for nonhuman rights! Now there can be no denying the fact that some of our 'persons' are even more capable than humans!"

"It took me by surprise," Roland said. "I had no idea that Alberta could have put that together. I saw the material she downloaded from Jacobs' phone and computer. Natsumi Mitchell looked at it. There's no way either of us could have figured it out."

"Alberta proves what we've been saying all along. We couldn't have asked for a better outcome," Davis continued. "Our government's failure to consider nonhuman rights became a real issue today. There are hundreds of chimps like Alberta still locked-up in school research facilities and at zoos all across the country today. At least they'll have a better chance now. We'll be bringing other cases."

"We can never take for granted the prejudice and inhumanity of humans," Roland said. "There are some who'll see always her as a threat, who'll never give her credit for having intelligence—let alone engage in a debate about her legal rights. Some would rather kill her than recognize her humanity."

"America just had a race war," Davis nodded. "People can't get along with each other. We still have a long way to go. Maybe *we* need a revolution."

"What are we going to do about Jacobs?" Roland asked. "According to Alberta's theory, he murdered Jennifer Alvarez, and he poses a danger to Alberta."

"She'll be safe," Davis answered. "I've got my best people looking for him. He'll be arrested as soon as they find him. The DA confirmed that to me an hour ago."

"Mr. Franklin," Roland ventured, nervous, "there's something I have to share with you about Alberta. She swore me to silence, but you're my employer. I hate to betray her, but I don't want you to see me is disloyal. I need this job."

"What is it, Roland?"

Roland bowed his head in hesitation, struggling within before finally blurting the words.

"Alberta's pregnant."

"Pregnant?" Davis asked, "how could that possibly be? She's had no exposure to a male chimp. Explain how she could be pregnant."

"As it turns out, Jacobs managed to get her artificially-inseminated during one of her check-ups when her regular doctor was on vacation," Roland answered. "And knowing Jacobs, he pre-selected the donor—

probably an Alberta relative somewhere in the U.S—to enhance the possibility of another Einstein brain. I'm sure he had plans for the baby."

"And Alberta?" Davis asked.

"She wants to have the baby. She's sure that she'll have the choice to keep it, because you've told her she is a legal person, and she believes you are a person of your word."

"There's the dilemma," Davis sighed. "We have a huge fight ahead of us. A baby chimp for Alberta would be a major distraction."

"I imagine she knew you'd feel that way. It's why she didn't want me to tell you."

"I'm glad you did. Thank you, Roland. We'll have to figure something out."

"So you're saying it's *not* her choice?" Roland asked. "That was her concern. Are you going to take the baby from her to advance your cause?"

"I don't know, but this is an unexpected wrinkle. When the media begins reporting that Alberta solved a murder case, we'll have all the publicity we need to take our cause nationwide, but a pregnancy would be a media distraction. Instead of the next Rosa Parks, she'd become the next Kim Kardashian."

"But you know Alberta," Roland warned. "I don't think she would take it well if you tried to take her baby away, regardless of how she came to be pregnant. It flies in the face of everything you've done to make her a legal person."

"Then we'll have to convince her that it's for the best," Davis said. "Kendrick owes me. It will be his job to make sure she understands that."

Franklin's next appointment was by telephone, as he did not want the scrutiny involved in a physical visit. Colin Stein-Whitaker was calling in from a burner phone.

"Mr. Stein-Whitaker, good to finally talk to you," Davis said. "I'm not certain you fully appreciate the amount of risk involved in our undertaking—for the both of us."

"You have more money than I do, Mr. Franklin, so you have more to risk on that front," Colin responded, "but this has become life and death for me. Luck has sent his people to kill me, shut me up or discredit me. I have to see this to its end."

"Do you know how hard it'll be to take down a billionaire?" Davis asked. "It's like overthrowing a foreign government. There are careers and entire economic markets at stake. Plus, the American government has a vested interest in people like him. Some federal interests will be affected."

"Of course they will," Colin shrugged, "but Luck has damaged American interests across the board. He caused this race war, and I'm going to make sure people understand that. I'm sure he'll try to divert blame or put his own spin on it, but he can't escape what we can put out there, whether you help me or not. The American people will turn on him and tear him to pieces."

"Okay, Colin," Davis said, "if that's really going to happen, why do you need me involved?"

"Because you are his equal or better. He'd try to pull me down with him. I need you to protect me, to focus public rage toward Luck and Cyanide. I want to be seen as an American patriot whose only involvement in this business was to reveal domestic traitors and their treachery toward the U.S."

"I understand," Davis nodded, "but you have to answer a question for me."

"What's that?"

"What about Cyanide?"

"You know better than that, Mr. Franklin. There's Cyanide's Ghost, and I was Cyanide's Avatar, but no one's ever met the real Cyanide—the God from the Machine."

"But now you've turned on Cyanide?" Davis asked. "You want to see Cyanide to go down with Luck?"

"No, Cyanide has a plan for every contingency. They can chase his ghost around, but they'll never put their hands on him. They'll only make him and his revolutionary street philosophy more famous when they write their stories. I'm done with being an avatar. I want to enjoy my money—start a new life."

"You're obviously a successful businessman, Colin," Davis continued, "so you understand there's always has to be a profit motive. Why don't you tell me how you think I'll benefit from the demise of Justin Luck?"

"You already know that, Mr. Franklin," Colin answered. "Huge insider trading tip—Justin Luck is arrested for treason tomorrow or the next day—an inconvenience that will drastically affect the value of all his properties, holdings and investments. If you're smart—as I know you are, you already have broker instructions in place to capitalize on his misfortune. I've done the same. I'll be glad to eat from his corpse."

"Based on the documents Sergeant Draco shared with me," Davis nodded, "I've decided to go forward with this. I'm in."

"That's good to know," Colin nodded, "and since you thought to ask me, I'm asking you the same question—do you know about Cyanide, Mr. Franklin? Better yet, are you Cyanide?"

"That would be impossible," Davis answered. "Believe me, I've done the research. My sources concluded that Cyanide is an urban legend, or he died on the battlefield in his short-lived revolution, but that's all a ruse. I believe Cyanide is a person—but not a person in the traditional sense. The real Cyanide will never die, because the real Cyanide is a 'nonhuman' person, a California corporation."

****

He had remained hidden inside the complex for most of the day. Five hours earlier, he parked a rented car a mile away and walked to the Oakland Hills home. Roland and Alberta had left for the preliminary hearing in San Francisco at ten that morning and would not be back until at least four that afternoon. Jacobs was certain he'd have time to be thorough.

He entered the home with the key code combination on the pad at the front door and disabled the alarm. Going directly to Alberta's door, he opened a wallet-sized case that contained handcrafted picks and tension wrenches. During his junior year of high school, Jacobs worked with his uncle Larry, who owned a locksmith business in Moorestown, Pennsylvania. He worked three years for his uncle before he was off for college, so he fancied picking locks as a lifelong hobby, giving him James Bond-like spy powers.

The lock on Alberta's door was large though simple. The fingers of chimpanzees lacked the dexterity that humans take for granted when keying open a lock, so the straight-forward design served for peace of mind rather than security.

Placing the tension wrench into the lower portion of the keyhole, he first made the determination that unlocking the door required turning the cylinder counterclockwise. Then it was a matter of torqueing the tension wrench in that direction and inserting the pick in the upper portion of the keyhole. The rest, for David, was art, which involved pushing the pins out of the cylinder. He opened the door in less than a minute.

Jacobs had been in Alberta's room only once before, so he wasn't sure what to expect. He was surprised by how neat and systematized the room was, since typical lab chimps had little sense of spatial organization. Even the bathroom was tidy and the marble sink countertop was spotless. *She lives in a higher style than I do! he thought. I deserve this, and better!*

Her computer was on the desk. First things first. Donning gloves, he opened his briefcase and retrieved a second set of tools—an assortment of small screwdrivers, sockets and wrenches purposed to remove the computer casing and access the hard disk drive. After another twenty minutes, he had opened the case, removed the magnets and taken out the platter—the prize.

He took the platter from the hard-drive to the garage floor, where he pounded it with a hammer until it was unrecognizable before wrapping it in a towel and placing it in his briefcase. He didn't believe it was necessary to put the computer back together sans hard-drive, but he did anyway before beginning his quest for Alberta's external storage devices. He found two, which also met their end on the garage floor.

He knew Alberta didn't have a smart phone since she couldn't vocalize, but he had seen an iPad. After searching for in her room for over an hour, he widened parameters and discovered it tucked in her bathroom, hidden in a case within the bottom vanity drawer. The iPad device destroyed, he focused on the possibility of data storage within a virtual cloud. The destruction of any possible virtual data she stored would be a more difficult matter and would require a more aggressive approach.

Jacobs had noticed that since the race war began, Roland had been spending more time away from the Oakland Hills home. Over the time that Jacobs had been there, he encouraged Roland to get out more, to pursue this new relationship. During Roland's absence, Alberta always locked herself in her room, while Jacobs spent time in the labs and in the front area of the house. The time for a direct conflict had arrived, and Jacobs wanted to act at the earliest opportunity. He was running out of time.

After restoring Alberta's room to its previous condition, which he compared to four smart photos he took when he first entered, he repeated the process in the garage, sweeping up and disposing of the glass and metal fragments remaining on the hard, cold cement floor. He was waiting, hidden in a laboratory closet, when Roland and Alberta arrived at 4:28, and he eavesdropped, using a baby monitor device hidden in the kitchen, as Roland explained that he would be gone for about three hours for an in-person meeting with Davis Franklin before dinner.

"Another precaution—we're going to start setting the alarm again."

Worried that Jacobs might return to the house, Roland changed the alarm code and called the police to request a patrol car drive-by once an hour. Reluctant to leave, he warned Alberta about the danger the doctor represented.

"You're the only person who can prove Jacobs killed Jennifer. If he were to come in here and kill you, Kendrick might go back to jail, and there'll be no nonhuman rights case for Davis Franklin in the foreseeable future. I've set up a 9-1-1 call on this phone—if he shows up or if you hear anything suspicious, all you have to do hit 'send.'"

Jacobs listened as Roland slammed the kitchen-garage door, started the car and drove off. He nodded as the roll-down garage door came to a stop. Exiting the closet, he loaded a full fifteen-round clip into magazine well of his black Glock-19 Gen 4 9-millimeter and chambered a round. Then he ventured out to the living room area, where he knew Alberta would come once she realized her computer was not working and there had been an intrusion in her room.

He waited. Nothing. She was in her room, listening to music and apparently smoking cigarettes. Jacobs recognized only one song—Mozart's *Violin Concerto No. 5 in A*, but only because it was his mother's favorite. Alberta exited the room at 5:30, cautiously inspecting the kitchen area.

"I'm here in the living room, Alberta," Jacobs announced, gun drawn, as he awaited her appearance.

He waited, though it took more than three minutes before she came into view, and once she saw the gun, she raised her arms. Out of his vision, he thought he heard her moving furniture or manipulating something before coming out.

"What were you doing back there?"

"Jacob is evil human. Alberta is afraid."

"You have nothing to be afraid about, Alberta," he answered, "as long as you do what I ask."

"What Jacob ask?"

"As you probably already know, I've destroyed the hard-drive from your computer and I've destroyed your storage devices. Whatever you think you downloaded from my devices—it doesn't exist anymore, so whatever you testified about at that hearing today—it's your word against mine, and you're just a chimp. You're intelligent compared to other chimps, but you're not as smart as the dumbest human. You're not even as smart as a moron."

"Moron is smarter than Jacob? Alberta is smarter than Jacob."

"Dumb ape! I underestimated you before when you drugged me and stole that data from me, but now I've corrected that error," Jacobs said. "You have nothing... unless it's in virtual cloud storage. So, I'll need you to give me the username and password for your virtual storage account."

"Jacob want to murder Alberta?"

"Murder? Impossible! You're just an ape. If I kill you, the law might consider it cruelty to animals, but not murder. I might pay a fine, but you'll be just another dead ape, and the 'Alberta personhood' cause will be over. We can all get back to business as usual."

"Maybe mi take chance. Maybe mi let Jacob shoot. Maybe mi let Davis Franklin be angry at Jacob. Him have money to punish Jacob. That is test of person. Mi give no password. Want all, lose all, Jacob. We see if it is murder to kill Alberta."

"Me killing you today serves neither of our purposes," Jacobs said. "My plan was to wait until we were seven or eight months into gestation. Now that would be a test worth the reward. I was going to shoot you and cut out the baby and put it in a facility that has successfully cared for prematurely-born chimps. You ruined that plan when you drugged me."

"Jacob rape mi, mi rape Jacob. Banana is Jacob boyfriend now."

"I've destroyed everything you took from me," the doctor continued. "I should kill you now, but I'll let you live if you provide the codes for your virtual storage... and I'll need you to sign a legal document, giving me custody of the baby from the day it is born. You'll die today if those two things don't happen."

"How human say? Go to hell, Jacob! You kill me anyway."

"I'll shoot you, you damned ape! I hate you!"

"Mi call Jacob bluff. Kill me, or murder me. Let human law decide!"

****

"What do we have going for damage control?" Luck asked. "There's got to be something someone can do to deflect or discredit what they're going to leak. Gordon? Bart, what do you got?"

"It's going to be pretty damaging, no matter how you parse it," Morton replied. "I think they're going directly to news sources, the news chiefs…"

"Who work for friends of mine!" Luck shouted. "Come on, this is totally fixable. Roberts—start getting station owners and network executives on the phone now. Tell em I want to speak to em directly. They all owe me favors. Today, I'm calling in all my markers."

"Yes sir, Mr. Luck," Roberts enthusiastically nodded. "I'll get right on it."

"The Luck empire is too big to fail," Luck repeated. "Bart, talking to these people won't be enough. What good is it to control power levers if you never use them? Talk to your friends. I want real pressure on any credible network decision-maker who is even willing to peek at those leaked documents. Make em understand that if they're in any way disloyal, they'll all have somethin to lose."

"You don't think you can control the entire media-at-large, do you, Justin?" Morton asked. "Someone's going to put this out there. The stories will get out."

"It won't matter," Luck retorted. "Let em do their worst. We'll just say the stories are false. They're fake news. Tell em there are alotta haters out there. We'll put our own stories and conspiracy theories out there—some even worse than what the Loverboys are saying. Our news and social media friends will help put so much fake news out there that nobody'll know what to believe. In the end, it won't hurt me. Get em going again in the Balkans. Spread a little money around over there. My friends are so loyal to me."

"You can just make up anything?" Morton persisted.

"There's no such thing as news anymore, it's all fact-free," Luck answered. "In America, everyone's a sellout."

Luck operatives went immediately to work, putting on the pressure, contacting friends, insiders and players in the news industry, ginning up their operatives who began immediately with stunning fake news stories that accused the President, Our Lives Matter and a group of rogue cops called "The Loverboys" for the race war. Other stories cast Justin Luck as an altruistic patriot who tried to prevent the war and who provided financial resources for wounded victims of the war. By 4 p.m., Facebook and Twitter were ablaze with theories, comments and statements that would seem to render any leak about Luck ineffective.

He left his lower Manhattan office at 8:30 p.m., intent on addressing followers in a series of interviews at the World Trade Center on Greenwich Street. He was pleased that the efforts to minimize damage to his person and to his brand were going so well. *After it all blows over*, he thought, *I'm going after that bastard, Colin, and his family, and every one of those Loverboys involved – but most of all, I'm going to get Davis Franklin!*

Yet even if he won the media war, there were some in government agencies who would surely seek to investigate the evidence and claims against him. If believed, the information could potentially result in his indictment and prosecution.

Fortunately, Luck knew where the evidence was—in Davis Franklin's possession, for the time being. He knew he would have to make the consequential call within hours to prevent the truth from being revealed, but he knew Franklin would succumb to the proper motivation. Franklin had a price, but Luck didn't know if he could afford it.

He had exited the limo and had just placed a call to Morton when it happened. It began with a phone call interruption from an international number.

"Hello, who's this and how did you get this number?"

"Must clean up loose end," the Eastern European-flavored male voice said. "*Dasvidania, Comrade Luck.*"

"Holy shit!"

It was probably best not to know—not to see it coming. He never felt a thing. In one moment, he was on top of the world, kicking ass as usual, while in the next, his eyes went dull and sank deep into their sockets. In one moment, he was striding in style, reporters crowded around, toward the front entrance of the Trade Center, while in the next, his body was hurled backward onto the sidewalk, where he lay still, bleeding from a huge chest-wound. A female aide, walking slightly behind him, was instantly dead and bleeding on the pavement as well.

Luck's guards sprang into action, using their own bodies to block the shooter from any further access to him while moving his body to a better location for protection. The rest of his entourage and the reporters, however, did not prove to be as brave. Screaming, scattering and ignoring their expensive equipment and clothing, they tripped over and into each other, scrambling to get away from the shooter's apparent target.

One block away, on the rooftop of a building on Sixth Avenue, a single sniper, American rifle rested, peered through a pair of 8x30 Russian military night vision binoculars to confirm his kill. Taking out a camera, he snapped a picture through the zoom lens. Sitting back against the wall on the roof with his gloves still on, he lit a Marlboro cigarette and smoked it slowly before packing up his camera and attachments. He would leave the rifle on the roof.

Grigori Sokolov did not know where the order came from, whether from the Americans, the Russians or the Ukrainians. He was anxious to leave America after having fired the first shot of the civil war. Grigori was at JFK in New York four days earlier, prepared to fly to London, when he got a message ordering him back to the hotel to await further instructions. The name of the target and the sniper platform location was revealed four hours earlier. He acted without passion, though he had heard, through dark networks, that Luck had ordered the death of Sergei Rahimkulov—his wife's younger brother.

Mission accomplished, he mashed out the cigarette on the cement next to the 50-caliber bullet casing—his personal signature. Away from the rifle, Grigori, dressed in black with a beanie on his head, could pass for a typical NYC tourist. He checked through the binoculars one final time to confirm that Justin Luck was dead, strapped the camera case around his neck and headed for the door to the stairs.

****

Natsumi promised to meet him at 5:30 at the restaurant in the Ritz-Carlton on Stockton Street in downtown San Francisco. She had dined with appreciative clients at the more casual lounge restaurant of the impressive hotel three years earlier, but Davis Franklin had booked the private dining room for the meeting. When she arrived, Davis was seated with several guests at a light-colored, myrtlewood table, set for ten.

She noticed her footsteps hardly made a sound on the hardwood floor as she admired the small, rectangular room. The walls seemed textured in a material that seemed like cloth, which was the same color as the table. When the host pulled out a wooden chair, its back and seat fashioned from brown, stitched leather, she noticed that Marybeth Wilke, the managing partner of the firm, would be at her left, while Davis Franklin was at her right.

There were two persons at the table she did not recognize, but she nodded toward public relations pro Miriam Wilke, her friend, who was seated across the table. She recognized Berkeley Professor Deuteronomy Saint Claire, her Aunt Destiny's friend—and apparently Franklin's friend, across the table. Roland was there. Kendrick Vesey sat at the far end, seeming despondent and aloof, the realization of his loss and a life without Jennifer weighing heavy on his mind. He was seated next to Police Inspector Dana Murphy. Natsumi had not realized how attractive Dana was until seeing her so dressed up that evening.

Davis, apparently sparing no expense, had asked the chef to put together a special 7-course menu, featuring a variety of local farm-to-fork and ocean-to-table entrees. The chef entered the room to welcome Davis' guests before describing each appetizer and entrée in tantalizing detail. He thanked all for coming and bowed before leaving.

But first a toast. After the last two guests arrived, a server brought in a tray with ten large crystal brandy snifters, each filled with two ounces of Louis XIII de Rémy Martin "Black Pearl" limited-edition cognac, at a cost of $550 per pour. A separate server presented the empty Baccarat dark crystal decanter to Davis, which he accepted and offered to Natsumi as a gift of appreciation.

"To Natsumi Mitchell's performance this afternoon…" he called out to the room, raising his snifter. His guests followed suit, raising their own glasses. "And to the beginning of a new era in the pursuit of nonhuman rights and protections! Without downplaying Dr. Kendrick Vesey's profoundly personal loss, I must say today was a victory of historic proportions. At that hearing, not only were we able to persuade the court to hear testimony from a nonhuman person, but by all accounts, Alberta solved a complex murder where San Francisco detectives were all stumped! Great work, Natsumi and Alberta!"

Others at the table called out various compliments before tapping glasses and sipping that very special old pale. The low, hollow vibration of crystal still reverberating in their ears, Davis continued.

"And to Kendrick Vesey!" Again, he raised his glass—this time in honor of the recently-released Berkeley professor, biological anthropologist, primate researcher and best-selling author. "We honor your loss! We never stopped believing in you! We sincerely welcome you back!"

Kendrick nodded as he and Dana tapped glasses, smiled toward each other and took a sip.

"This is just the beginning," Davis continued, "and for that reason, Natsumi, I've shared a special request proposal with Marybeth concerning you, and Marybeth of course, being gracious, indicated she would support my proposal—for the good of all. Therefore Natsumi, I would like to offer you an executive position at NonHumanPersons Incorporated, a new division of the Tomorrow Foundation, specifically dedicated to the advancement of the nonhuman rights and protections for cognitively complex animals all over the world."

Natsumi looked toward Marybeth and then to Miriam, wondering how long beforehand they had known about Davis' proposal. Sitting there irritated, Natsumi felt betrayed, like there had been a *quid pro quo*—that the firm had offered her and her services as a token of loyalty to the generous billionaire who had supported Wilke and Reed and its causes over so many years.

Franklin was obviously excited—especially after Alberta's performance at the preliminary hearing. Her testimony had already engendered a global fascination with her, leading to legal debates on nonhuman rights that played out on cable and Internet broadcasts across the country. In the meantime, as news spread across the globe about a chimpanzee who had solved a murder case that had stumped the city of San Francisco's best detectives, YouTube videos featuring Alberta and Natsumi went viral.

Downloads quickly surged after over two hundred million views. In a few short hours, Alberta and Natsumi had become social media mega-celebrities. Thirty minutes later at 6:15, Alberta launched her first Tweet from @realAlbertaNHP, lighting up the Twitter Sphere and creating millions of Alberta followers within the hour.

The number of email messages and social media invites on Natsumi's phone indicated a groundswell of interest in her and her relationship with Alberta, while "Alberta" and "nonhuman rights" dominated Internet search engine requests—but "nonhuman rights" was Davis Franklin's cause, his passion. To Natsumi, the background and legal issues involved in his fight were unfamiliar, unanticipated and intimidating. She wasn't certain that she was up for the challenge. Nonhuman rights made for interesting debate, but her heart wasn't in it.

Our Lives Matter was still busy engaging federal and state legislatures and legislators, still working to propose solutions. Natsumi had not been significantly involved in many of the organization's activities during the hearing, but she hoped to re-involve herself with the executive committee once Vesey's legal matters were fully resolved.

Over the course of dinner, Davis explained that he wanted to become more involved in helping Our Lives Matter push their political agenda and at efforts involving legislative and policy changes for law enforcement agencies across the country. He also announced that he was funding two scholarships for Bay-Area low-income girls—two in Queen Shabaz's name, and another two for young women Dreamers, in Jennifer Alvarez's name.

"I know you're not in it for the money, Natsumi" Davis said, "but believe me, money does help—especially when your goal is to assist those who are less fortunate. I'm prepared to pay you one and a half million a year, plus incentives and bonuses."

"You're right, Mr. Franklin. It's not about the money," she repeated, "but I already have a cause."

"I admire and will always support Our Lives Matter," he insisted, "but you're wasting your time and talent there."

"Excuse me!" she interrupted, "You're a rich and powerful white man, but you can't just change people's lives, rewrite their dreams by waving your money wand. You can't arrange people on your board like tiny chess pieces.

What if I said the same thing about you—that maybe you're wasting your time on nonhuman rights? It'll be years before anyone in this country ever seriously decides to take up that issue."

"Civil rights attorneys come a dime a dozen," he countered. "Every year, law schools crank out tens of thousands of idealists who think they're going to change the world, and they do the best they can, but most will never make a difference. Unfortunately, dreams take years to wither and die, along with dreamers. I'll be honest, Natsumi. Today, you outgrew Our Lives Matter, just as it's grown away from you—it's taken a life of its own. Its new leaders can get along just fine without Natsumi Mitchell. It's time for the next big challenge in your life. Tonight, I'm offering you the opportunity to make a *real* difference in the world."

"I am making a real difference."

"You're different than the fifty thousand other civil rights attorneys out there, fighting the good fight. I see the fire in your soul, and I know you're capable of much more. Your friends—they'll all either give up, sell out or become cynical. It's the natural progression of activism. They're civil rights automatons, not innovators."

"Seriously? And you really want me to work for you?"

"It's your best and highest use, Natsumi. Stop settling. You're better than that!"

"Mr. Franklin, I am honored you've thought to consider me in such a significant capacity at your foundation, but I'm not ready to take up a whole new cause. I'm a civil rights lawyer, and that's it. I don't know enough about nonhuman rights and what you're trying to accomplish."

"Of course you do," Davis countered, still smiling. "We're still talking about civil rights, because civil rights are the rights of persons. Look at what you already accomplished today! Come on, take advantage of the opportunity here. You'll be breaking new legal ground. Wouldn't you rather work in an area where you'll be changing the very definition of personhood?"

"I've done a little research on nonhuman rights, sir, so I know what you're up against. The opposition would be overwhelming, and attitudes are slow to change. At best, you'll probably be waiting ten or more years before any significant nonhuman rights case ever goes up before a U.S. court."

"You're selling yourself short," he responded. "Something as unique as nonhuman rights is your higher calling. We're talking about a nascent movement, something truly on the cutting edge. Consider history. Do you want to be a Jesse Jackson, an Al Sharpton, a Queen Shabaz—or would you rather be the next Martin Luther King, Jr? Stop settling!"

"It's one thing allowing a chimp to testify at a preliminary hearing," she answered, "but wholesale rights and protections across the country? I respect your passion and appreciate your attempt to inspire me, Mr. Franklin, but I don't want to spend half my career waiting for something that might not ever happen—no matter how much you offer to pay me."

****

"You're picking up the bad habits of the humans you associate with, Alberta," Jacobs continued, gun still drawn. "You're bluffing. You don't want to die, and you don't want your baby to die. I don't want that either. I don't want to kill you, but I will if I have to!"

Kapowww!

He fired the gun into the fireplace, startling her, watching as she shrieked in response to the violent explosion, cringing in fear, her hands covering her ears.

"Again, I need you to do two things for me—I need the codes for your virtual storage, and I need you to sign a legal document giving me custody of your baby."

"Why do you do this?" Alberta signed desperately.

"Because I'm the one who discovered you and lost you. I was robbed. I got no recognition for it."

"No money!"

"That too, and when that happened, I lost everything—the only woman who ever loved me, my family. Everything."

"Alberta is person. Mi baby is person."

"Nonsense! You're just a chimp, and your baby'll be nothing more than a chimp. I don't buy any of Franklin's crap about nonhuman persons. He's just out to make money off you."

"Why Alberta is not a person?"

"Because persons have to be humans. Persons must have souls. God made humans with souls—but no other animal. Apes belong in cages, every last one of them."

"Many human is in cage, in prison. Them not have souls? Them is not a person?"

"No, they aren't persons," Jacobs sneered. "Criminals, felons, lost souls—they're animals who belong there, in locked cages. They're sub-human, like you—they don't deserve to have rights. And you think you should have more status than them?"

"What crime mi do? Crime to be born chimp? What crime mi baby do?"

"I can't believe I'm arguing with an ape. Look—humans are the dominant species, period. It's our world. We make the rules."

"Sometime rule is wrong. White human make black human slave, put black human in cage, in jail—kill black human on street. That is human law rule, but rule is wrong. Black have no soul? Black is criminal? Human rule is immoral."

"Oh," Jacobs groaned, "morality is just one of those fancy words Vesey tried to teach you, but you can't begin to conceive of morality. You're an ape!"

"Mi understand Jacob is immoral. Jacob want mi baby for money."

Kapowww!

Jacobs fired the gun again into the fireplace, startling Alberta.

"You want me to show you immoral? I'm two seconds away from putting a bullet in your hairy black hide. Stop stalling."

Gun still raised, he tossed a document, a pen and an inkpad on the couch before backing away.

"I know your signature, your 'A.' I need you to put that and your fingerprint on the signature line and initial each page—everywhere you see yellow. Do it, now."

"If mi is not person, signature not mean nothing."

"I'm betting on Davis Franklin. I'm betting he'll find some animal activist judge out there who'll grant you some form of legal rights, which will make that document legal. Now sign it!"

Jacobs aimed the gun at Alberta's head as she moved toward the couch.

"Make one move toward me—and your world-famous brain will be splattered on that wall. Don't even twitch my way."

Pen in her trembling hand, Alberta proceed to make an 'A' on the signature line, and she slowly made 'A's in all the yellowed spaces for initials Then she opened the inkpad and carefully placed an index fingerprint next to each initial.

"Now back away."

Jacobs retrieved the document after Alberta was a safe distance away. Eyes darting down to the pages and back towards Alberta, he checked to make certain every page had her initial. Making sure he had at least a 30-foot space cushion, he opened his briefcase and returned the document to its file. Maintaining this cushion, he opened his laptop.

"Now give me the codes for your virtual cloud storage."

"Mi got no cloud storage."

"You're lying," Jacobs said, perplexed. "Vesey and Hughes insist you aren't capable of lying, but I know you're lying. If you can lie, what else are you capable of? That's why you belong in a cage. Give me those damn codes, Alberta. Now!

"Mi no lie. Mi forget code."

"Then you must have them written somewhere."

"Mi think in library."

"Then let's go to the library," Jacobs demanded. "You first."

Arms in the air, Alberta headed down the hallway toward the library. She turned the knob and entered. Ignoring Kendrick's larger bureau, she went to a smaller desk and opened the drawer, taking out a small sheet of paper.

"Stay there!" Jacobs warned as he sat in the chair by the door. "Stay behind that desk." Gun still aimed at the chimp, he opened his laptop and looked back toward her, gauging her to be at least 20 feet away, a safe enough distance. "Website address!"

"Microsoft."

"Good. I use that one too."

He moved a potted plant off a low table, pulled it close and placed the laptop there, typing with his left hand, glancing up after every letter.

"Username!"

"#1NHPerson."

"Figures!" he said as the typed on the keyboard. "Password!"

"AlbertaloveKendrick."

"That's a sick thought!" Jacobs groaned as he typed the long password. Looking up, he sighed. "That's the wrong password."

"No 's' in password," she signed.

Gun still aimed at Alberta, Jacobs typed in the password again.

"There's only one document listed. What is this?" he said as he clicked on the file with an flv. extension.

He flinched when he saw the video image of himself. There he was on the living room floor, prone, pants around his ankles, and there was Alberta, with a huge plantain in her right hand, just beginning to insert it.

Enraged, he stood to better aim the gun. *You're a dead ape!*

Kapowww!

The loud explosion startled him. Looking toward Alberta, Jacobs could not believe his eyes, and then he looked down toward his right shoulder, where he saw the blood. He tasted blood in his mouth. The concussive force of the bullet had knocked the gun from his right hand. Still in shock, he looked back toward the ape in disbelief. Alberta was still aiming the gun at him—aiming his own gun—the one she stole from him when she drugged him. Alberta had shot him in the shoulder!

"You shot me!" he screamed, his back against the wall, blood trailing down his arm. "You could have killed me with that thing! Put that gun down!"

She continued aiming, though she signed the demand "sit" with her left hand. Only after he was seated did she lower the gun.

"Who is smarter now?" she signed, directly confronting Jacobs.

"You, you shot me…" he groaned. "I'm shot! I need medical attention. I need to call…"

"No," she gestured before tapping the gun with her fingers. "Jacob sit him bumboclaat ass down!"

His cell phone was in his right-side pant pocket, but due to his right shoulder injury, it was out of reach."

"What do you want, Alberta?" Jacobs yelled. "Are you going to let me bleed to death here?"

"I take my chances," she signed, "You said those same words, Jacobs. Remember? You said, 'I'll take my chances.'"

"What are you talking about?"

"If I let you live, Jacobs, then you'll come back. You'll do everything in your power to kill me and take my baby. You'll use human prejudice and laws against me."

"No, I would never do that!" Jacobs insisted. "No! Please forgive me. *Kipekee!*"

"You lie. You are not a human, a person. You are a snake. This is what I will do."

Raising the Springfield Armory 9-millimeter pistol, she carefully approached Kendrick's desk. Seated on the desktop, she placed the gun at her right side, keeping it close as she signed.

"If I kill Jacobs in the way an ape would kill a human—physical, with my hands and teeth, using blood and violence—then that would make me a savage animal, and humans would kill me the way they would kill a dangerous animal."

"You, you're going to kill me?" the doctor exclaimed.

"But if use my brain and I kill you, in the same way that a human would kill a human—with a gun—then what will human law do? I'll take my chance to test human law, to see if I am a person after I kill a human with a gun. Davis Franklin will be happy."

"Alberta, please!" Jacobs pleaded. "I'm sorry! Please! I promise I'll go away and you'll never see me again! I promise!"

"Jacobs tries to kill Alberta, but Alberta kills Jacobs. That is self-defense protection. That is human law."

"I discovered you, Alberta," Jacobs continued. "I'm, I'm like your father. I care about you like a daughter. You wouldn't even have the opportunity for personhood without me!"

"Yes mi would. Mi is born a person. No human make mi person, fassyhole!"

At that moment, Dr. David Jacobs realized that within her brutish, animal, simian heart, Alberta was intent on killing him. Sitting before him was the result of Franklin and Vesey's respondent conditioning, made to approximate a person, though without a trace of humanity. She was incapable of empathy or compassion, a cruel, savage animal who had been trained to apply cold, efficient logic.

Although the pain in his shoulder was agonizing, he knew he would have to risk some bold action in order to live. He'd have to overwhelm her logic by doing something unexpected. His only hope would be to get to his gun, which was ten feet away, next to the wall.

Shooting with his left hand would be a challenge, but he had done regular work with his left at the gun range, so he knew that if he could get to the gun, his chances would improve.

The bullet she fired had hit him in the shoulder, but was she aiming for his shoulder? Had she hit him by accident? She was an ape. Could she have taught herself to shoot that gun? Could she hit a moving target?

If he could make a break and get the gun, he could shoot her dead, but how would he explain his blood in the room and his own gunshot injury? He thought for a moment. He would tell police that when he went to the house to pick up some documents that he left in the library, Alberta shot him with a gun she stole from him weeks earlier, and he was forced to kill her in self-defense.

With Alberta dead, the only way to preserve his investment would be to take mature somatic cells and eggs from her body for use in cloning. He would also take the unborn fetus. Jacobs was in negotiations with two facilities outside the U.S. who had expressed an interest in cloning Alberta.

One far East company had offered him $2.5 million for a genetic sample that resulted in an Alberta clone, a half-million for each successful future Alberta clone and one million dollars for the fetus and placenta from her body. As cruel as it seemed, killing her and cutting the baby out would not constitute a crime. She was an animal, after all. She wasn't a person!

Alberta watched Jacobs' eyes when he glanced over at the gun, preparing to lunge.

"Mi give Jacob chance…"

Shoving his laptop in her direction to distract her, Jacobs went for the gun. He was surprised when he reached the weapon that she hadn't shot at him. Scrambling to his feet, he aimed toward her with his left hand and fired.

Kapowww!

He didn't know if he had hit her because she was no longer on the desk. Was she dead? Her body blown across the room? Was she back there, on the other side of the desk, bloodied and sprawled on the floor?

He laughed, relieved, and then he saw movement in his left periphery. When he turned, his facial expression morphed to one of terror.

"God help me!"

Kapowww!

Alberta fired the bullet from five feet away, directly into his heart.

From the Author
Become Part of a Best-Seller!

If you have enjoyed this book, the best thing you can do for me as the author is to tell your friends about Alberta, or better yet, embrace me as a friend. Over many years of marketing books, I have isolated seven specific things that communities (or supporters) can do to become an essential part of an author's success story:

1 – Instead of buying one book—Buy Two. It doubles the impact of your support, and one of your friends will certainly appreciate the thoughtful gift.

2 – Share out my marketing campaigns on Social Media. Most of us underappreciate the power that we possess through our everyday connections. On my Author Platform (Website) under "Sharing," I will provide specific materials to be shared out to Facebook, Twitter and other platforms. All I ask is that you share them every other week for three months. Beyond that, it's mutual cooperation.

3 – Visit my Website every other week. Promote it to your friends and encourage them to join the discussion. In essence—become a part of my success so that I can become a part of yours. Let's be real friends. Let's exchange ideas. I promise: There will be much to explore when you visit www.marcusmcgee.net. Stop by and say "Hello" on a regular basis.

4 – Buy the Print Book and eBook of *Alberta* only at Barnes & Noble. The success of a book has everything to do with numbers—numbers are all that buyers and reviewers recognize. Buying from a single retailer consolidates the numbers, providing greater impact, and increases a book and author's opportunity for success. Best-Seller Threshold: 50,000 books.

5 – Take the time and effort to write a review on Amazon or Barnes & Noble. With newsprint circulation shrinking, most people do not comprehend the power of a single on-line review. Readers are now more powerful than reviewers!

6 – Think out-of-the-box. There is no silver bullet for book marketing, so success is a matter always considering new ideas, approaches and opportunities. Share yours with me, and I'll share mine with you.

7 – Tell me what you need me to do for you. I've spent two pages telling you what I need you to do. Many authors do not fully appreciate the power of "The Ask." If you want (or you need) others to become a part of your success, then you cannot be shy about making specific requests. Remember—You are in control. Ask for what you need.

I don't expect anyone to do all the things I have asked for, but I'm urging my friends and family to do at least four of the items listed above. I promise to Pay It Forward. We'll be much more Successful Together!

OTHER TITLES BY MARCUS MCGEE

LEGAL THRILLER
(Suspense thriller, 439 pages paperback, eBook)
Murder mystery set in San Francisco

MURDER FROM THE GRAVE
(Suspense thriller, 425 pages paperback, eBook)
Berkeley professor-turned-SF police detective matches wits with a killer who wants to commit seven murders after he is already dead

VIRAL VECTOR
(Suspense thriller, 378 pages paperback, eBook)
Group of billionaires seek to control world using futuristic DNA weapon

TWO MATADORS
(Novella, drama, 126 pages paperback, eBook)
An ancient Matador tells an epic story of living a life of love and passion!

FOUR STORIES
(Short Stories, 210 pages paperback, eBook)
Humorous collection of short stories

SYNCHRONICITY
(Short Stories, 298 pages paperback, eBook)
"The Club," "Anthropophagi" and other stories

THE SILK NOOSE
(Short Stories, essays, 217 pages paperback, eBook)
"Denouément," "On Niggers and Squirrels," and others

SHADOW IN THE SKY
(Suspense thriller, 263 pages paperback, eBook)
Asteroid threatens Earth, Last year of life

MOMENT OF TRUTH
(Suspense thriller, 265 pages paperback, eBook)
Societies deal with end of Earth, Book Two of The Last Year Trilogy

HOW TO EAT AN ELEPHANT
The Secret for How Ordinary People Can Accomplish Extraordinary Things
(Short Story, 8,870 words, eBook)

ON NIGGERS AND SQUIRRELS
An Examination of the Relationship Between Police and Black/Brown Males
#1 Amazon Best Seller for Two Years
(Essay, 11,030 words, eBook)

ON WHAT THEY CALL US
A Historical Perspective about the Illusion of Race in America.
(Essay, 11,050 words, eBook)

ON THE SEVEN-YEAR HITCH
A Discussion on the Efficacy of Long-Term Marriage in an Impermanent Society.
(Essay, 4,050 words, eBook)

WILLIE – THE MAN, THE MYTH & THE ERA

Texas Roots/California Dreams
Three chapters detailing Willie Brown's background and his earliest influences
(Biography, 15,760 words, eBook)
The Speakership Battles
Willie's ascension to the speakership and his efforts over insurmountable odds
Biography, 40,740 words, eBook)
California's Initiatives
Willie's influence on the history of the initiative process as practiced in California
Biography, 39,940 words, eBook)
Conspiracy and The Sting
Calculated attempts to depose or destroy the State's most brilliant politician
Biography, 17,540 words, eBook)

visit www.pegasusbooks.net

spend an afternoon or evening with Marcus

www.marcusmcgee.net

www.ingramcontent.com/pod-product-compliance
Lightning Source LLC
Chambersburg PA
CBHW031146270326
41931CB00006B/165